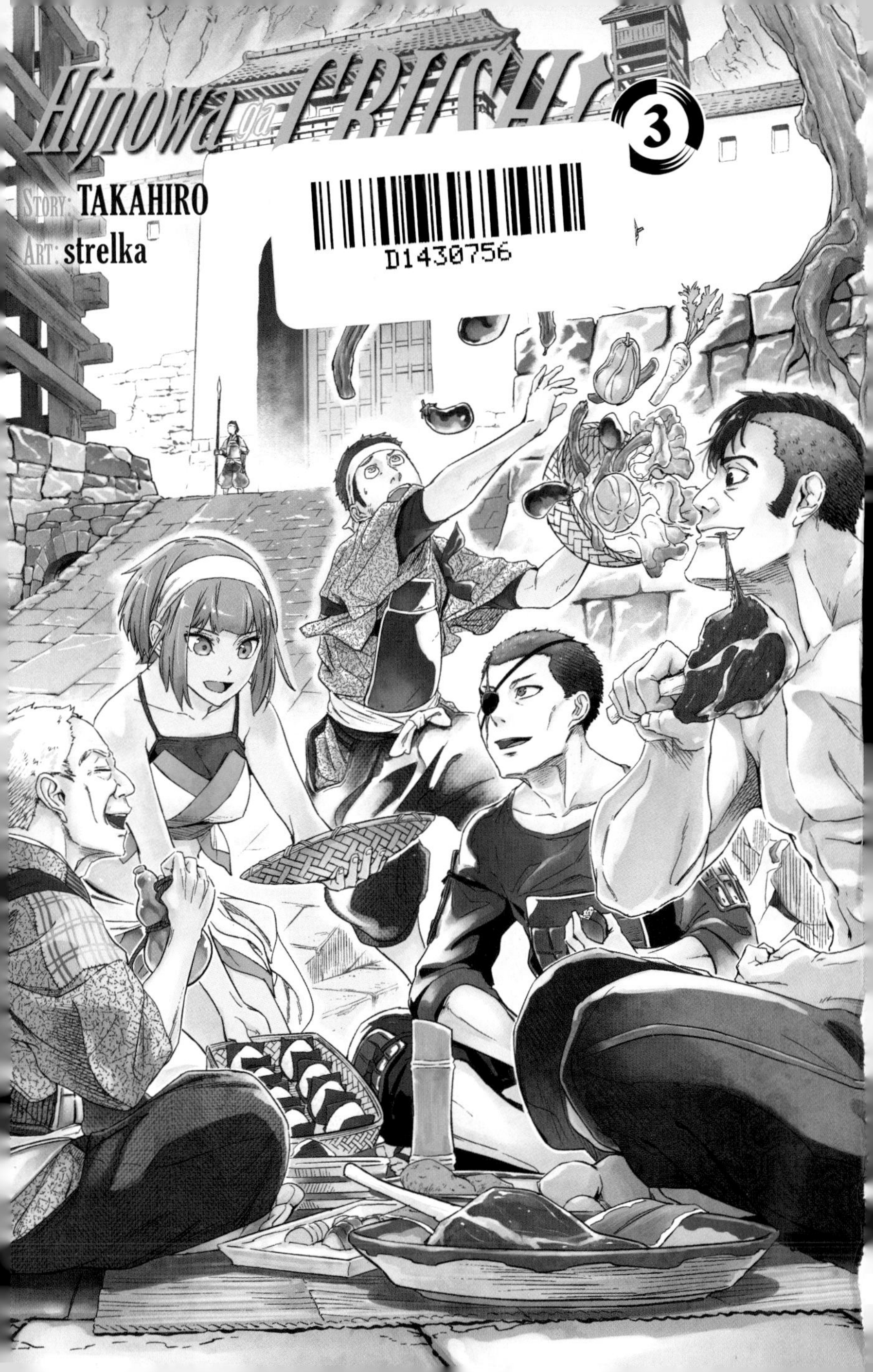
Hinowa ga CRUSH
3
Story: TAKAHIRO
Art: strelka

Contents

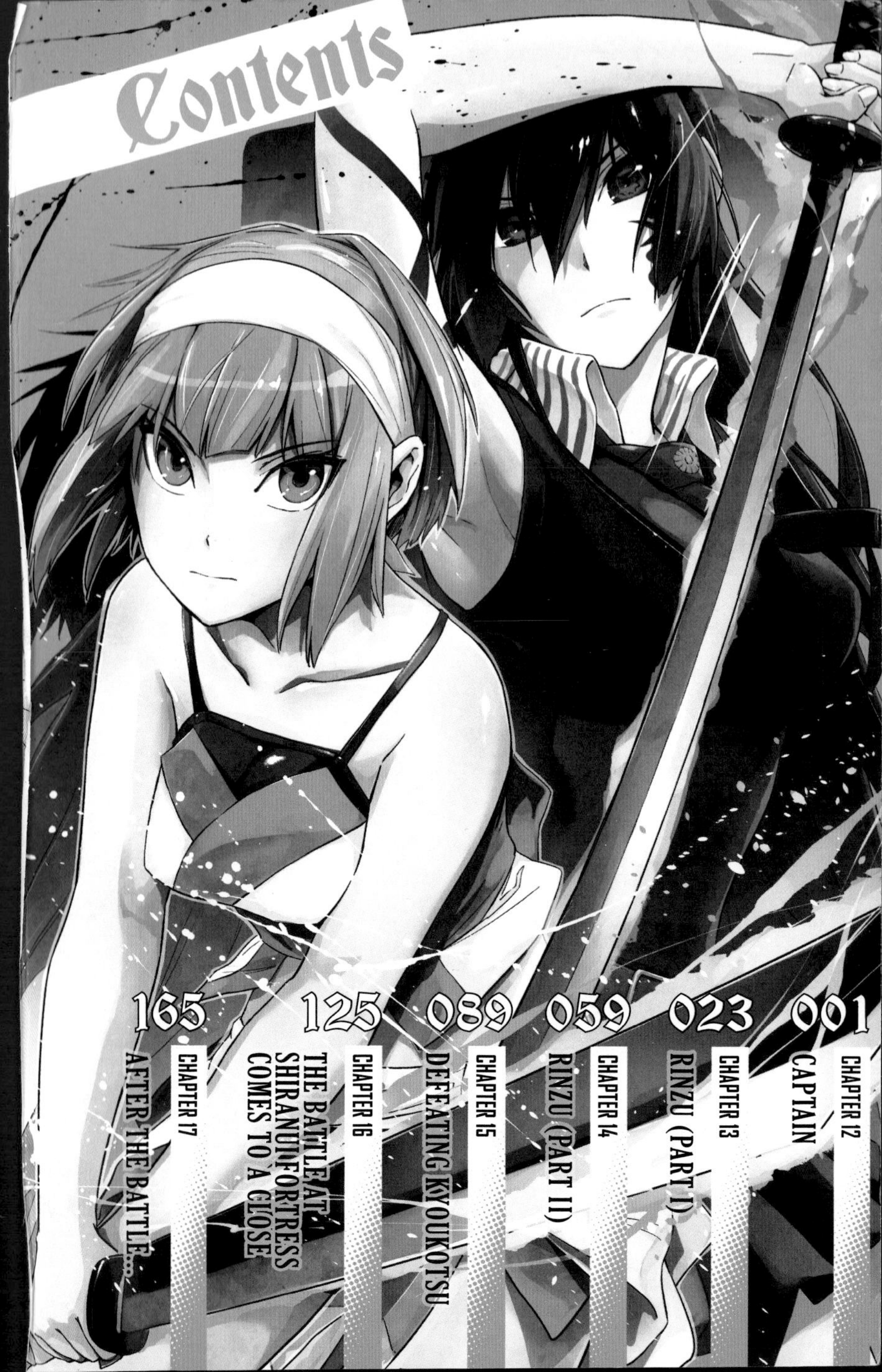

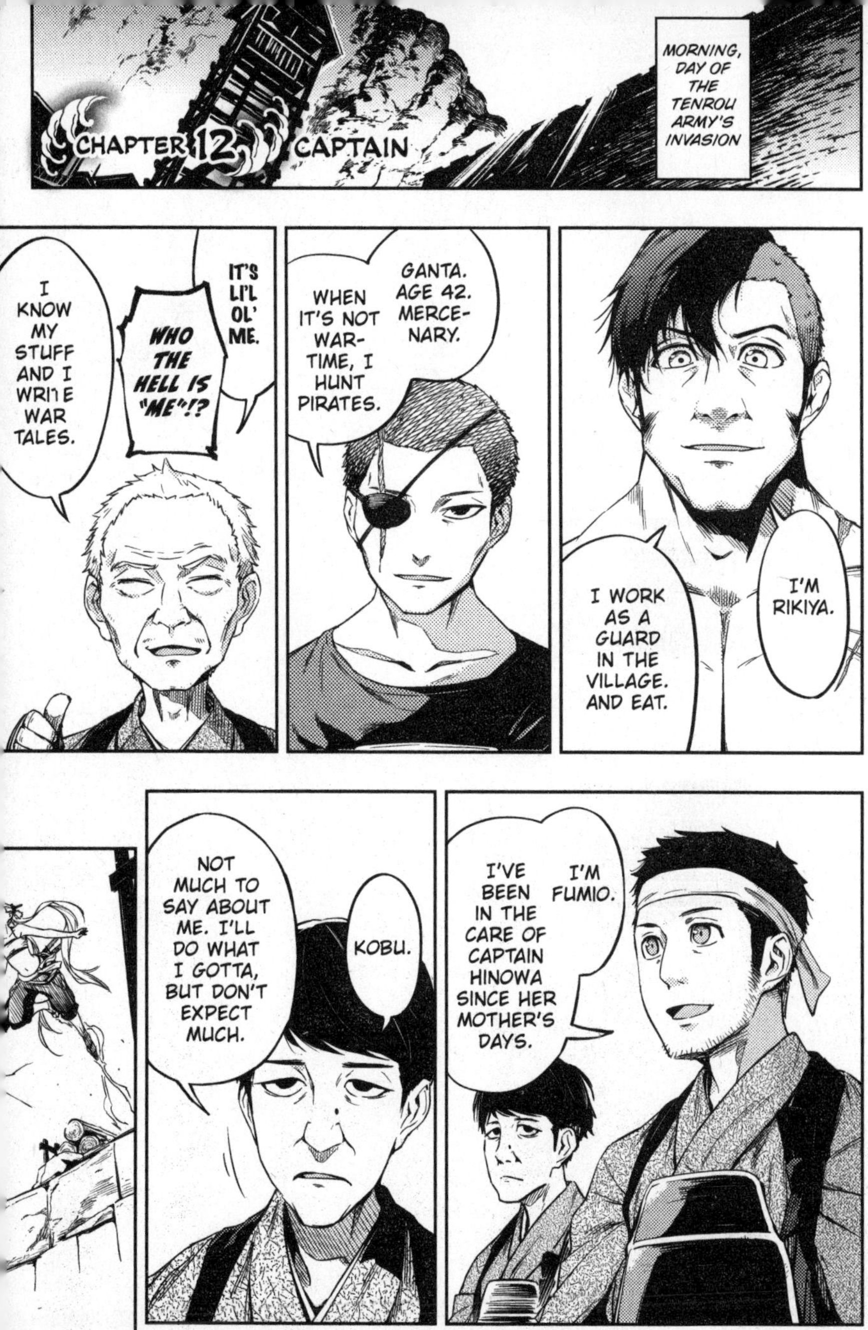
MORNING, DAY OF THE TENROU ARMY'S INVASION
CHAPTER 12 CAPTAIN
I'M RIKIYA.
I WORK AS A GUARD IN THE VILLAGE. AND EAT.
GANTA. AGE 42. MERCENARY.
WHEN IT'S NOT WARTIME, I HUNT PIRATES.
IT'S LI'L OL' ME.
WHO THE HELL IS "ME"!?
I KNOW MY STUFF AND I WRITE WAR TALES.
I'M FUMIO.
I'VE BEEN IN THE CARE OF CAPTAIN HINOWA SINCE HER MOTHER'S DAYS.
KOBU.
NOT MUCH TO SAY ABOUT ME. I'LL DO WHAT I GOTTA, BUT DON'T EXPECT MUCH.

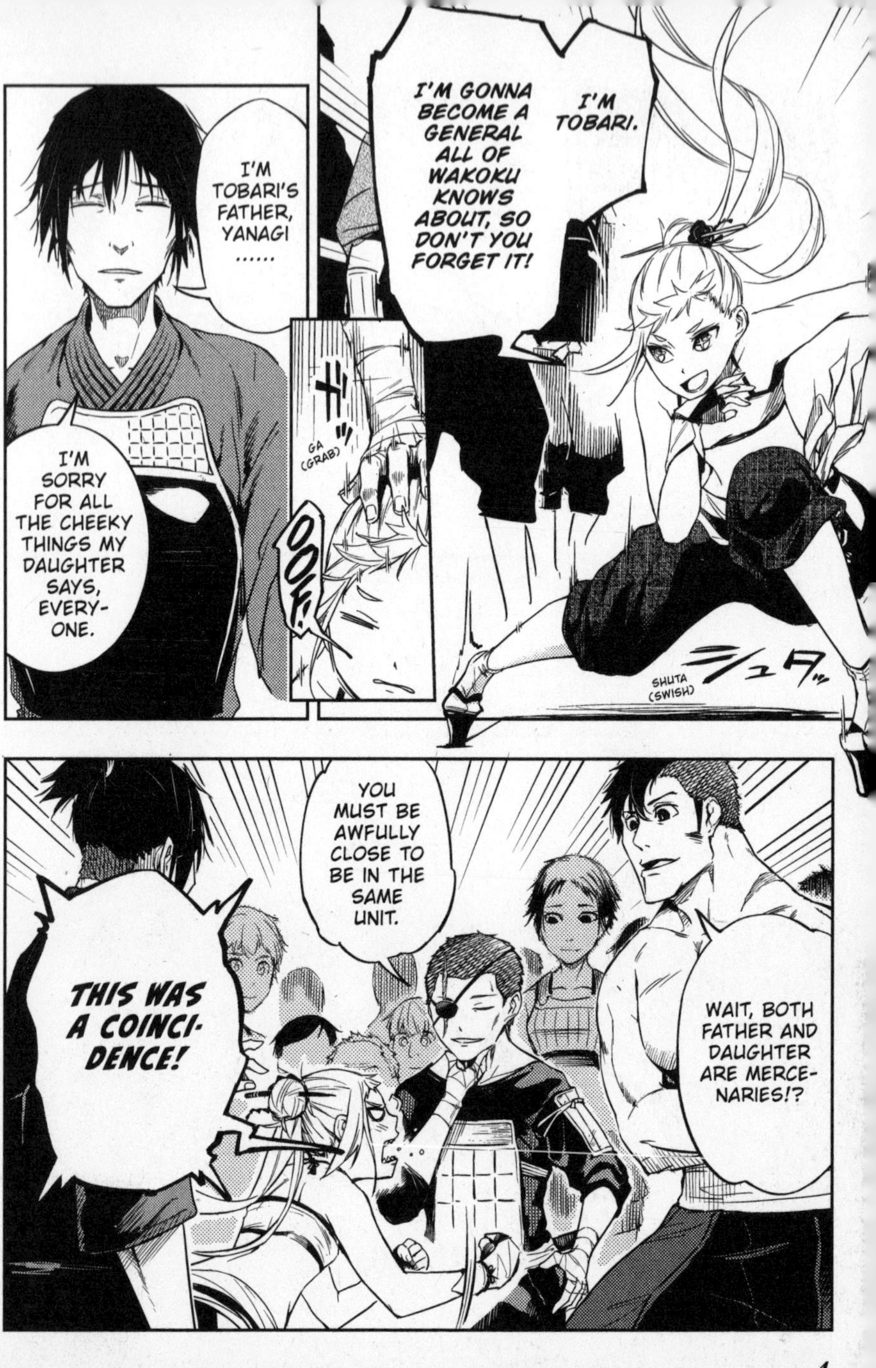
I'M TOBARI.
I'M GONNA BECOME A GENERAL ALL OF WAKOKU KNOWS ABOUT, SO DON'T YOU FORGET IT!
SHUTA (SWISH)
GA (GRAB)
OOF!
I'M TOBARI'S FATHER, YANAGI ......
I'M SORRY FOR ALL THE CHEEKY THINGS MY DAUGHTER SAYS, EVERY-ONE.
WAIT, BOTH FATHER AND DAUGHTER ARE MERCE-NARIES!?
YOU MUST BE AWFULLY CLOSE TO BE IN THE SAME UNIT.
THIS WAS A COINCI-DENCE!

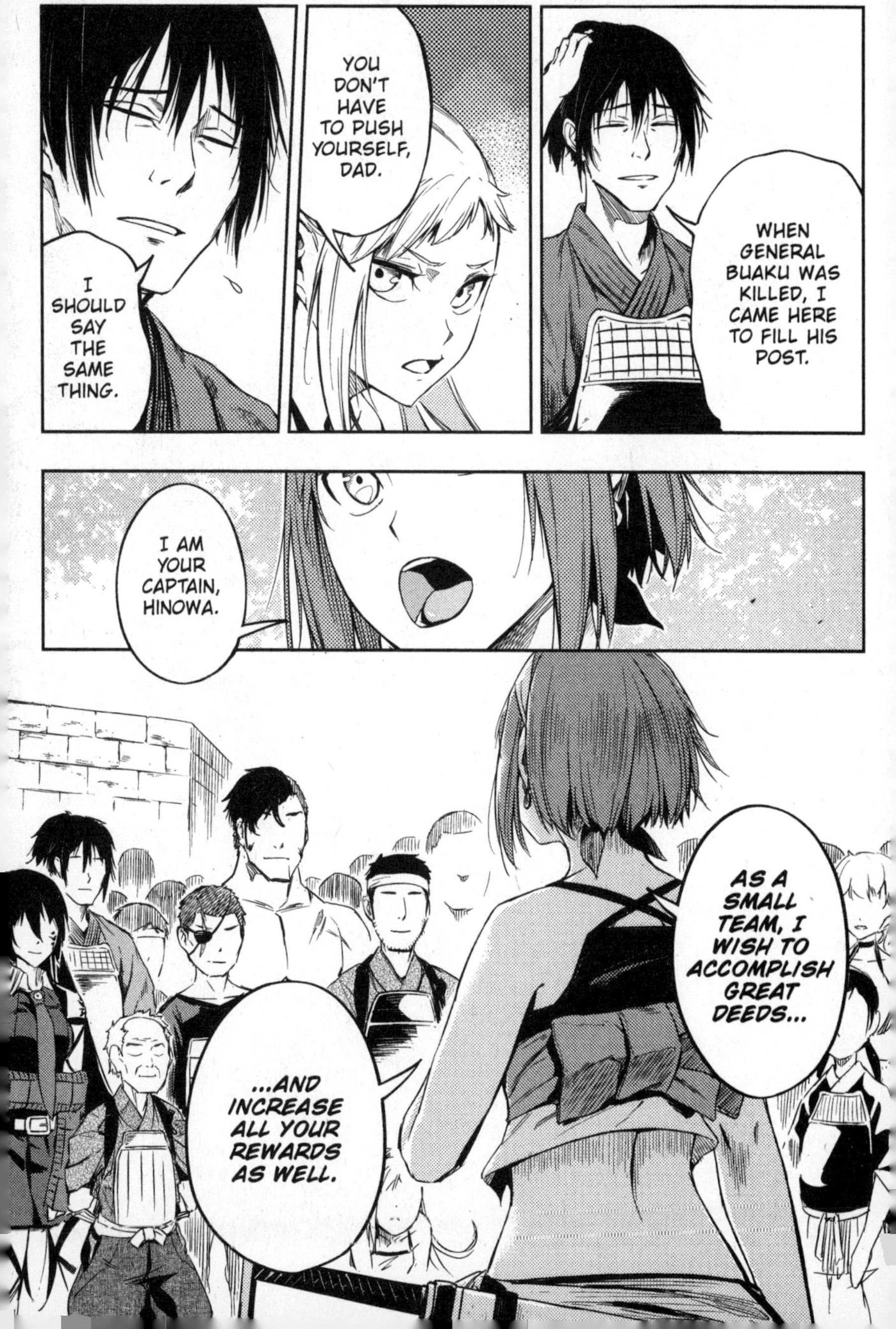
WHEN GENERAL BUAKU WAS KILLED, I CAME HERE TO FILL HIS POST.
YOU DON'T HAVE TO PUSH YOURSELF, DAD.
I SHOULD SAY THE SAME THING.
I AM YOUR CAPTAIN, HINOWA.
AS A SMALL TEAM, I WISH TO ACCOMPLISH GREAT DEEDS...
...AND INCREASE ALL YOUR REWARDS AS WELL.

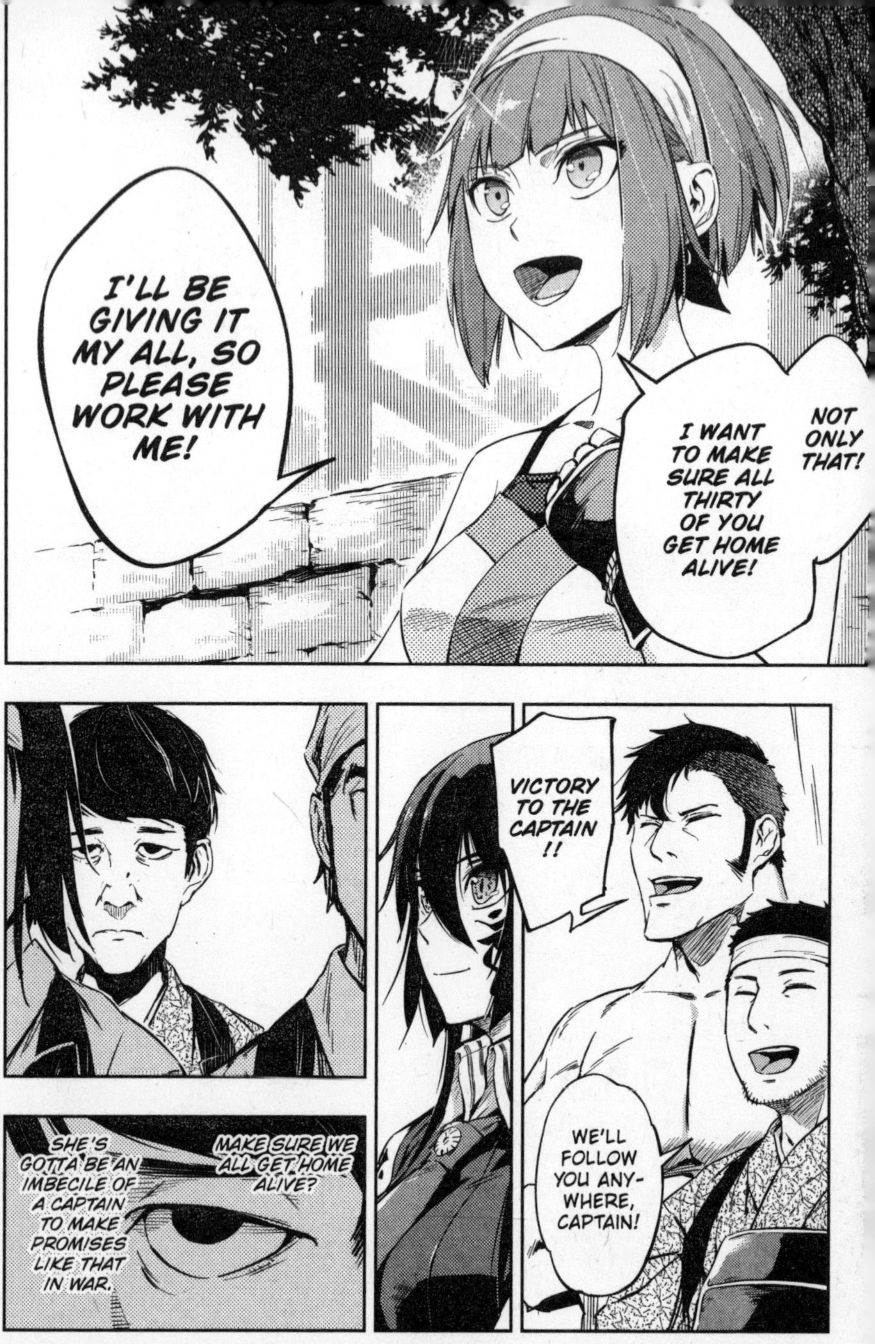
I'LL BE GIVING IT MY ALL, SO PLEASE WORK WITH ME!
NOT ONLY THAT!
I WANT TO MAKE SURE ALL THIRTY OF YOU GET HOME ALIVE!
VICTORY TO THE CAPTAIN!!
WE'LL FOLLOW YOU ANY-WHERE, CAPTAIN!
MAKE SURE WE ALL GET HOME ALIVE?
SHE'S GOTTA BE AN IMBECILE OF A CAPTAIN TO MAKE PROMISES LIKE THAT IN WAR.

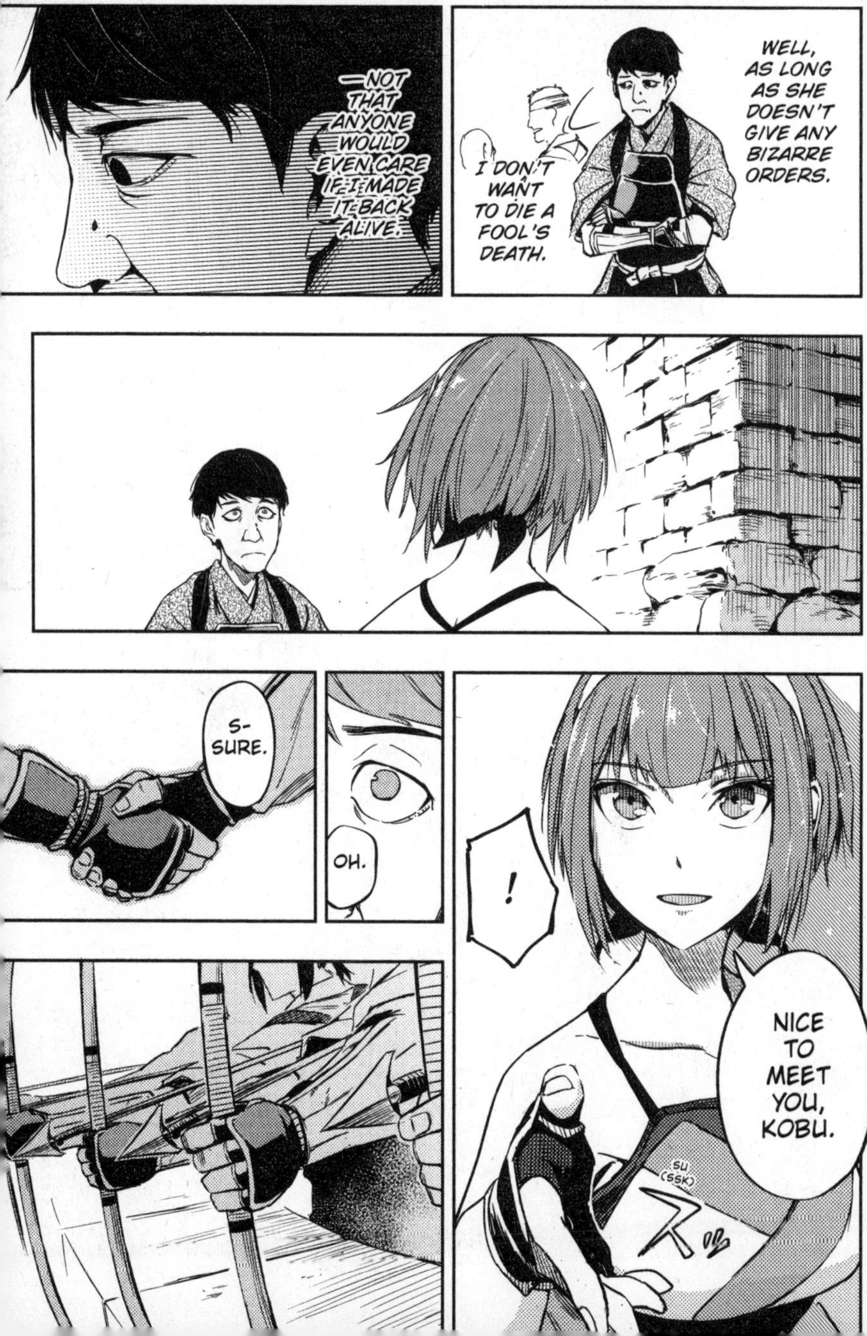
WELL, AS LONG AS SHE DOESN'T GIVE ANY BIZARRE ORDERS.
I DON'T WANT TO DIE A FOOL'S DEATH.
—NOT THAT ANYONE WOULD EVEN CARE IF I MADE IT BACK ALIVE.
!
NICE TO MEET YOU, KOBU.
SU (SSK)
OH.
S-SURE.

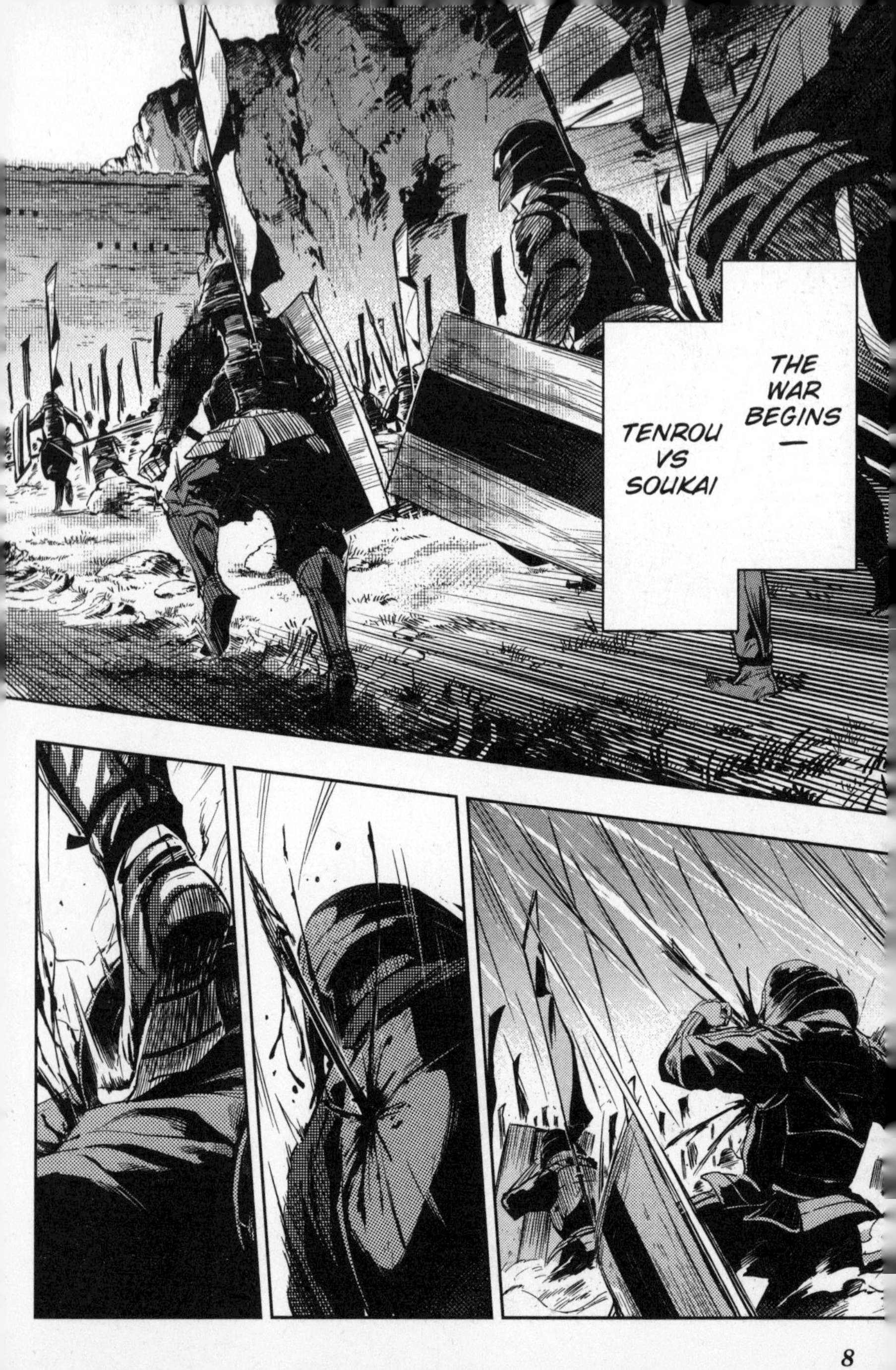
THE WAR BEGINS —
TENROU VS SOUKAI

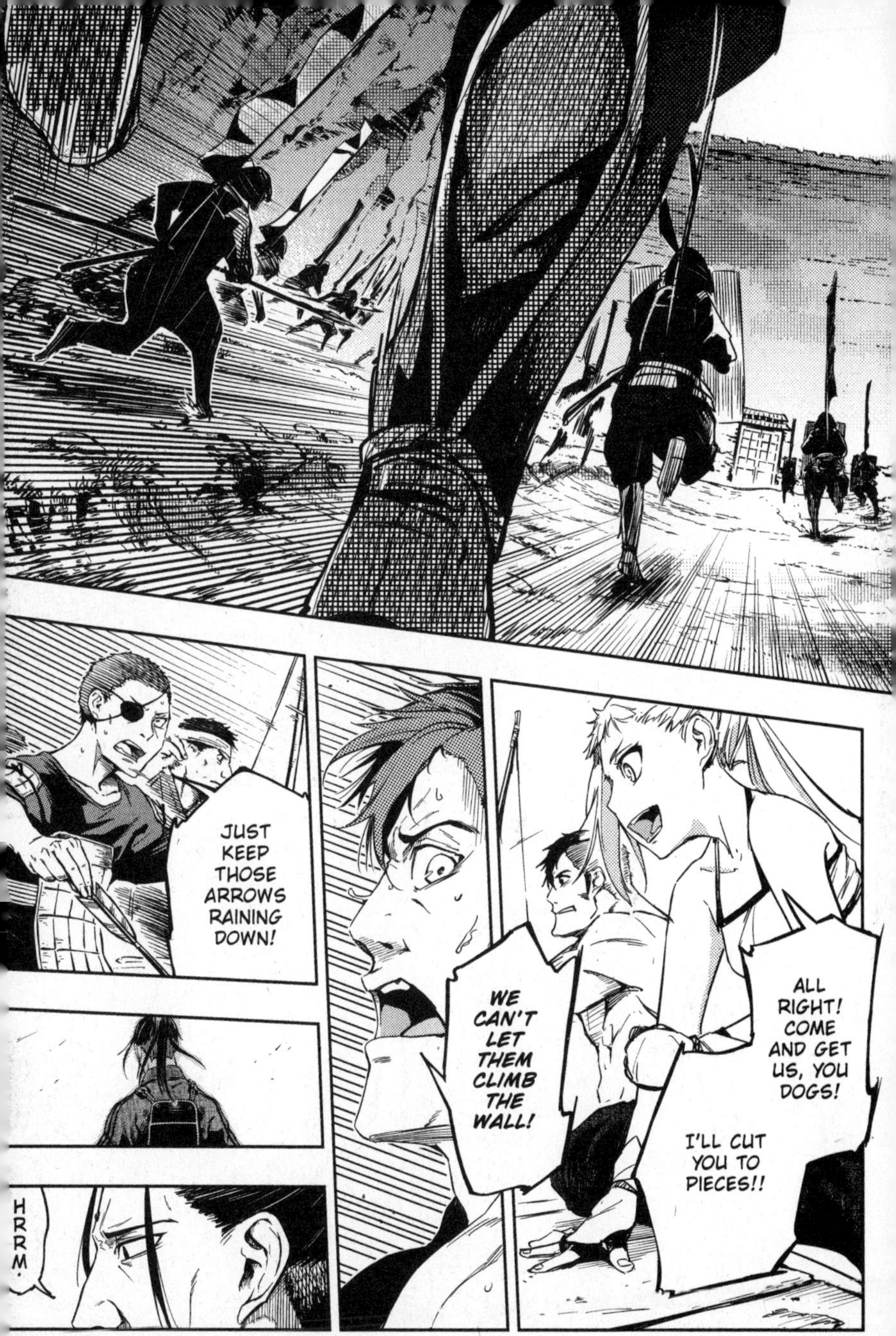
ALL RIGHT! COME AND GET US, YOU DOGS!
I'LL CUT YOU TO PIECES!!
WE CAN'T LET THEM CLIMB THE WALL!
JUST KEEP THOSE ARROWS RAINING DOWN!
HRRM.

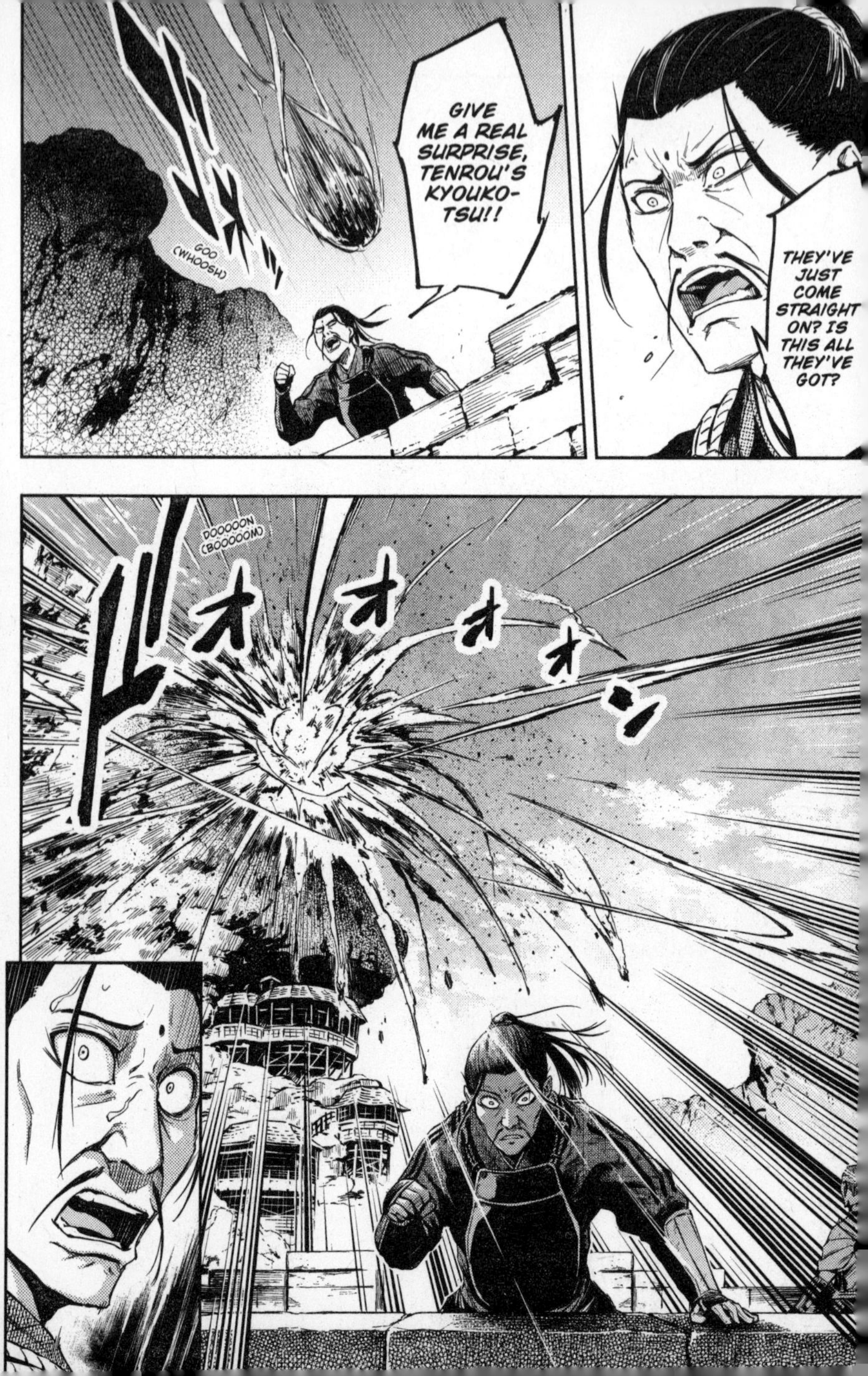

THEY'VE JUST COME STRAIGHT ON? IS THIS ALL THEY'VE GOT?
GIVE ME A REAL SURPRISE, TENROU'S KYOUKO-TSU!!
GOO (WHOOSH)
DOOOOON (BOOOOOM)

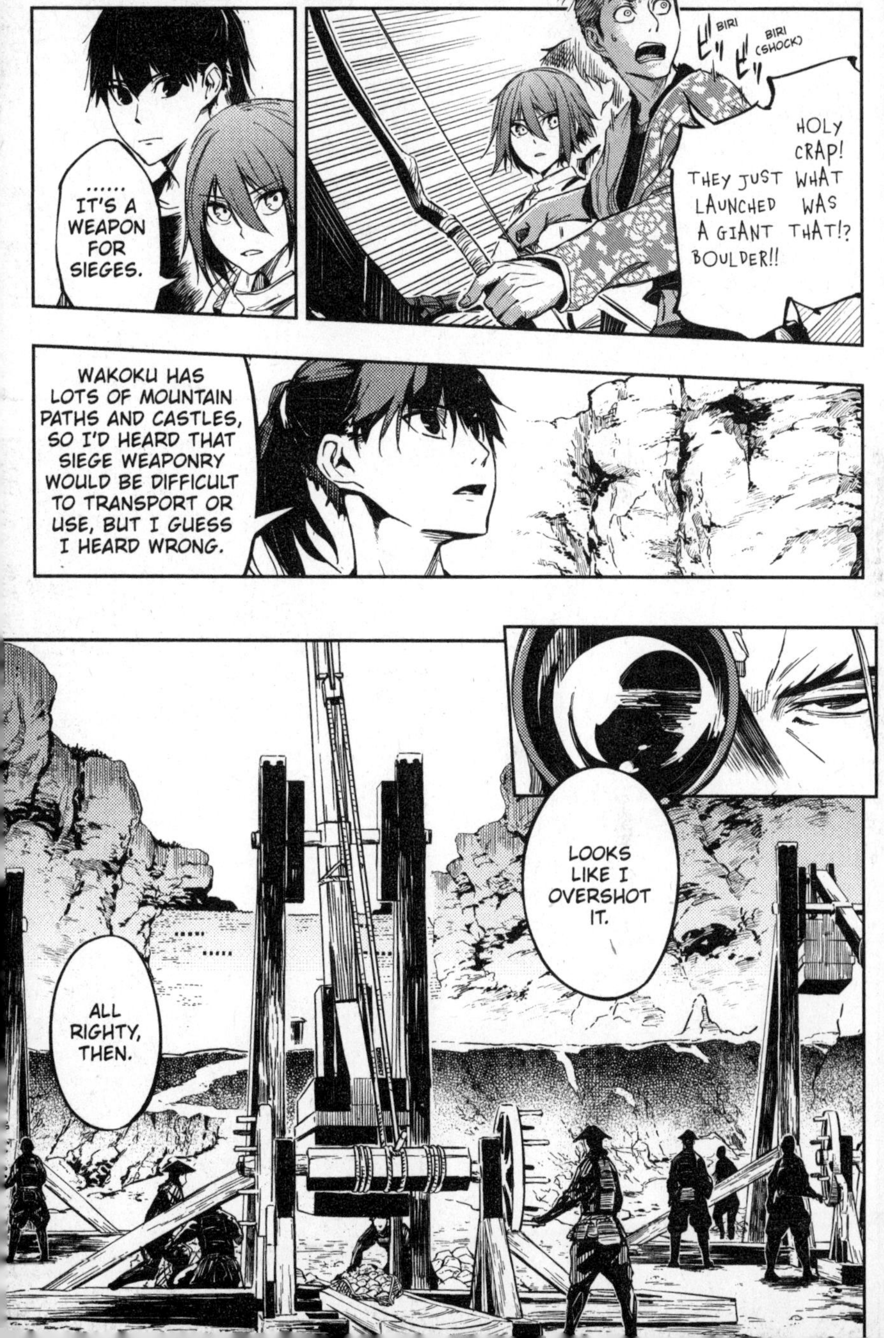
BIRI BIRI (SHOCK)
HOLY CRAP! WHAT WAS THAT!?
THEY JUST LAUNCHED A GIANT BOULDER!!
...... IT'S A WEAPON FOR SIEGES.
WAKOKU HAS LOTS OF MOUNTAIN PATHS AND CASTLES, SO I'D HEARD THAT SIEGE WEAPONRY WOULD BE DIFFICULT TO TRANSPORT OR USE, BUT I GUESS I HEARD WRONG.
LOOKS LIKE I OVERSHOT IT.
ALL RIGHTY, THEN.

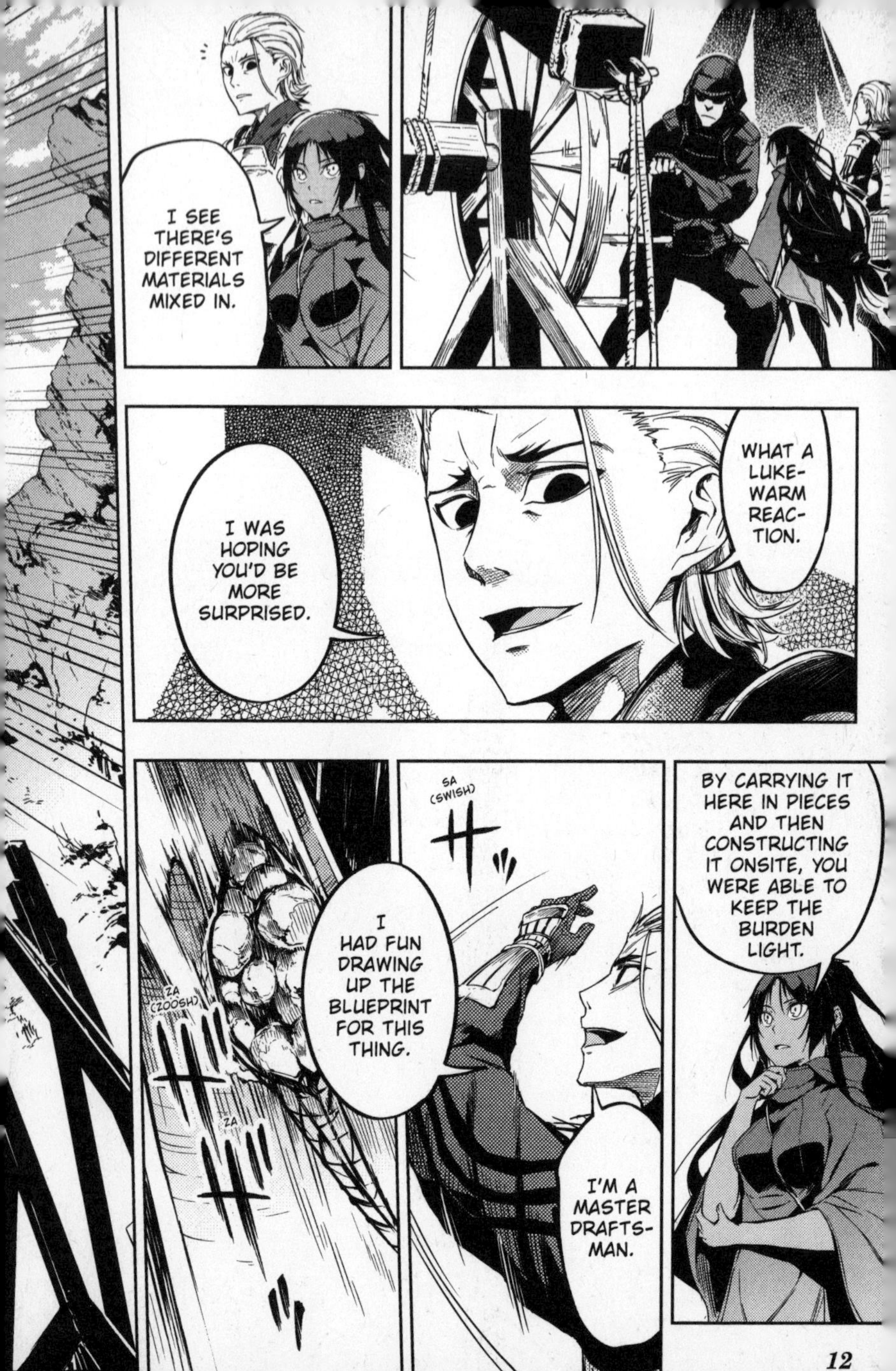
I SEE THERE'S DIFFERENT MATERIALS MIXED IN.
WHAT A LUKE-WARM REACTION.
I WAS HOPING YOU'D BE MORE SURPRISED.
BY CARRYING IT HERE IN PIECES AND THEN CONSTRUCTING IT ONSITE, YOU WERE ABLE TO KEEP THE BURDEN LIGHT.
SA (SWISH)
I HAD FUN DRAWING UP THE BLUEPRINT FOR THIS THING.
I'M A MASTER DRAFTS-MAN.
ZA (ZOOSH)
ZA

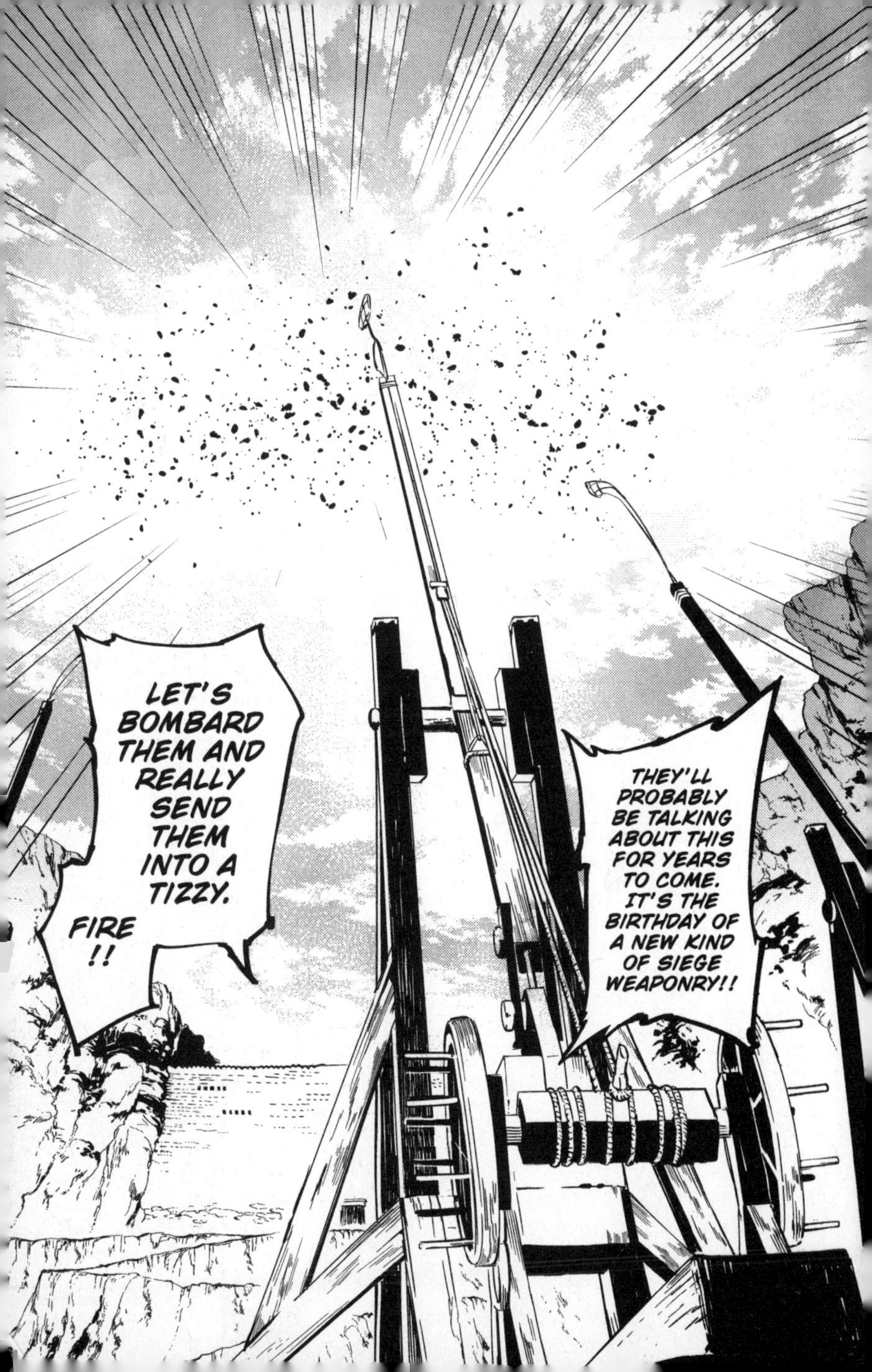
THEY'LL PROBABLY BE TALKING ABOUT THIS FOR YEARS TO COME. IT'S THE BIRTHDAY OF A NEW KIND OF SIEGE WEAPONRY!!
LET'S BOMBARD THEM AND REALLY SEND THEM INTO A TIZZY.
FIRE!!

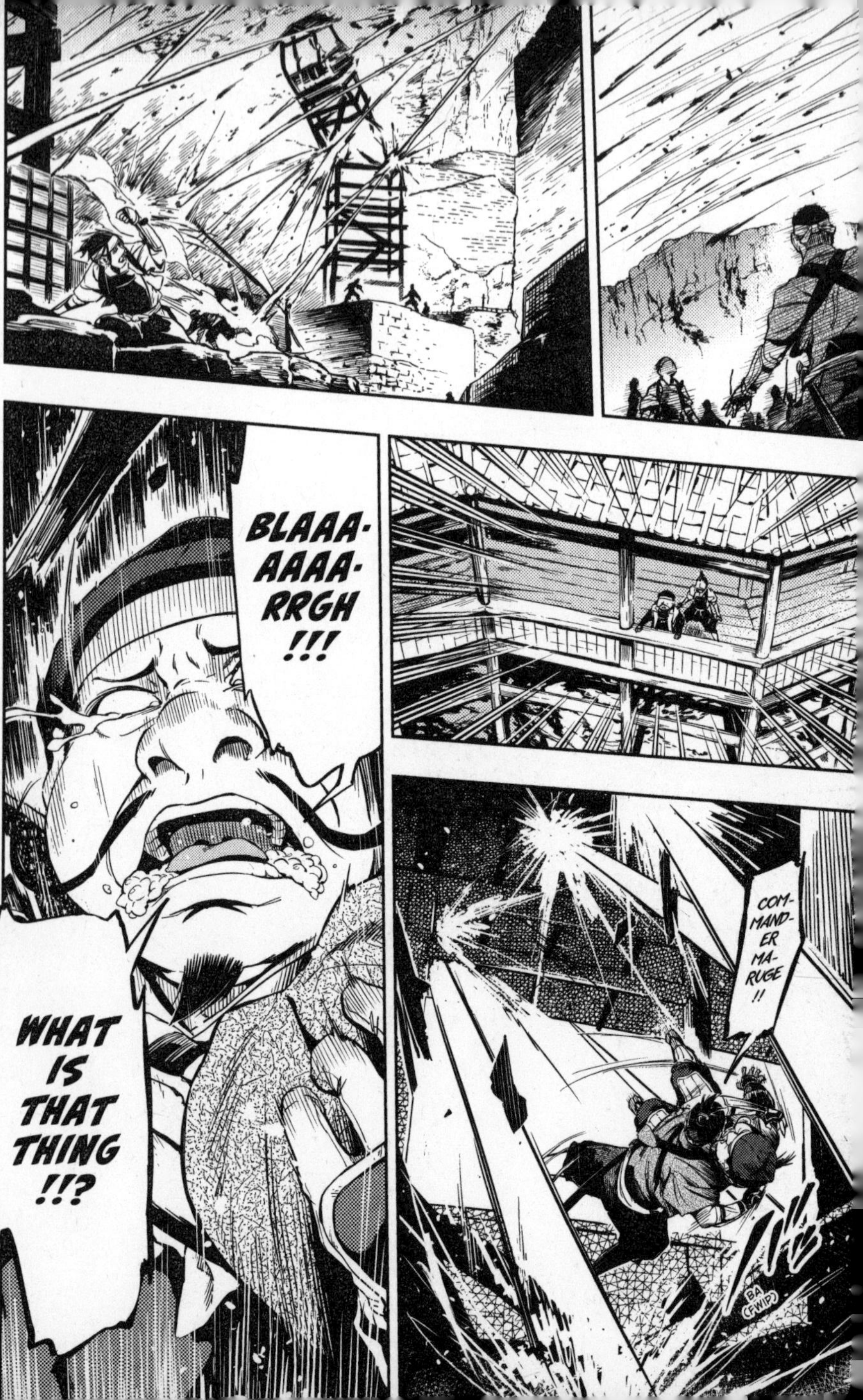
COMMANDER MARUGE!!
BA (FWIP)
BLAAAAAAARRGH!!!
WHAT IS THAT THING!!?

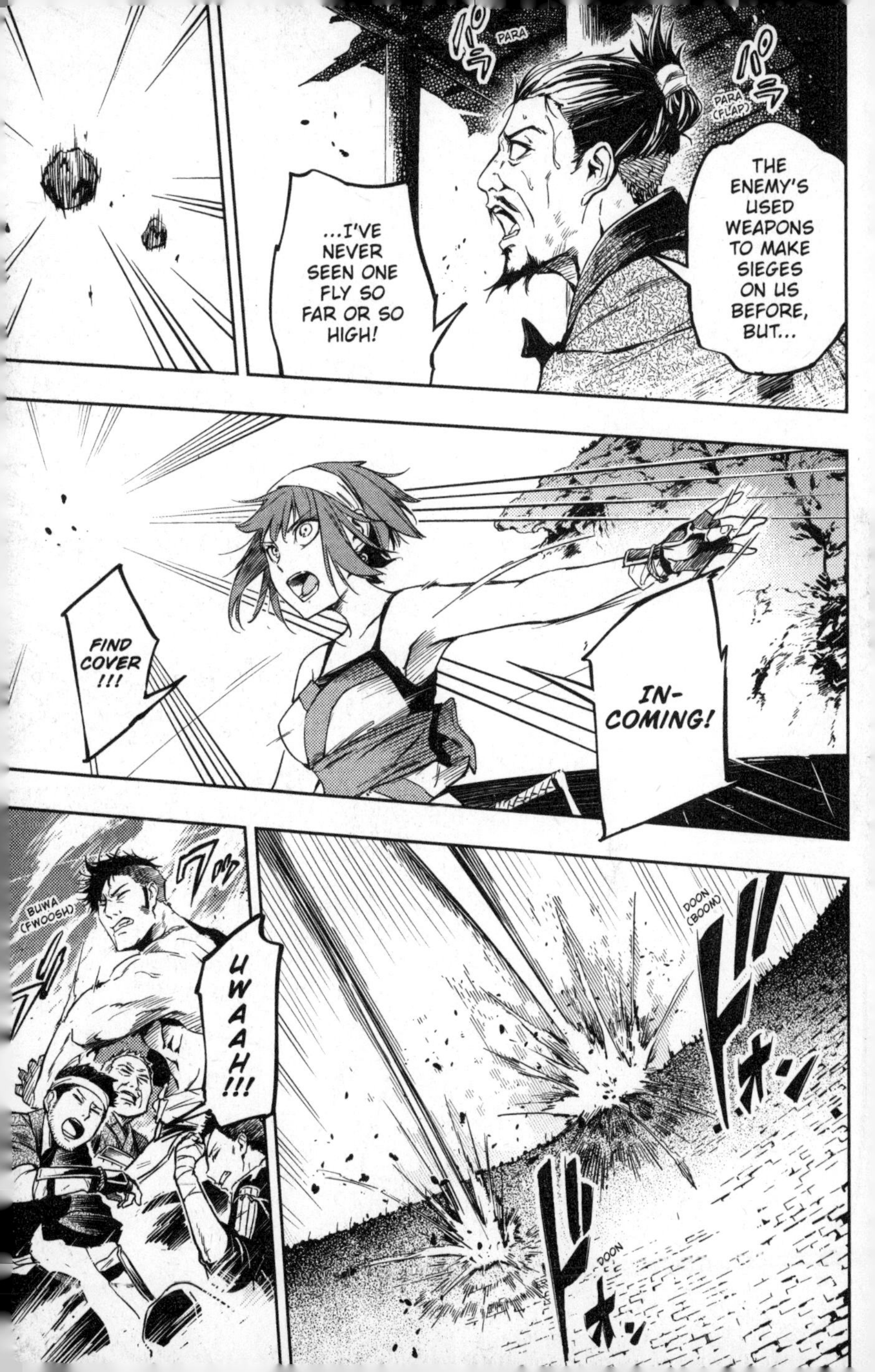
PARA
PARA (FLAP)
THE ENEMY'S USED WEAPONS TO MAKE SIEGES ON US BEFORE, BUT...
...I'VE NEVER SEEN ONE FLY SO FAR OR SO HIGH!
IN-COMING!
FIND COVER!!!
DOON (BOOM)
DOON
BUWA (FWOOSH)
UWAAAH!!!

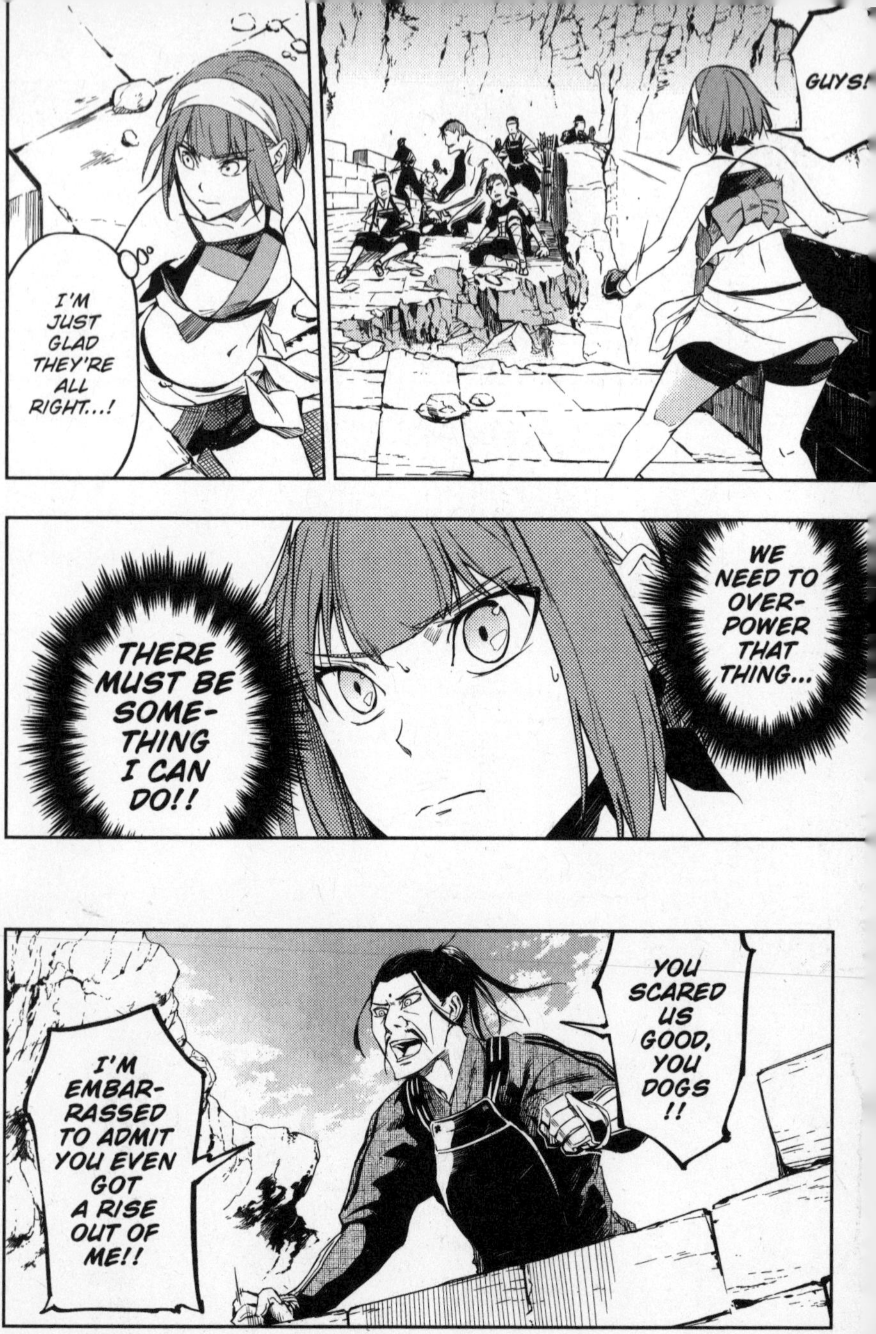
GUYS!
I'M JUST GLAD THEY'RE ALL RIGHT...!
WE NEED TO OVER-POWER THAT THING...
THERE MUST BE SOME-THING I CAN DO!!
YOU SCARED US GOOD, YOU DOGS!!
I'M EMBAR-RASSED TO ADMIT YOU EVEN GOT A RISE OUT OF ME!!

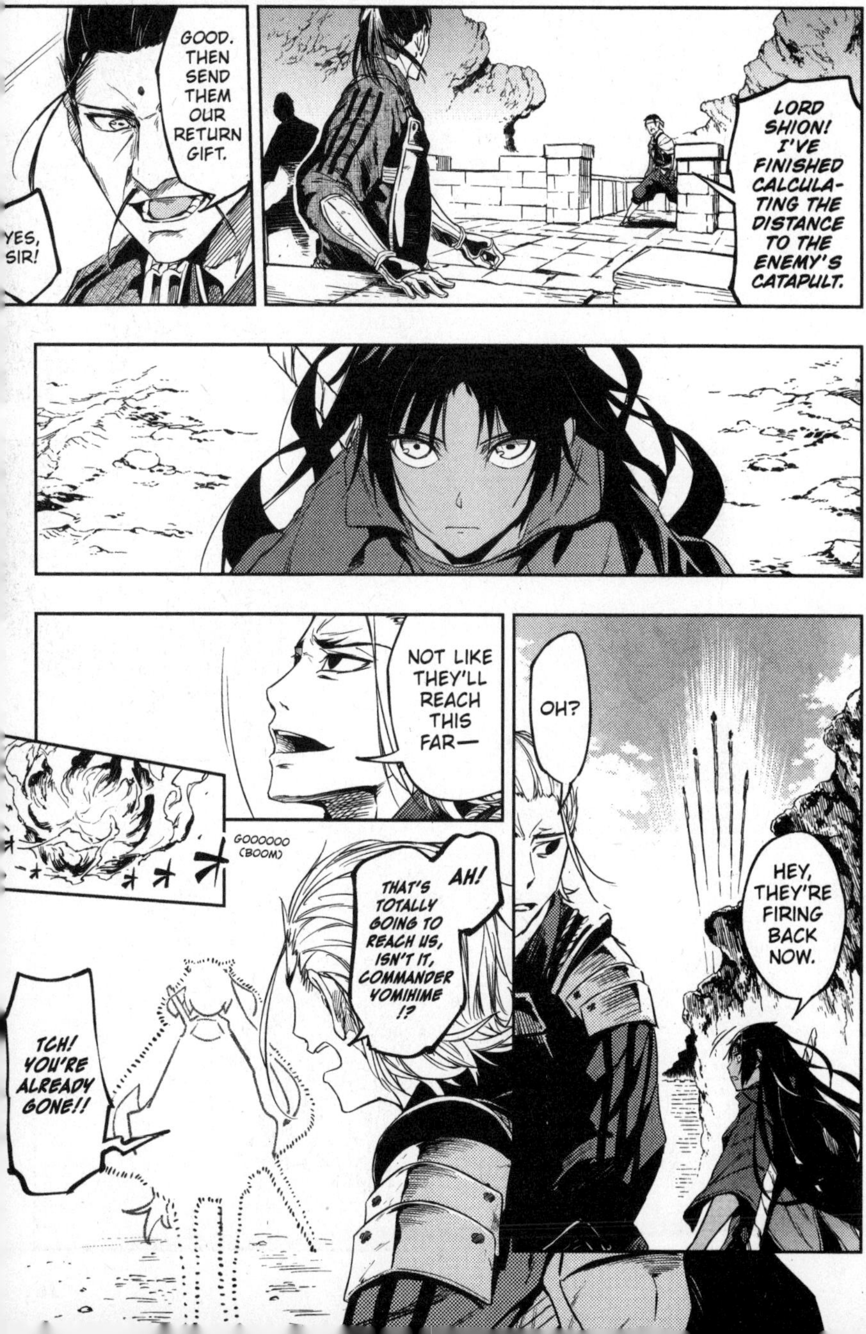
LORD SHION! I'VE FINISHED CALCULATING THE DISTANCE TO THE ENEMY'S CATAPULT.
GOOD. THEN SEND THEM OUR RETURN GIFT.
YES, SIR!
OH?
HEY, THEY'RE FIRING BACK NOW.
NOT LIKE THEY'LL REACH THIS FAR—
GOOOOOO (BOOM)
AH!
THAT'S TOTALLY GOING TO REACH US, ISN'T IT, COMMANDER YOMIHIME!?
TCH! YOU'RE ALREADY GONE!!

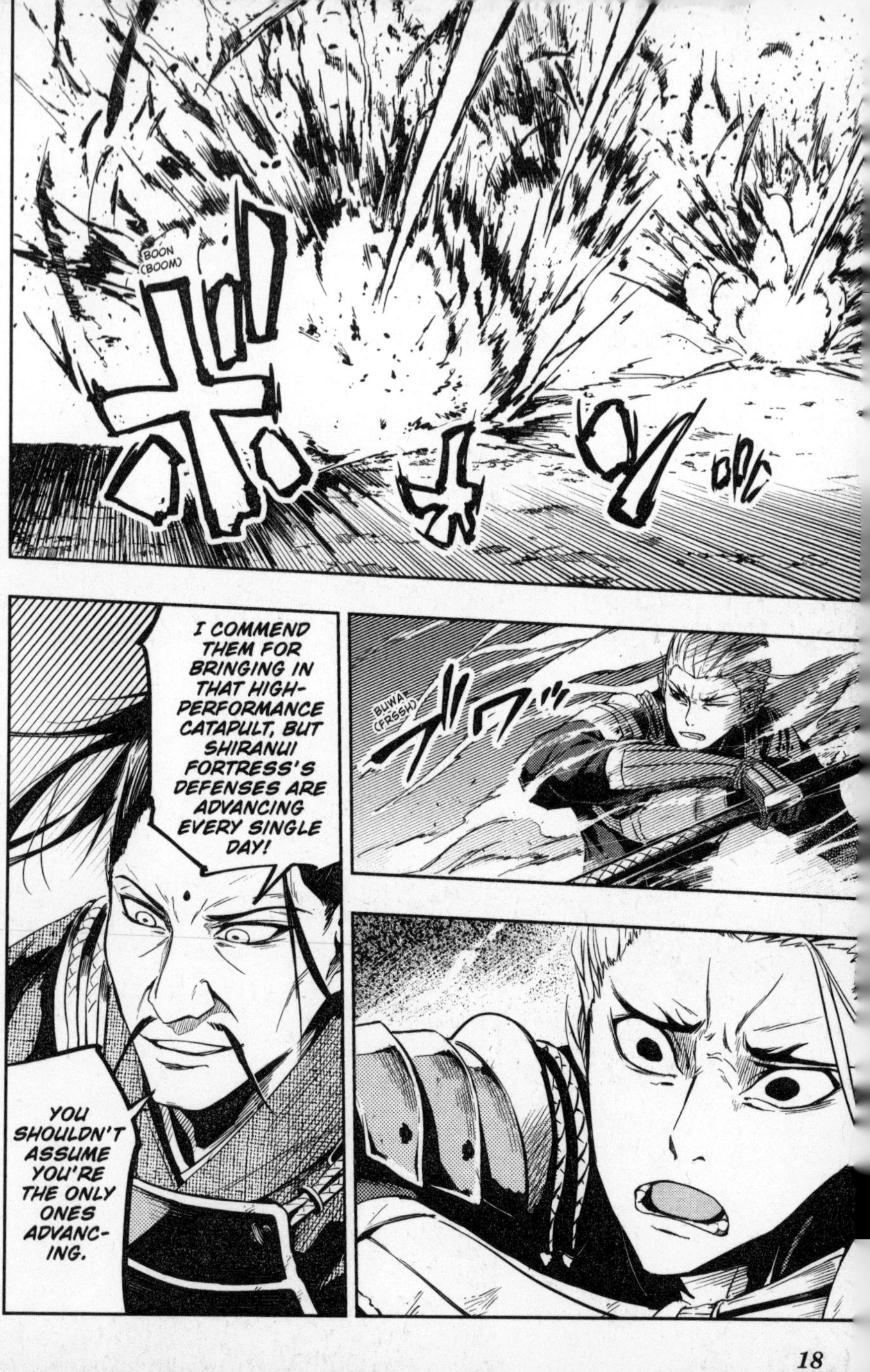
BOON (BOOM)
BUWA (FRSSH)
I COMMEND THEM FOR BRINGING IN THAT HIGH-PERFORMANCE CATAPULT, BUT SHIRANUI FORTRESS'S DEFENSES ARE ADVANCING EVERY SINGLE DAY!
YOU SHOULDN'T ASSUME YOU'RE THE ONLY ONES ADVANC-ING.

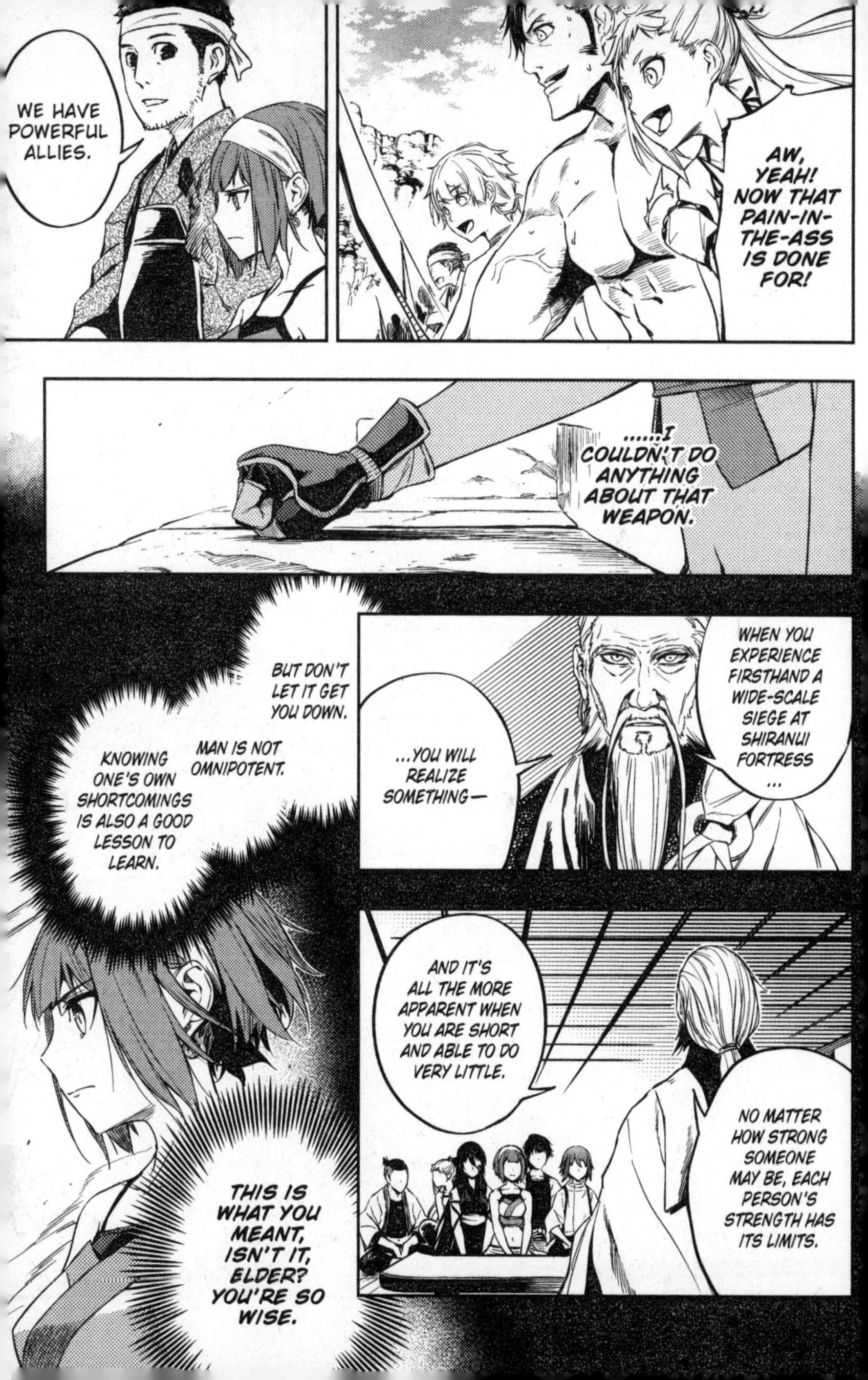

AW, YEAH! NOW THAT PAIN-IN-THE-ASS IS DONE FOR!
WE HAVE POWERFUL ALLIES.
......I COULDN'T DO ANYTHING ABOUT THAT WEAPON.
WHEN YOU EXPERIENCE FIRSTHAND A WIDE-SCALE SIEGE AT SHIRANUI FORTRESS ...
...YOU WILL REALIZE SOMETHING—
NO MATTER HOW STRONG SOMEONE MAY BE, EACH PERSON'S STRENGTH HAS ITS LIMITS.
AND IT'S ALL THE MORE APPARENT WHEN YOU ARE SHORT AND ABLE TO DO VERY LITTLE.
BUT DON'T LET IT GET YOU DOWN.
MAN IS NOT OMNIPOTENT.
KNOWING ONE'S OWN SHORTCOMINGS IS ALSO A GOOD LESSON TO LEARN.
THIS IS WHAT YOU MEANT, ISN'T IT, ELDER? YOU'RE SO WISE.

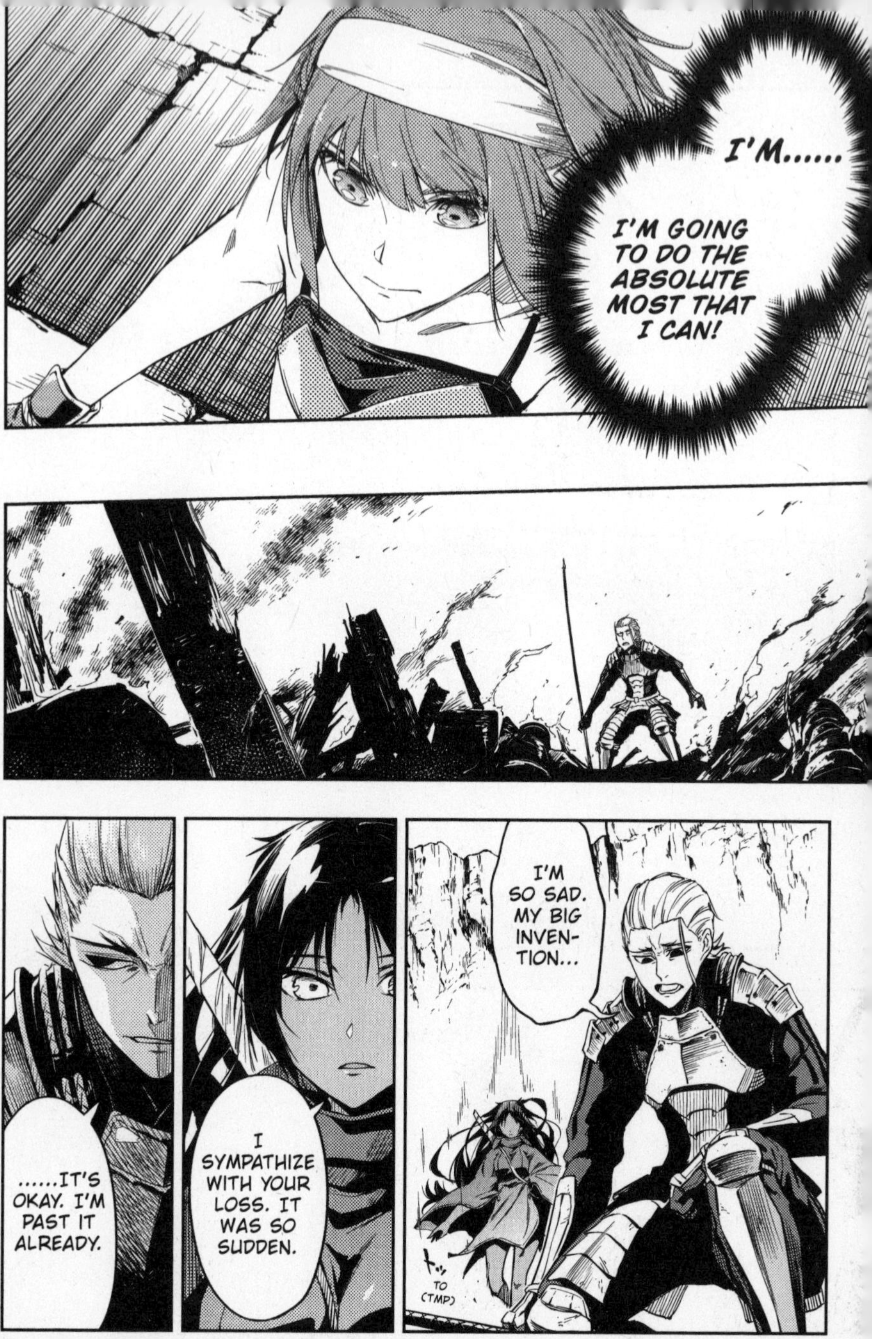
I'M......
I'M GOING TO DO THE ABSOLUTE MOST THAT I CAN!
I'M SO SAD. MY BIG INVEN- TION...
トッ
TO (TMP)
I SYMPATHIZE WITH YOUR LOSS. IT WAS SO SUDDEN.
......IT'S OKAY. I'M PAST IT ALREADY.

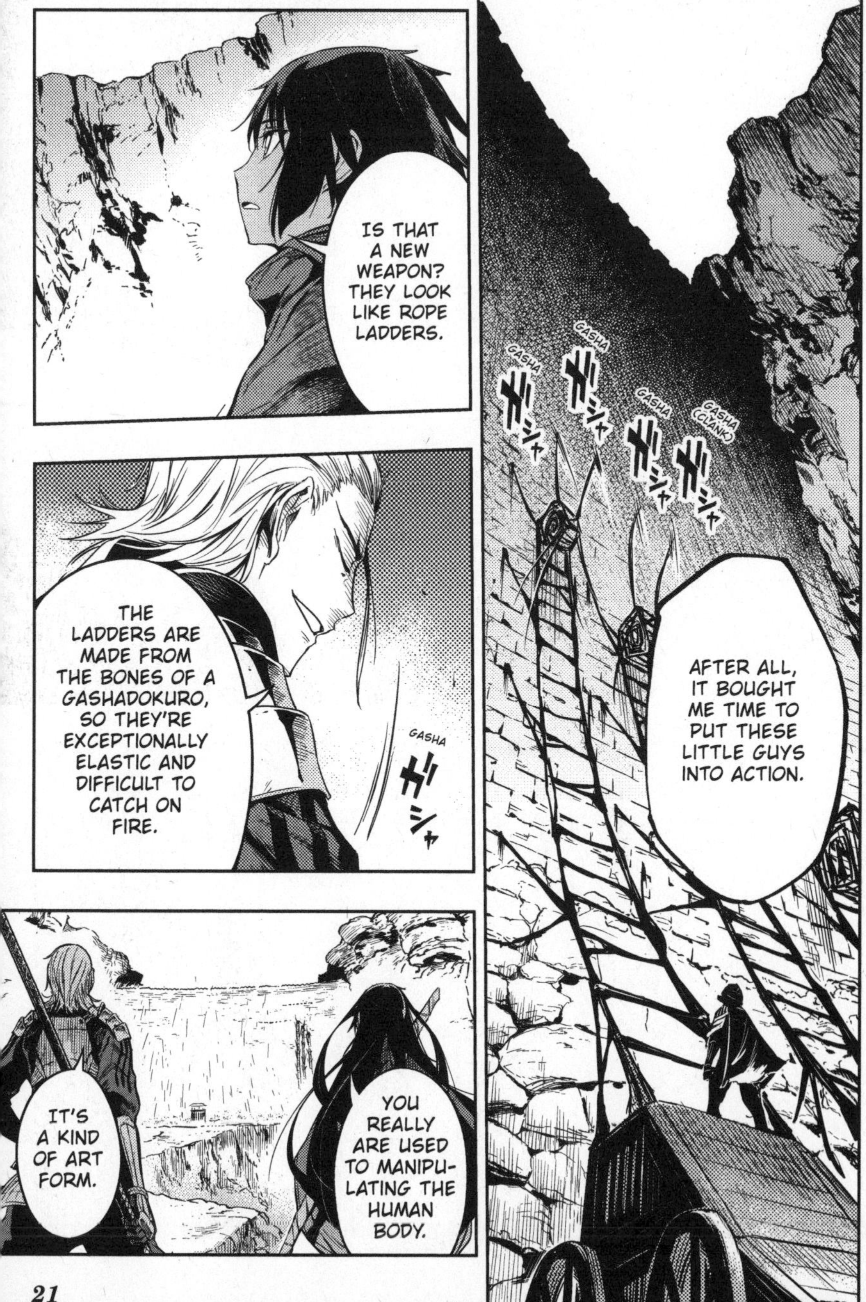
GASHA
GASHA
GASHA
GASHA (CLANK)
AFTER ALL, IT BOUGHT ME TIME TO PUT THESE LITTLE GUYS INTO ACTION.
IS THAT A NEW WEAPON? THEY LOOK LIKE ROPE LADDERS.
THE LADDERS ARE MADE FROM THE BONES OF A GASHADOKURO, SO THEY'RE EXCEPTIONALLY ELASTIC AND DIFFICULT TO CATCH ON FIRE.
GASHA
YOU REALLY ARE USED TO MANIPULATING THE HUMAN BODY.
IT'S A KIND OF ART FORM.

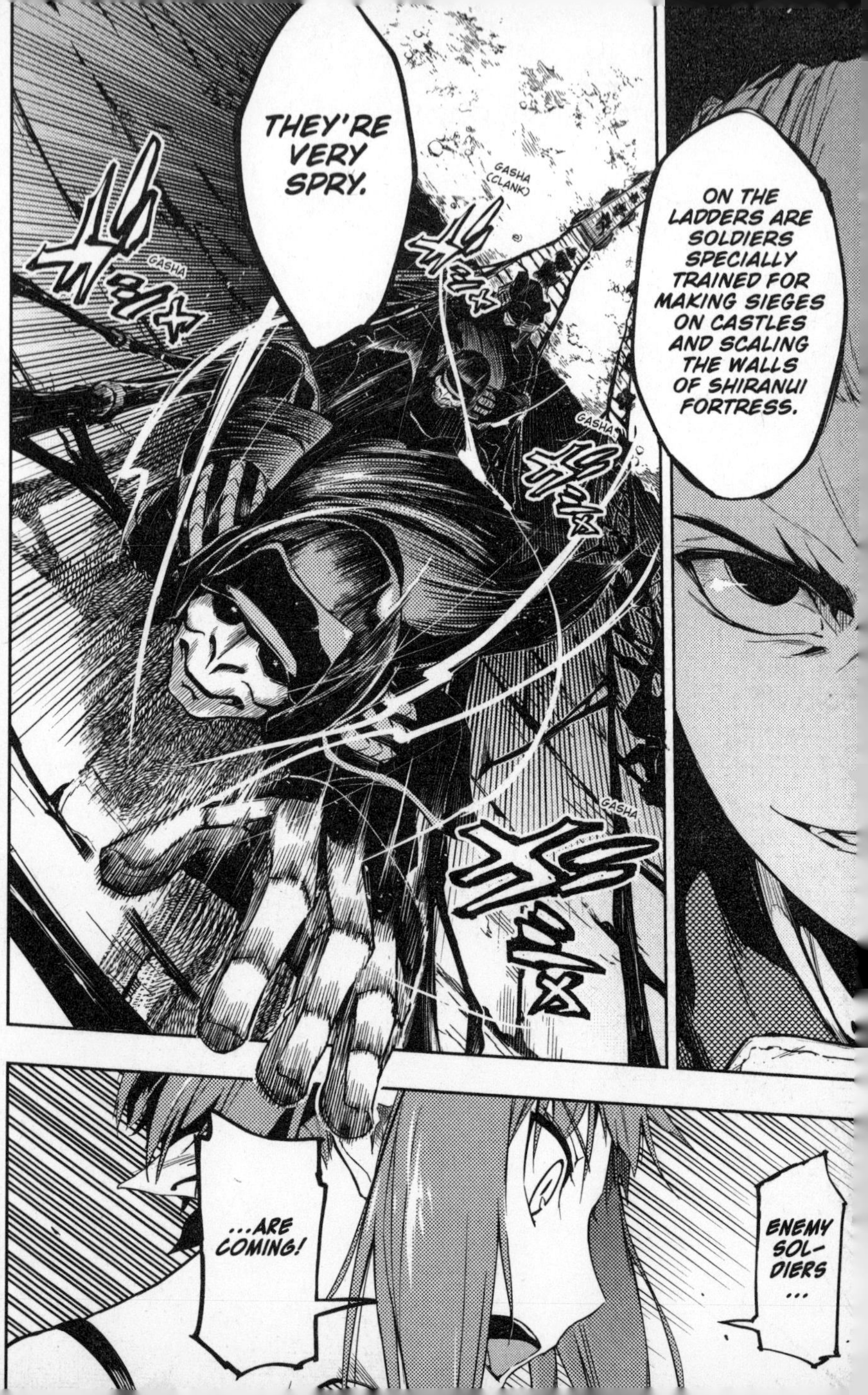
ON THE LADDERS ARE SOLDIERS SPECIALLY TRAINED FOR MAKING SIEGES ON CASTLES AND SCALING THE WALLS OF SHIRANUI FORTRESS.
THEY'RE VERY SPRY.
GASHA (CLANK)
GASHA
GASHA
GASHA
ENEMY SOL-DIERS ...
...ARE COMING!

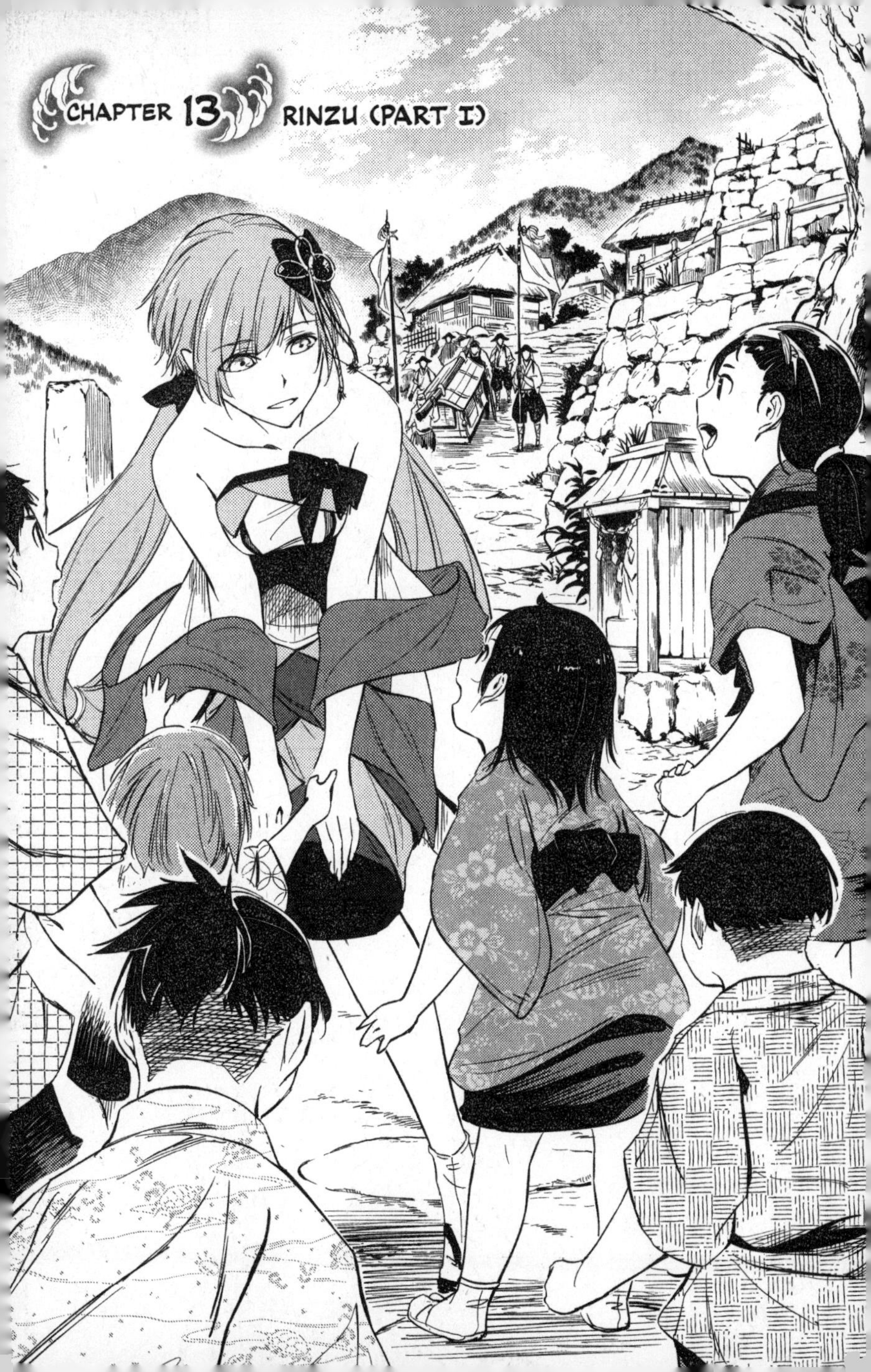
CHAPTER 13
RINZU (PART I)

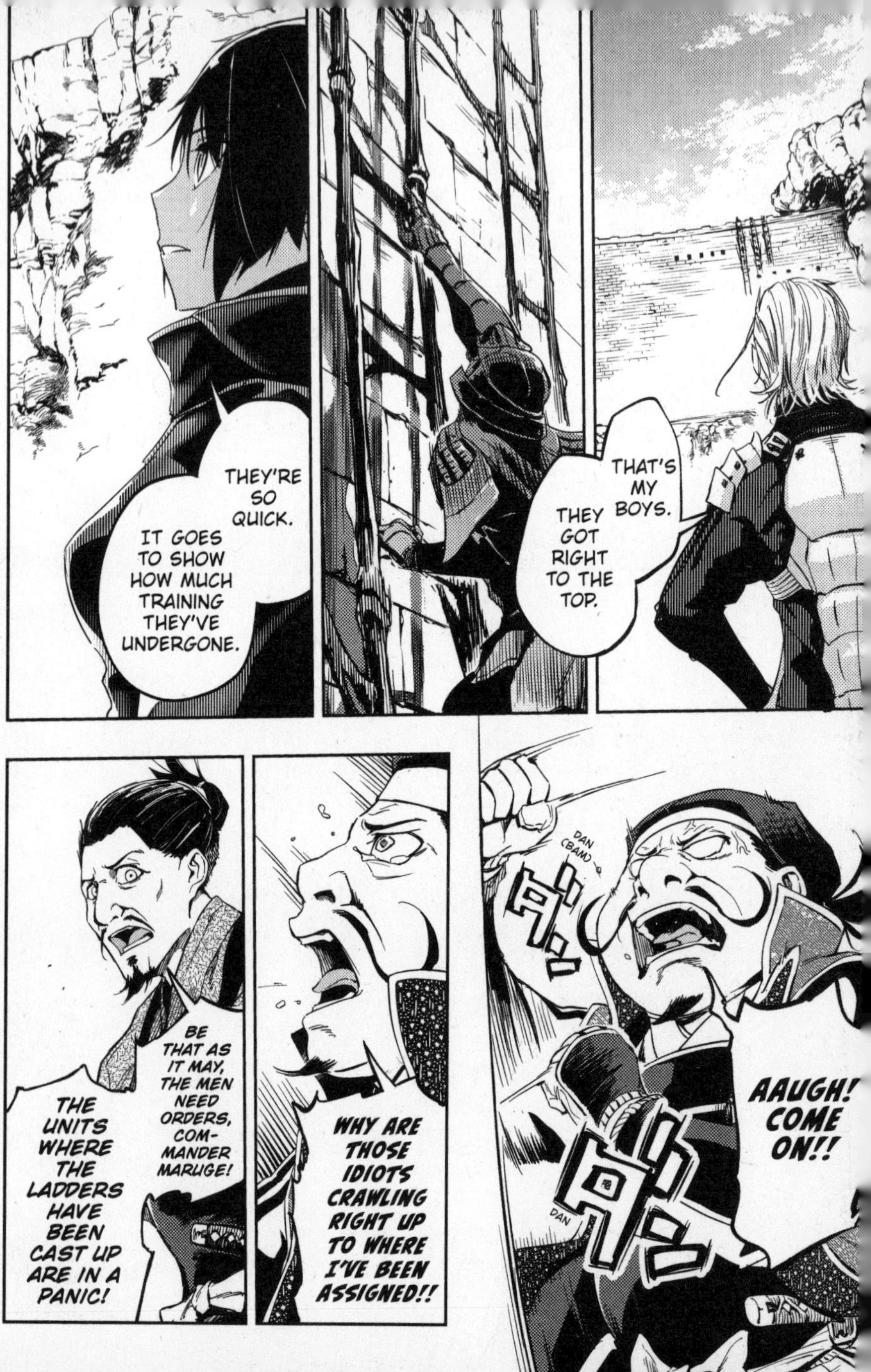
THAT'S MY BOYS.
THEY GOT RIGHT TO THE TOP.
THEY'RE SO QUICK.
IT GOES TO SHOW HOW MUCH TRAINING THEY'VE UNDERGONE.
DAN (BAM)
AAUGH! COME ON!!
DAN
WHY ARE THOSE IDIOTS CRAWLING RIGHT UP TO WHERE I'VE BEEN ASSIGNED!!
BE THAT AS IT MAY, THE MEN NEED ORDERS, COM-MANDER MARUGE!
THE UNITS WHERE THE LADDERS HAVE BEEN CAST UP ARE IN A PANIC!

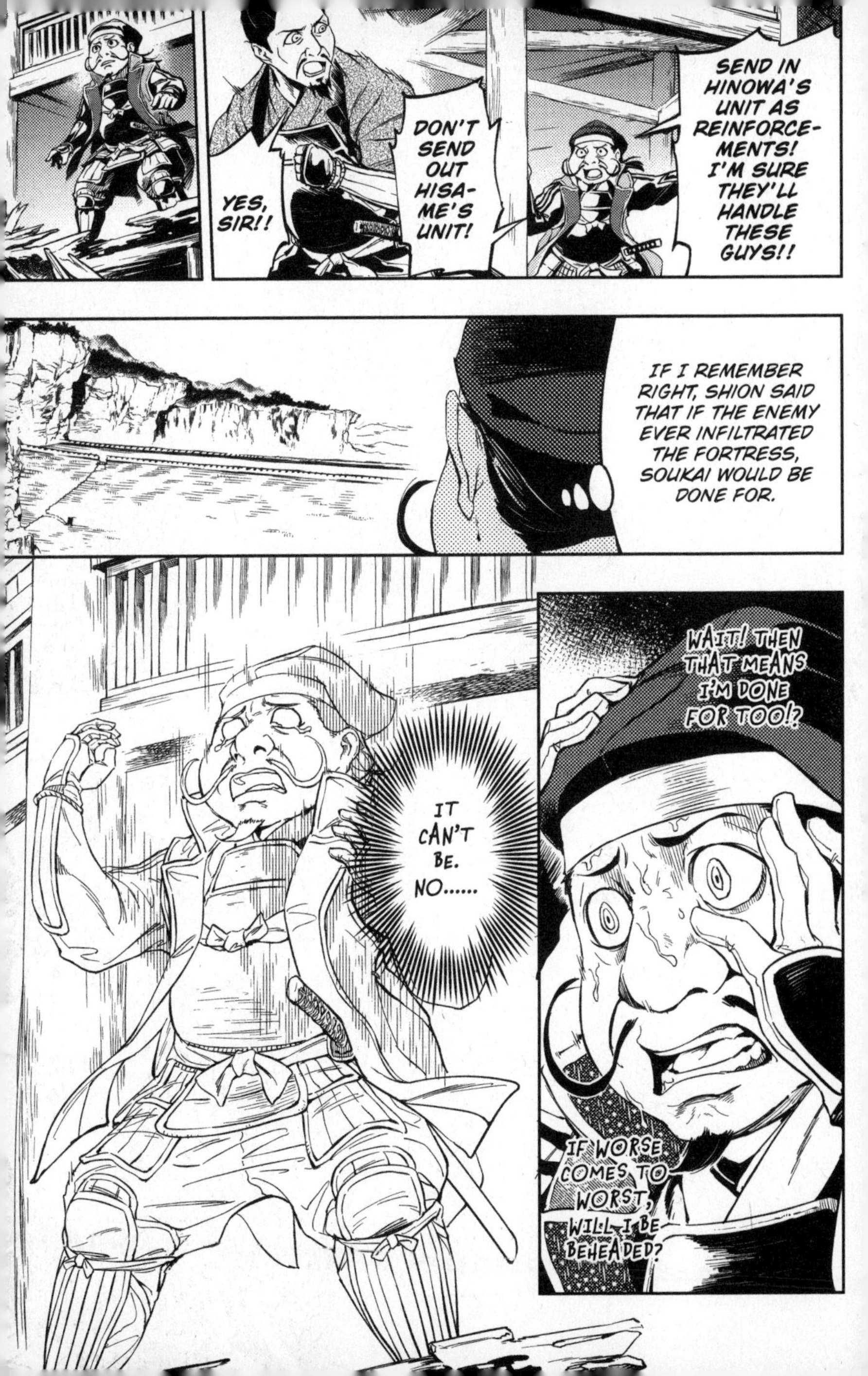
SEND IN HINOWA'S UNIT AS REINFORCEMENTS! I'M SURE THEY'LL HANDLE THESE GUYS!!
DON'T SEND OUT HISAME'S UNIT!
YES, SIR!!
IF I REMEMBER RIGHT, SHION SAID THAT IF THE ENEMY EVER INFILTRATED THE FORTRESS, SOUKAI WOULD BE DONE FOR.
WAIT! THEN THAT MEANS I'M DONE FOR TOO!?
IF WORSE COMES TO WORST, WILL I BE BEHEADED?
IT CAN'T BE. NO......

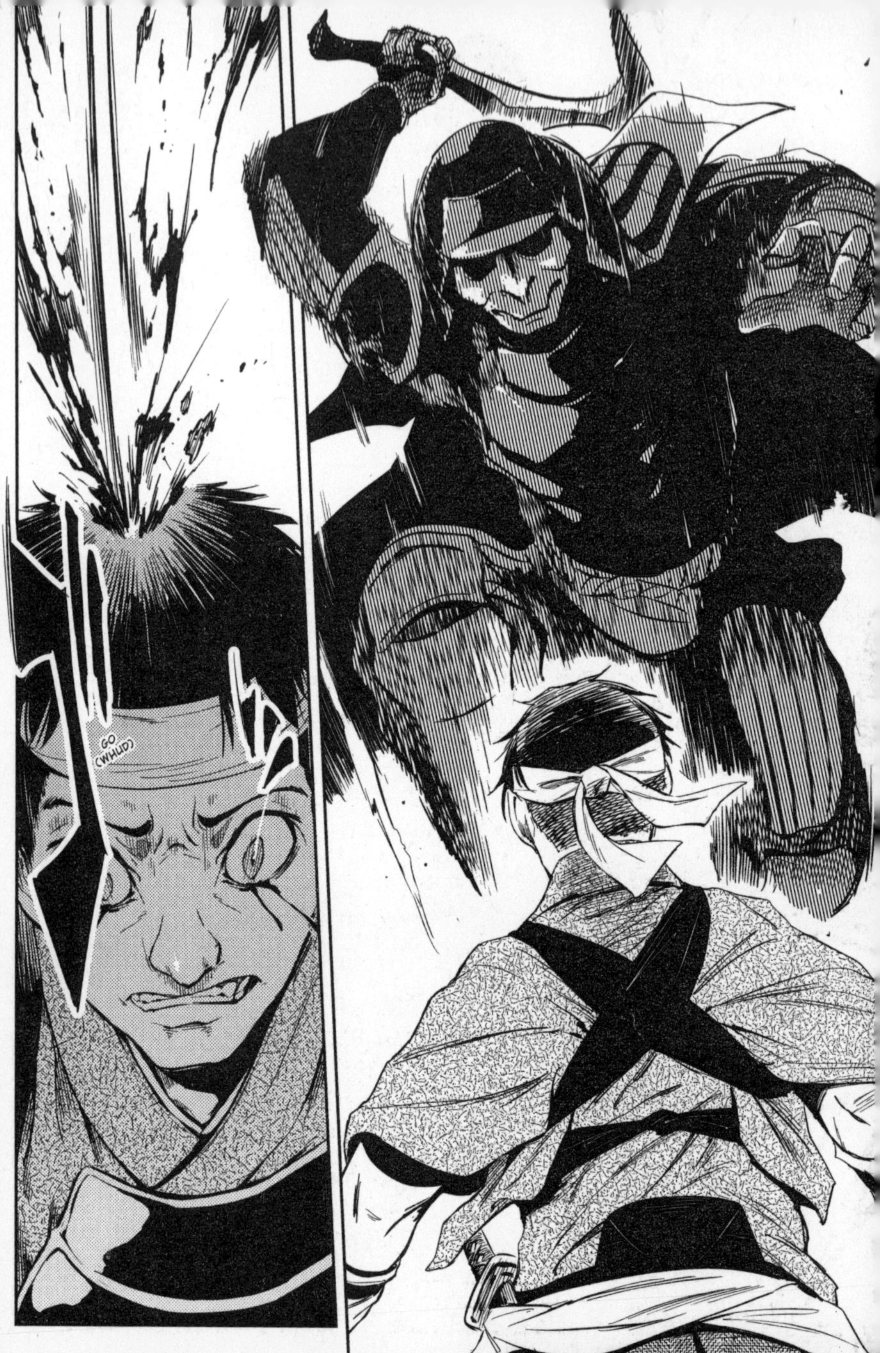
GO
(WHUD)

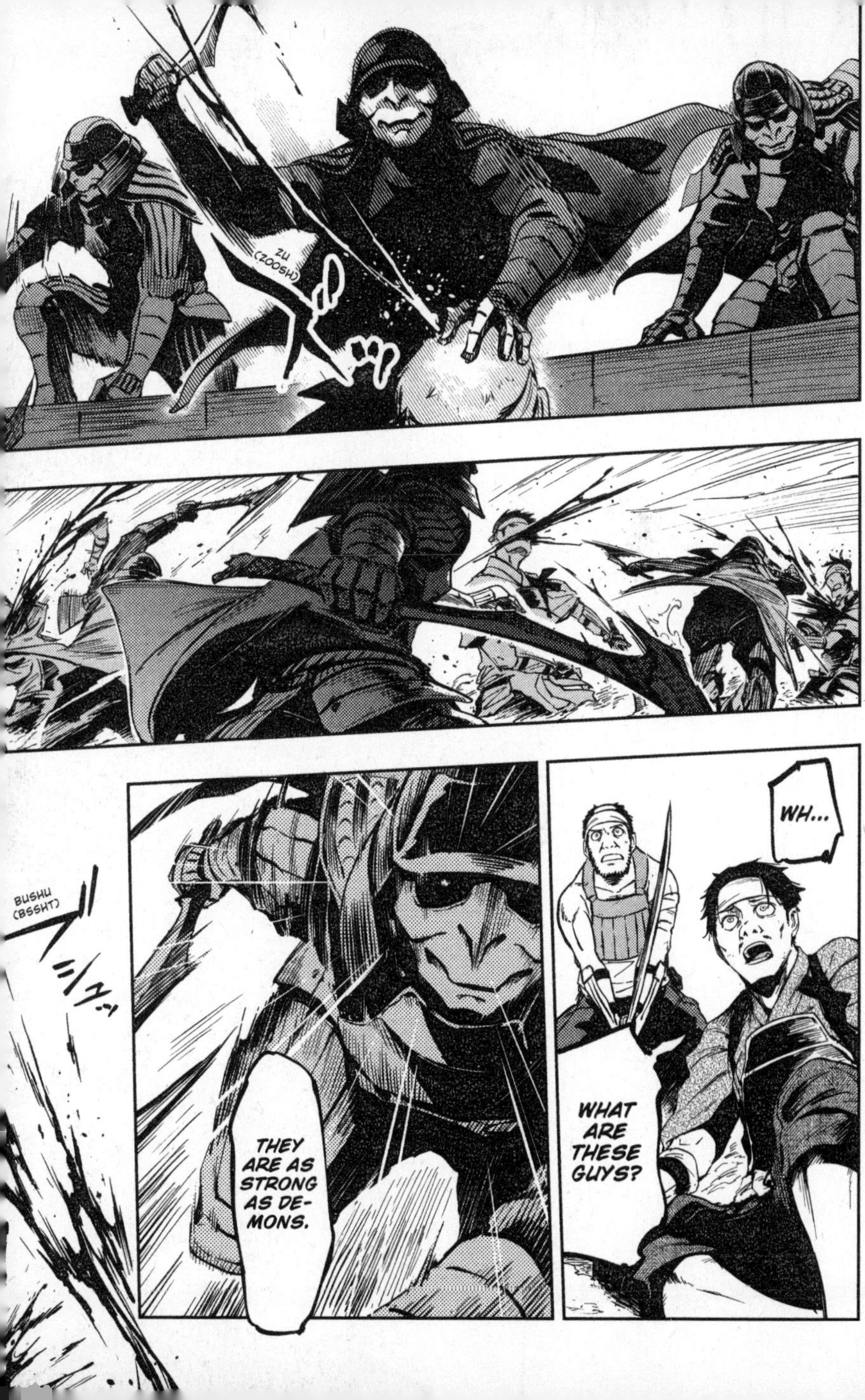
ZU
(ZOOSH)
WH...
WHAT ARE THESE GUYS?
BUSHU
(BSSHT)
THEY ARE AS STRONG AS DE-MONS.

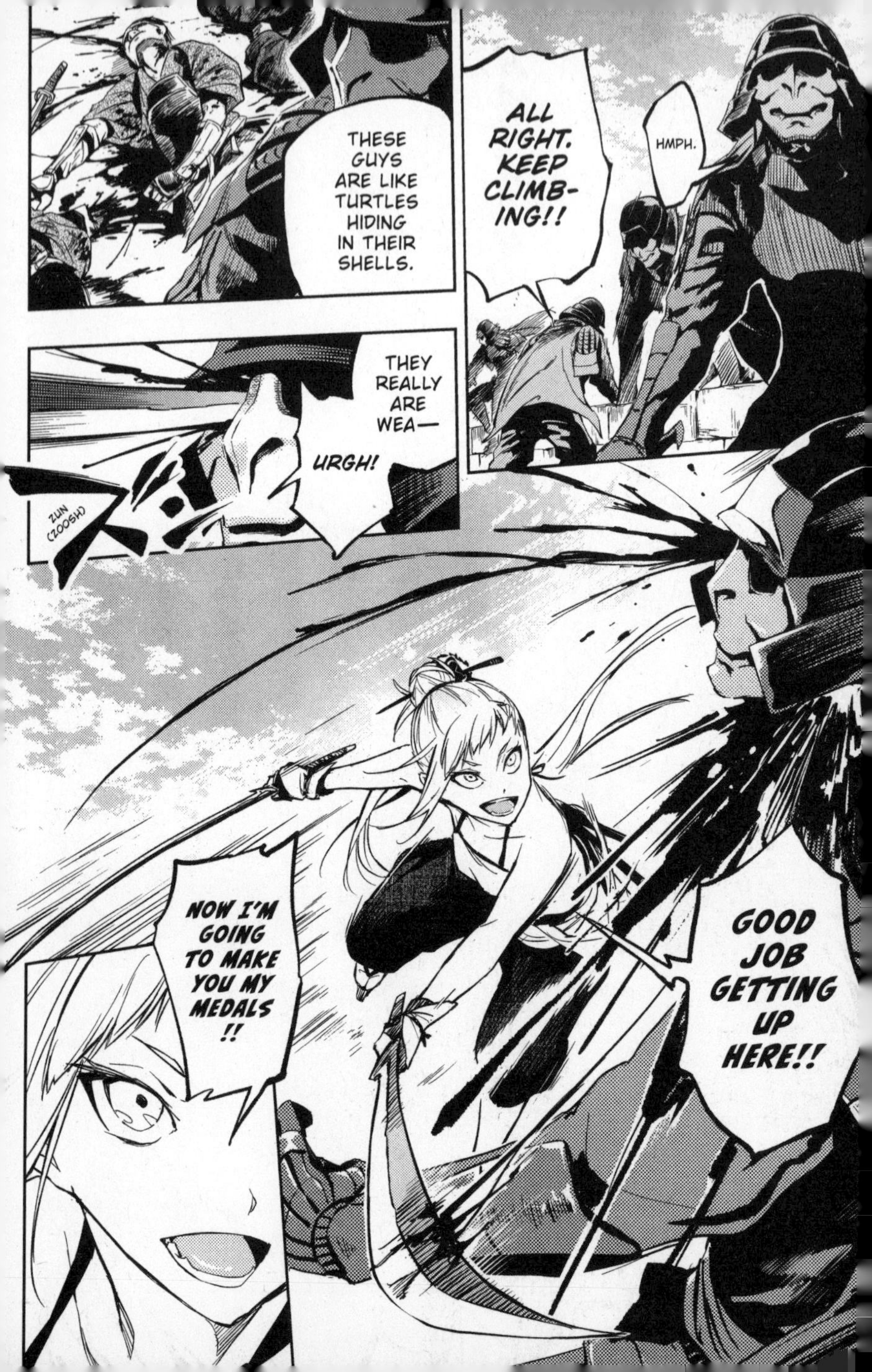
HMPH.
ALL RIGHT. KEEP CLIMB-ING!!
THESE GUYS ARE LIKE TURTLES HIDING IN THEIR SHELLS.
THEY REALLY ARE WEA—
URGH!
ZUN (ZOOSH)
GOOD JOB GETTING UP HERE!!
NOW I'M GOING TO MAKE YOU MY MEDALS!!

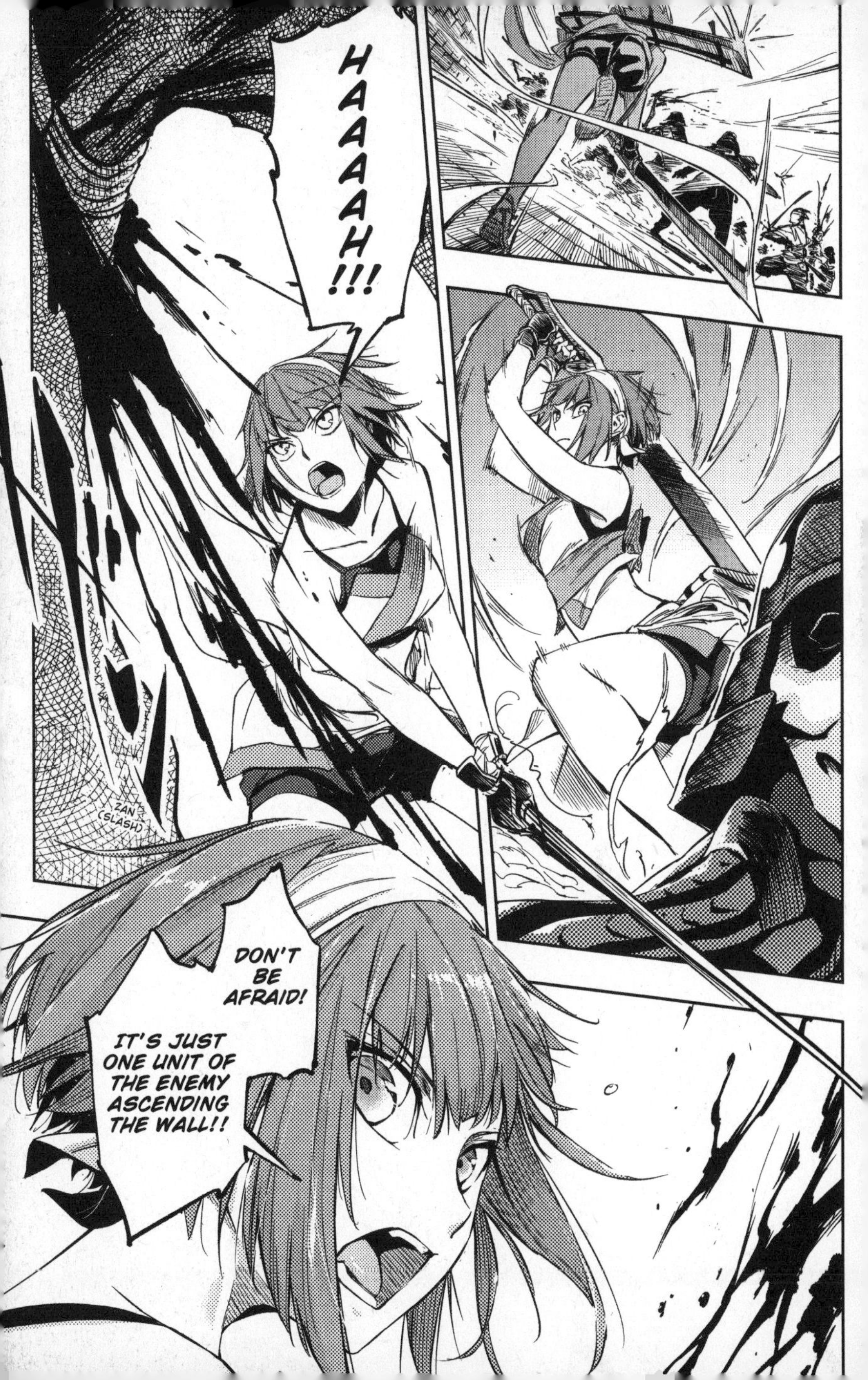
HAAAAAH!!!
ZAN (SLASH)
DON'T BE AFRAID!
IT'S JUST ONE UNIT OF THE ENEMY ASCENDING THE WALL!!

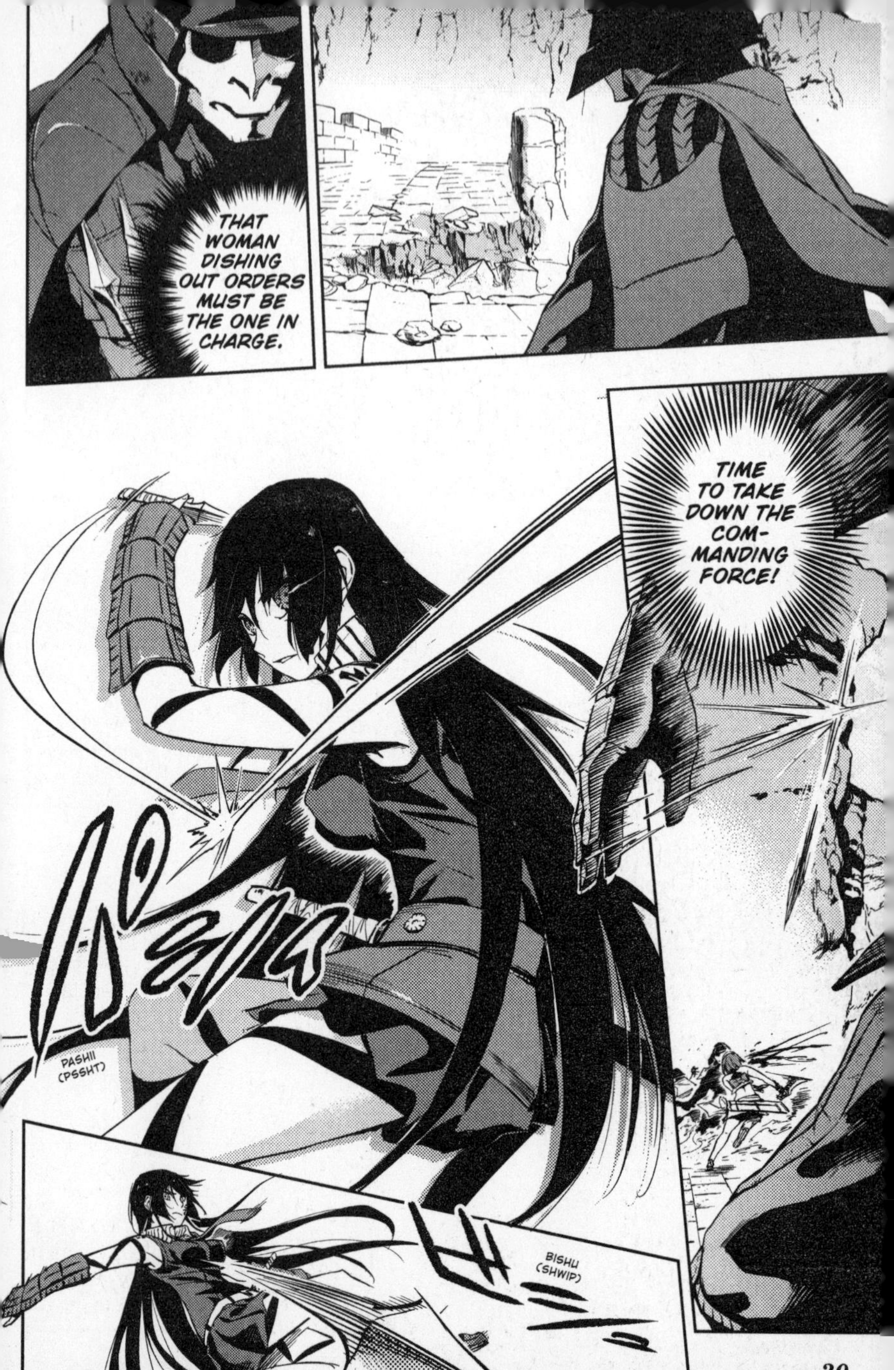
THAT WOMAN DISHING OUT ORDERS MUST BE THE ONE IN CHARGE.
TIME TO TAKE DOWN THE COM-MANDING FORCE!
PASHII (PSSHT)
BISHU (SHWIP)

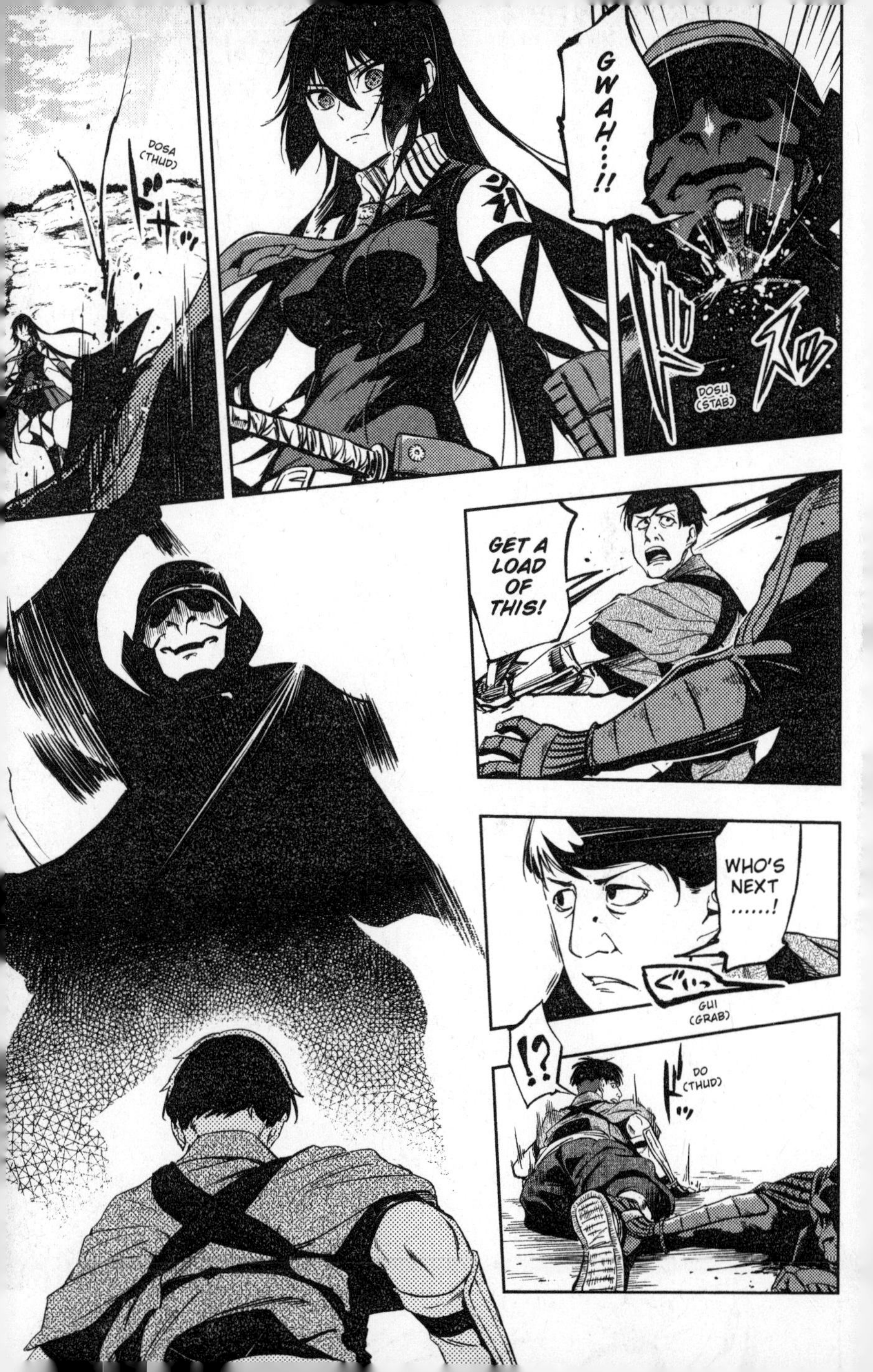
GWAH...!!
DOSU (STAB)
DOSA (THUD)
GET A LOAD OF THIS!
WHO'S NEXT......!
ぐいっ
GUI (GRAB)
!?
DO (THUD)

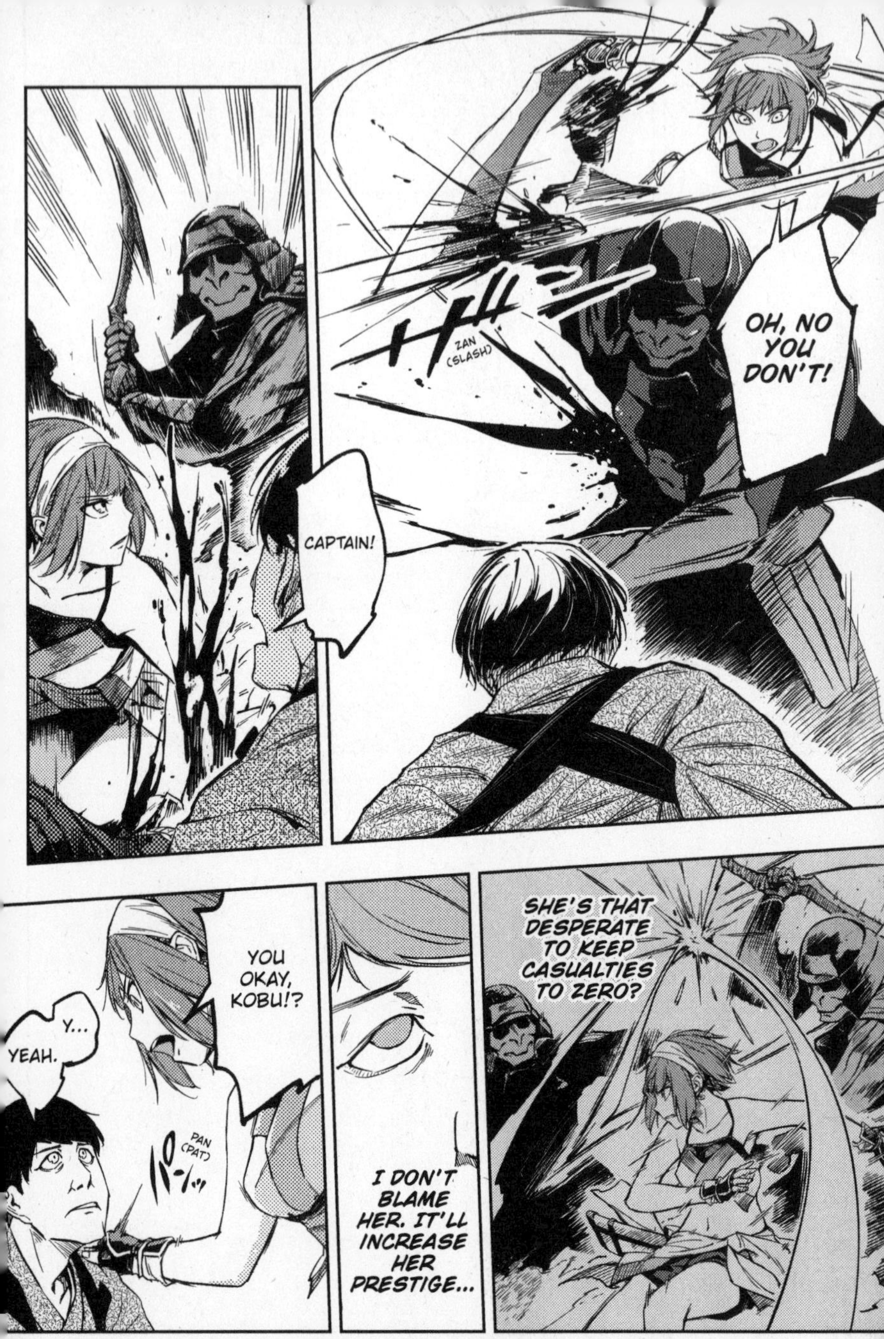
OH, NO YOU DON'T!
ZAN (SLASH)
CAPTAIN!
SHE'S THAT DESPERATE TO KEEP CASUALTIES TO ZERO?
I DON'T BLAME HER. IT'LL INCREASE HER PRESTIGE...
YOU OKAY, KOBU!?
Y... YEAH.
PAN (PAT)

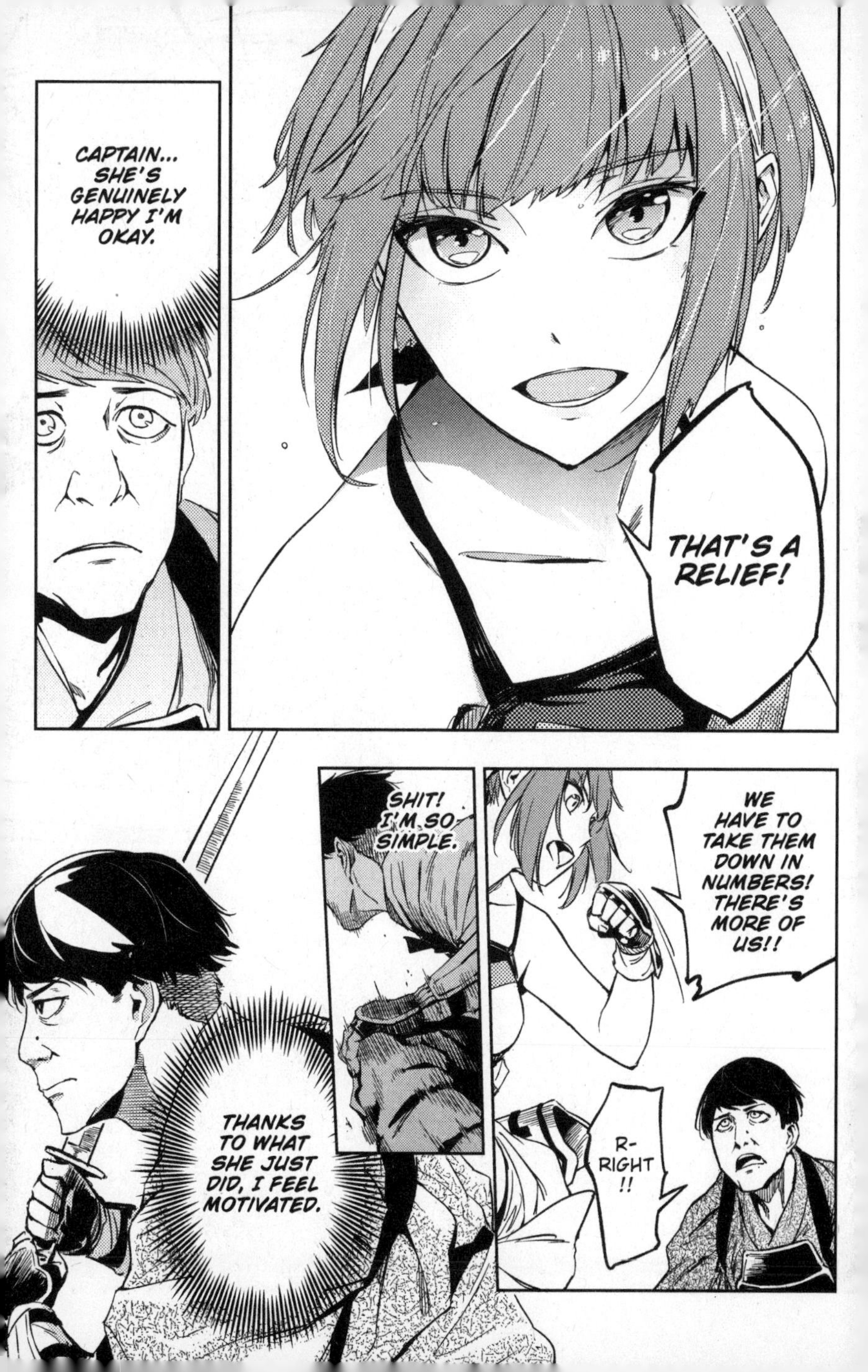
THAT'S A RELIEF!
CAPTAIN... SHE'S GENUINELY HAPPY I'M OKAY.
WE HAVE TO TAKE THEM DOWN IN NUMBERS! THERE'S MORE OF US!!
R-RIGHT!!
SHIT! I'M SO SIMPLE.
THANKS TO WHAT SHE JUST DID, I FEEL MOTIVATED.

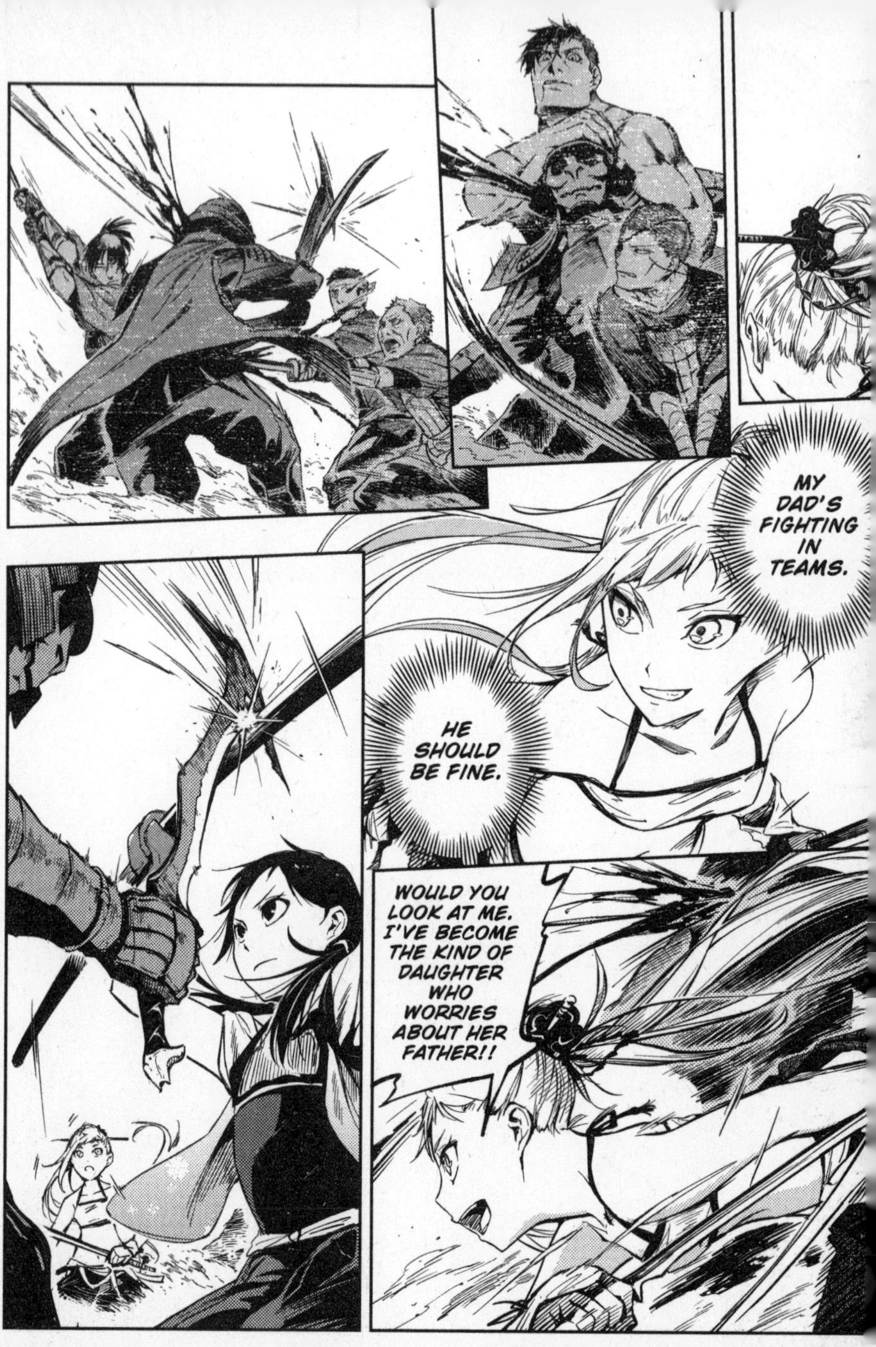
MY DAD'S FIGHTING IN TEAMS.
HE SHOULD BE FINE.
WOULD YOU LOOK AT ME. I'VE BECOME THE KIND OF DAUGHTER WHO WORRIES ABOUT HER FATHER!!

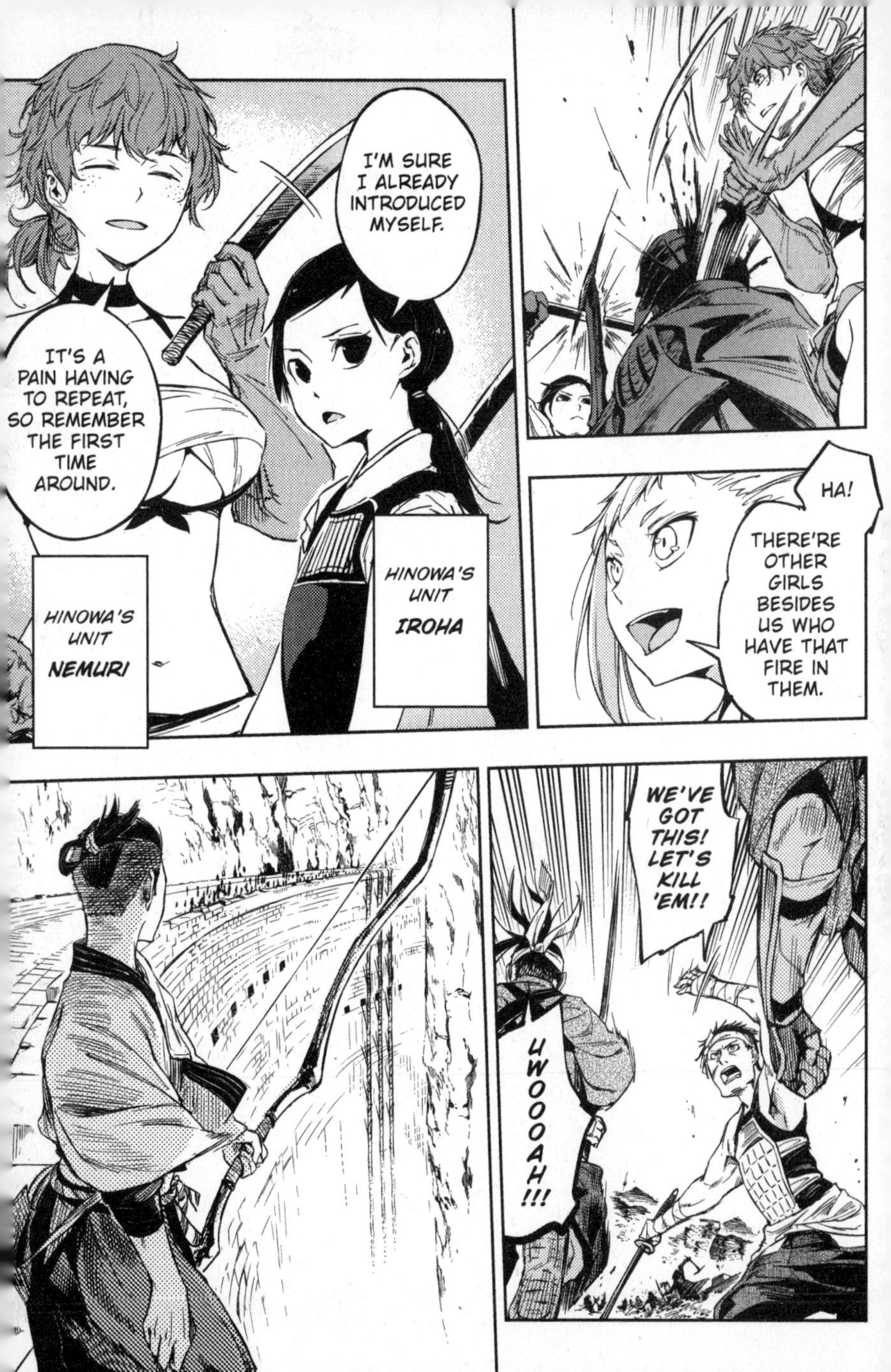
HA!
THERE'RE OTHER GIRLS BESIDES US WHO HAVE THAT FIRE IN THEM.
I'M SURE I ALREADY INTRODUCED MYSELF.
IT'S A PAIN HAVING TO REPEAT, SO REMEMBER THE FIRST TIME AROUND.
HINOWA'S UNIT IROHA
HINOWA'S UNIT NEMURI
WE'VE GOT THIS! LET'S KILL 'EM!!
UWOOOOAH!!!

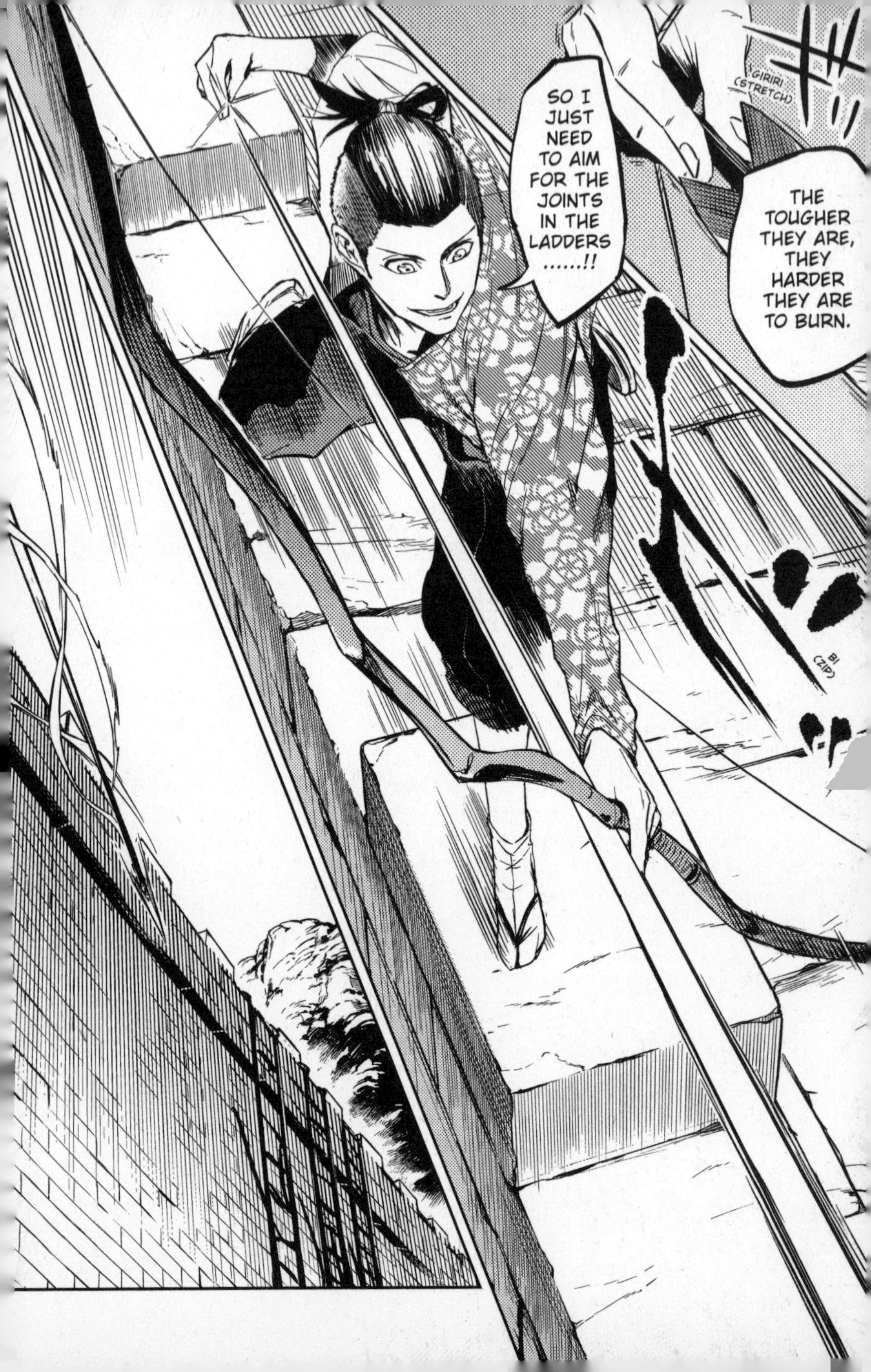
GIRIRI (STRETCH)
THE TOUGHER THEY ARE, THEY HARDER THEY ARE TO BURN.
SO I JUST NEED TO AIM FOR THE JOINTS IN THE LADDERS ......!!
BI (ZIP)

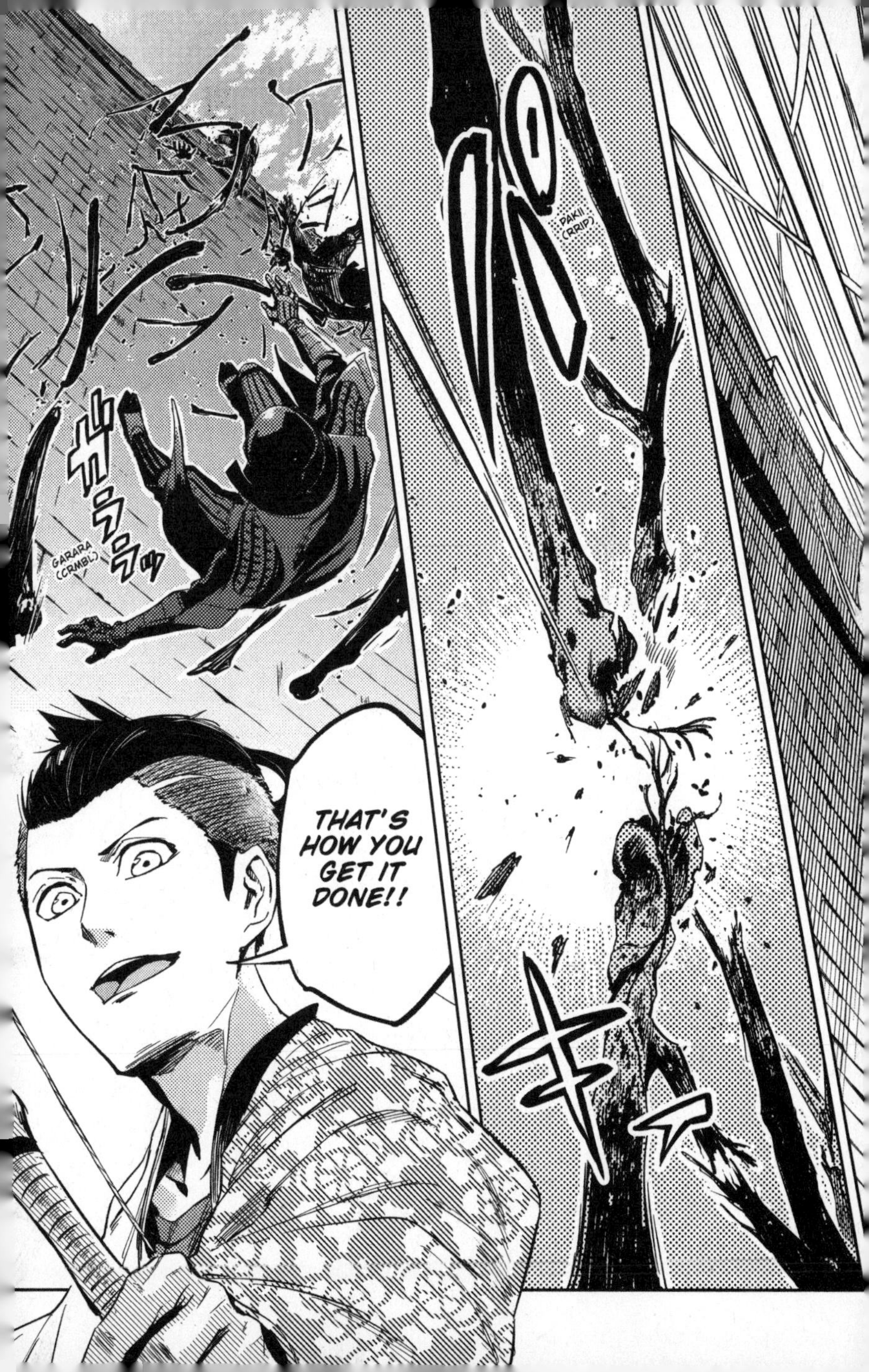
PAKII (RRIP)
GARARA (CRMBL)
THAT'S HOW YOU GET IT DONE!!

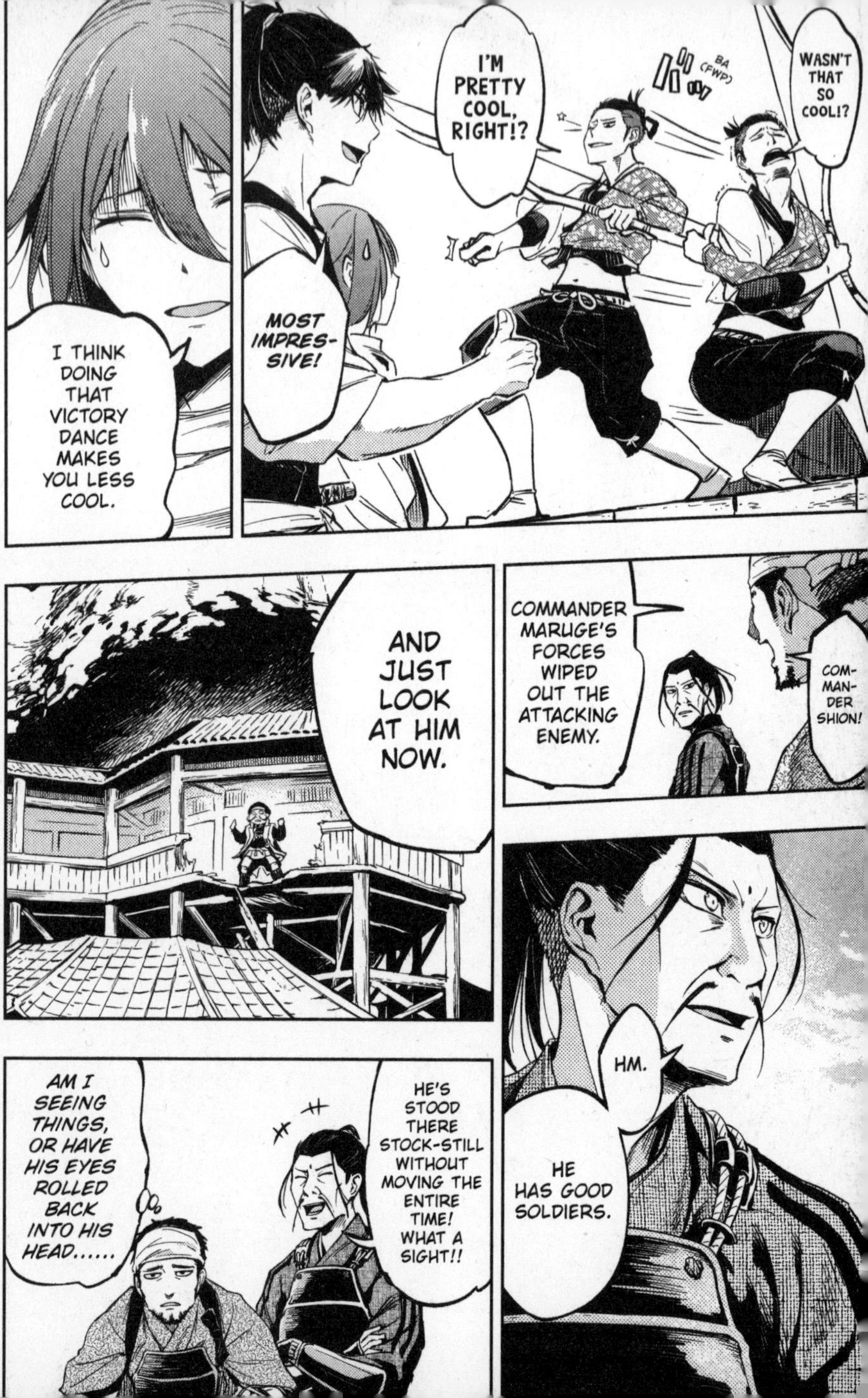
WASN'T THAT SO COOL!?
BA (FWP)
I'M PRETTY COOL, RIGHT!?
MOST IMPRES-SIVE!
I THINK DOING THAT VICTORY DANCE MAKES YOU LESS COOL.
COM-MAN-DER SHION!
COMMANDER MARUGE'S FORCES WIPED OUT THE ATTACKING ENEMY.
HM.
HE HAS GOOD SOLDIERS.
AND JUST LOOK AT HIM NOW.
HE'S STOOD THERE STOCK-STILL WITHOUT MOVING THE ENTIRE TIME! WHAT A SIGHT!!
AM I SEEING THINGS, OR HAVE HIS EYES ROLLED BACK INTO HIS HEAD......

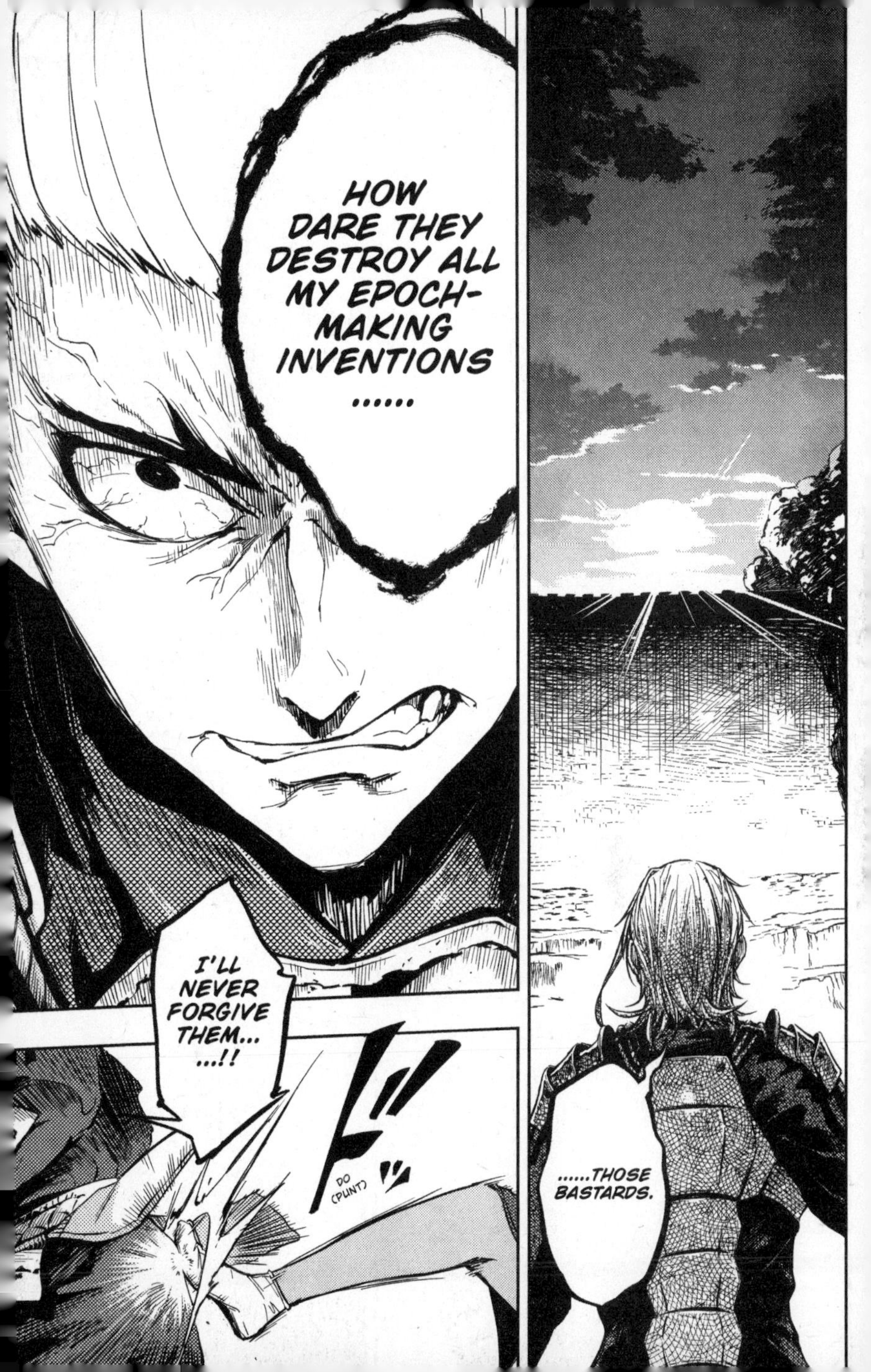
......THOSE BASTARDS.
HOW DARE THEY DESTROY ALL MY EPOCH-MAKING INVENTIONS ......
I'LL NEVER FORGIVE THEM... ...!!
DO (PUNT)

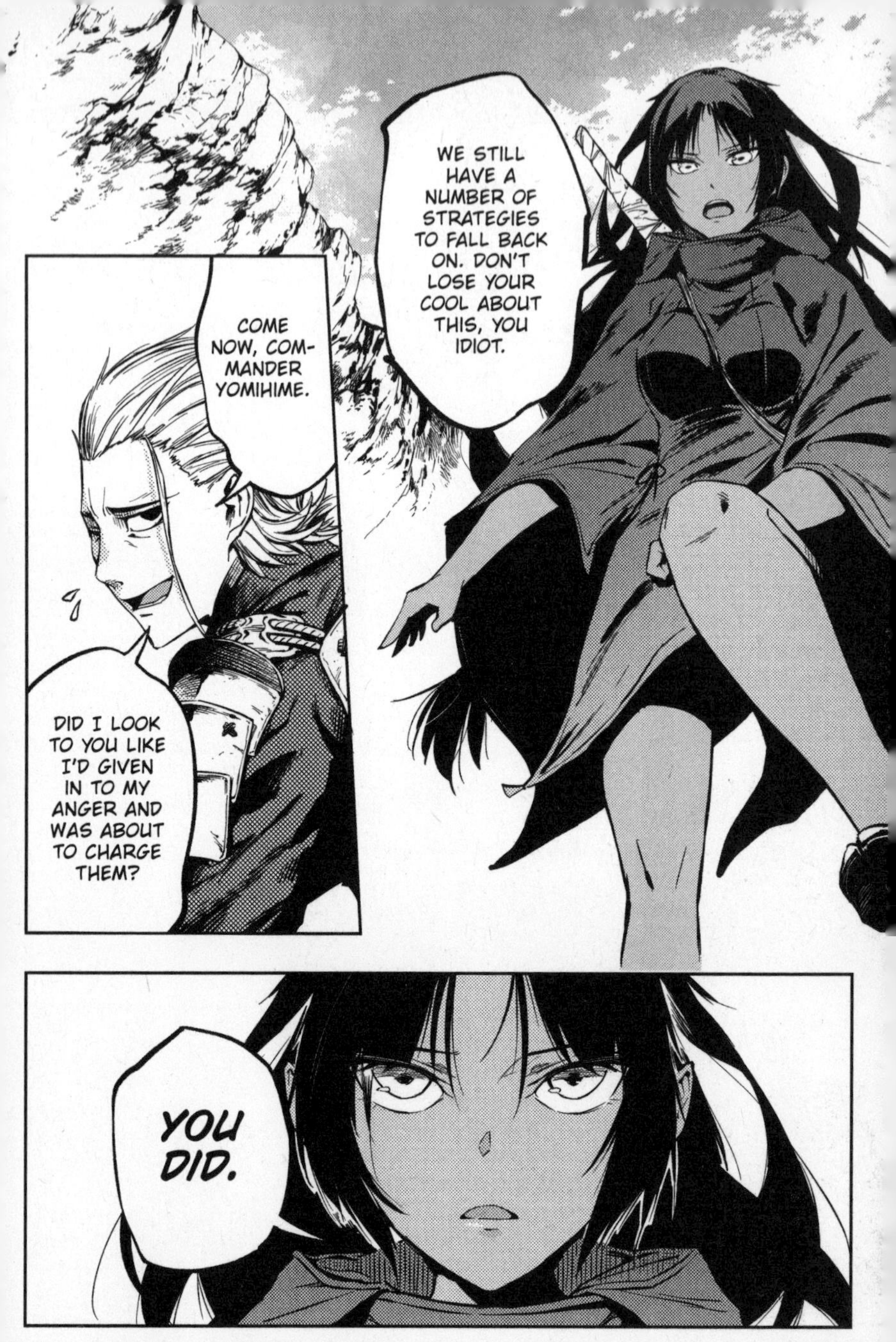
WE STILL HAVE A NUMBER OF STRATEGIES TO FALL BACK ON. DON'T LOSE YOUR COOL ABOUT THIS, YOU IDIOT.
COME NOW, COM-MANDER YOMIHIME.
DID I LOOK TO YOU LIKE I'D GIVEN IN TO MY ANGER AND WAS ABOUT TO CHARGE THEM?
YOU DID.

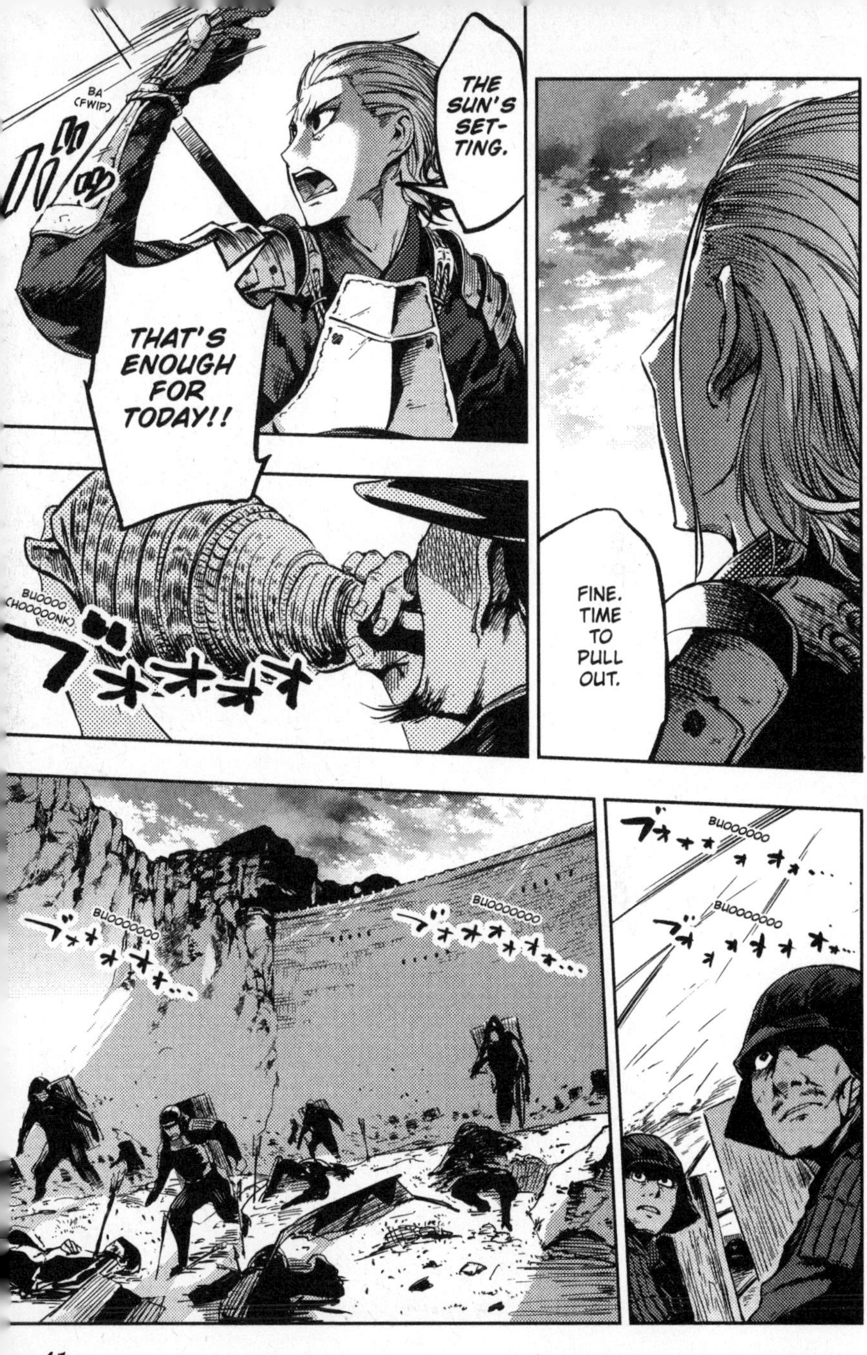
FINE. TIME TO PULL OUT.
THE SUN'S SET-TING.
BA (FWIP)
THAT'S ENOUGH FOR TODAY!!
BUOOOO (HOOOOONK)
BUOOOOOO
BUOOOOOOO
BUOOOOOOO
BUOOOOOOO

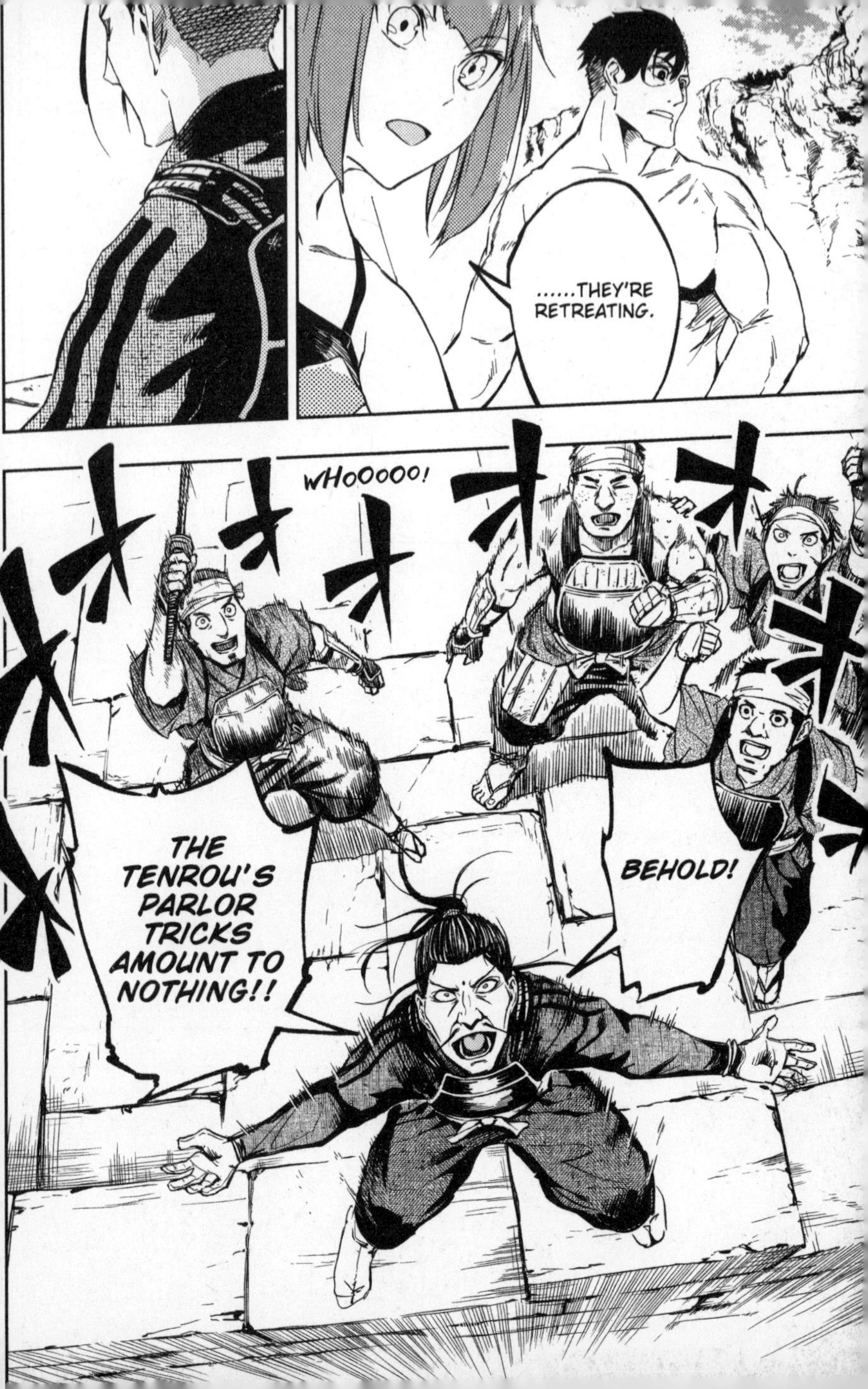
......THEY'RE RETREATING.
WHOOOOO!
BEHOLD!
THE TENROU'S PARLOR TRICKS AMOUNT TO NOTHING!!

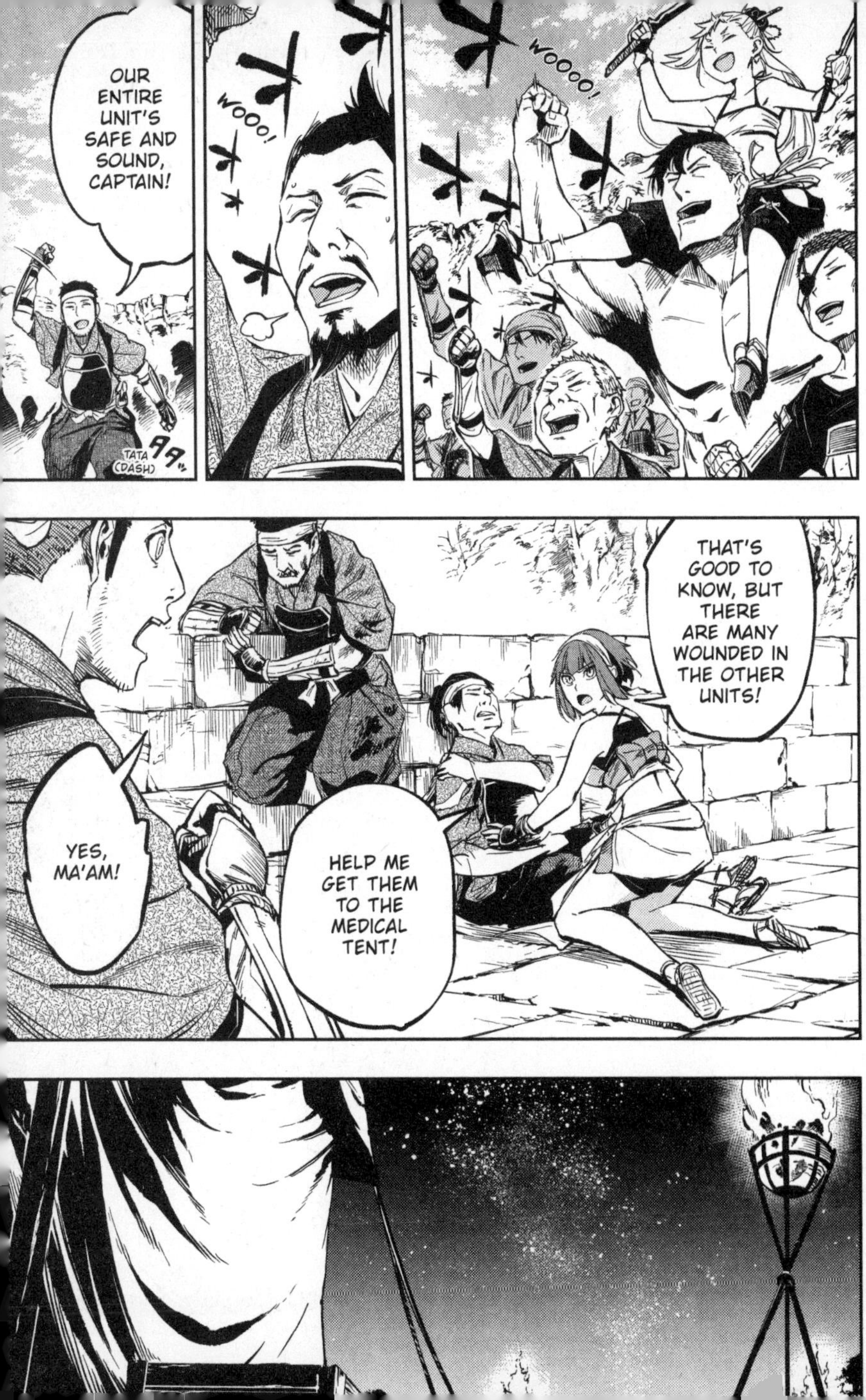
WOOOO!
WOOO!
OUR ENTIRE UNIT'S SAFE AND SOUND, CAPTAIN!
TATA (DASH)
THAT'S GOOD TO KNOW, BUT THERE ARE MANY WOUNDED IN THE OTHER UNITS!
HELP ME GET THEM TO THE MEDICAL TENT!
YES, MA'AM!

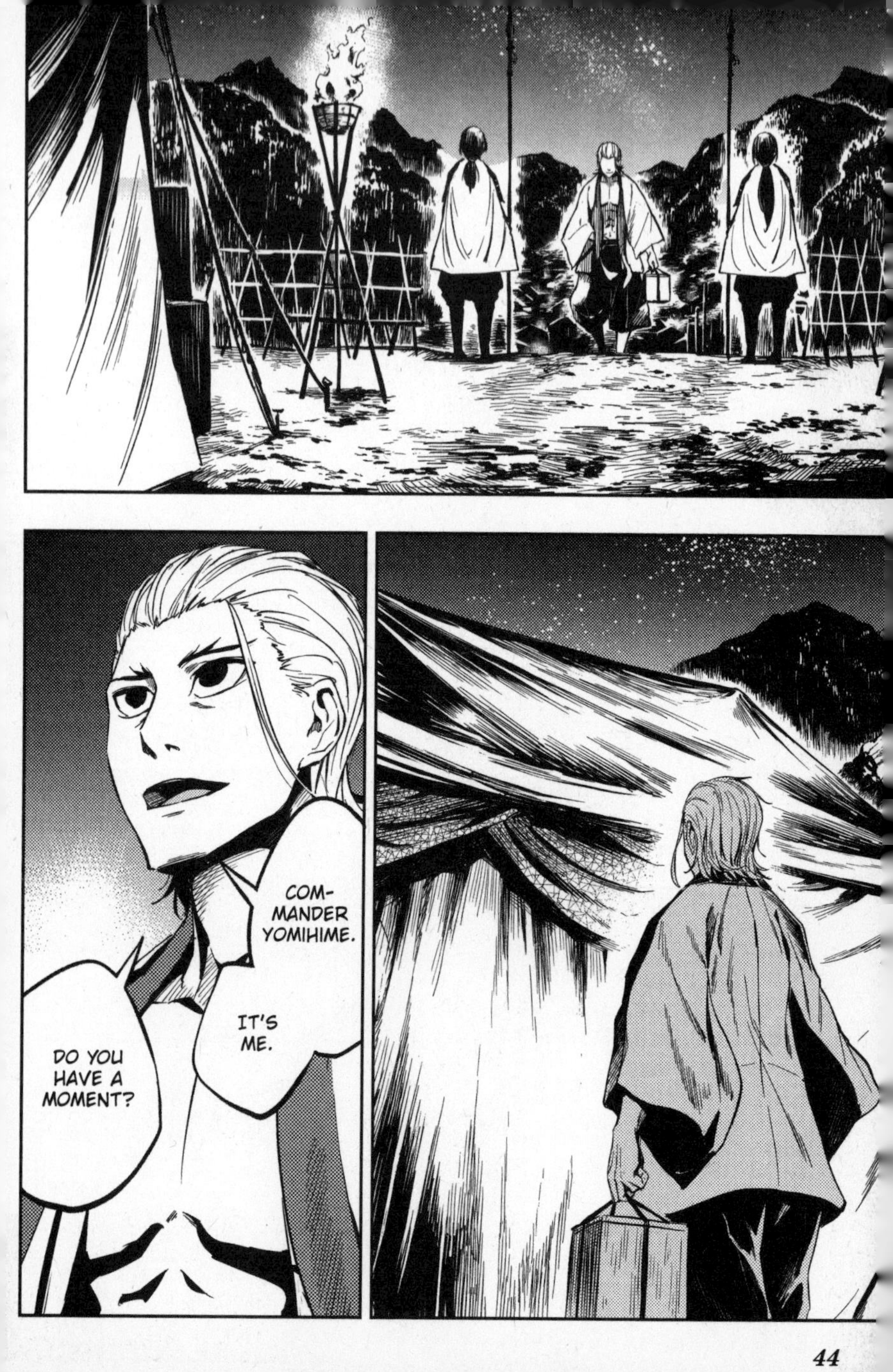
COM-MANDER YOMIHIME.
IT'S ME.
DO YOU HAVE A MOMENT?

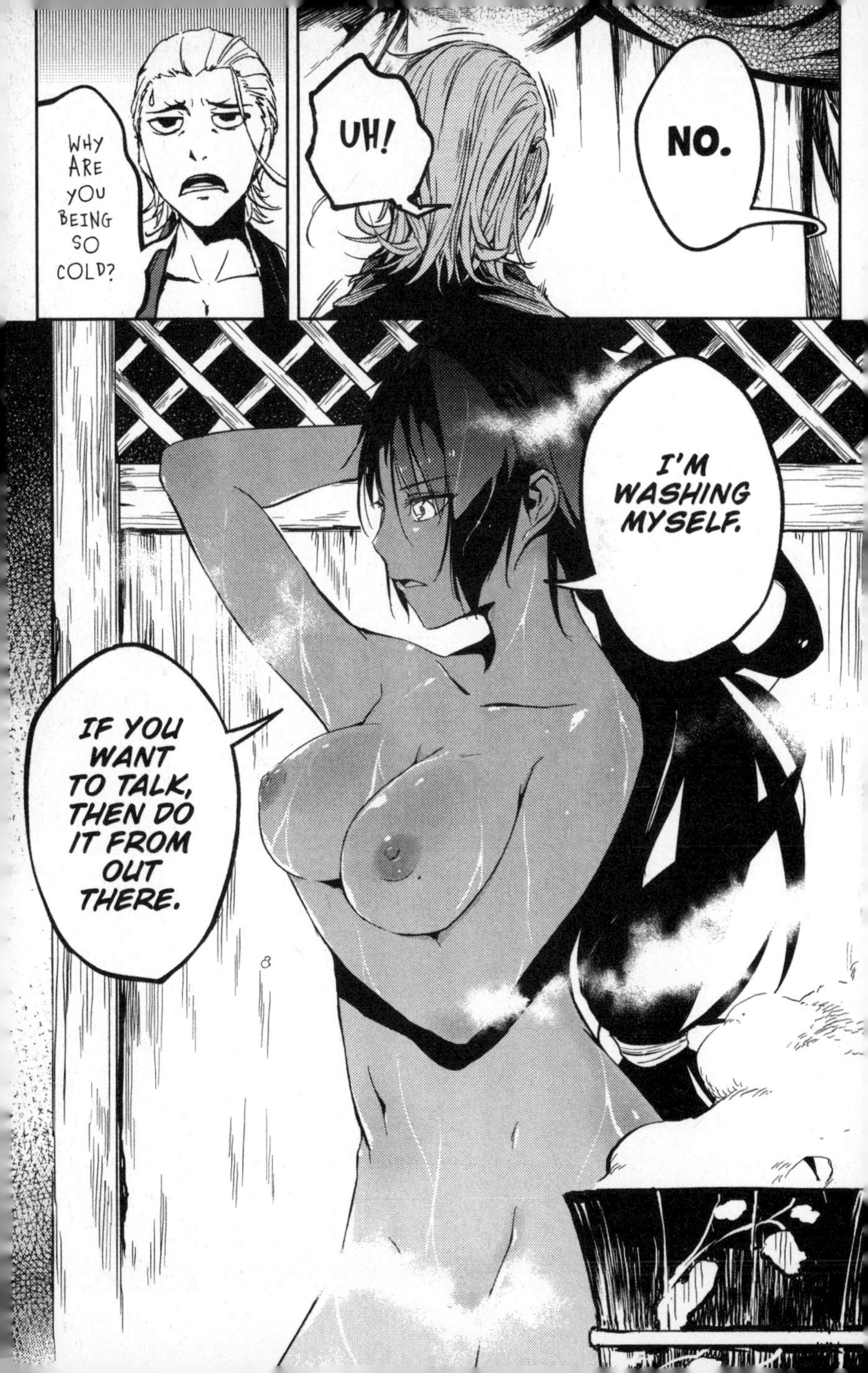
NO.
UH!
WHY ARE YOU BEING SO COLD?
I'M WASHING MYSELF.
IF YOU WANT TO TALK, THEN DO IT FROM OUT THERE.

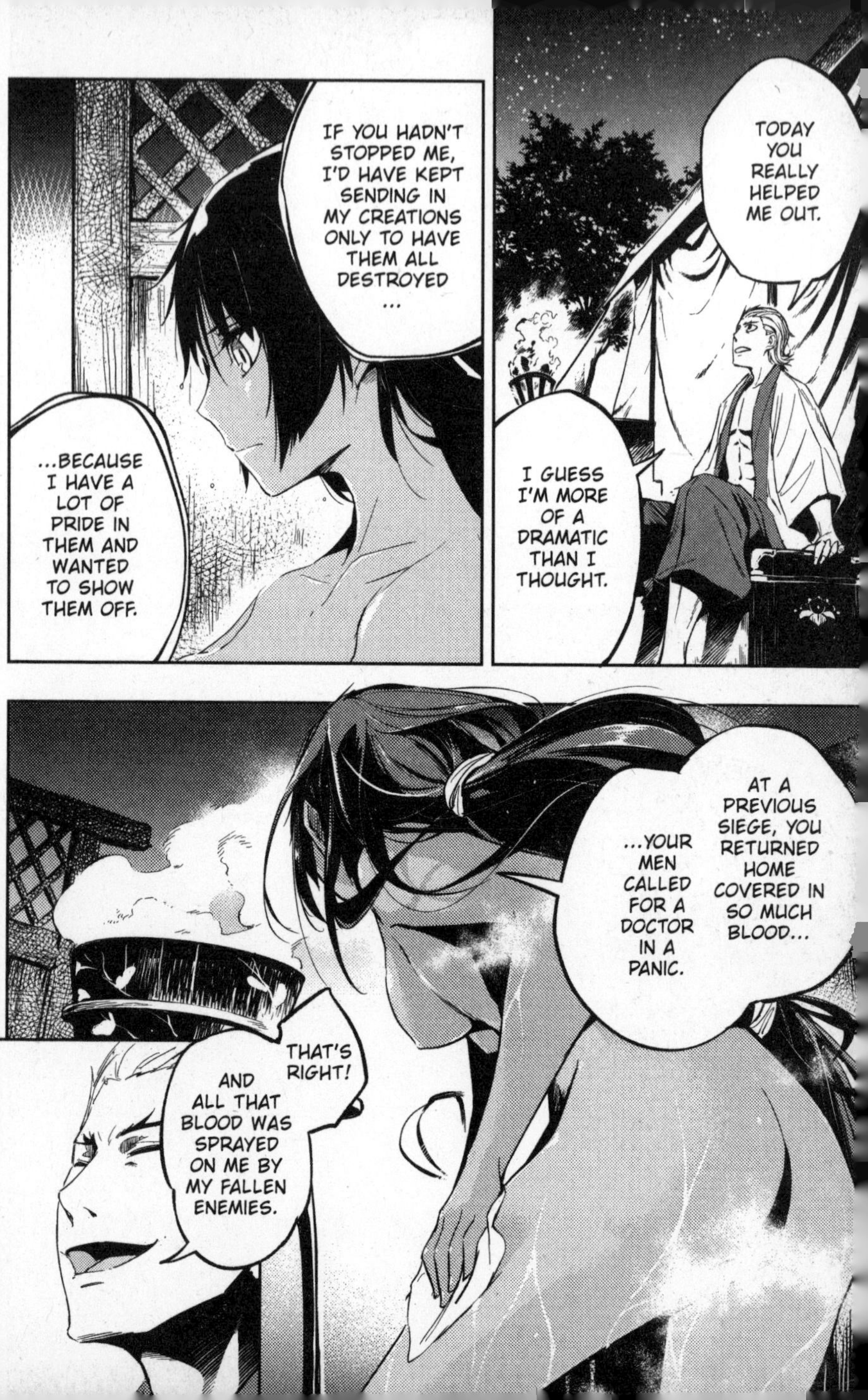
TODAY YOU REALLY HELPED ME OUT.
I GUESS I'M MORE OF A DRAMATIC THAN I THOUGHT.
IF YOU HADN'T STOPPED ME, I'D HAVE KEPT SENDING IN MY CREATIONS ONLY TO HAVE THEM ALL DESTROYED ...
...BECAUSE I HAVE A LOT OF PRIDE IN THEM AND WANTED TO SHOW THEM OFF.
AT A PREVIOUS SIEGE, YOU RETURNED HOME COVERED IN SO MUCH BLOOD...
...YOUR MEN CALLED FOR A DOCTOR IN A PANIC.
THAT'S RIGHT!
AND ALL THAT BLOOD WAS SPRAYED ON ME BY MY FALLEN ENEMIES.

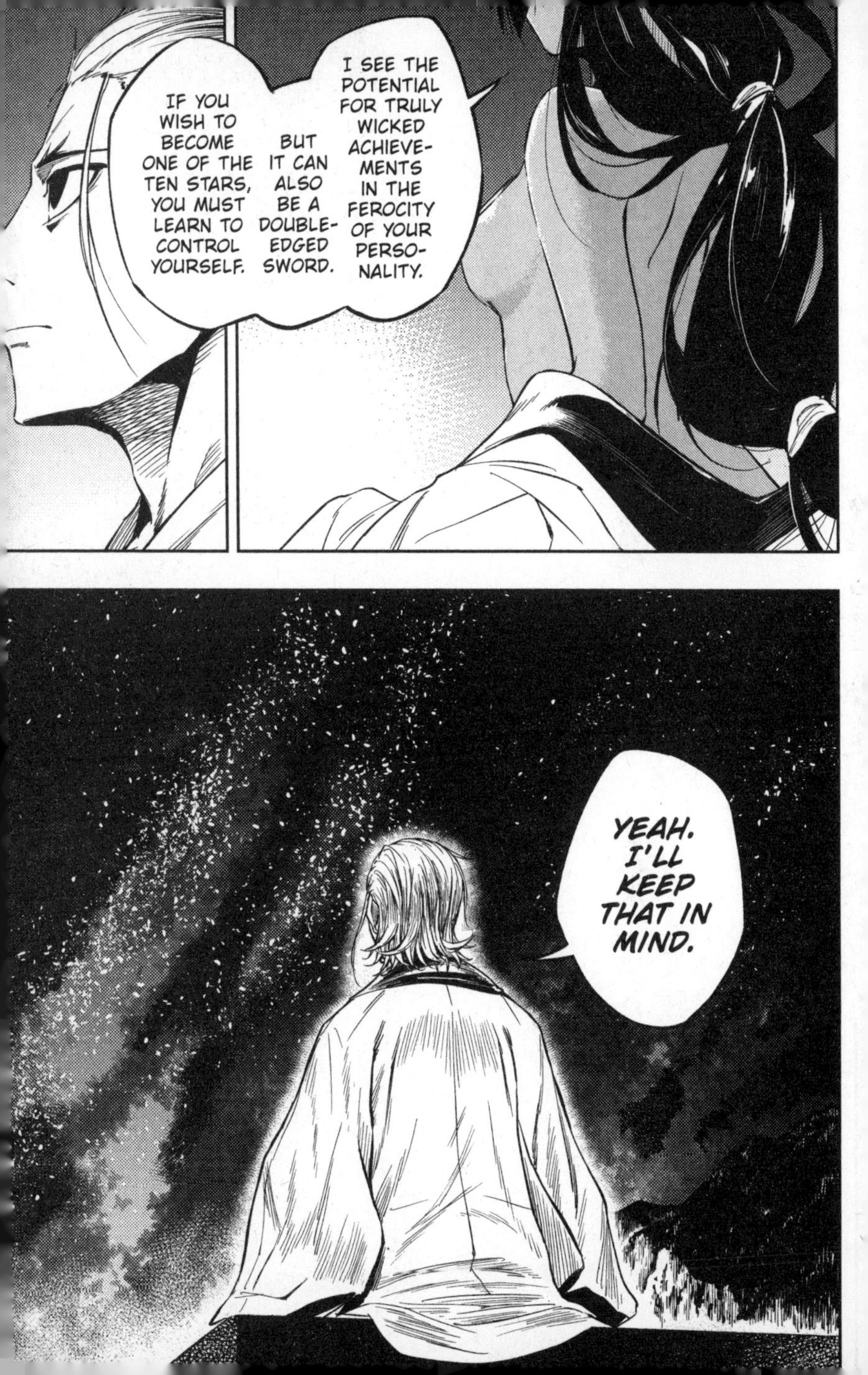
I SEE THE POTENTIAL FOR TRULY WICKED ACHIEVEMENTS IN THE FEROCITY OF YOUR PERSONALITY.
BUT IT CAN ALSO BE A DOUBLE-EDGED SWORD.
IF YOU WISH TO BECOME ONE OF THE TEN STARS, YOU MUST LEARN TO CONTROL YOURSELF.
YEAH. I'LL KEEP THAT IN MIND.

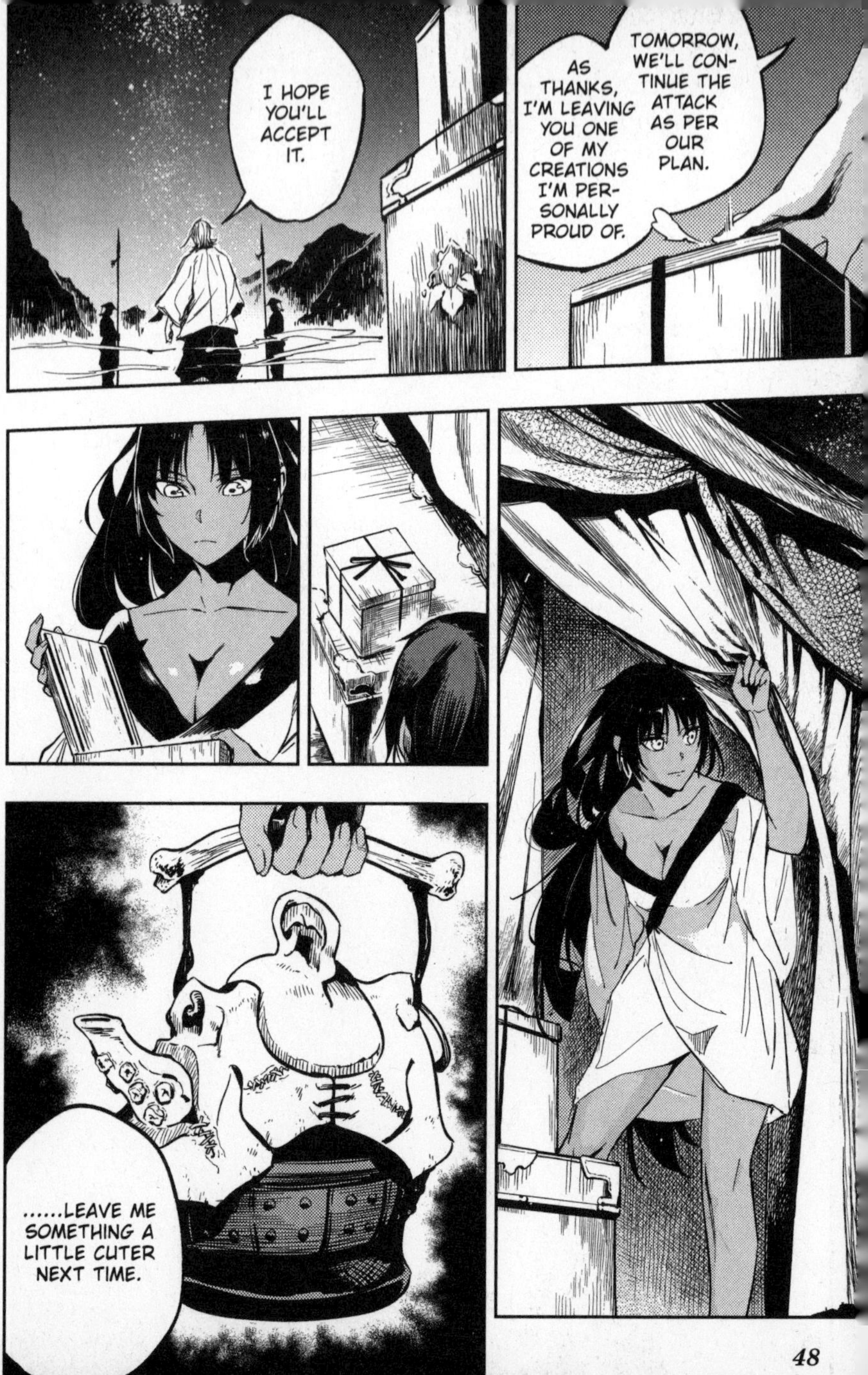
TOMORROW, WE'LL CON-TINUE THE ATTACK AS PER OUR PLAN.
AS THANKS, I'M LEAVING YOU ONE OF MY CREATIONS I'M PER-SONALLY PROUD OF.
I HOPE YOU'LL ACCEPT IT.
......LEAVE ME SOMETHING A LITTLE CUTER NEXT TIME.

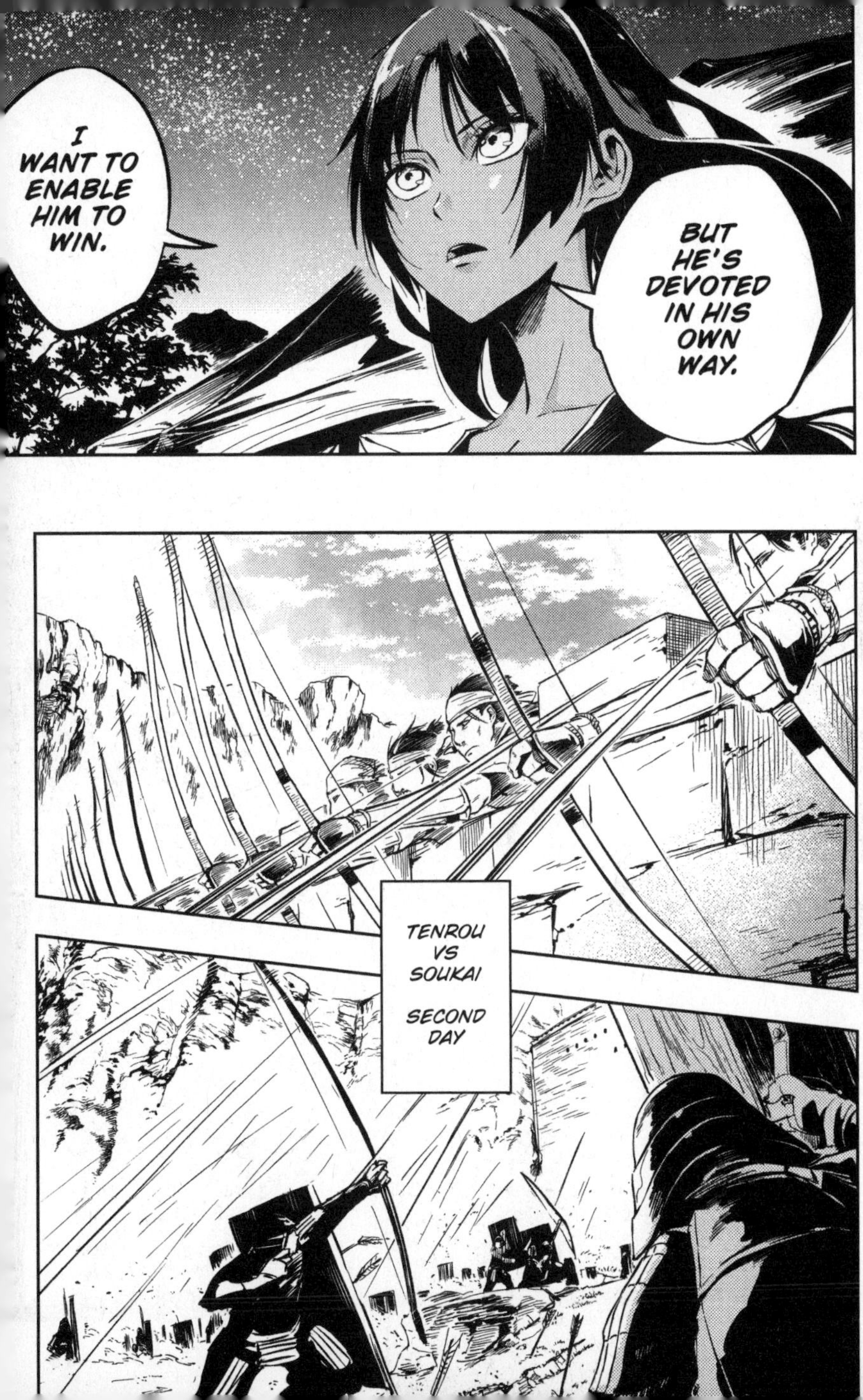
BUT HE'S DEVOTED IN HIS OWN WAY.
I WANT TO ENABLE HIM TO WIN.
TENROU VS SOUKAI
SECOND DAY

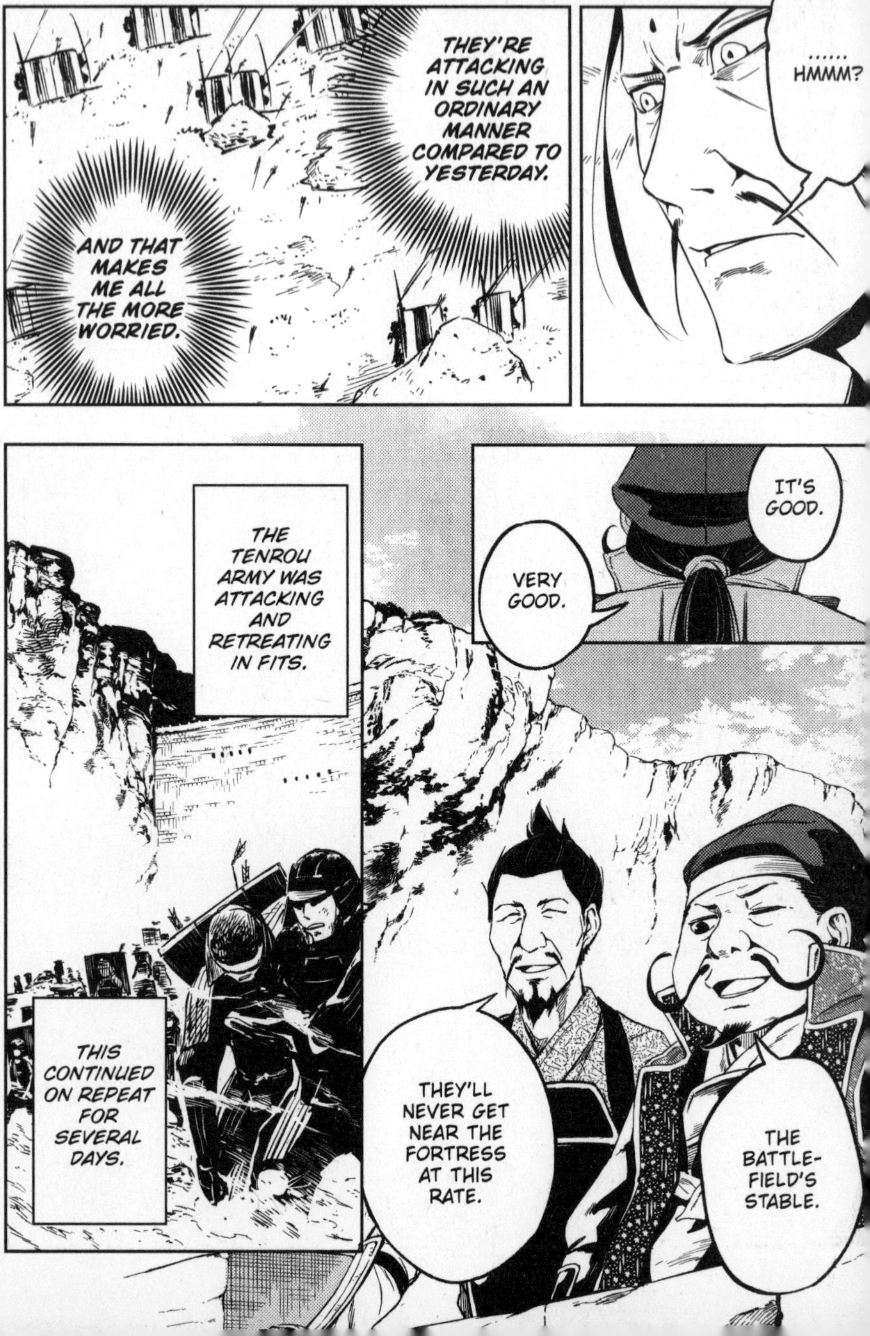

......
HMMM?
THEY'RE ATTACKING IN SUCH AN ORDINARY MANNER COMPARED TO YESTERDAY.
AND THAT MAKES ME ALL THE MORE WORRIED.
IT'S GOOD.
VERY GOOD.
THE BATTLE-FIELD'S STABLE.
THEY'LL NEVER GET NEAR THE FORTRESS AT THIS RATE.
THE TENROU ARMY WAS ATTACKING AND RETREATING IN FITS.
THIS CONTINUED ON REPEAT FOR SEVERAL DAYS.

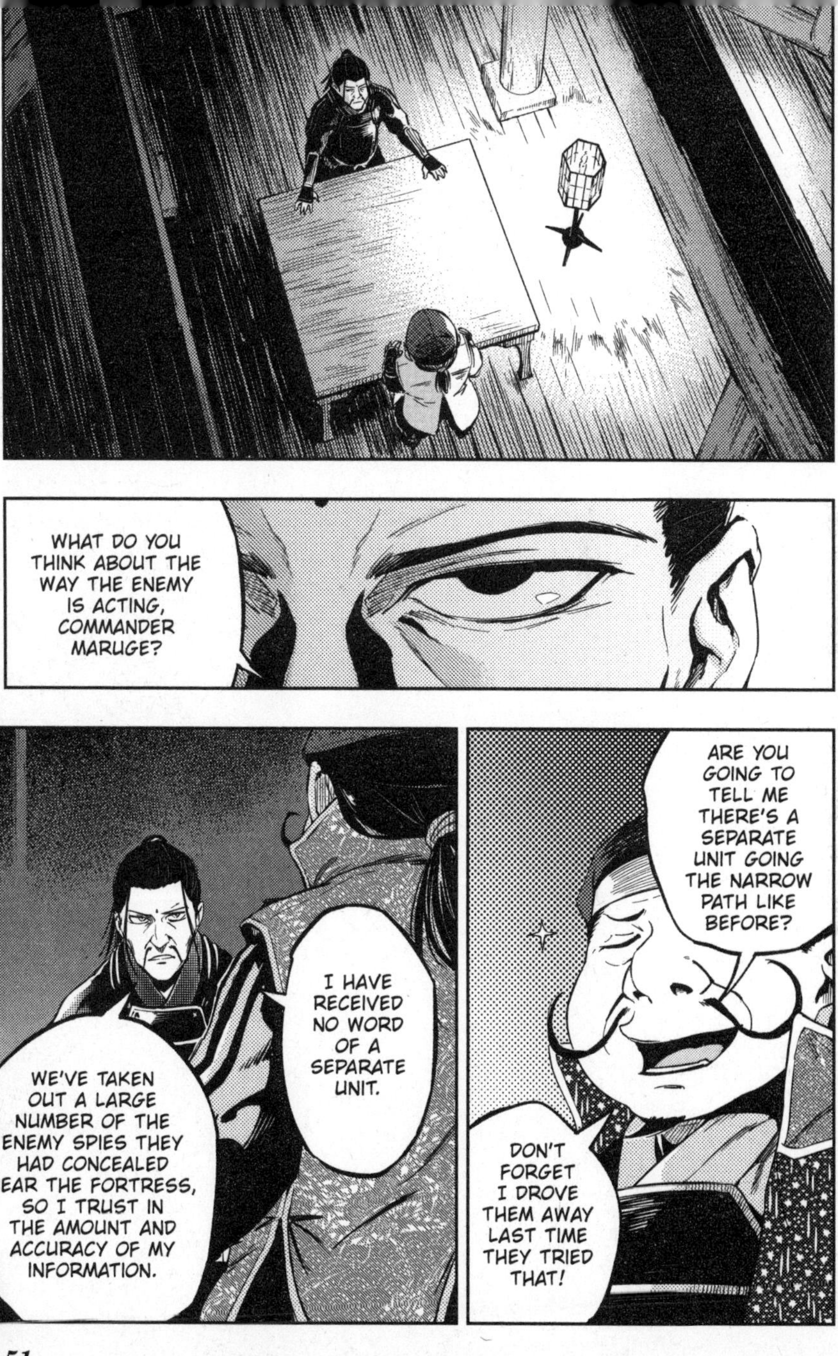
WHAT DO YOU THINK ABOUT THE WAY THE ENEMY IS ACTING, COMMANDER MARUGE?
ARE YOU GOING TO TELL ME THERE'S A SEPARATE UNIT GOING THE NARROW PATH LIKE BEFORE?
DON'T FORGET I DROVE THEM AWAY LAST TIME THEY TRIED THAT!
I HAVE RECEIVED NO WORD OF A SEPARATE UNIT.
WE'VE TAKEN OUT A LARGE NUMBER OF THE ENEMY SPIES THEY HAD CONCEALED NEAR THE FORTRESS, SO I TRUST IN THE AMOUNT AND ACCURACY OF MY INFORMATION.

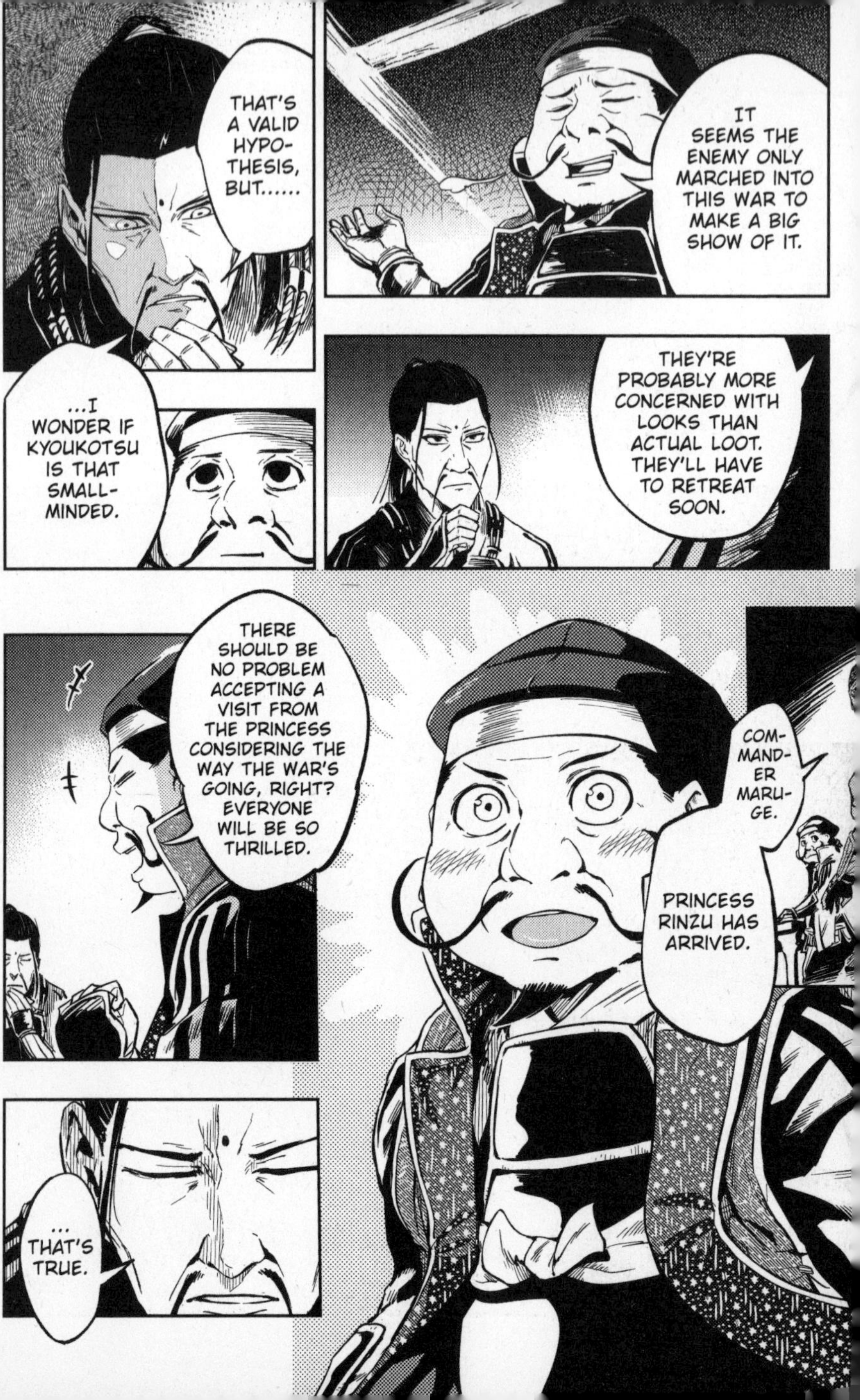
IT SEEMS THE ENEMY ONLY MARCHED INTO THIS WAR TO MAKE A BIG SHOW OF IT.
THAT'S A VALID HYPOTHESIS, BUT......
THEY'RE PROBABLY MORE CONCERNED WITH LOOKS THAN ACTUAL LOOT. THEY'LL HAVE TO RETREAT SOON.
...I WONDER IF KYOUKOTSU IS THAT SMALL-MINDED.
COMMANDER MARUGE.
PRINCESS RINZU HAS ARRIVED.
THERE SHOULD BE NO PROBLEM ACCEPTING A VISIT FROM THE PRINCESS CONSIDERING THE WAY THE WAR'S GOING, RIGHT? EVERYONE WILL BE SO THRILLED.
... THAT'S TRUE.

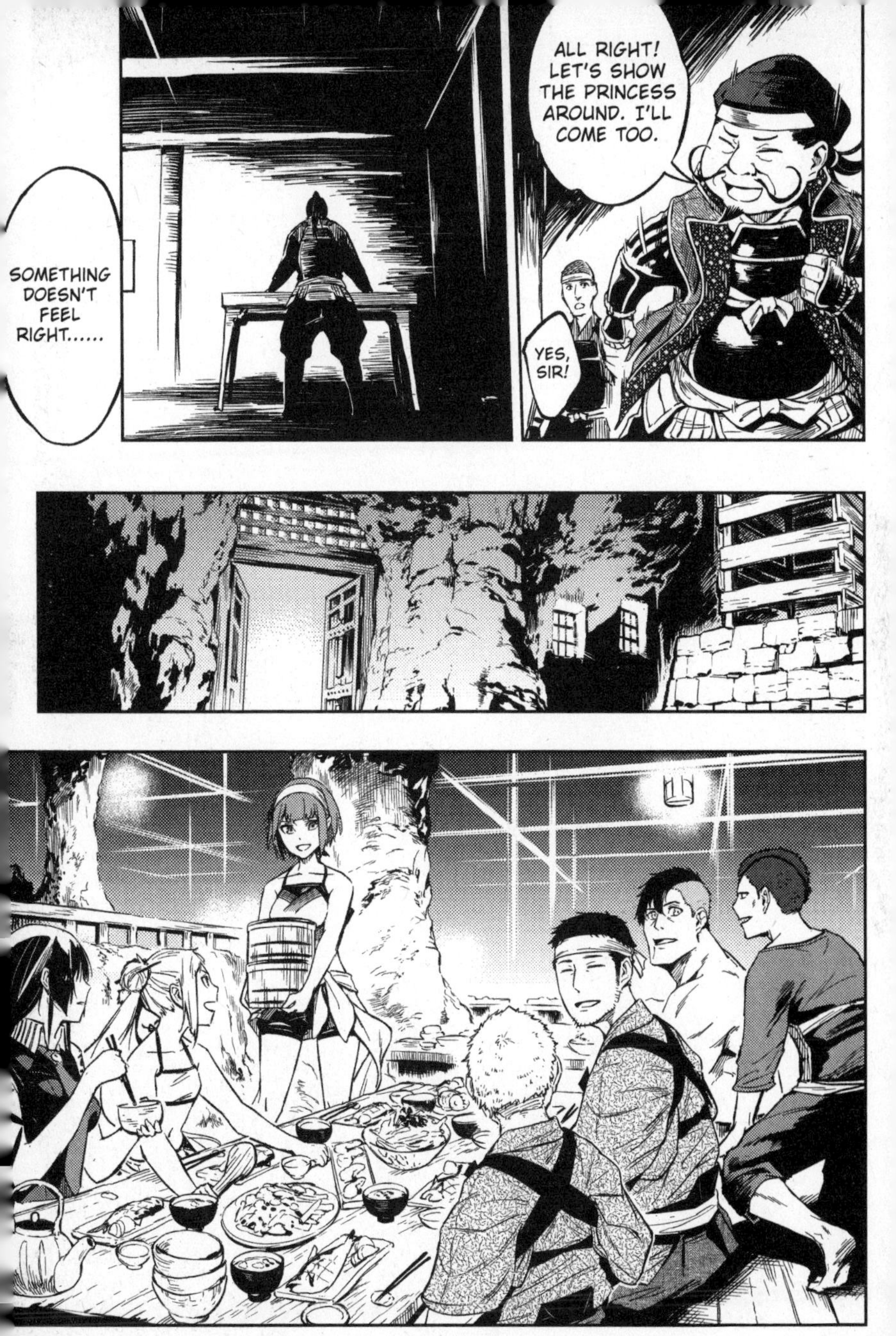
ALL RIGHT! LET'S SHOW THE PRINCESS AROUND. I'LL COME TOO.
YES, SIR!
SOMETHING DOESN'T FEEL RIGHT......

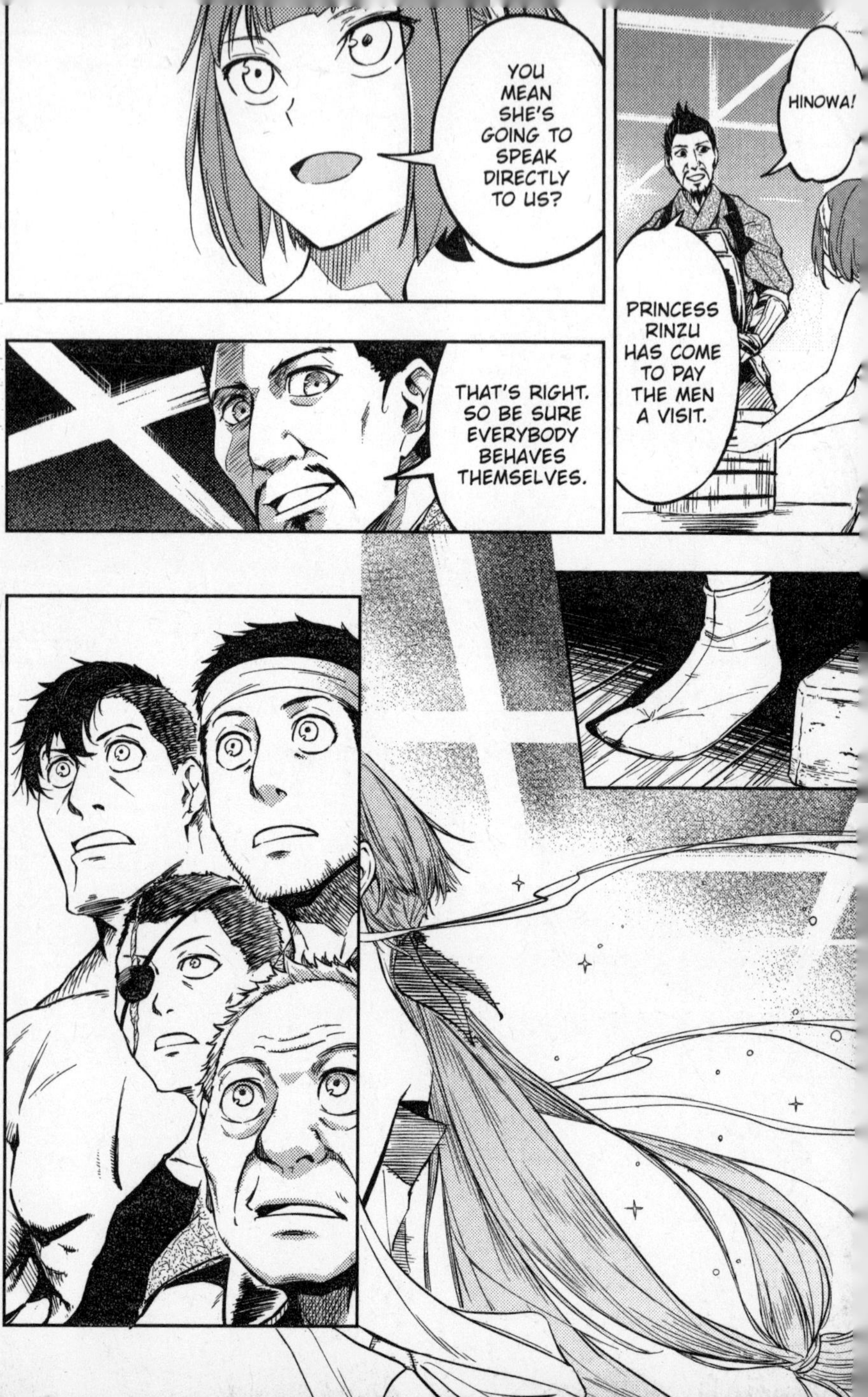
HINOWA!
PRINCESS RINZU HAS COME TO PAY THE MEN A VISIT.
YOU MEAN SHE'S GOING TO SPEAK DIRECTLY TO US?
THAT'S RIGHT. SO BE SURE EVERYBODY BEHAVES THEMSELVES.

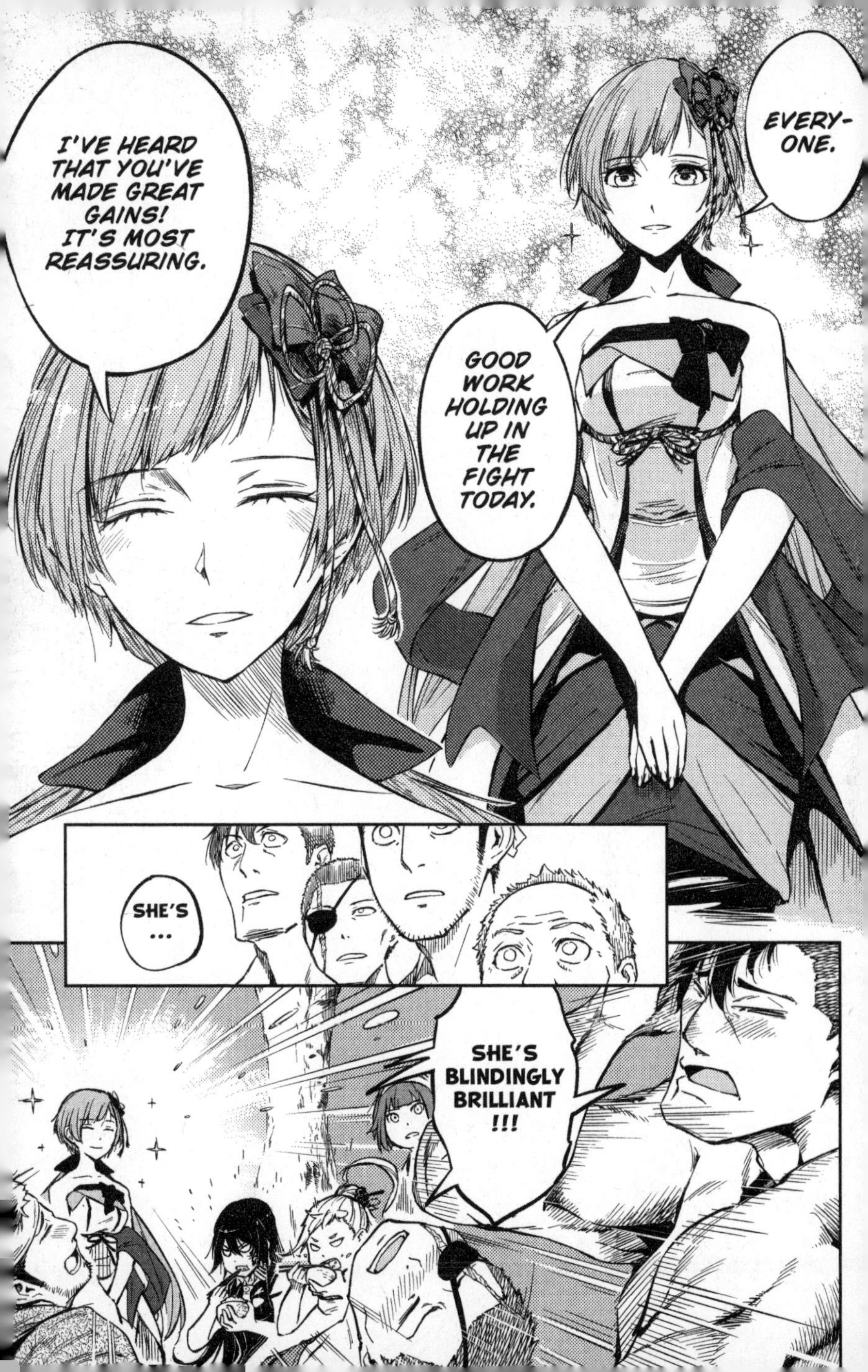
EVERY-ONE.
GOOD WORK HOLDING UP IN THE FIGHT TODAY.
I'VE HEARD THAT YOU'VE MADE GREAT GAINS! IT'S MOST REASSURING.
SHE'S ...
SHE'S BLINDINGLY BRILLIANT !!!

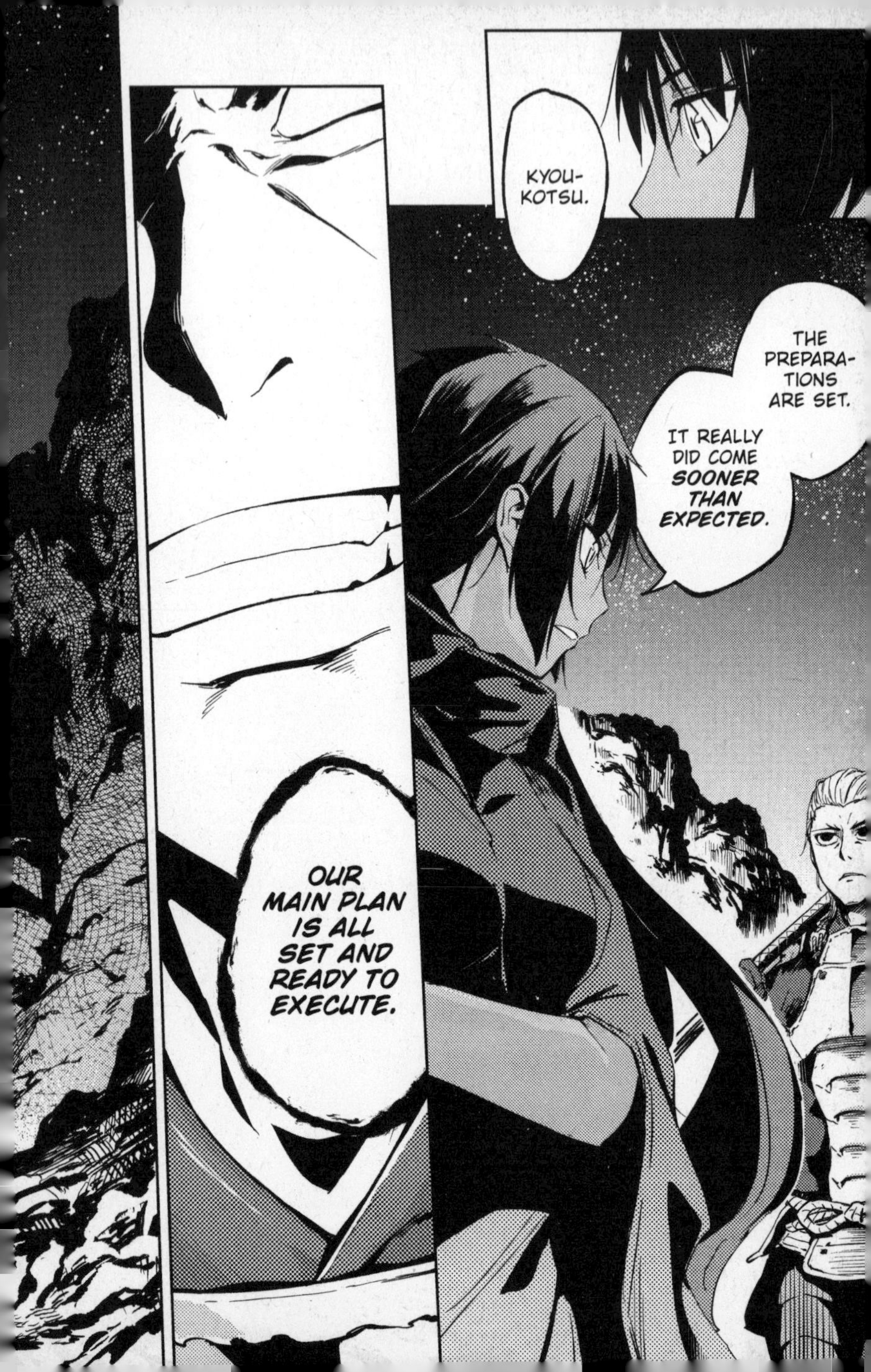
KYOU-KOTSU.
THE PREPARATIONS ARE SET.
IT REALLY DID COME SOONER THAN EXPECTED.
OUR MAIN PLAN IS ALL SET AND READY TO EXECUTE.

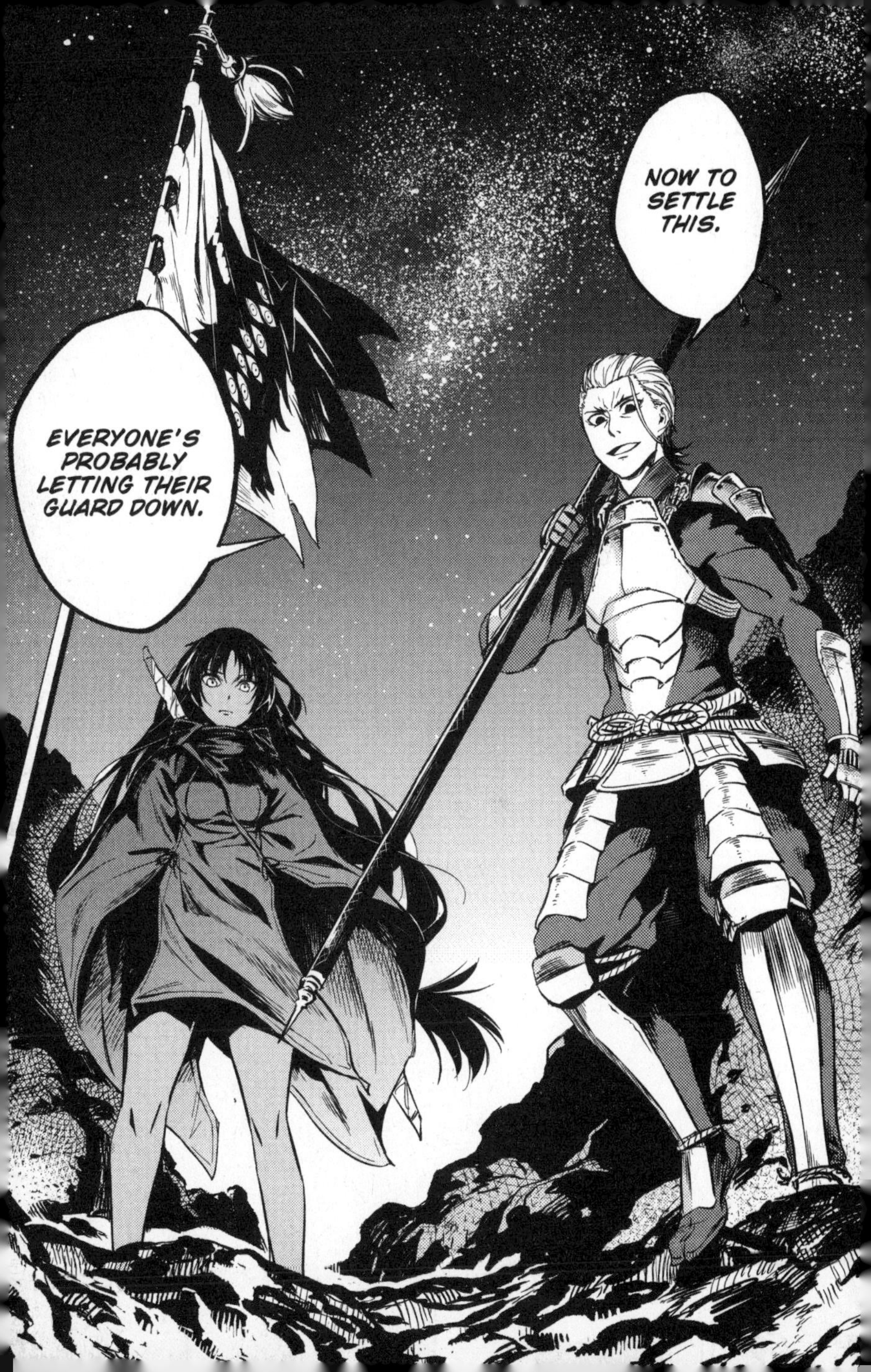
NOW TO SETTLE THIS.
EVERYONE'S PROBABLY LETTING THEIR GUARD DOWN.

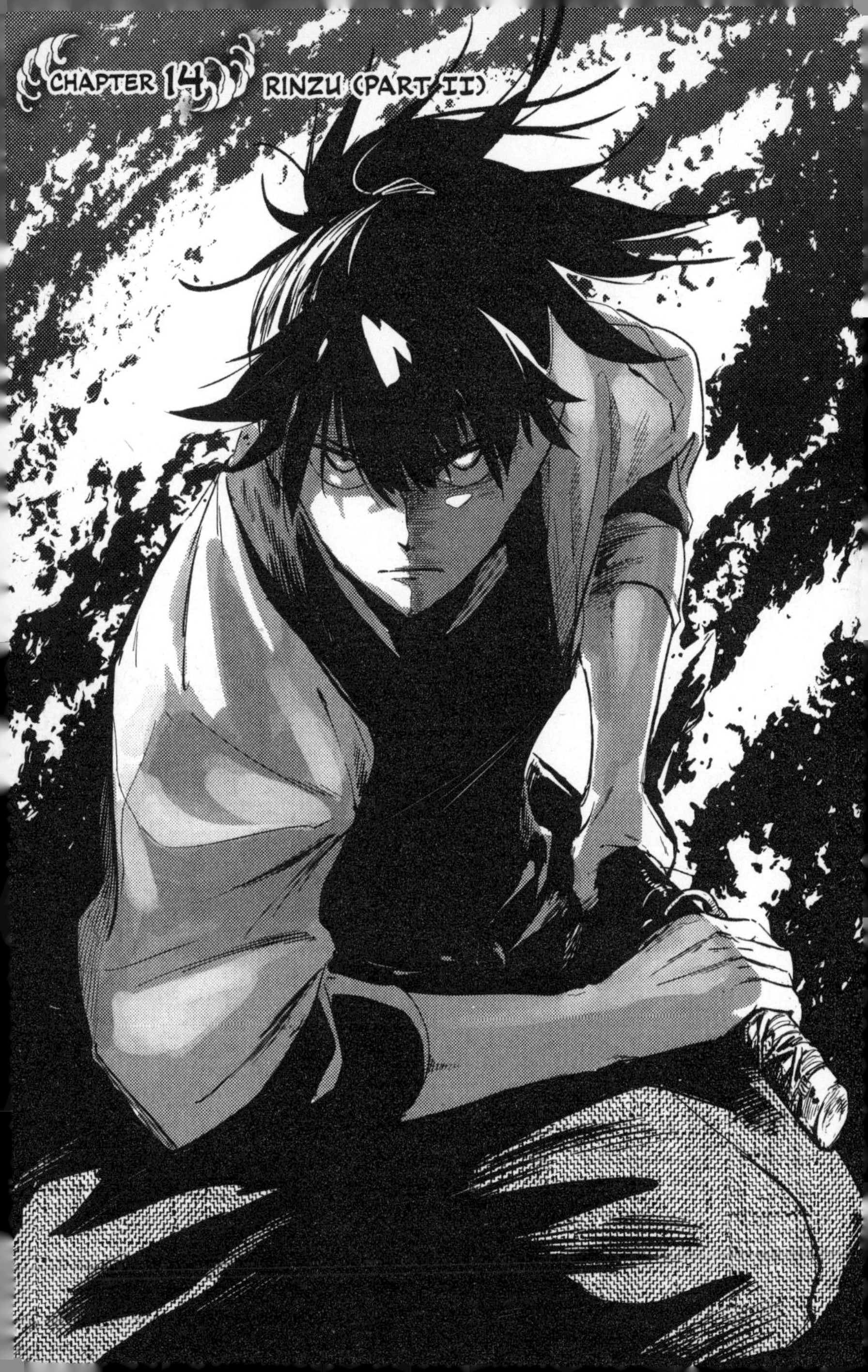
CHAPTER 14
RINZU (PART II)

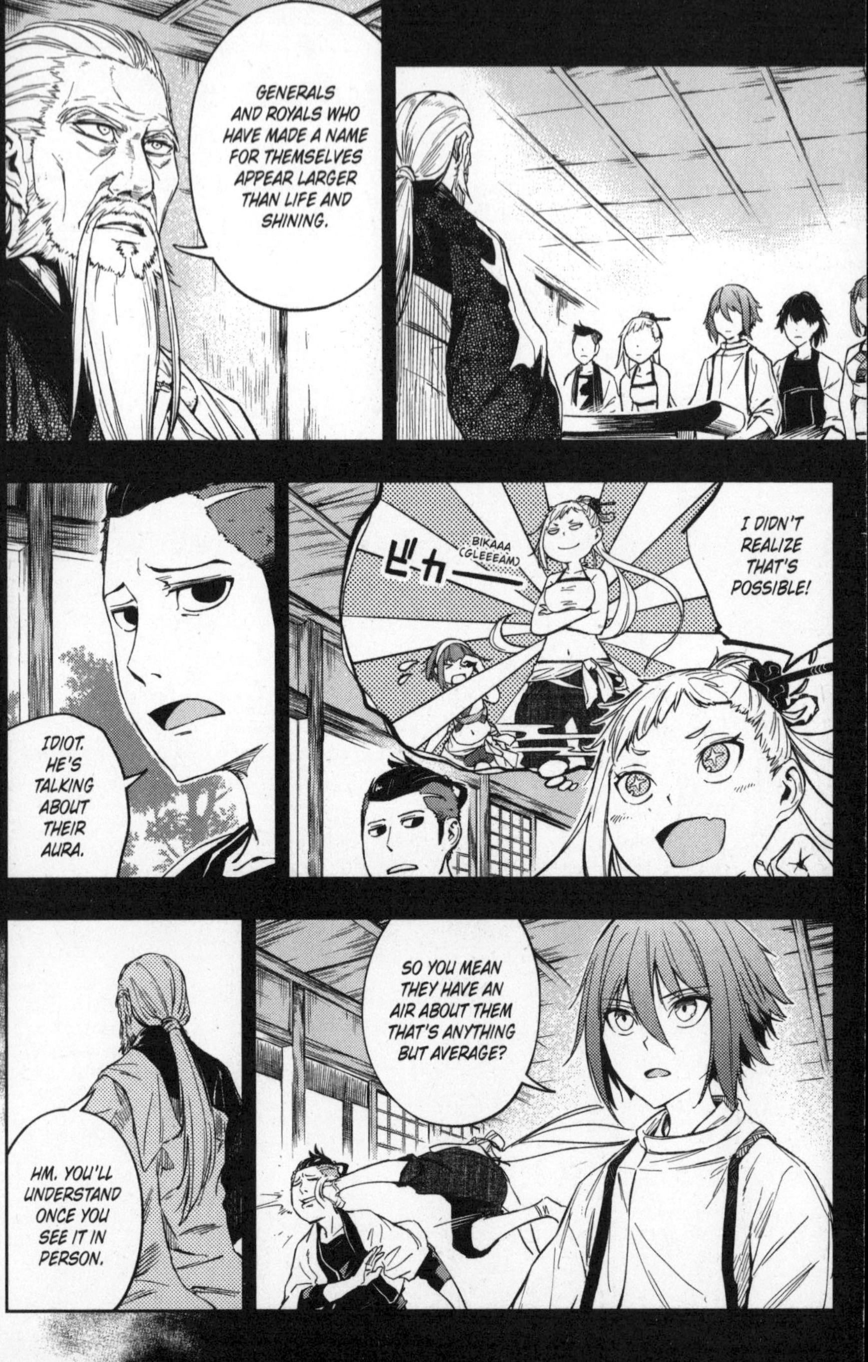
GENERALS AND ROYALS WHO HAVE MADE A NAME FOR THEMSELVES APPEAR LARGER THAN LIFE AND SHINING.
I DIDN'T REALIZE THAT'S POSSIBLE!
ビカー
BIKAAA (GLEEEAM)
IDIOT. HE'S TALKING ABOUT THEIR AURA.
SO YOU MEAN THEY HAVE AN AIR ABOUT THEM THAT'S ANYTHING BUT AVERAGE?
HM. YOU'LL UNDERSTAND ONCE YOU SEE IT IN PERSON.

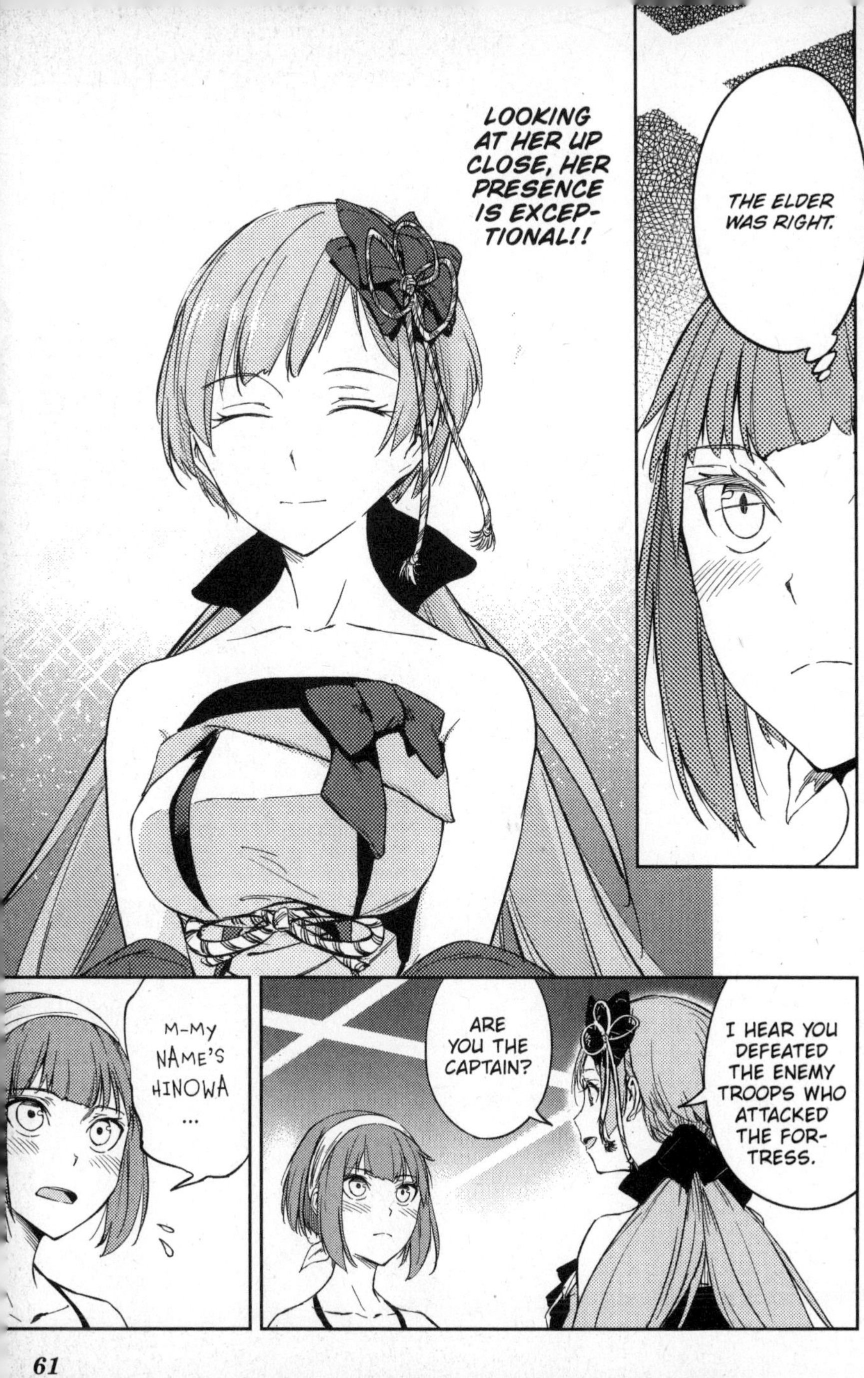
THE ELDER WAS RIGHT.
LOOKING AT HER UP CLOSE, HER PRESENCE IS EXCEP-TIONAL!!
I HEAR YOU DEFEATED THE ENEMY TROOPS WHO ATTACKED THE FOR-TRESS.
ARE YOU THE CAPTAIN?
M-MY NAME'S HINOWA ...

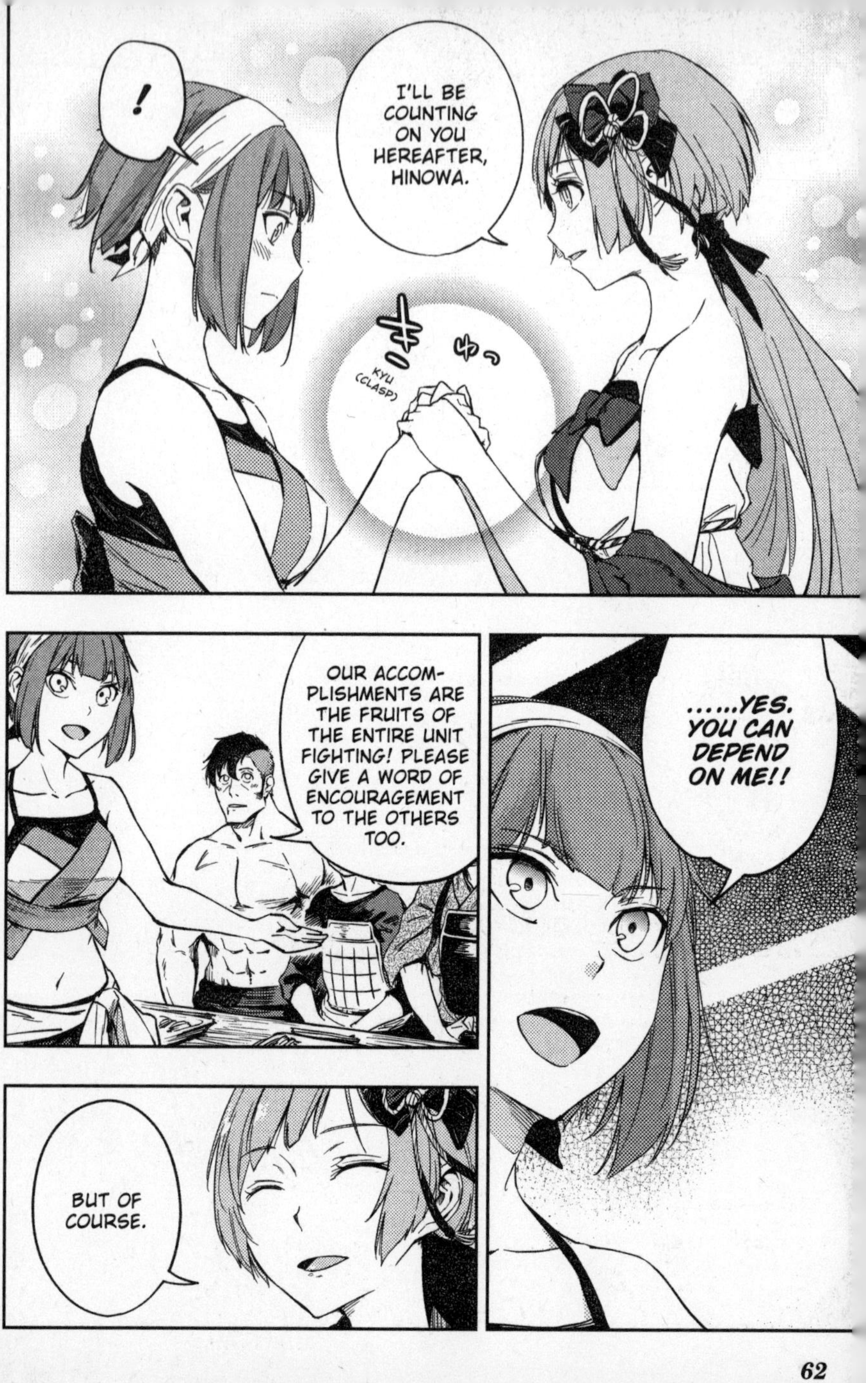
I'LL BE COUNTING ON YOU HEREAFTER, HINOWA.
きゅっ
KYU (CLASP)
!
......YES. YOU CAN DEPEND ON ME!!
OUR ACCOM-PLISHMENTS ARE THE FRUITS OF THE ENTIRE UNIT FIGHTING! PLEASE GIVE A WORD OF ENCOURAGEMENT TO THE OTHERS TOO.
BUT OF COURSE.

EVERYONE, YOU TRULY DID A HARD DAY'S WORK TODAY.

KYUUUN
(SWOOOOON)

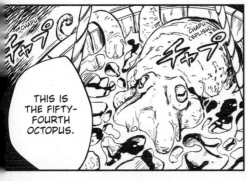

CHAPU

CHAPU
(SPLISH)

THIS IS THE FIFTY-FOURTH OCTOPUS.

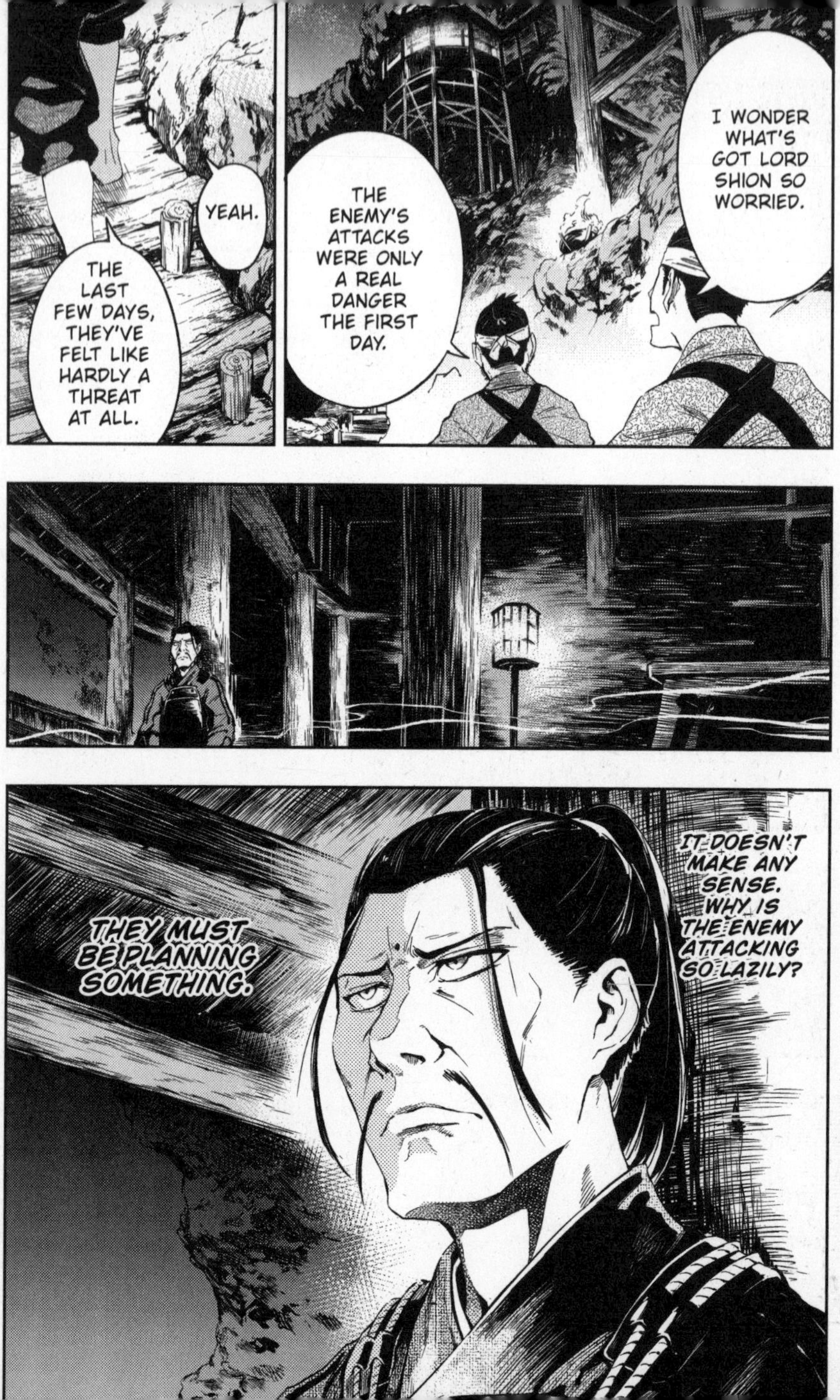
I WONDER WHAT'S GOT LORD SHION SO WORRIED.
THE ENEMY'S ATTACKS WERE ONLY A REAL DANGER THE FIRST DAY.
YEAH.
THE LAST FEW DAYS, THEY'VE FELT LIKE HARDLY A THREAT AT ALL.
IT DOESN'T MAKE ANY SENSE. WHY IS THE ENEMY ATTACKING SO LAZILY?
THEY MUST BE PLANNING SOMETHING.

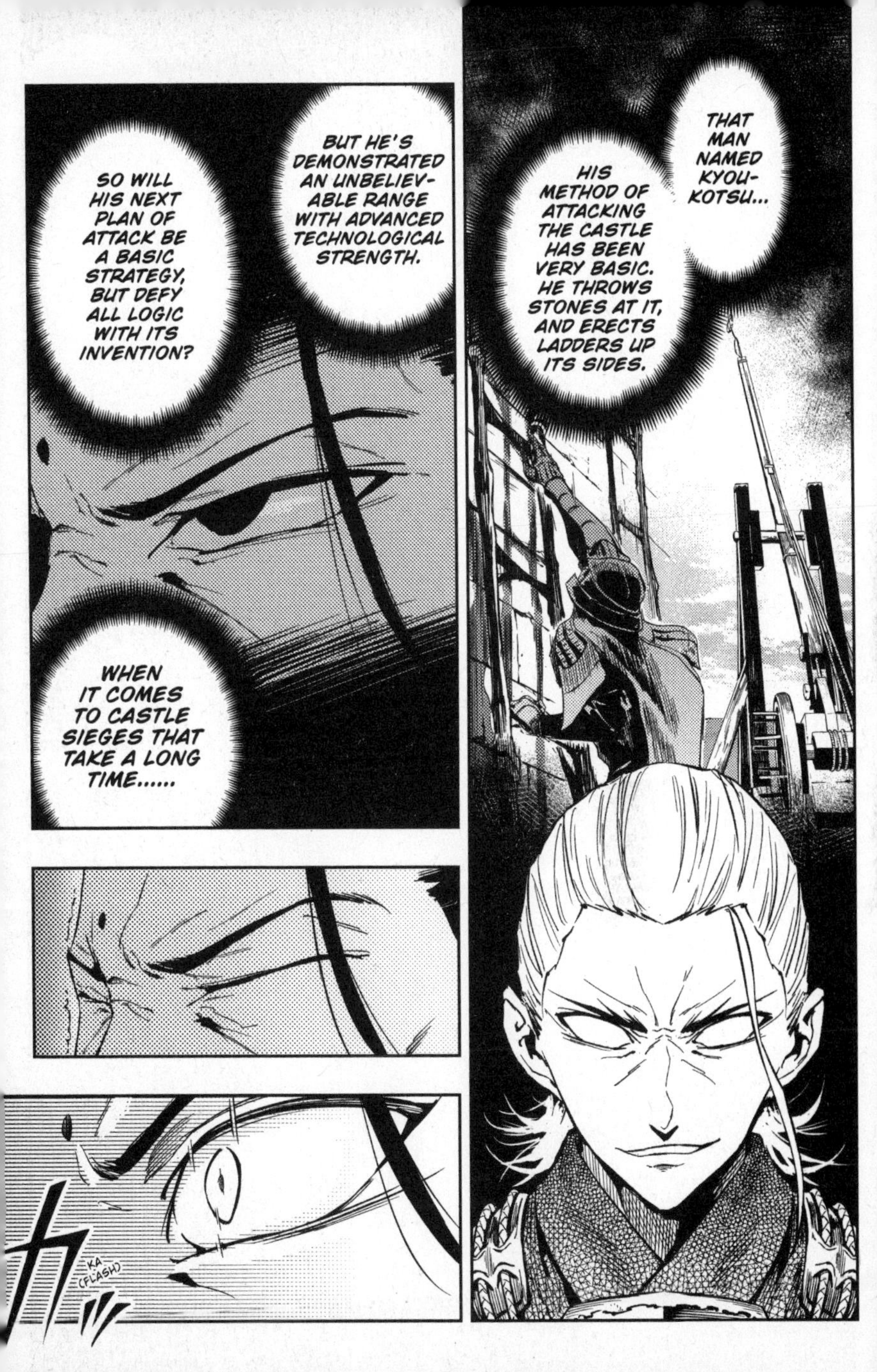
THAT MAN NAMED KYOU-KOTSU...
HIS METHOD OF ATTACKING THE CASTLE HAS BEEN VERY BASIC. HE THROWS STONES AT IT, AND ERECTS LADDERS UP ITS SIDES.
BUT HE'S DEMONSTRATED AN UNBELIEV-ABLE RANGE WITH ADVANCED TECHNOLOGICAL STRENGTH.
SO WILL HIS NEXT PLAN OF ATTACK BE A BASIC STRATEGY, BUT DEFY ALL LOGIC WITH ITS INVENTION?
WHEN IT COMES TO CASTLE SIEGES THAT TAKE A LONG TIME......
KA (FLASH)

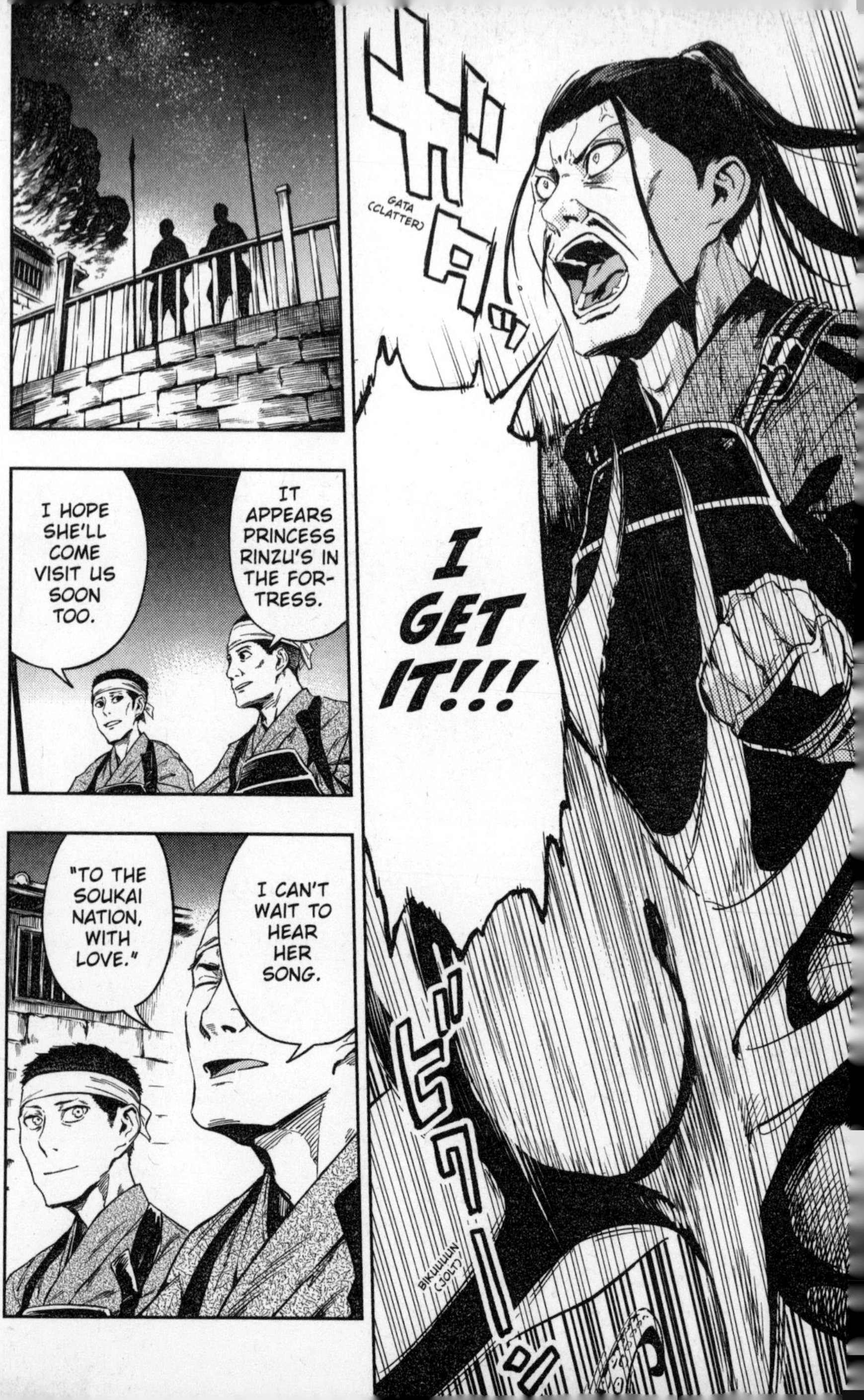
GATA (CLATTER)
I GET IT!!!
BIKUUUUN (JOLT)
IT APPEARS PRINCESS RINZU'S IN THE FORTRESS.
I HOPE SHE'LL COME VISIT US SOON TOO.
I CAN'T WAIT TO HEAR HER SONG.
"TO THE SOUKAI NATION, WITH LOVE."

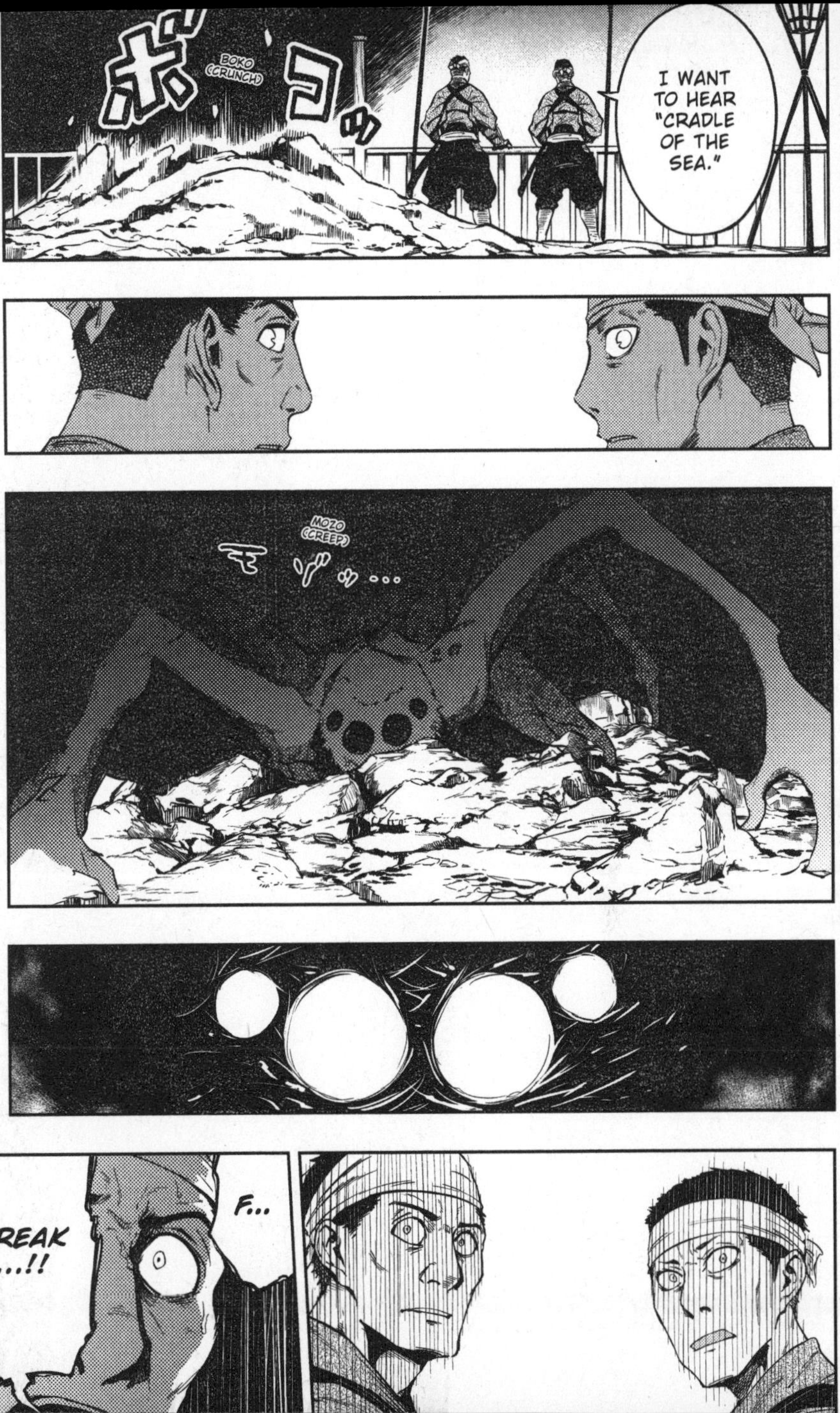
I WANT TO HEAR "CRADLE OF THE SEA."
ボコッ
BOKO (CRUNCH)
モゾッ...
MOZO (CREEP)
F...
FREAK ...!!

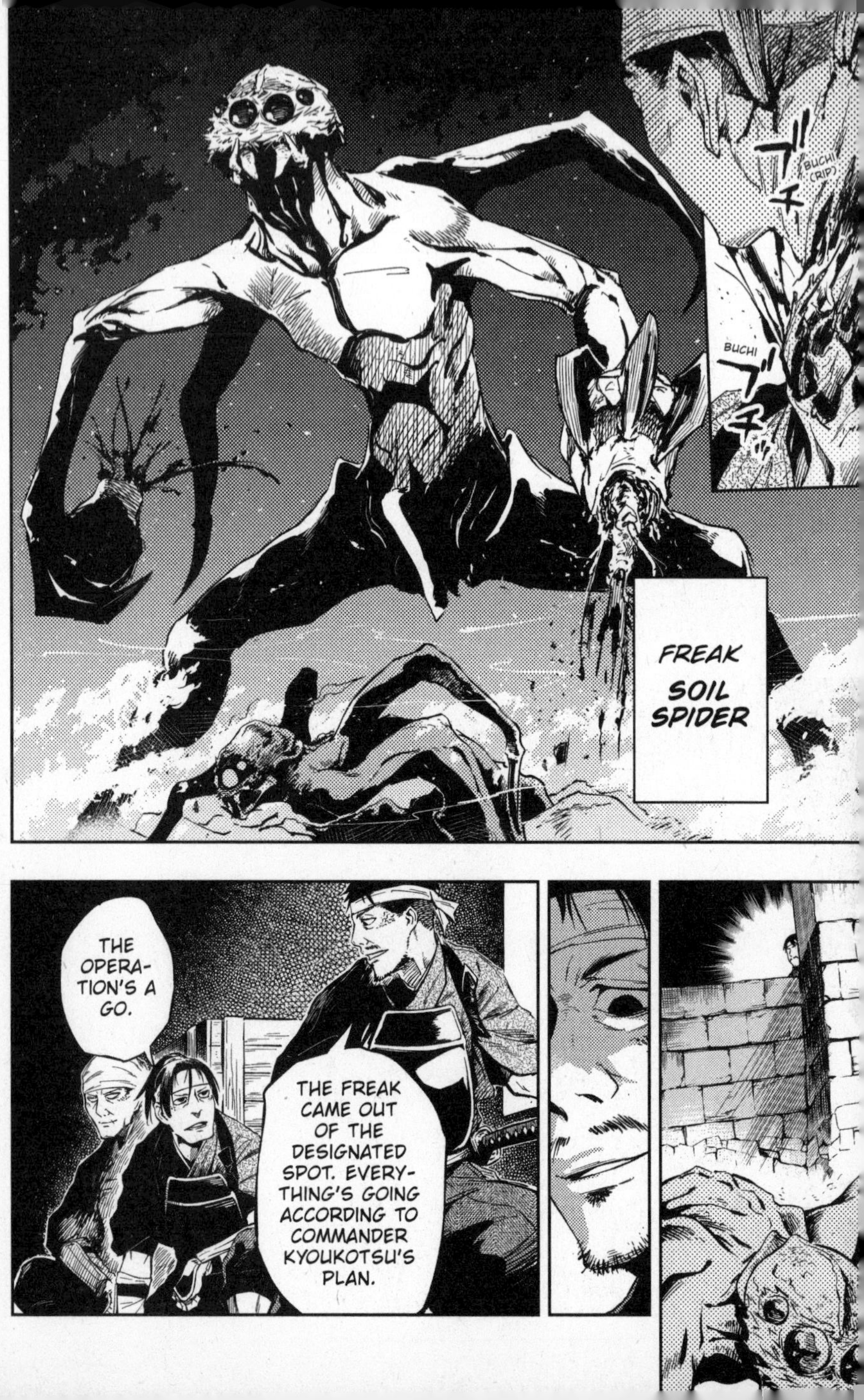
ブチ
BUCHI (RIP)
ブチッ
BUCHI
FREAK
SOIL SPIDER
THE OPERATION'S A GO.
THE FREAK CAME OUT OF THE DESIGNATED SPOT. EVERYTHING'S GOING ACCORDING TO COMMANDER KYOUKOTSU'S PLAN.

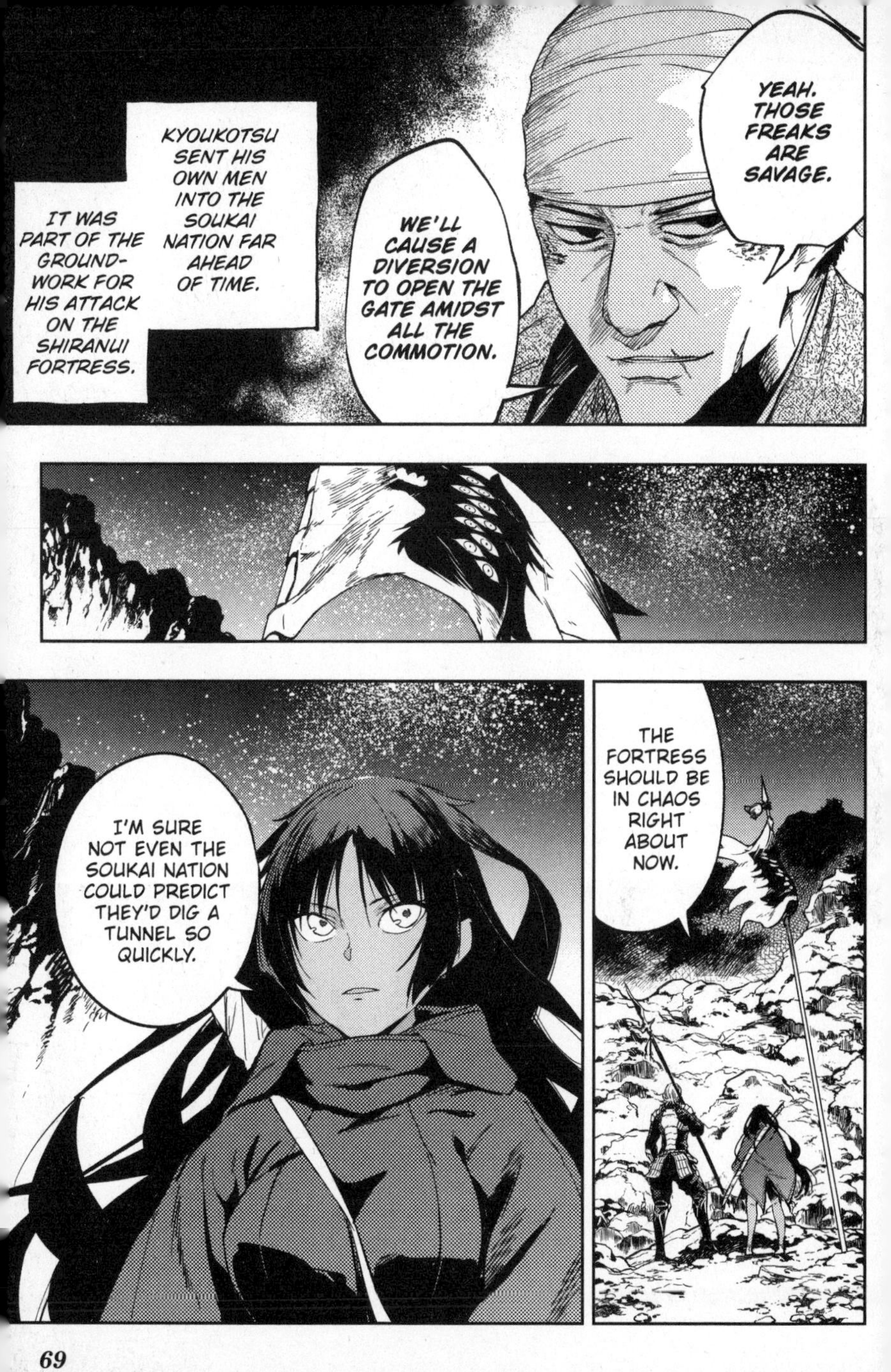
YEAH. THOSE FREAKS ARE SAVAGE.
WE'LL CAUSE A DIVERSION TO OPEN THE GATE AMIDST ALL THE COMMOTION.
KYOUKOTSU SENT HIS OWN MEN INTO THE SOUKAI NATION FAR AHEAD OF TIME.
IT WAS PART OF THE GROUND-WORK FOR HIS ATTACK ON THE SHIRANUI FORTRESS.
THE FORTRESS SHOULD BE IN CHAOS RIGHT ABOUT NOW.
I'M SURE NOT EVEN THE SOUKAI NATION COULD PREDICT THEY'D DIG A TUNNEL SO QUICKLY.

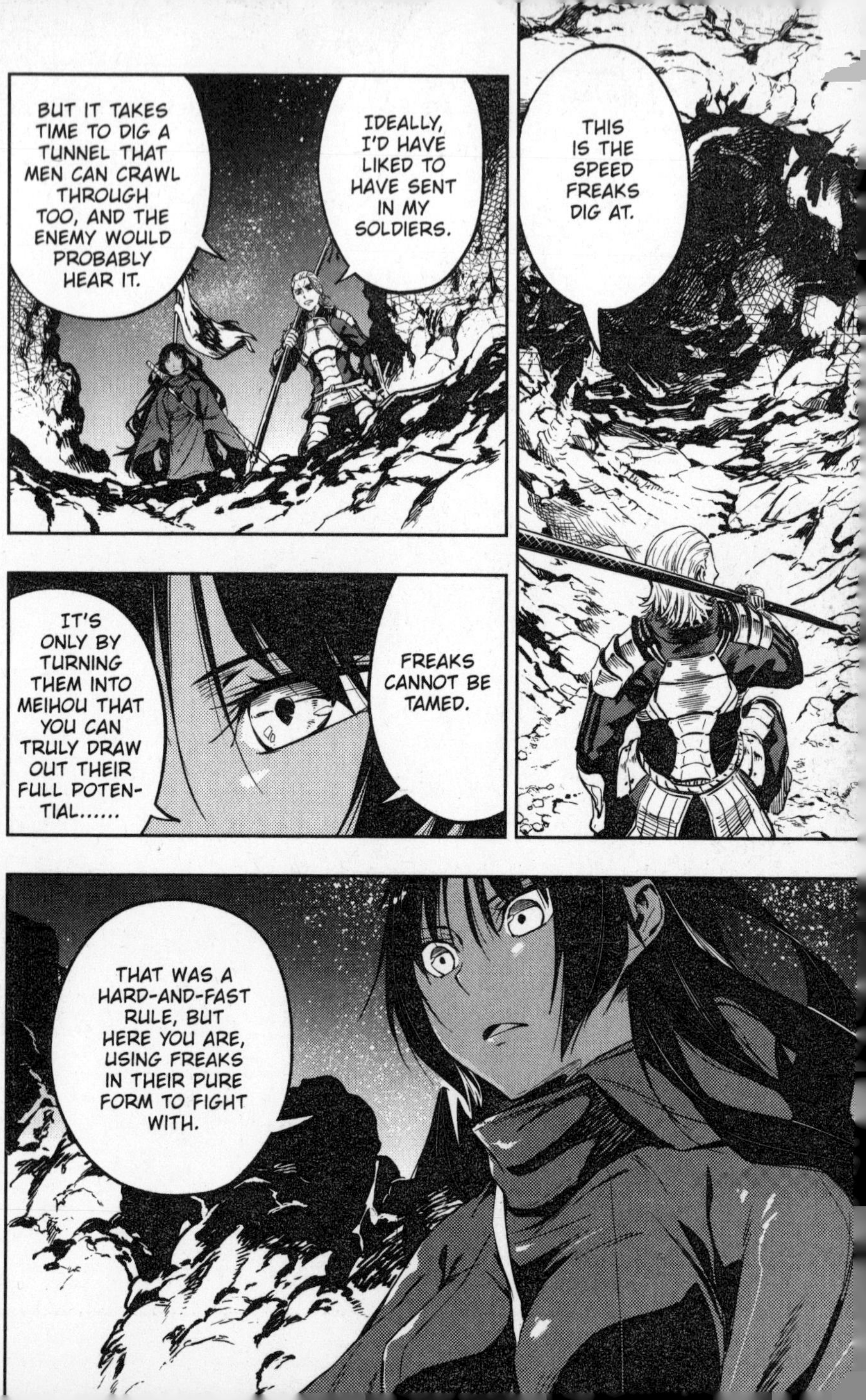
THIS IS THE SPEED FREAKS DIG AT.
IDEALLY, I'D HAVE LIKED TO HAVE SENT IN MY SOLDIERS.
BUT IT TAKES TIME TO DIG A TUNNEL THAT MEN CAN CRAWL THROUGH TOO, AND THE ENEMY WOULD PROBABLY HEAR IT.
FREAKS CANNOT BE TAMED.
IT'S ONLY BY TURNING THEM INTO MEIHOU THAT YOU CAN TRULY DRAW OUT THEIR FULL POTEN-TIAL......
THAT WAS A HARD-AND-FAST RULE, BUT HERE YOU ARE, USING FREAKS IN THEIR PURE FORM TO FIGHT WITH.

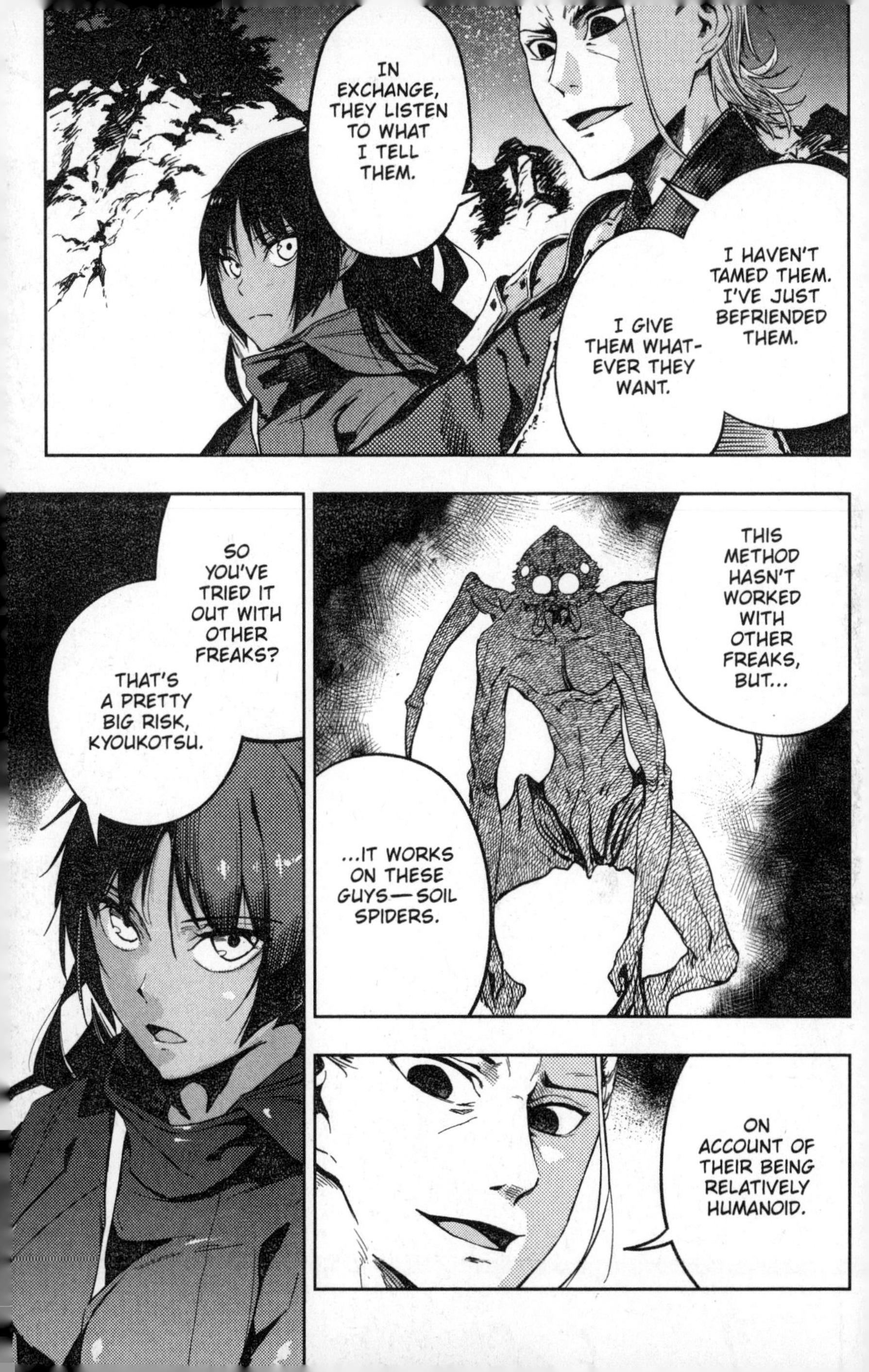
I HAVEN'T TAMED THEM. I'VE JUST BEFRIENDED THEM.
I GIVE THEM WHATEVER THEY WANT.
IN EXCHANGE, THEY LISTEN TO WHAT I TELL THEM.
THIS METHOD HASN'T WORKED WITH OTHER FREAKS, BUT...
...IT WORKS ON THESE GUYS—SOIL SPIDERS.
ON ACCOUNT OF THEIR BEING RELATIVELY HUMANOID.
SO YOU'VE TRIED IT OUT WITH OTHER FREAKS?
THAT'S A PRETTY BIG RISK, KYOUKOTSU.

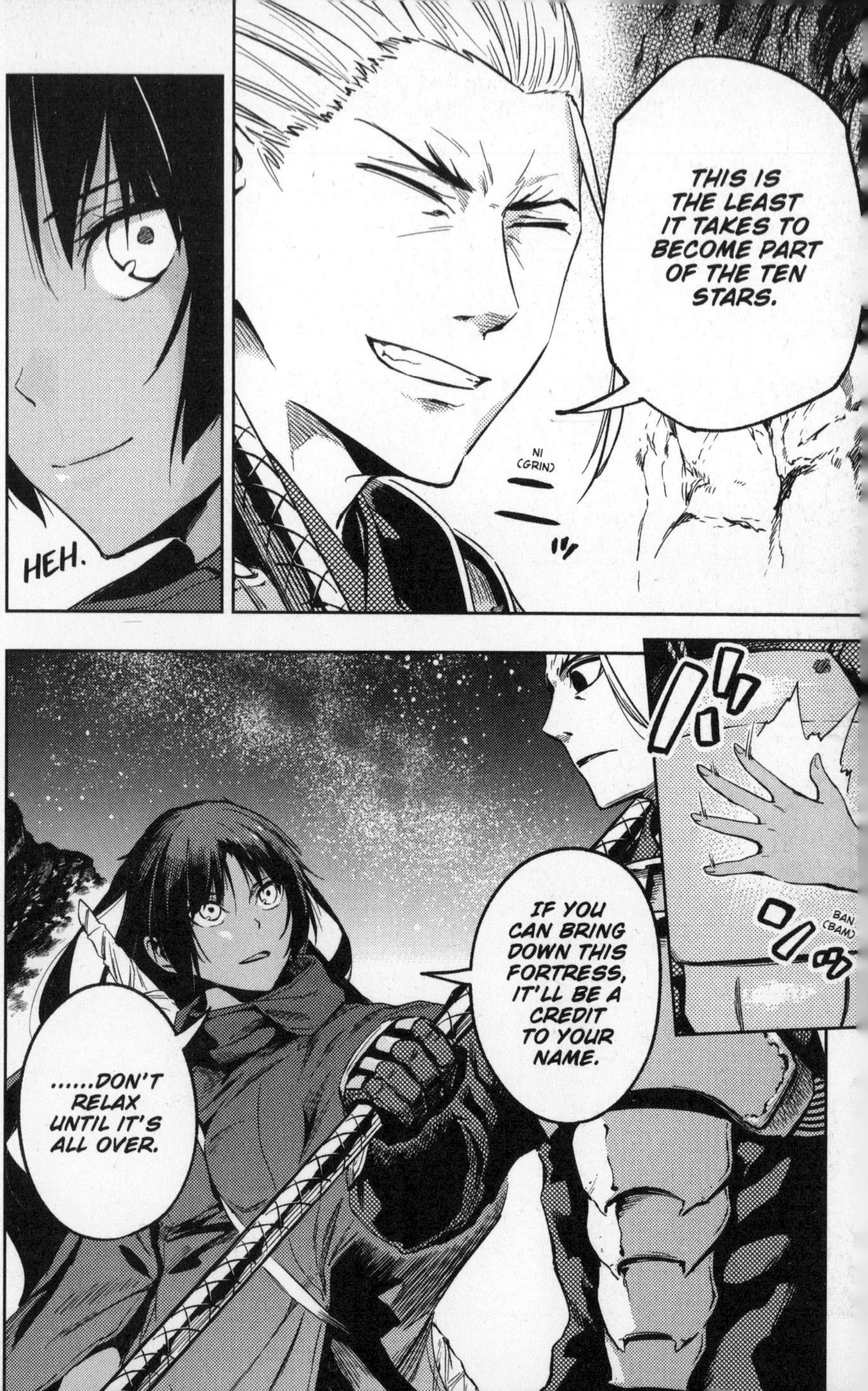
THIS IS THE LEAST IT TAKES TO BECOME PART OF THE TEN STARS.
NI (GRIN)
HEH.
BAN (BAM)
IF YOU CAN BRING DOWN THIS FORTRESS, IT'LL BE A CREDIT TO YOUR NAME.
......DON'T RELAX UNTIL IT'S ALL OVER.

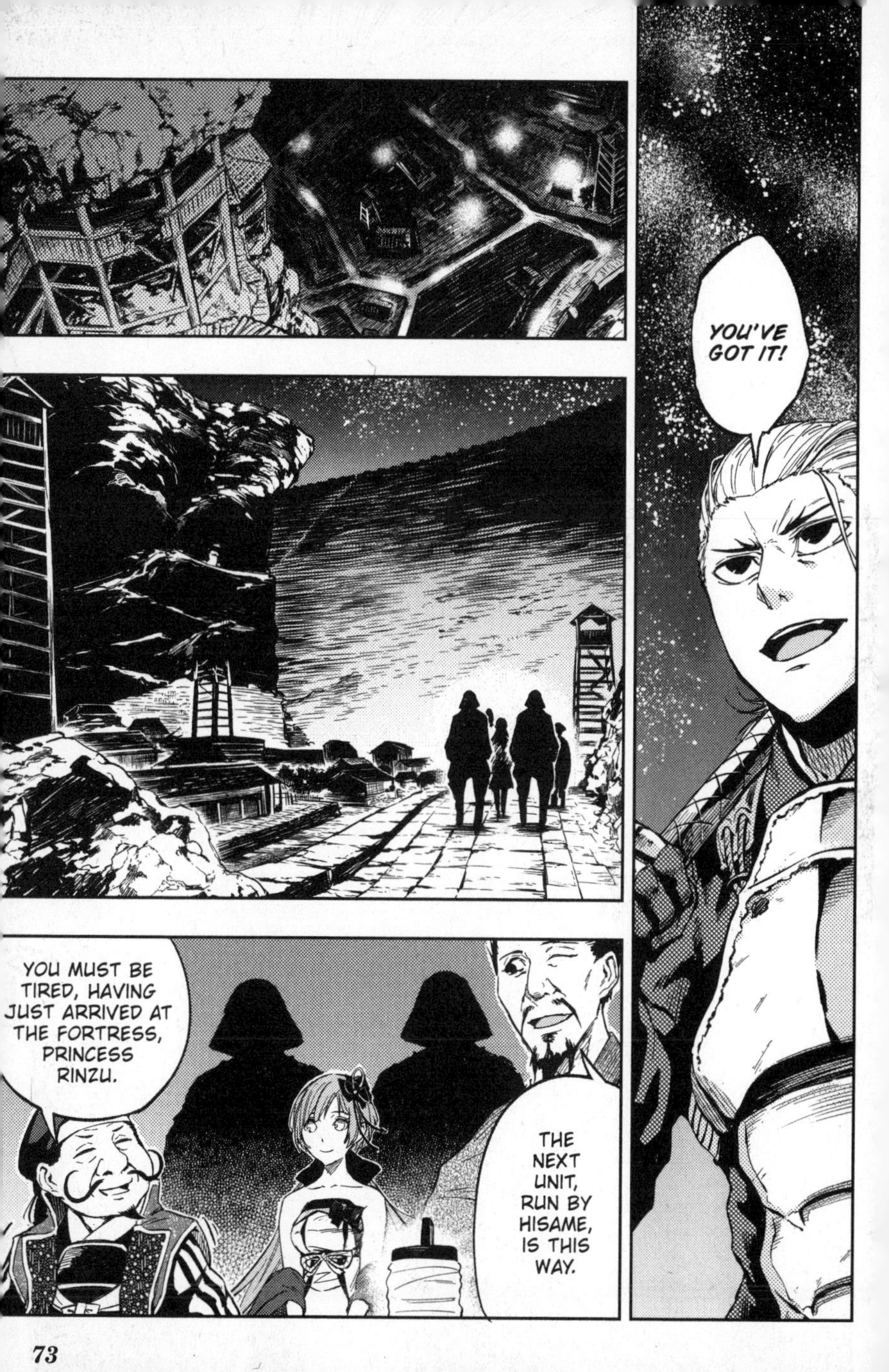
YOU'VE GOT IT!
YOU MUST BE TIRED, HAVING JUST ARRIVED AT THE FORTRESS, PRINCESS RINZU.
THE NEXT UNIT, RUN BY HISAME, IS THIS WAY.

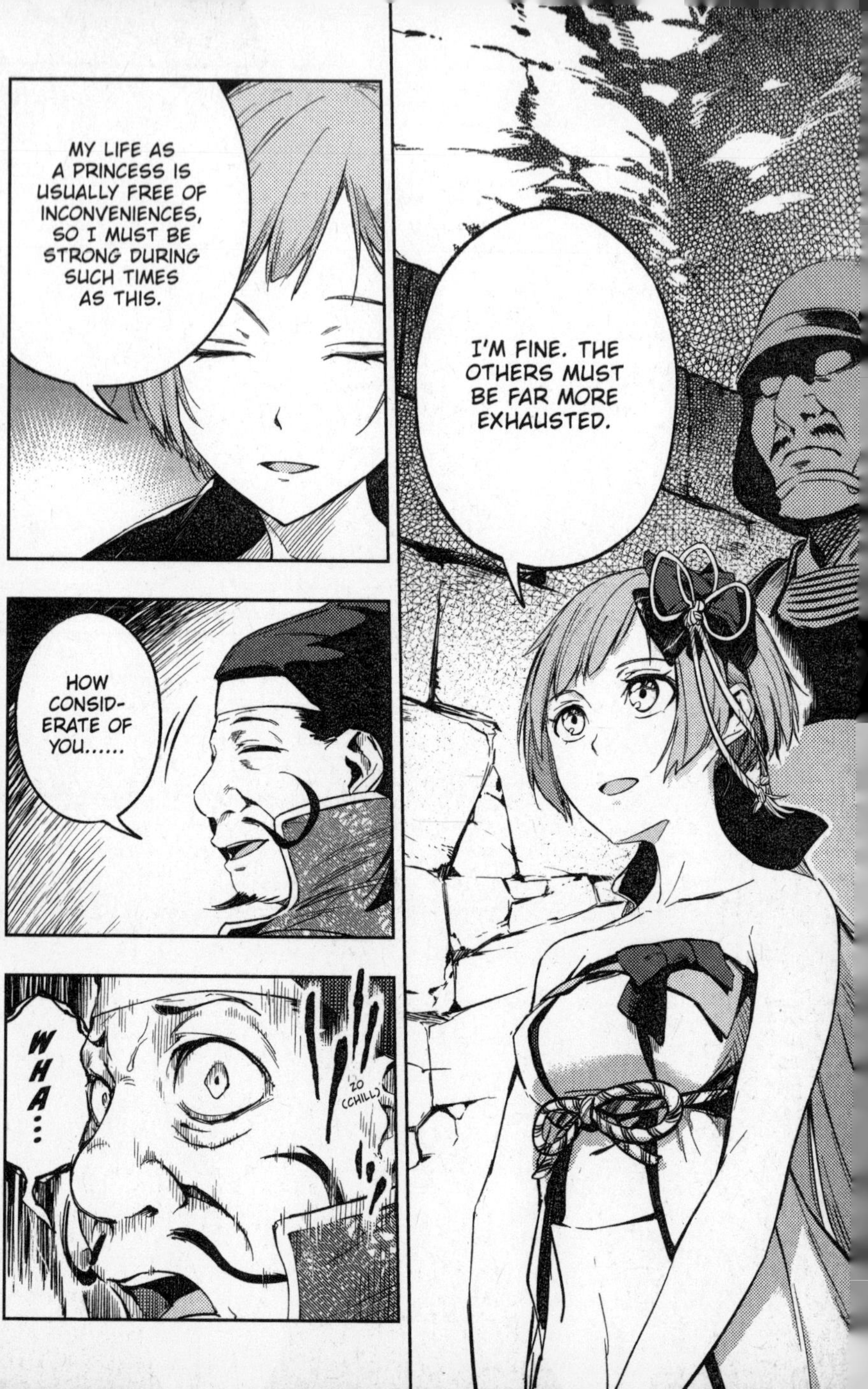
I'M FINE. THE OTHERS MUST BE FAR MORE EXHAUSTED.
MY LIFE AS A PRINCESS IS USUALLY FREE OF INCONVENIENCES, SO I MUST BE STRONG DURING SUCH TIMES AS THIS.
HOW CONSID- ERATE OF YOU......
ZO (CHILL)
WHA...

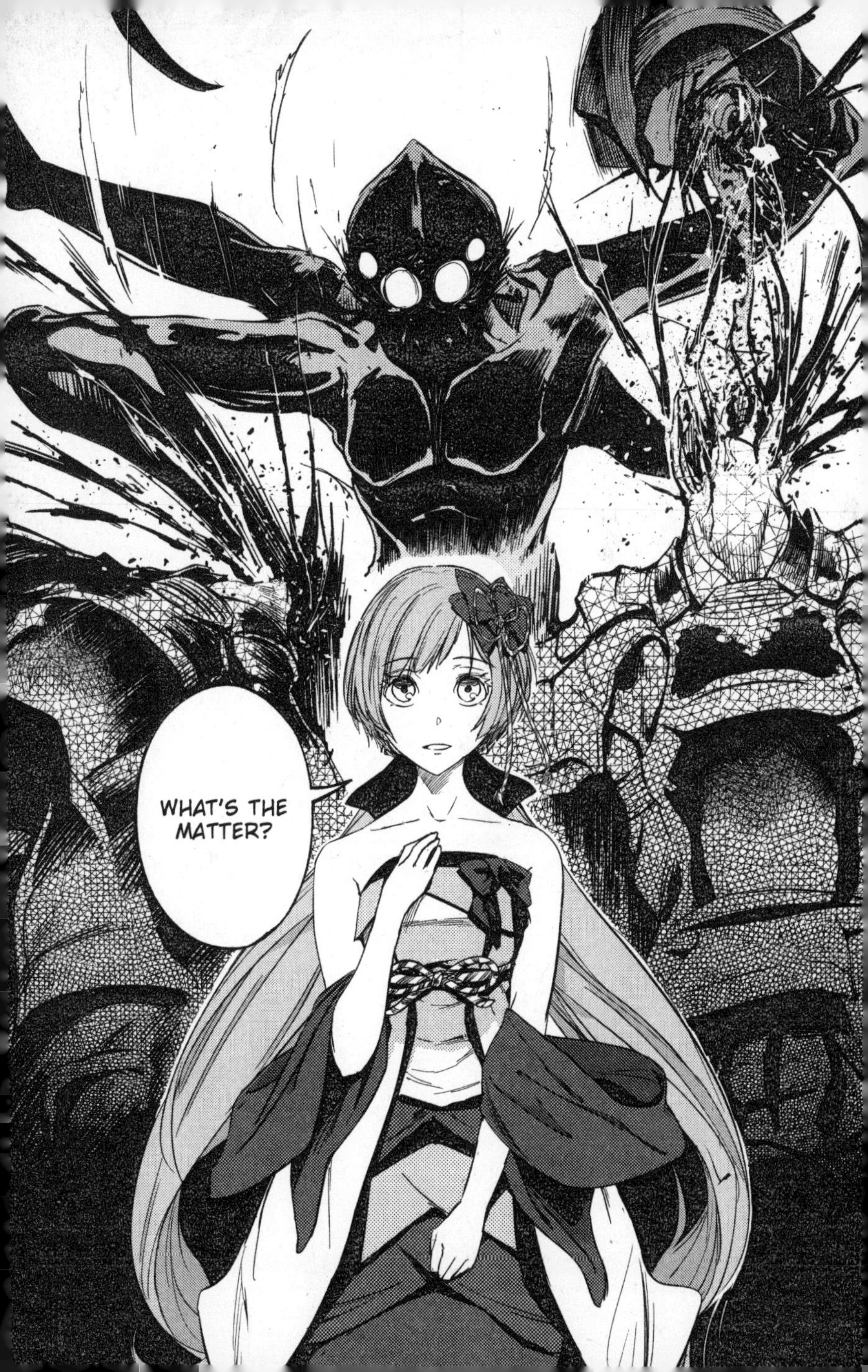
WHAT'S THE MATTER?

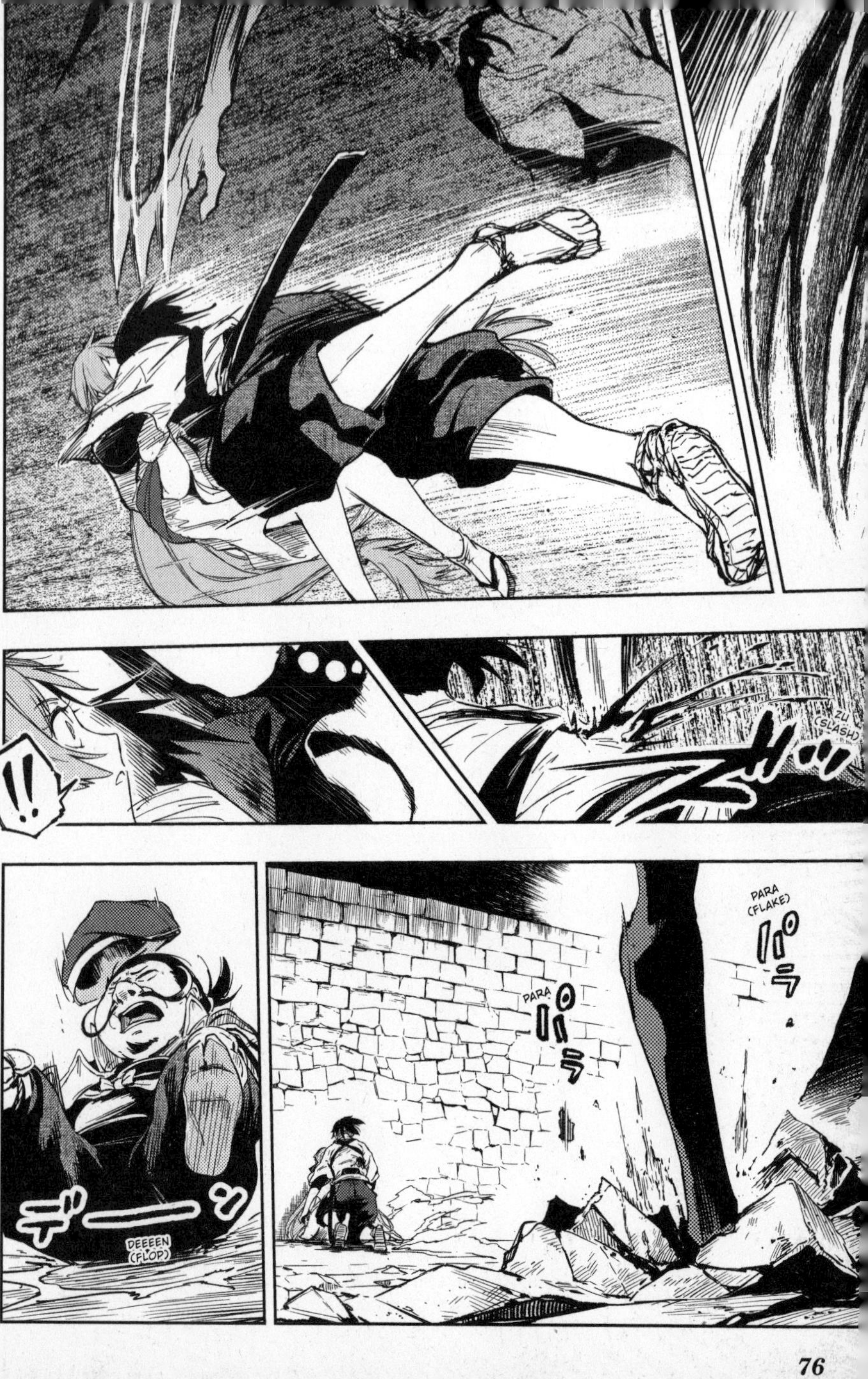
ZU (SLASH)
!!
PARA (FLAKE)
PARA
DEEEEN (FLOP)

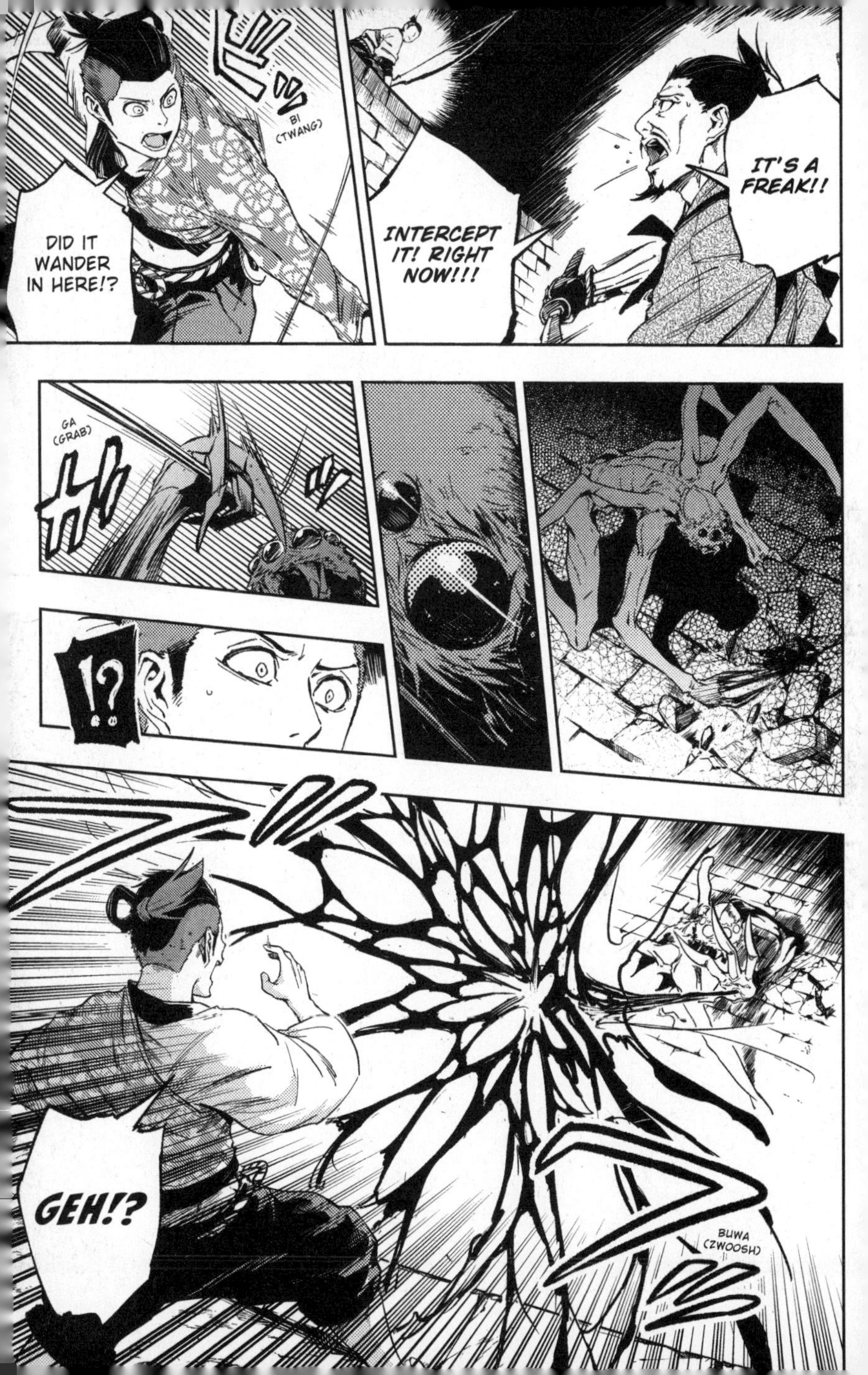
IT'S A FREAK!!
INTERCEPT IT! RIGHT NOW!!!
BI (TWANG)
DID IT WANDER IN HERE!?
GA (GRAB)
!?
BUWA (ZWOOSH)
GEH!?

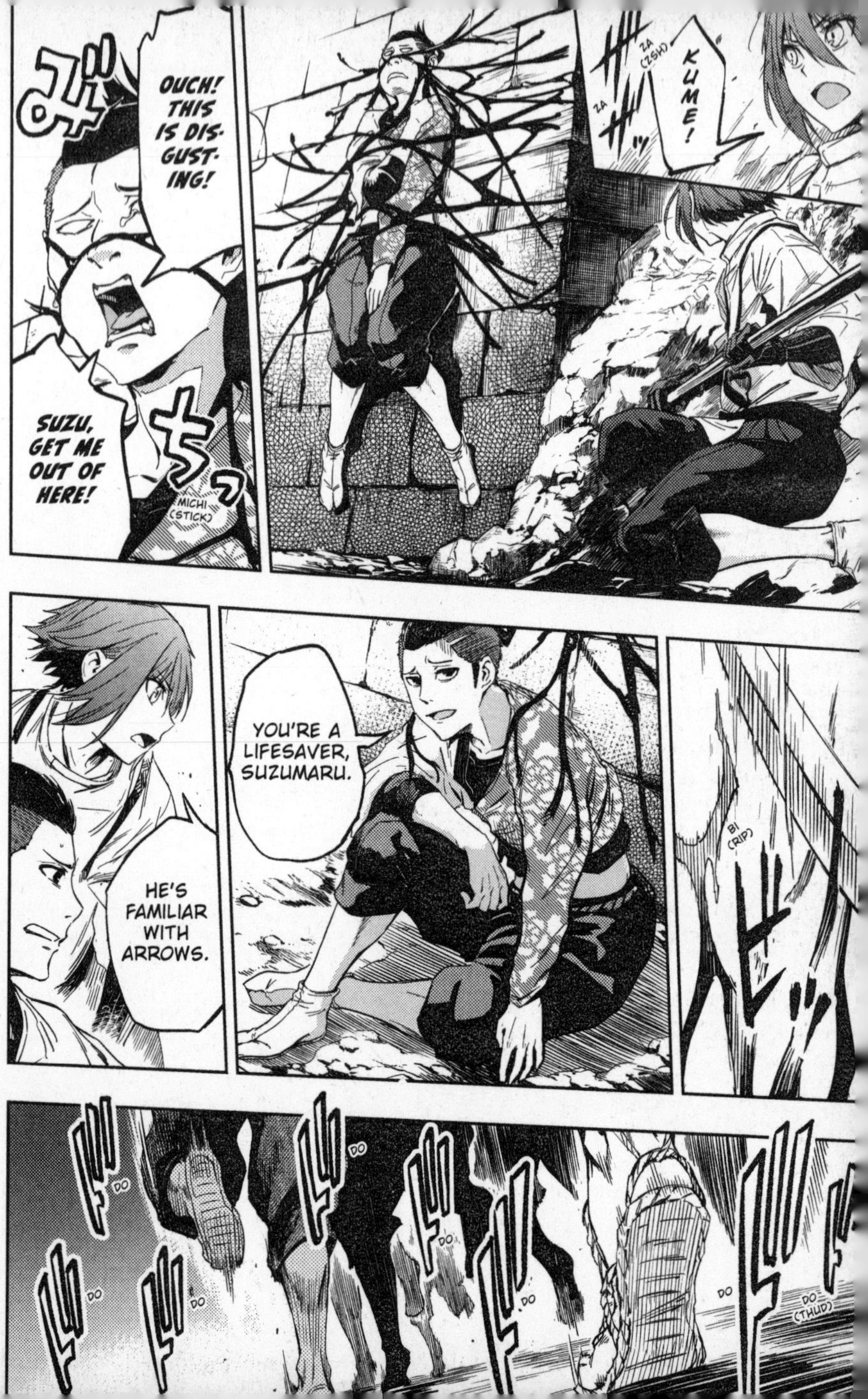
ZA (ZSH)
ZA
KUME!
OUCH! THIS IS DIS-GUST-ING!
SUZU, GET ME OUT OF HERE!
MICHI (STICK)
BI (RIP)
YOU'RE A LIFESAVER, SUZUMARU.
HE'S FAMILIAR WITH ARROWS.
DO (THUD)
DO
DO
DO
DO
DO
DO

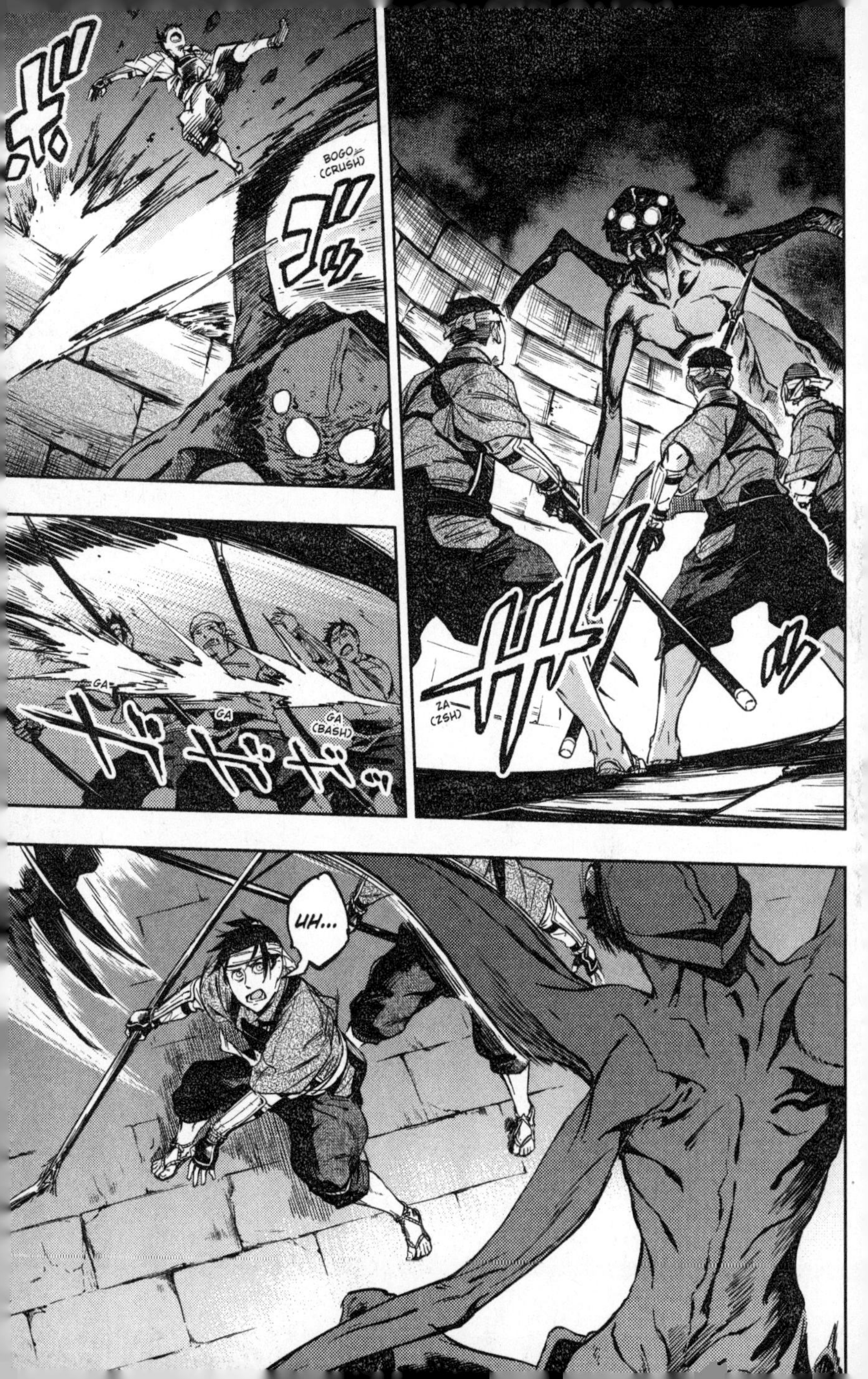
ZA (ZSH)
BOGO (CRUSH)
GA
GA
GA (BASH)
UH...

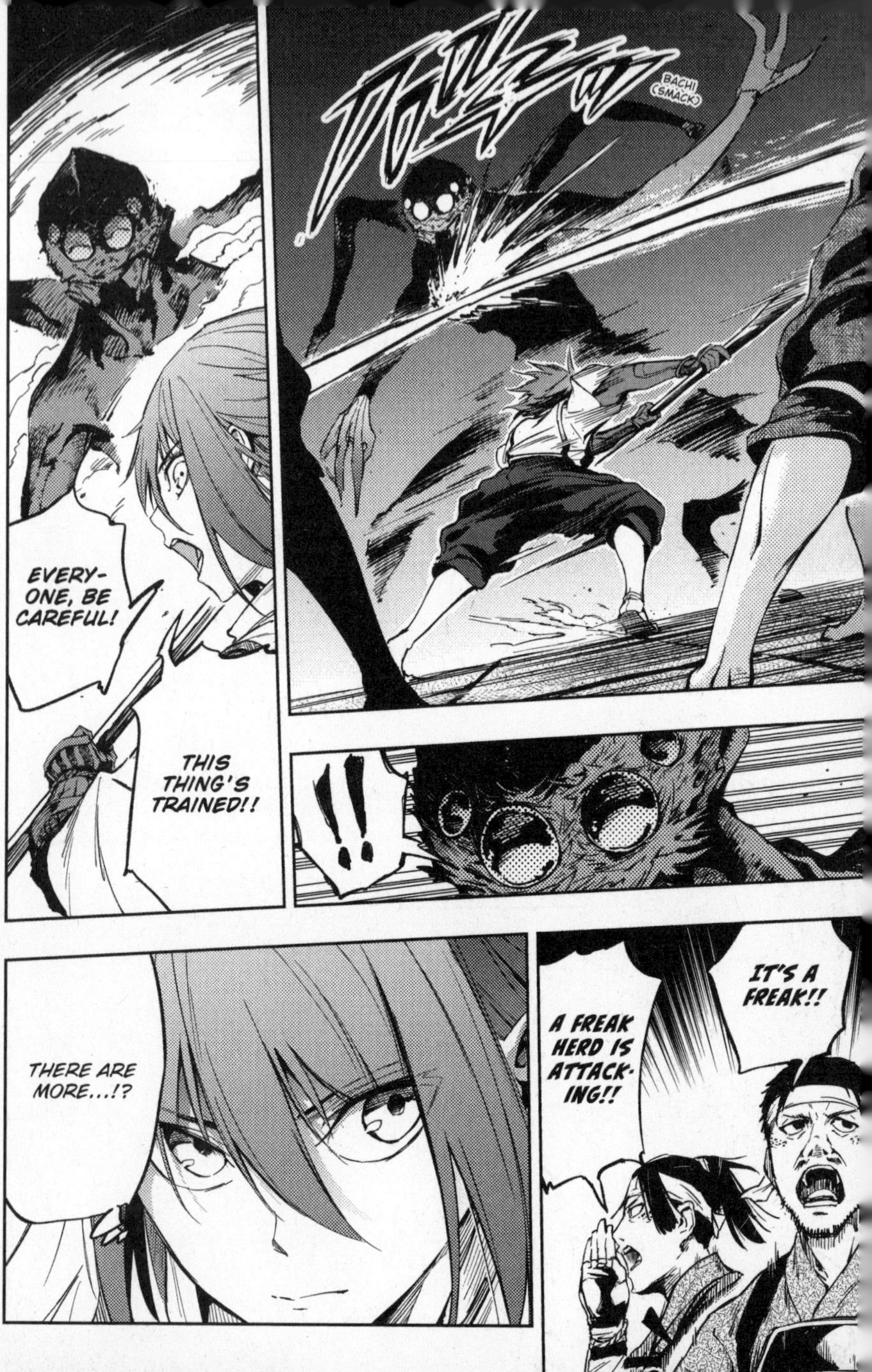
BACHI (SMACK)
!!
EVERY-ONE, BE CAREFUL!
THIS THING'S TRAINED!!
IT'S A FREAK!!
A FREAK HERD IS ATTACK-ING!!
THERE ARE MORE...!?

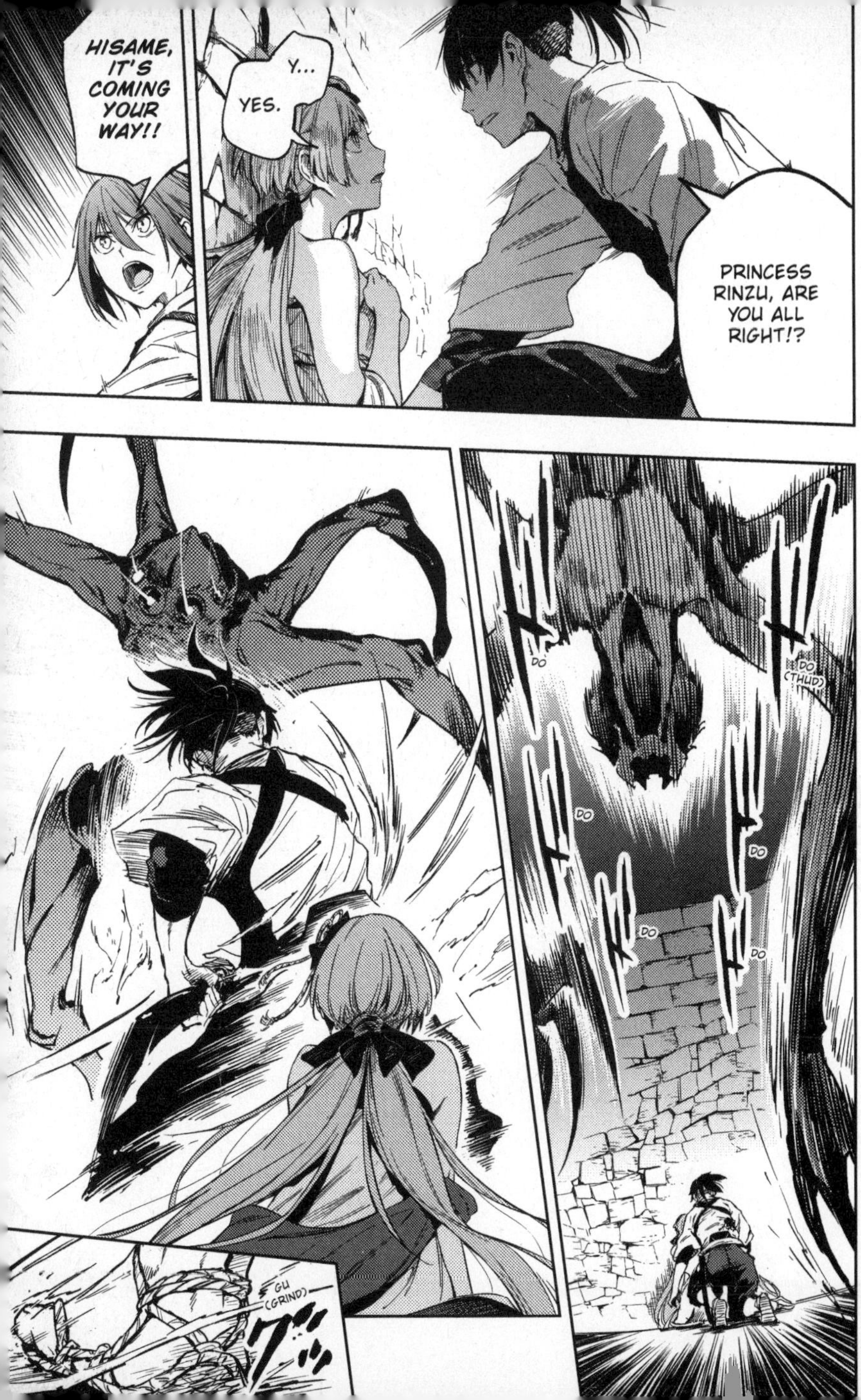
PRINCESS RINZU, ARE YOU ALL RIGHT!?
Y... YES.
HISAME, IT'S COMING YOUR WAY!!
DO (THUD)
DO
DO
DO
DO
DO
GU (GRIND)

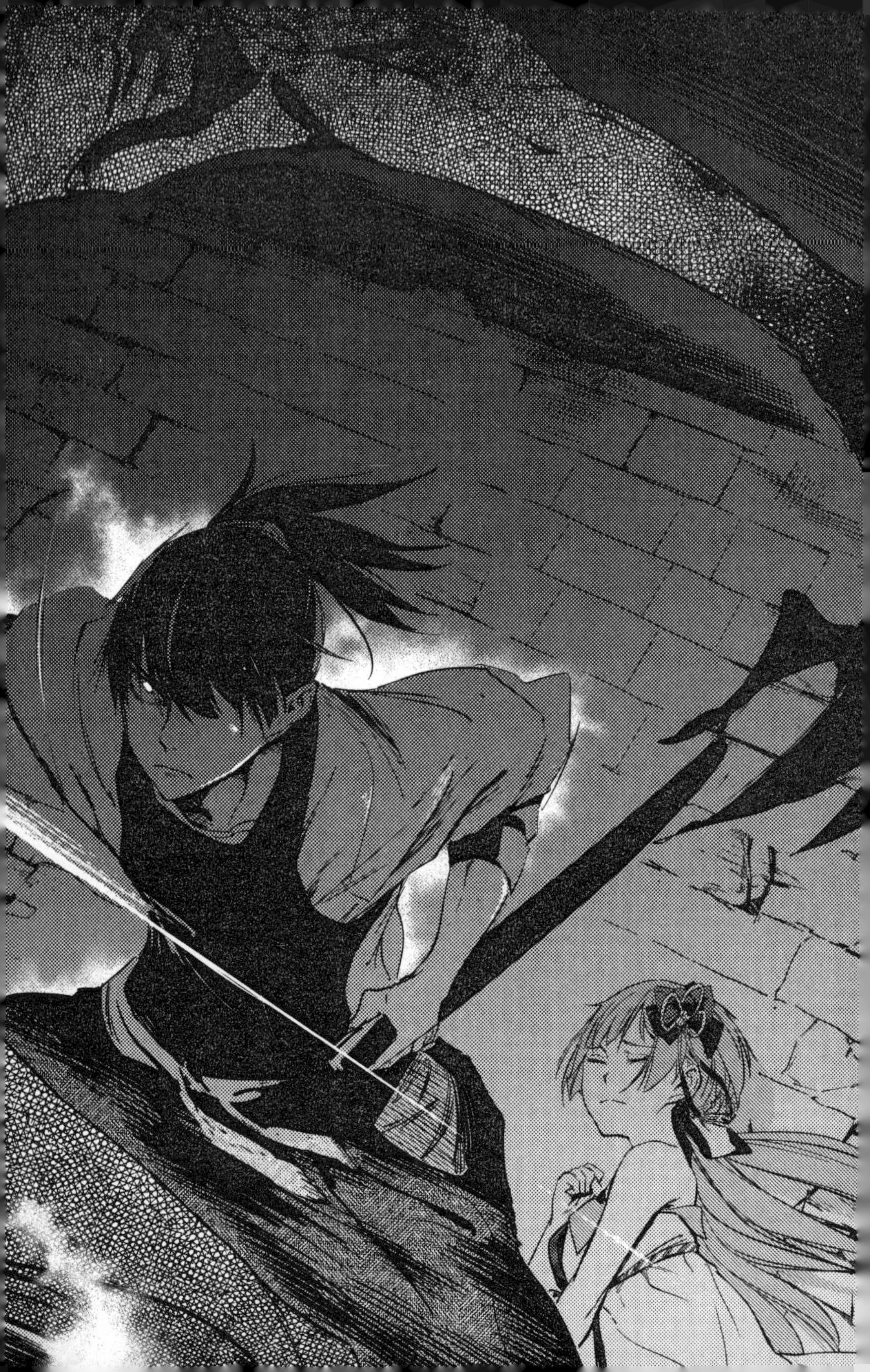

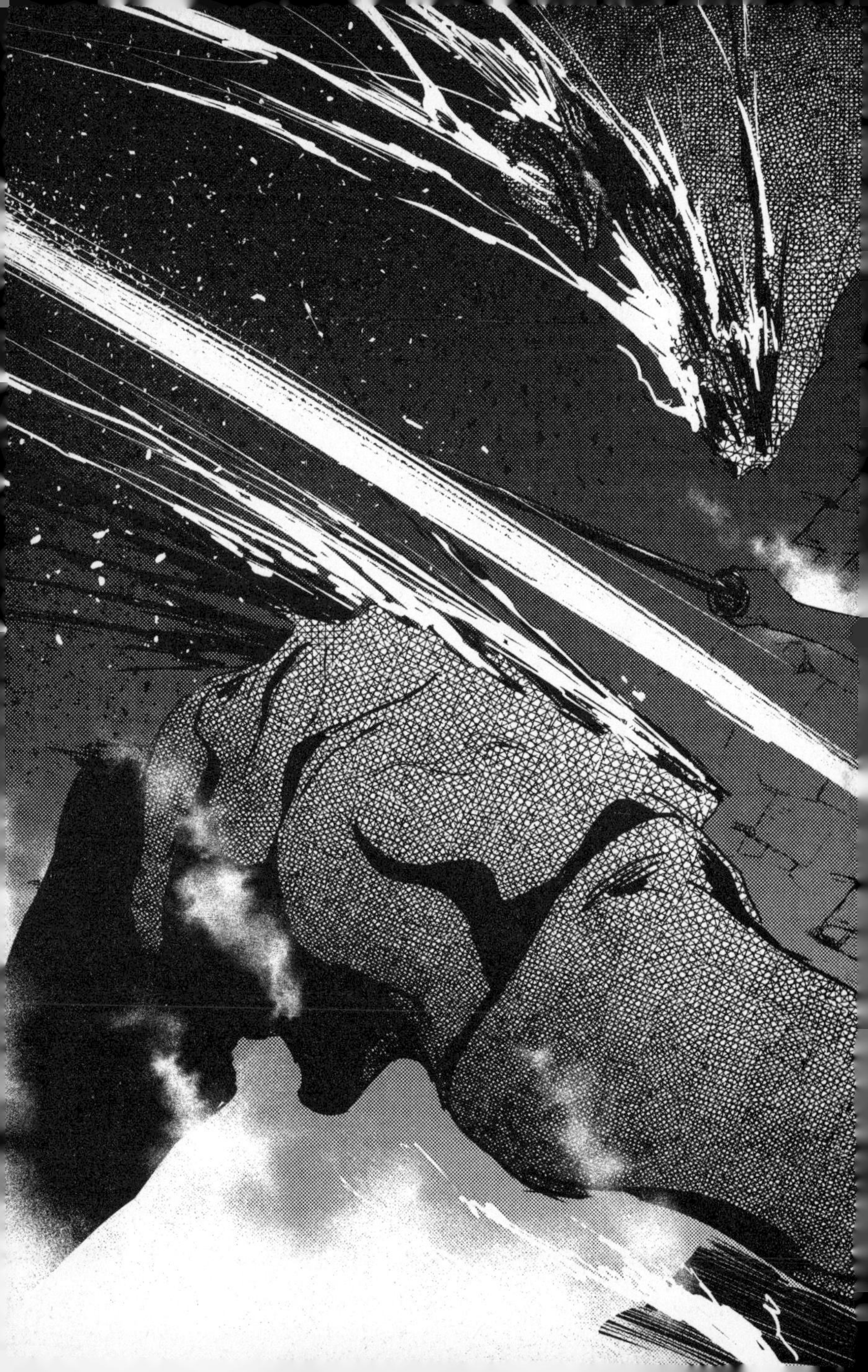

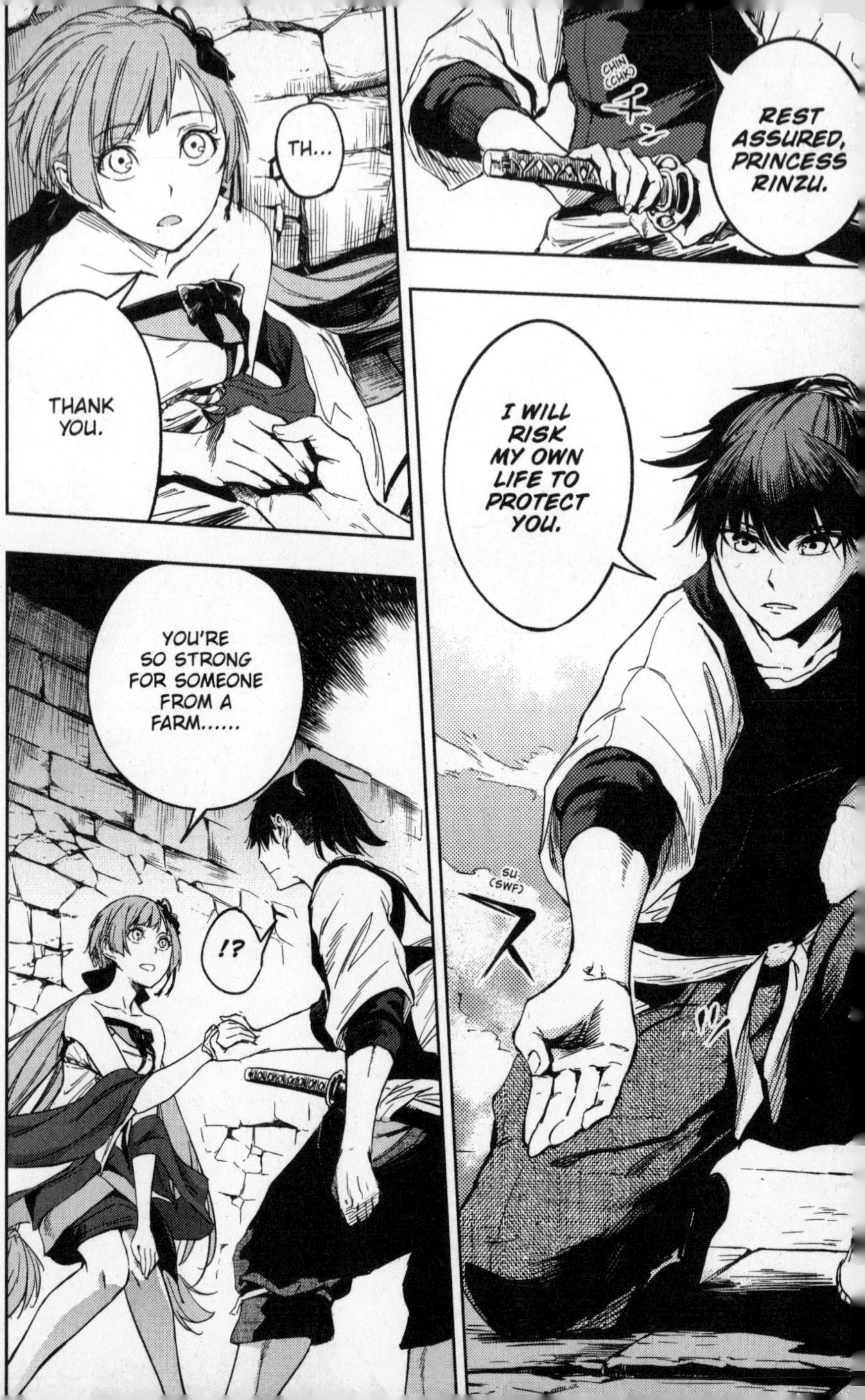
CHIN (CHK)
REST ASSURED, PRINCESS RINZU.
I WILL RISK MY OWN LIFE TO PROTECT YOU.
SU (SWF)
TH...
THANK YOU.
YOU'RE SO STRONG FOR SOMEONE FROM A FARM......
!?

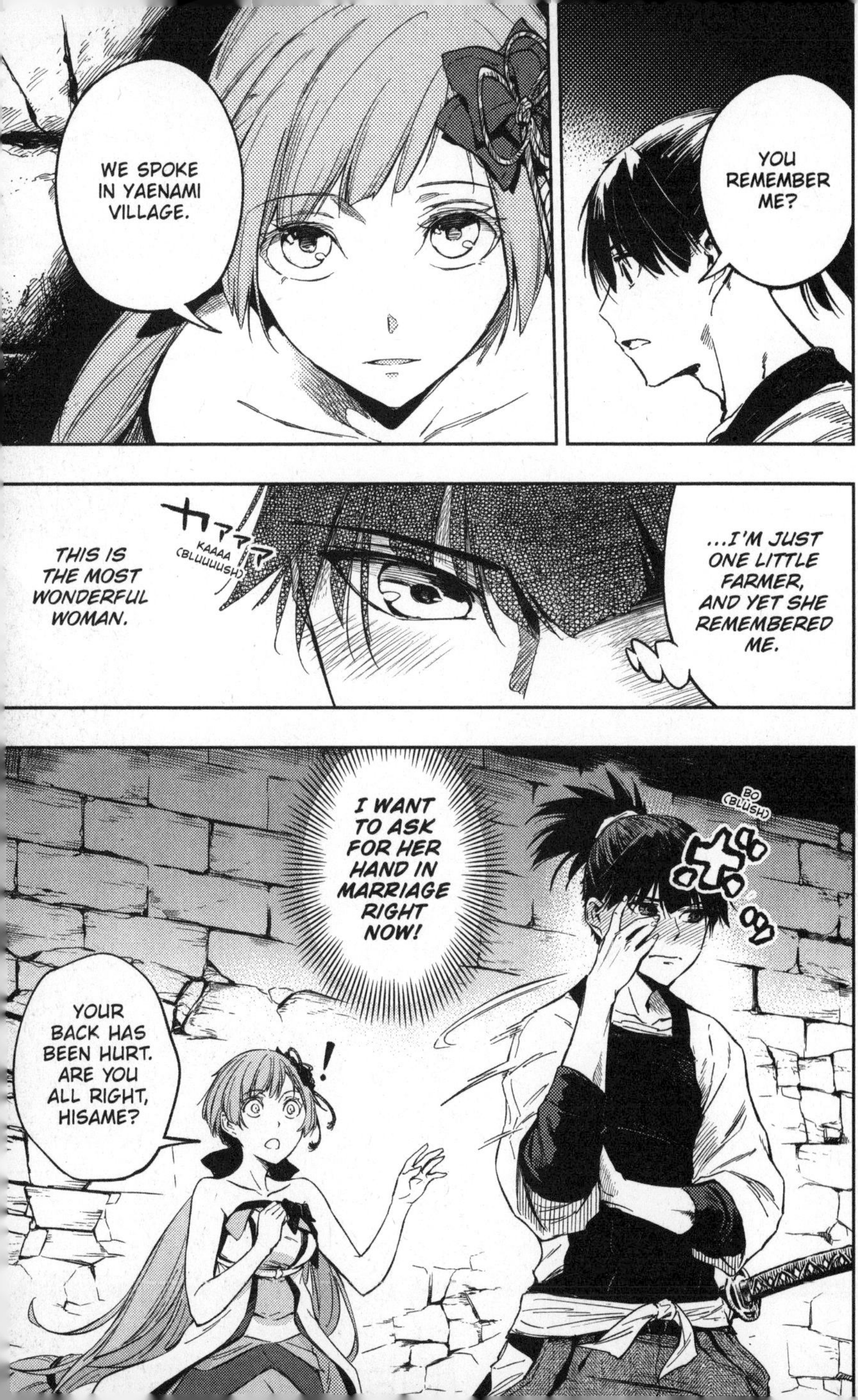
YOU REMEMBER ME?
WE SPOKE IN YAENAMI VILLAGE.
...I'M JUST ONE LITTLE FARMER, AND YET SHE REMEMBERED ME.
KAAAA (BLUUUUSH)
THIS IS THE MOST WONDERFUL WOMAN.
BO (BLUSH)
I WANT TO ASK FOR HER HAND IN MARRIAGE RIGHT NOW!
YOUR BACK HAS BEEN HURT. ARE YOU ALL RIGHT, HISAME?
!

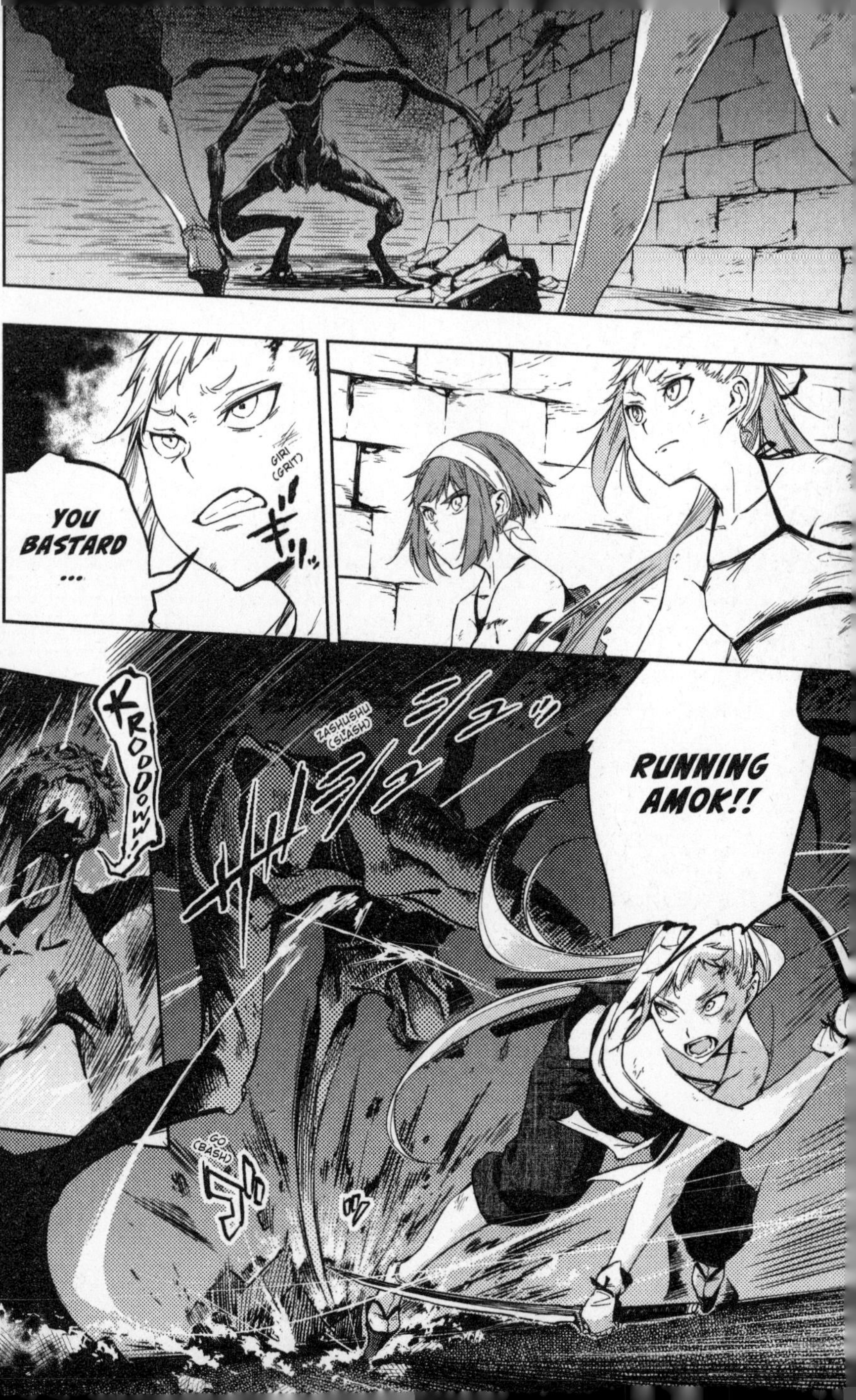
GIRI (GRIT)
YOU BASTARD ...
RUNNING AMOK!!
ZASHUSHU (SLASH)
KROOOOWW!
GO (BASH)

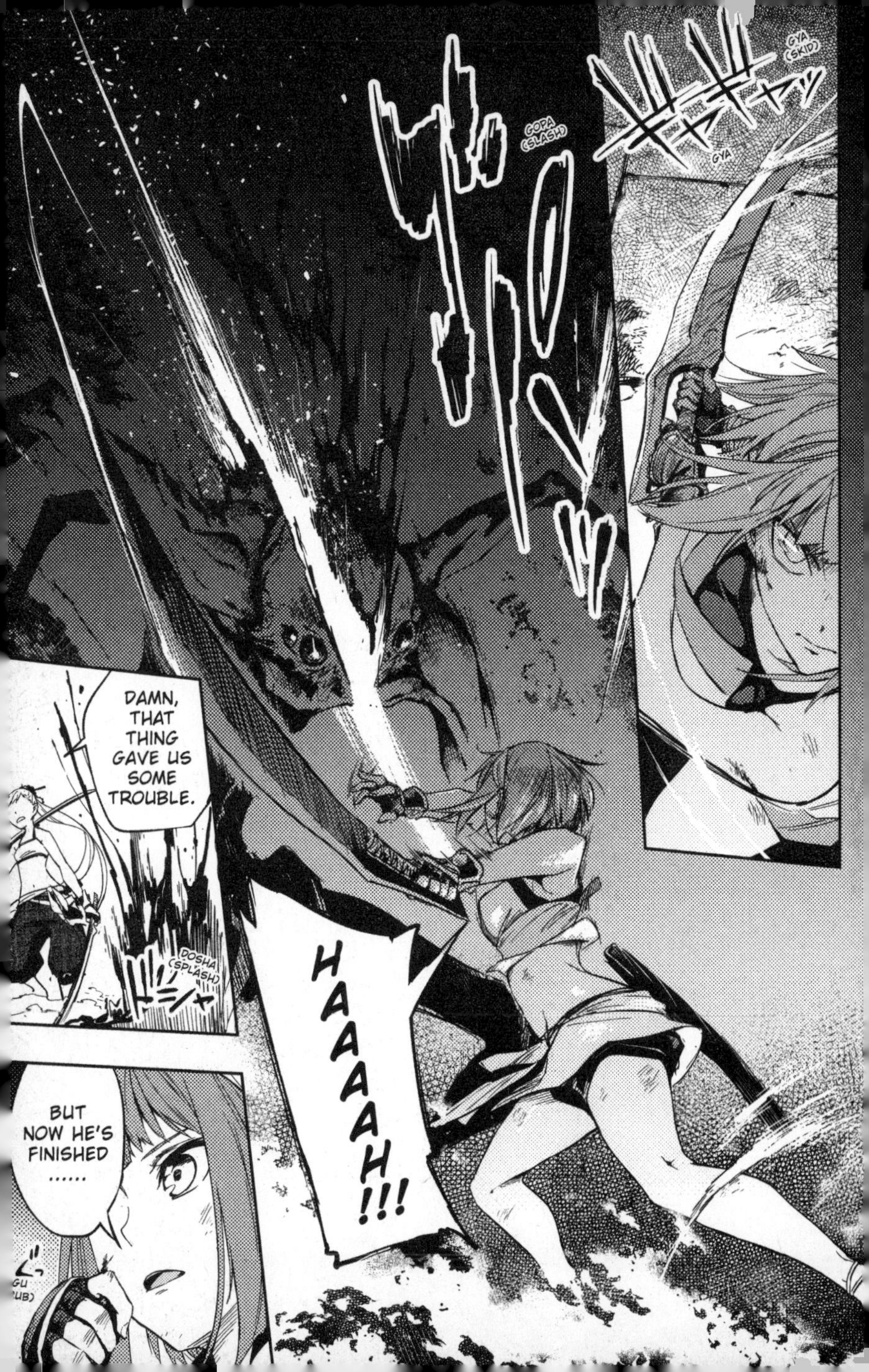
GYA (SKID)
GYA
GOPA (SLASH)
HAAAAAH!!!
DAMN, THAT THING GAVE US SOME TROUBLE.
DOSHA (SPLASH)
BUT NOW HE'S FINISHED ......
GU

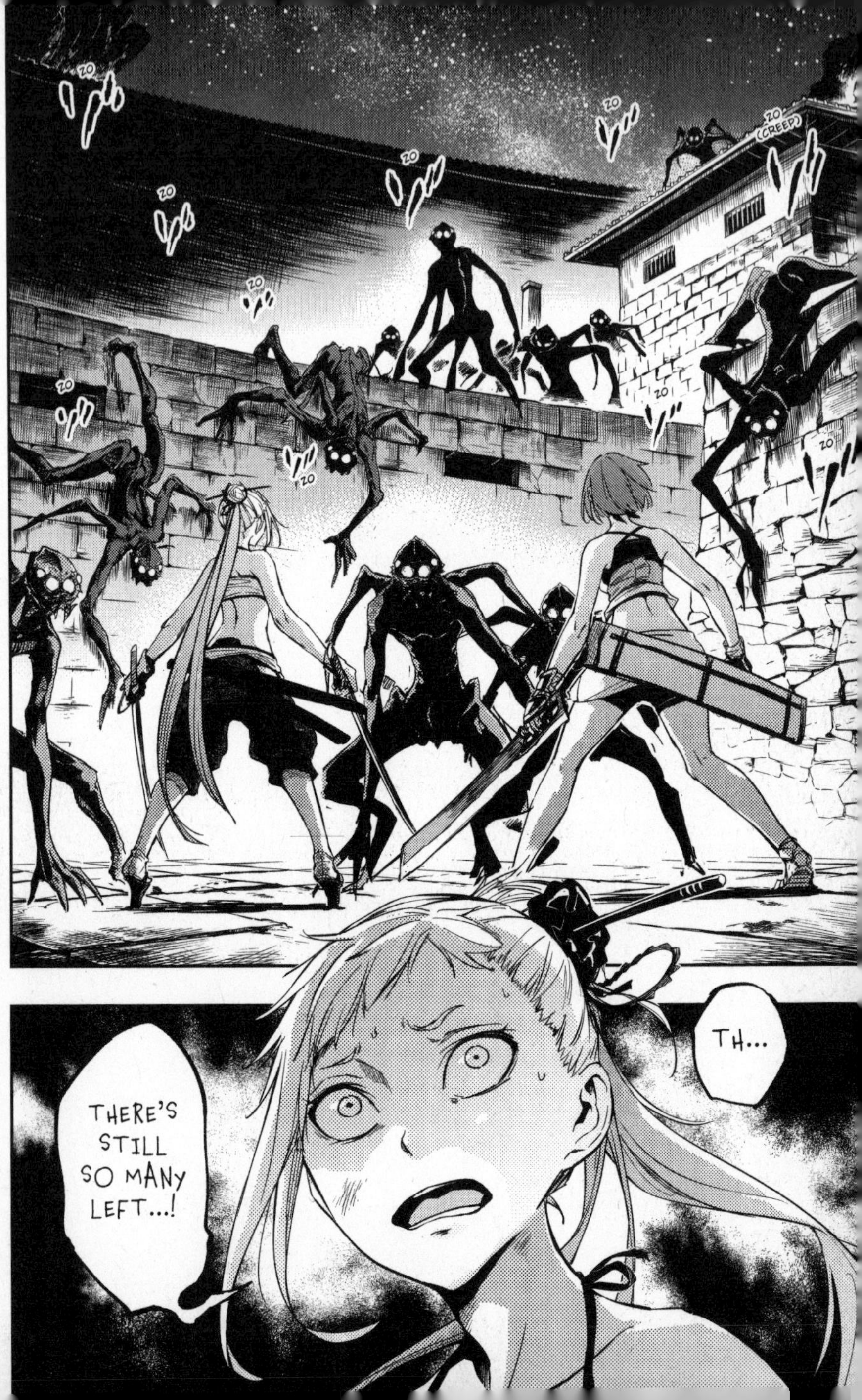
ZO (CREEP)
ZO
ZO
ZO
ZO
ZO
ZO
ZO
ZO
ZO
TH...
THERE'S STILL SO MANY LEFT...!

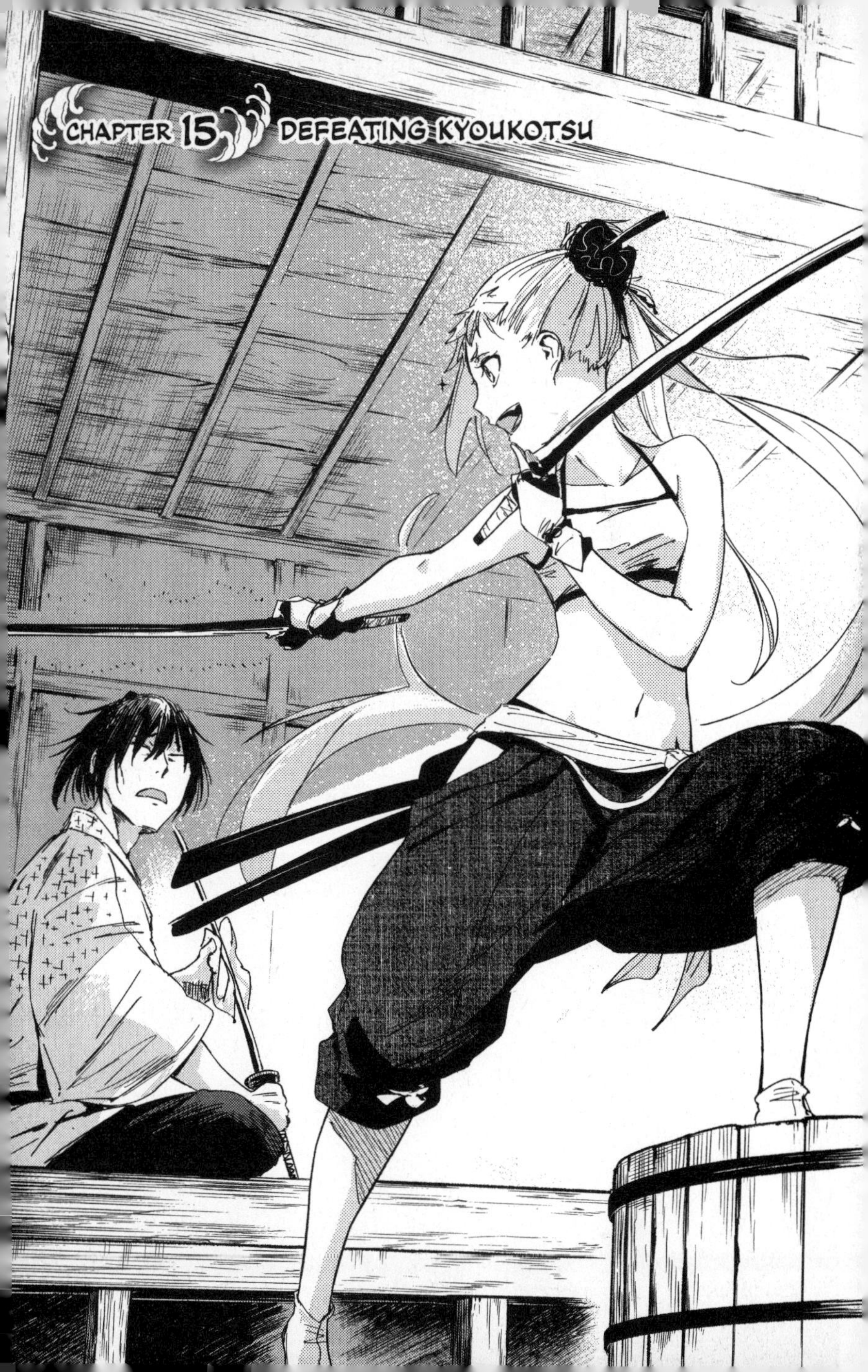
CHAPTER 15
DEFEATING KYOUKOTSU

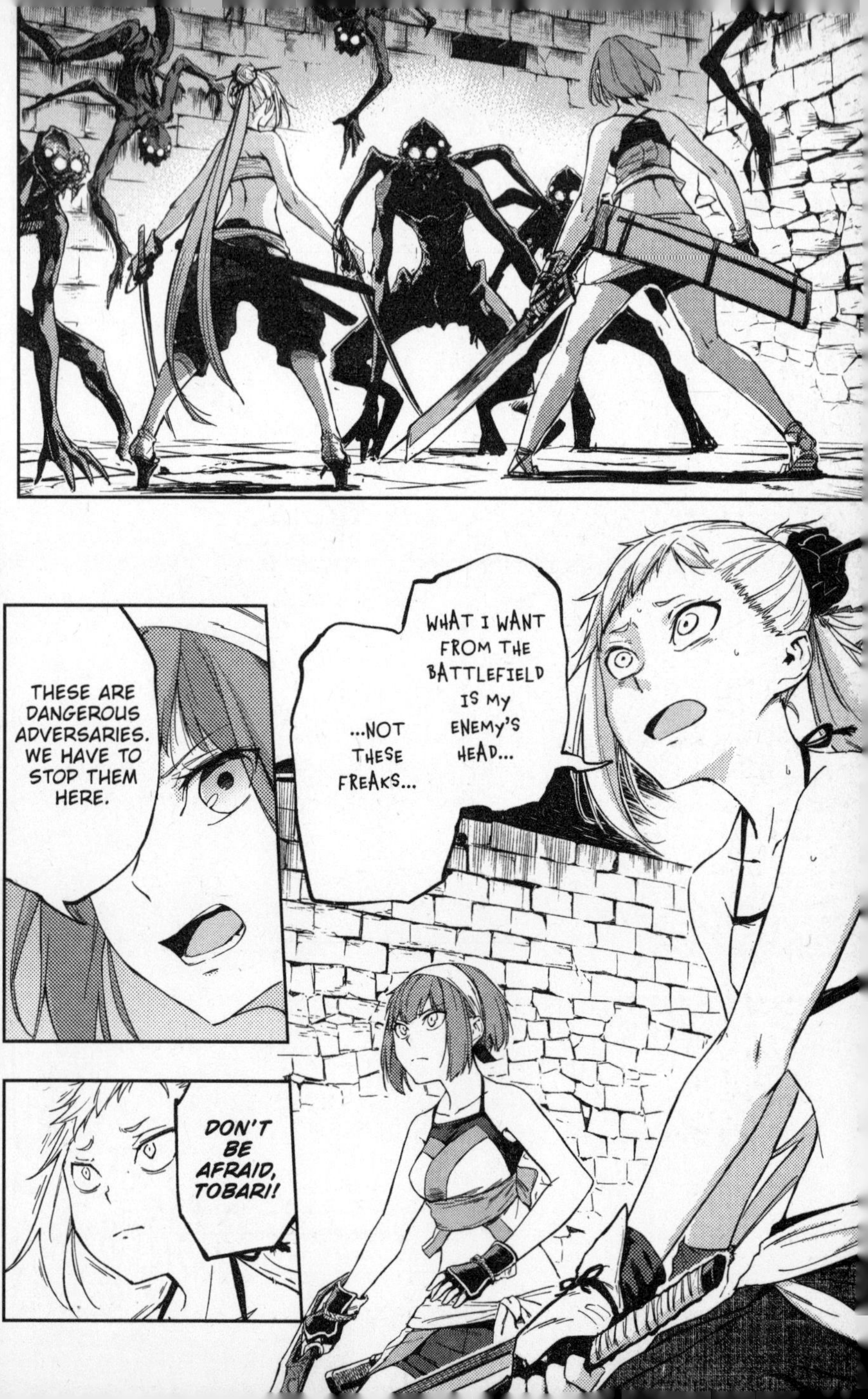
WHAT I WANT FROM THE BATTLEFIELD IS MY ENEMY'S HEAD...
...NOT THESE FREAKS...
THESE ARE DANGEROUS ADVERSARIES. WE HAVE TO STOP THEM HERE.
DON'T BE AFRAID, TOBARI!

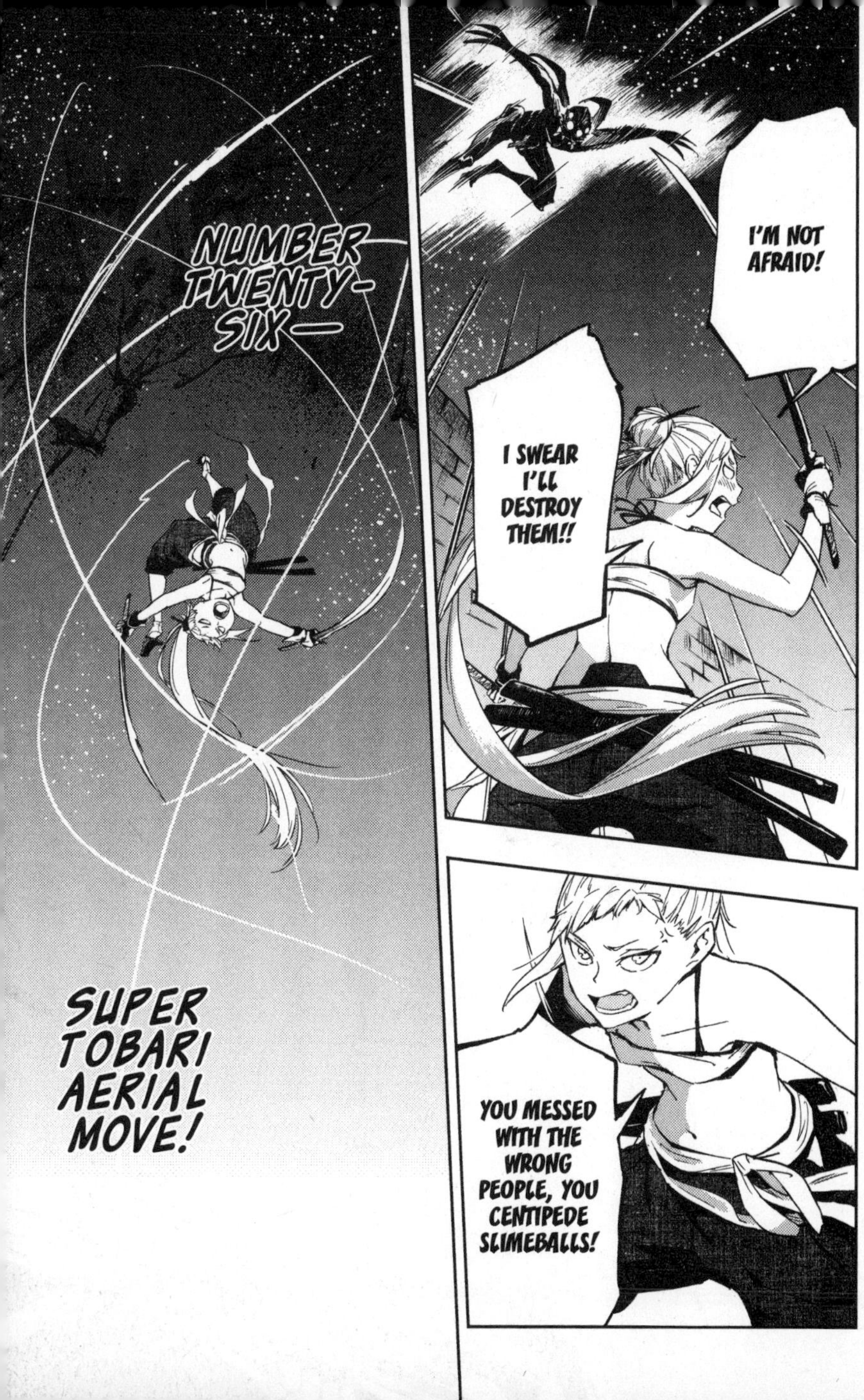
I'M NOT AFRAID!
I SWEAR I'LL DESTROY THEM!!
YOU MESSED WITH THE WRONG PEOPLE, YOU CENTIPEDE SLIMEBALLS!
NUMBER TWENTY-SIX—
SUPER TOBARI AERIAL MOVE!

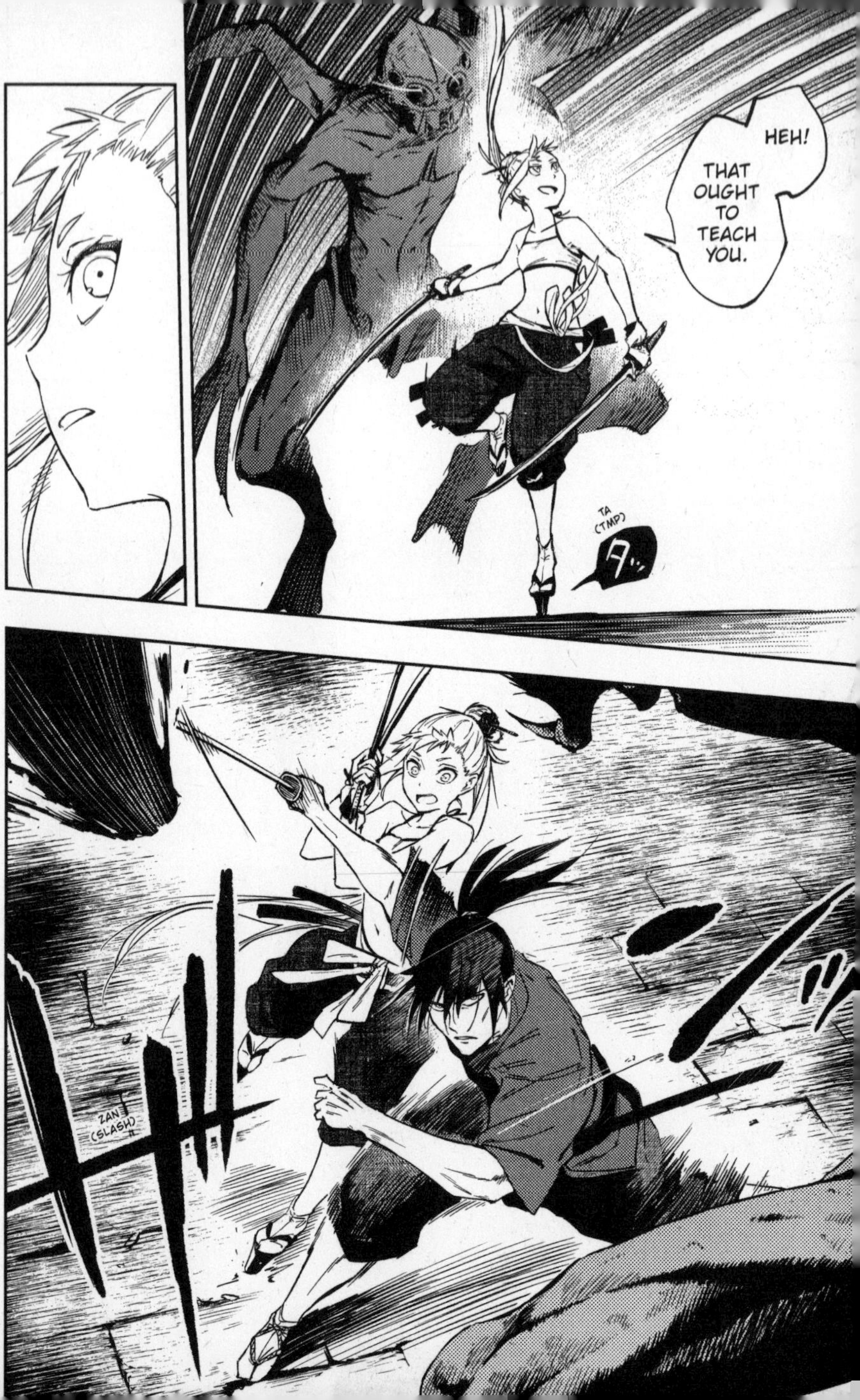
HEH!
THAT OUGHT TO TEACH YOU.
TA (TMP)
ZAN (SLASH)

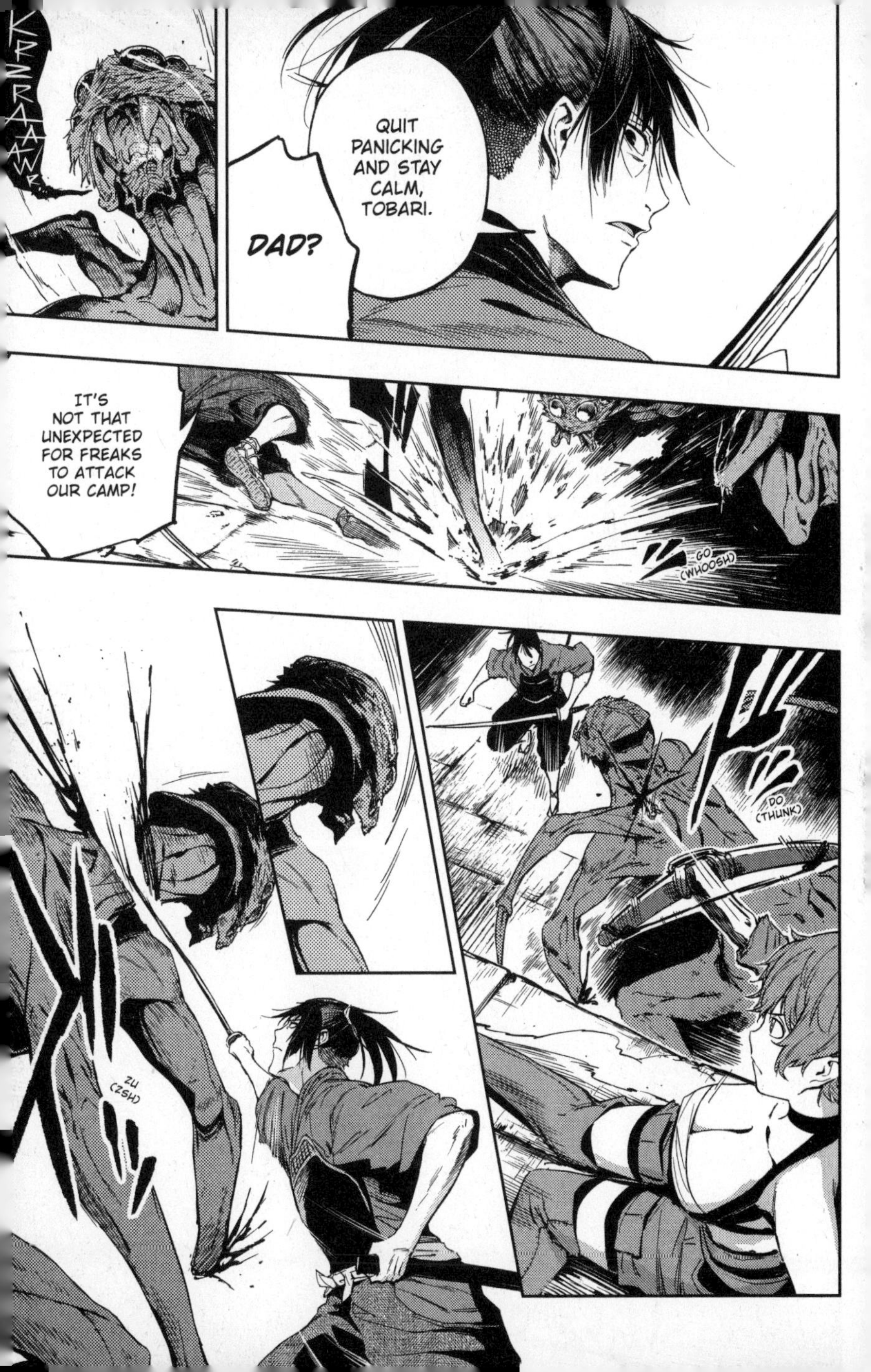

QUIT PANICKING AND STAY CALM, TOBARI.
DAD?
KRZRAAAWR
GO (WHOOSH)
IT'S NOT THAT UNEXPECTED FOR FREAKS TO ATTACK OUR CAMP!
DO (THUNK)
ZU (ZSH)

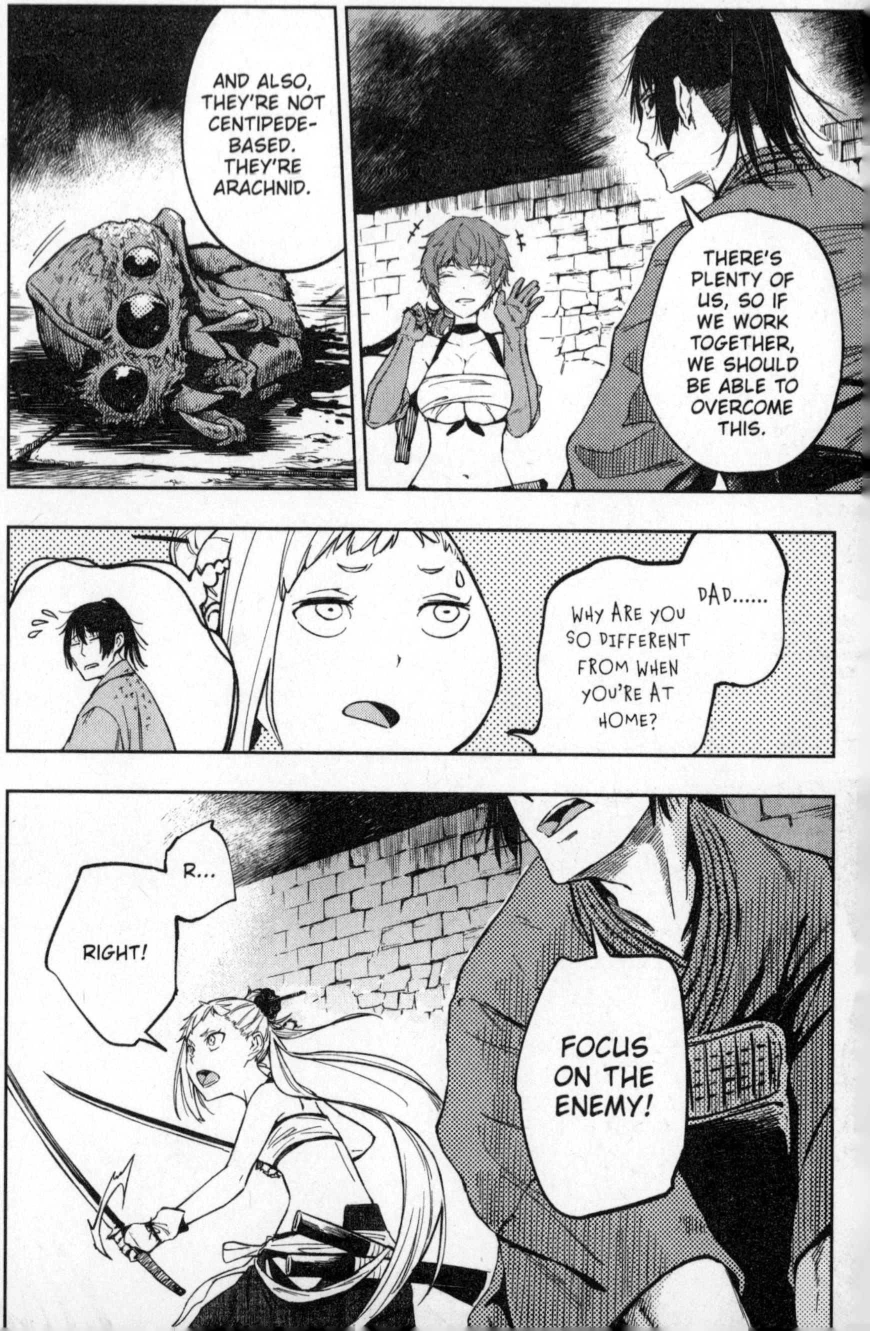
THERE'S PLENTY OF US, SO IF WE WORK TOGETHER, WE SHOULD BE ABLE TO OVERCOME THIS.
AND ALSO, THEY'RE NOT CENTIPEDE-BASED. THEY'RE ARACHNID.
DAD......
WHY ARE YOU SO DIFFERENT FROM WHEN YOU'RE AT HOME?
FOCUS ON THE ENEMY!
R...
RIGHT!

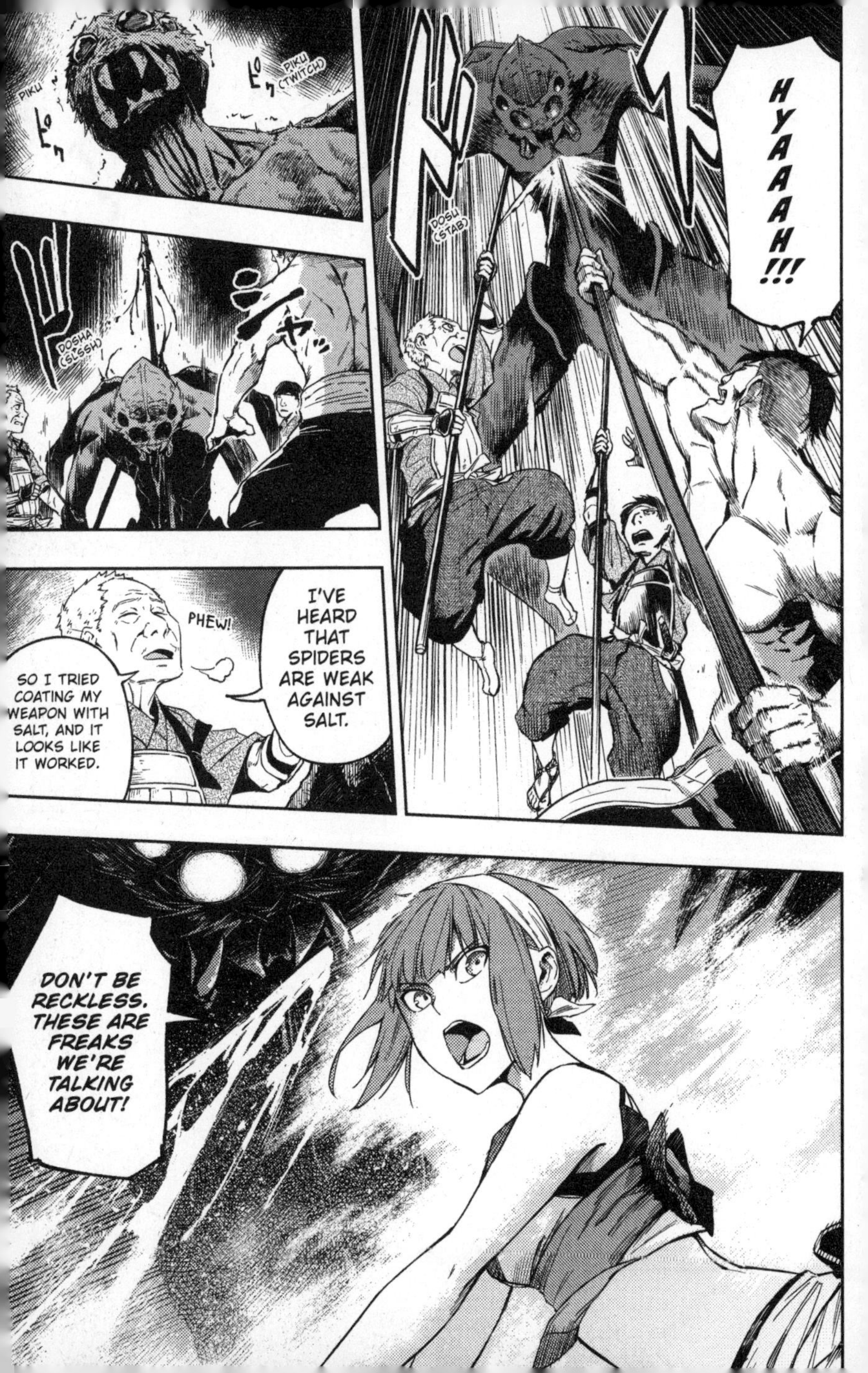
HYAAAAH!!!
DOSU (STAB)
PIKU
PIKU (TWITCH)
DOSHA (SLSSH)
I'VE HEARD THAT SPIDERS ARE WEAK AGAINST SALT.
PHEW!
SO I TRIED COATING MY WEAPON WITH SALT, AND IT LOOKS LIKE IT WORKED.
DON'T BE RECKLESS. THESE ARE FREAKS WE'RE TALKING ABOUT!

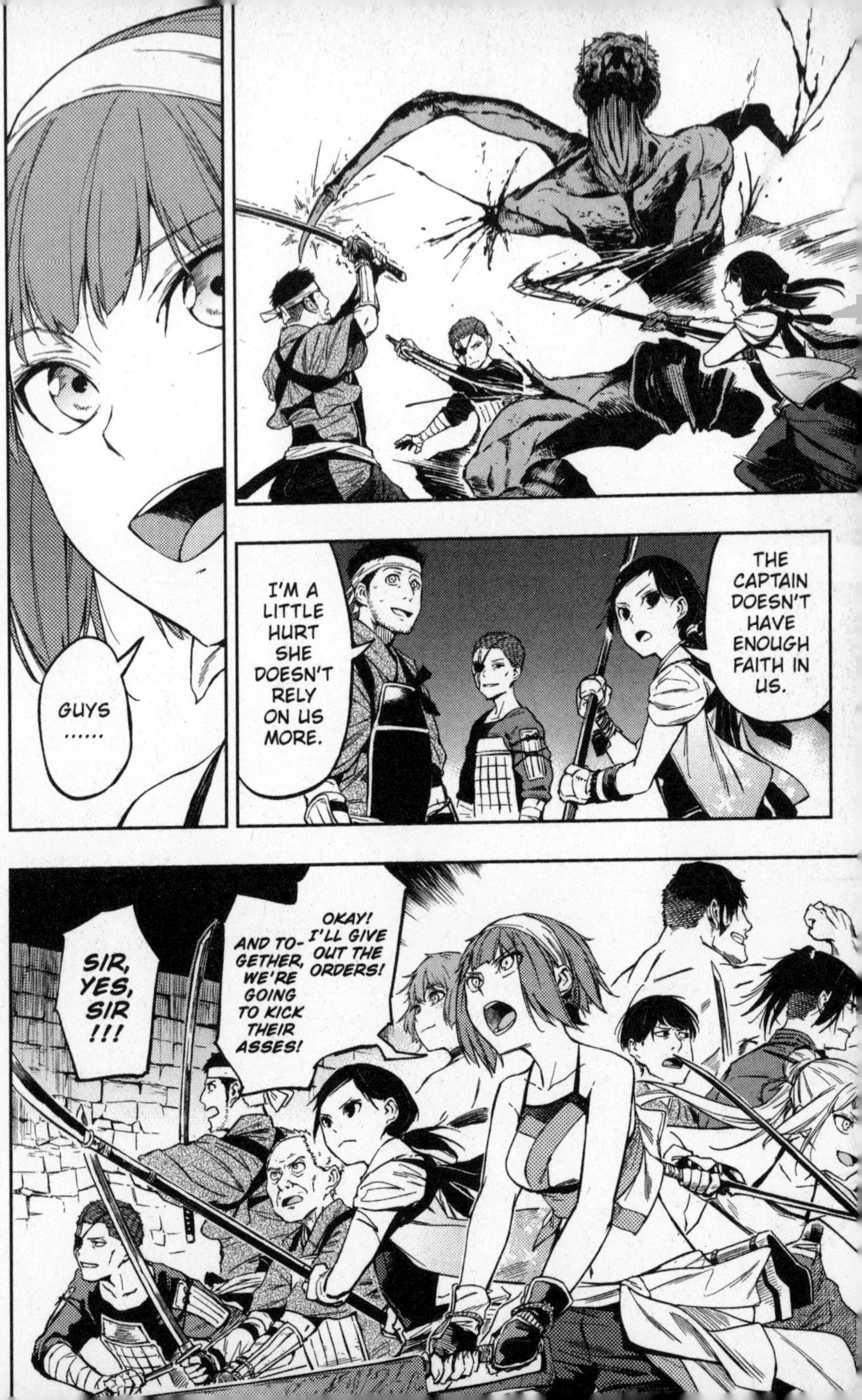
THE CAPTAIN DOESN'T HAVE ENOUGH FAITH IN US.
I'M A LITTLE HURT SHE DOESN'T RELY ON US MORE.
GUYS ......
OKAY! I'LL GIVE OUT THE ORDERS! AND TO-GETHER, WE'RE GOING TO KICK THEIR ASSES!
SIR, YES, SIR!!!

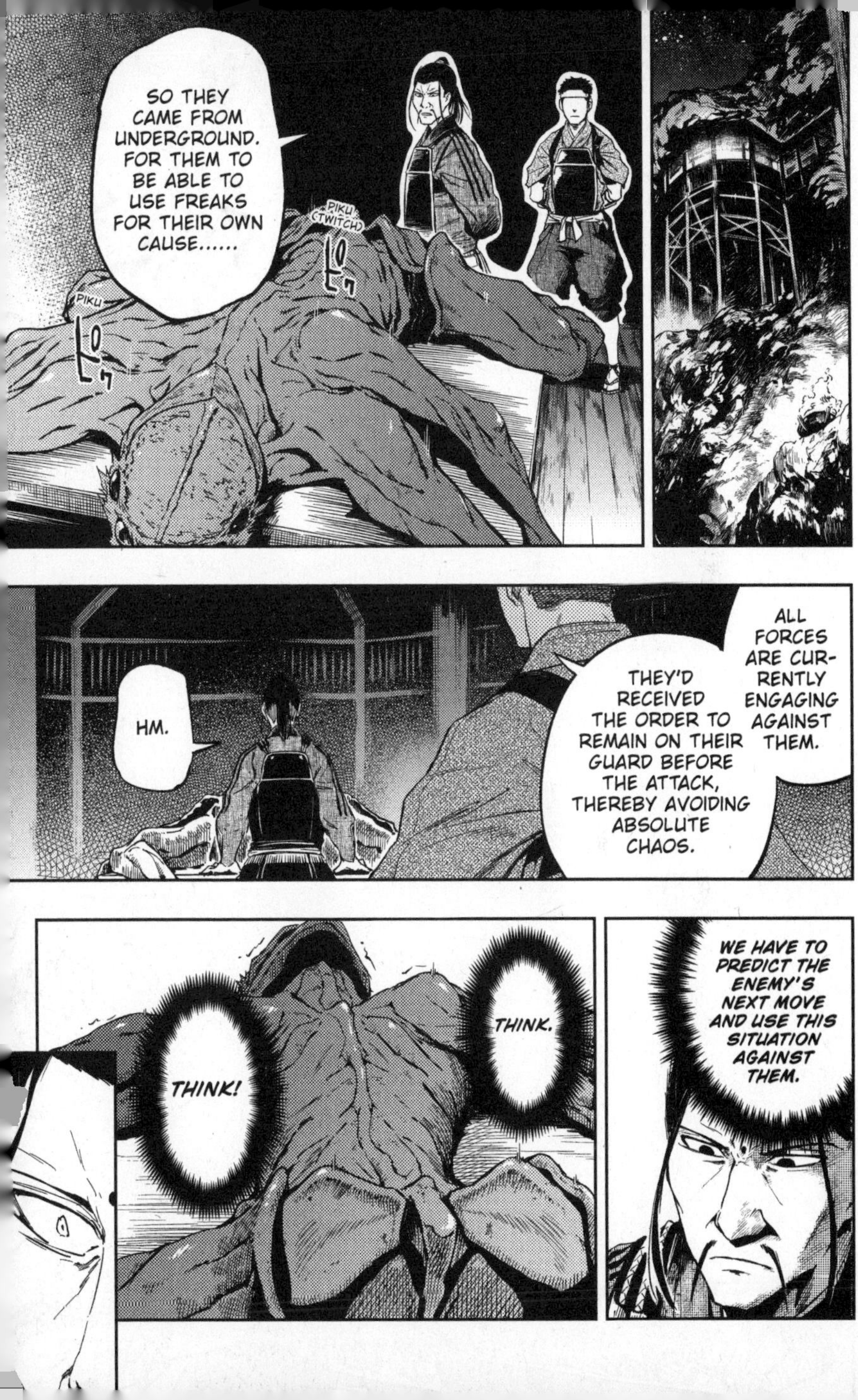
SO THEY CAME FROM UNDERGROUND. FOR THEM TO BE ABLE TO USE FREAKS FOR THEIR OWN CAUSE......
PIKU (TWITCH)
PIKU
ALL FORCES ARE CUR-RENTLY ENGAGING AGAINST THEM.
THEY'D RECEIVED THE ORDER TO REMAIN ON THEIR GUARD BEFORE THE ATTACK, THEREBY AVOIDING ABSOLUTE CHAOS.
HM.
WE HAVE TO PREDICT THE ENEMY'S NEXT MOVE AND USE THIS SITUATION AGAINST THEM.
THINK.
THINK!

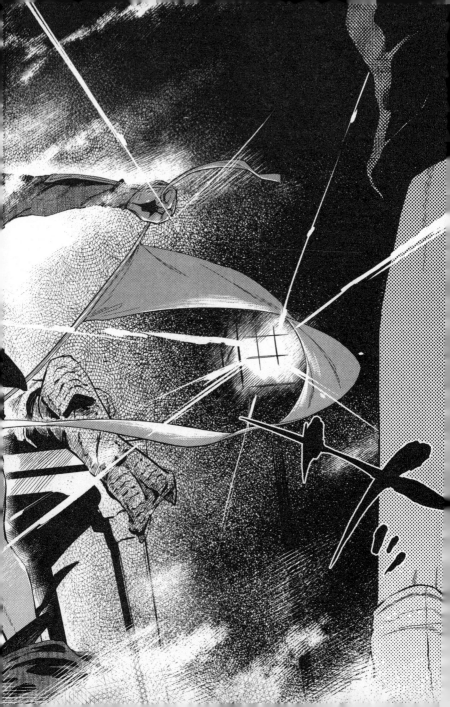

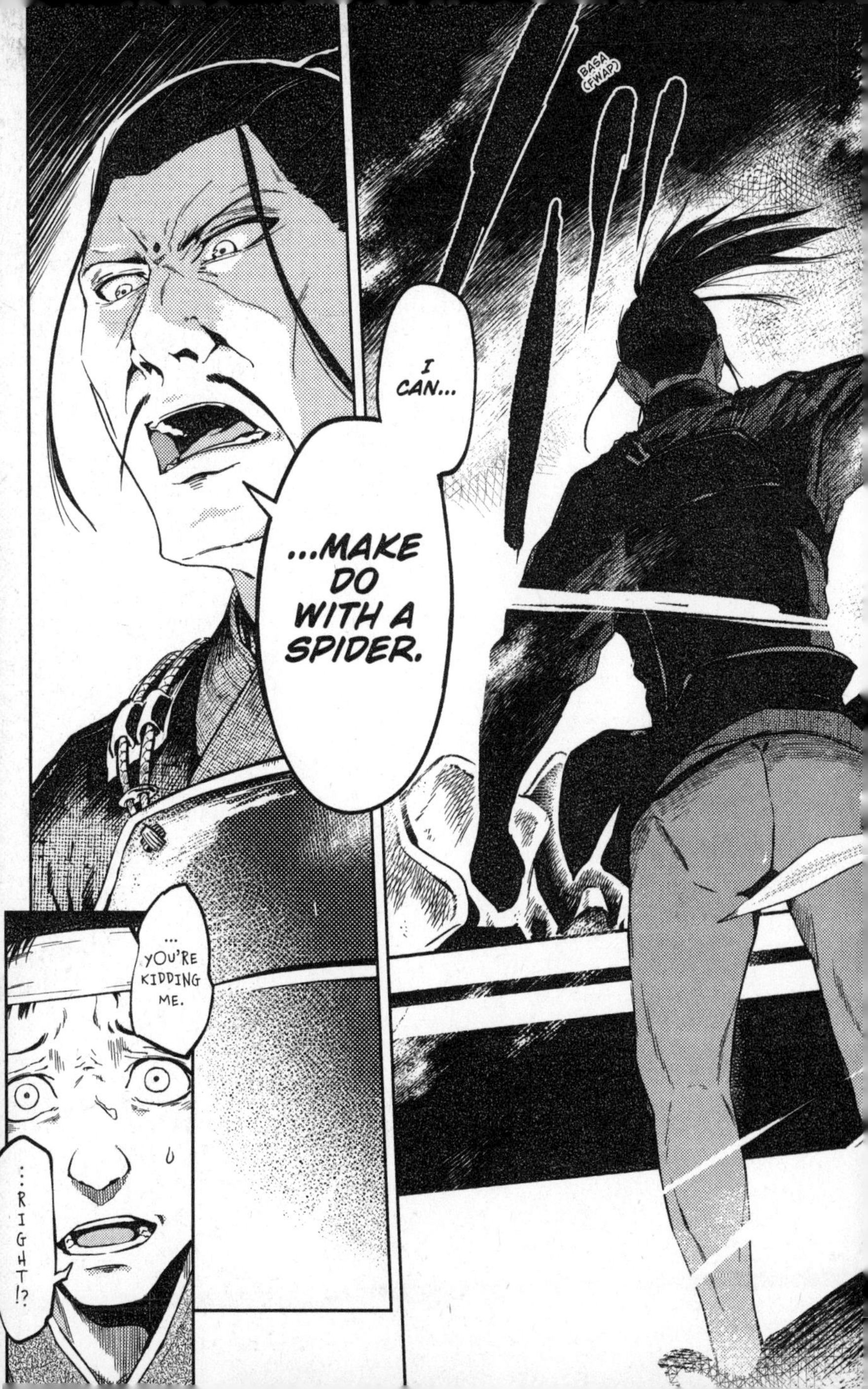
BASA (FWAP)
I CAN...
...MAKE DO WITH A SPIDER.
...YOU'RE KIDDING ME.
...RIGHT!?

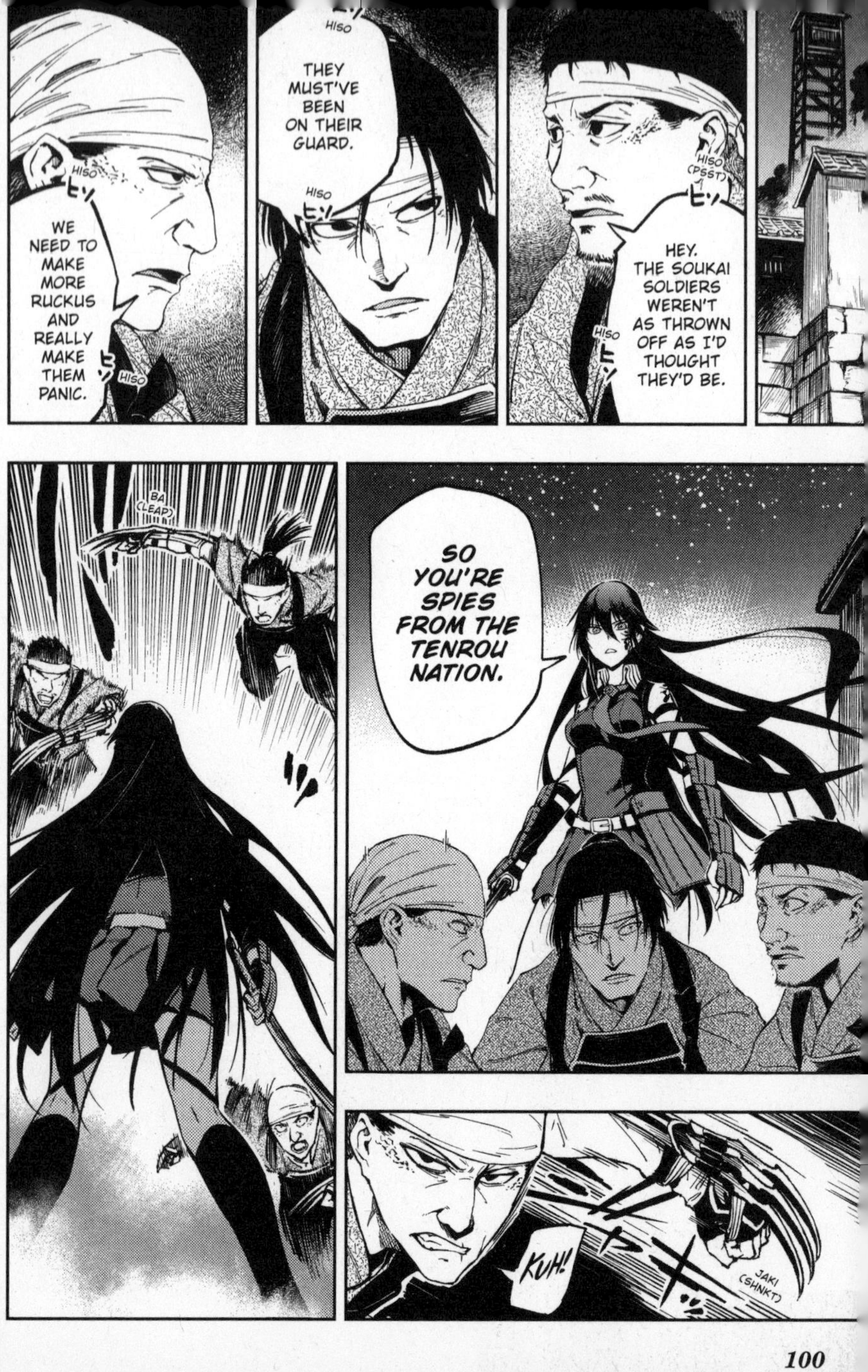
HISO (PSST)
ヒソ
HISO
ヒソ
HEY. THE SOUKAI SOLDIERS WEREN'T AS THROWN OFF AS I'D THOUGHT THEY'D BE.
HISO
HISO
ヒソ
THEY MUST'VE BEEN ON THEIR GUARD.
HISO
ヒソ
HISO
ヒソ
WE NEED TO MAKE MORE RUCKUS AND REALLY MAKE THEM PANIC.
SO YOU'RE SPIES FROM THE TENROU NATION.
KUH!
JAKI (SHNKT)
BA (LEAP)

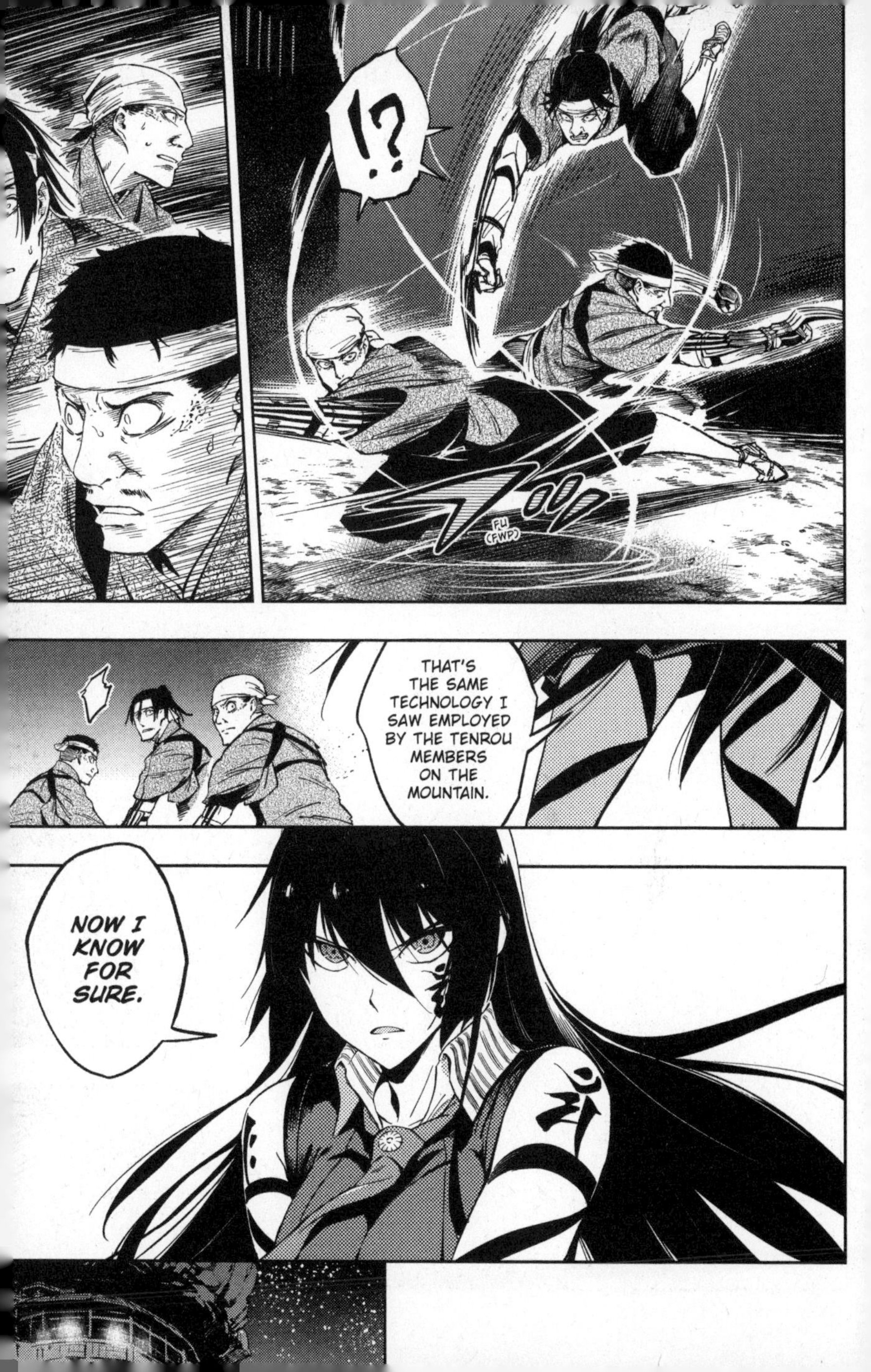
!?
FU (FWP)
THAT'S THE SAME TECHNOLOGY I SAW EMPLOYED BY THE TENROU MEMBERS ON THE MOUNTAIN.
NOW I KNOW FOR SURE.

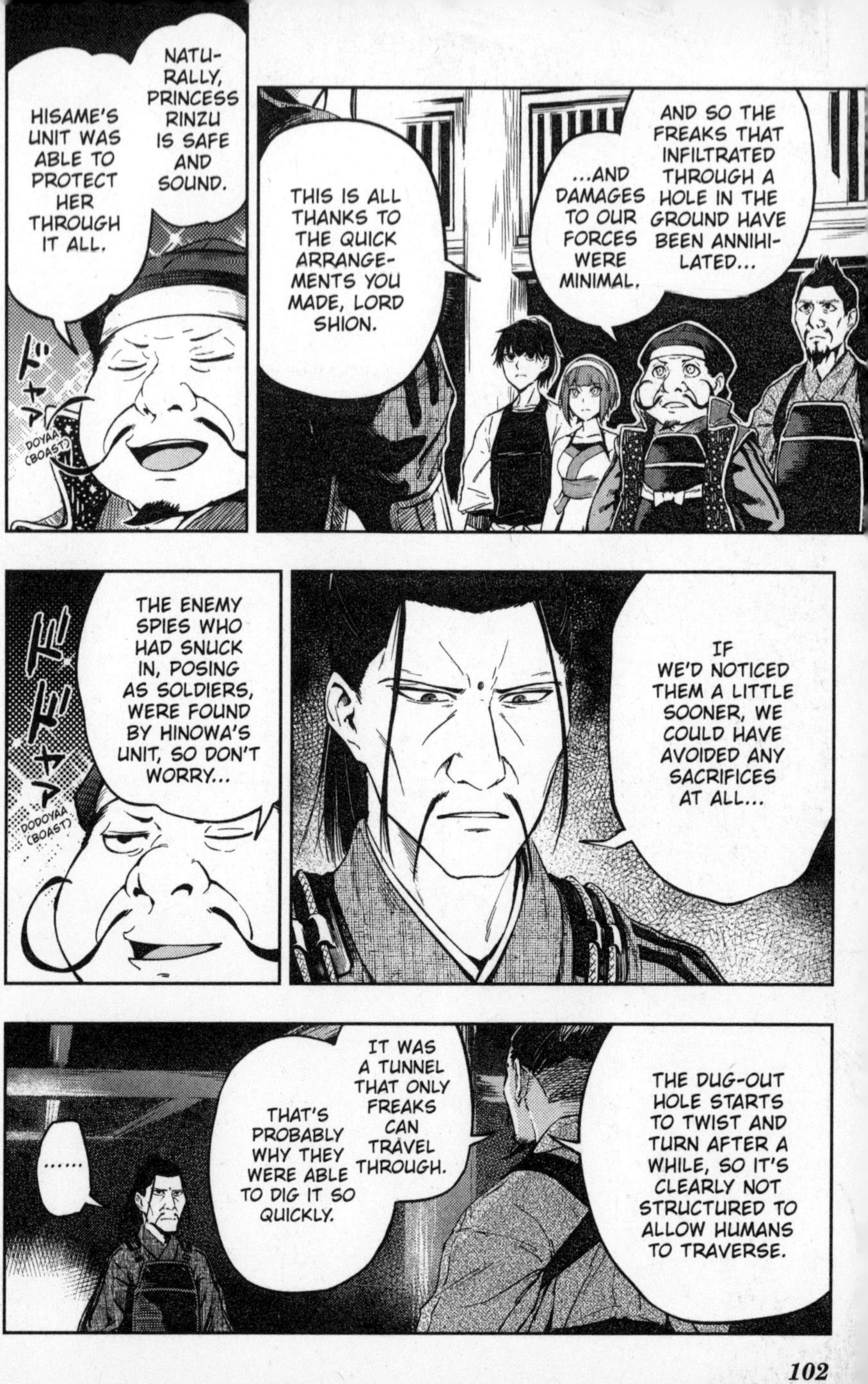
AND SO THE FREAKS THAT INFILTRATED THROUGH A HOLE IN THE GROUND HAVE BEEN ANNIHILATED...
...AND DAMAGES TO OUR FORCES WERE MINIMAL.
THIS IS ALL THANKS TO THE QUICK ARRANGEMENTS YOU MADE, LORD SHION.
NATURALLY, PRINCESS RINZU IS SAFE AND SOUND.
HISAME'S UNIT WAS ABLE TO PROTECT HER THROUGH IT ALL.
ドヤァ
DOYAA (BOAST)
IF WE'D NOTICED THEM A LITTLE SOONER, WE COULD HAVE AVOIDED ANY SACRIFICES AT ALL...
THE ENEMY SPIES WHO HAD SNUCK IN, POSING AS SOLDIERS, WERE FOUND BY HINOWA'S UNIT, SO DON'T WORRY...
ドドヤァ
DODOYAA (BOAST)
THE DUG-OUT HOLE STARTS TO TWIST AND TURN AFTER A WHILE, SO IT'S CLEARLY NOT STRUCTURED TO ALLOW HUMANS TO TRAVERSE.
IT WAS A TUNNEL THAT ONLY FREAKS CAN TRAVEL THROUGH.
THAT'S PROBABLY WHY THEY WERE ABLE TO DIG IT SO QUICKLY.
......

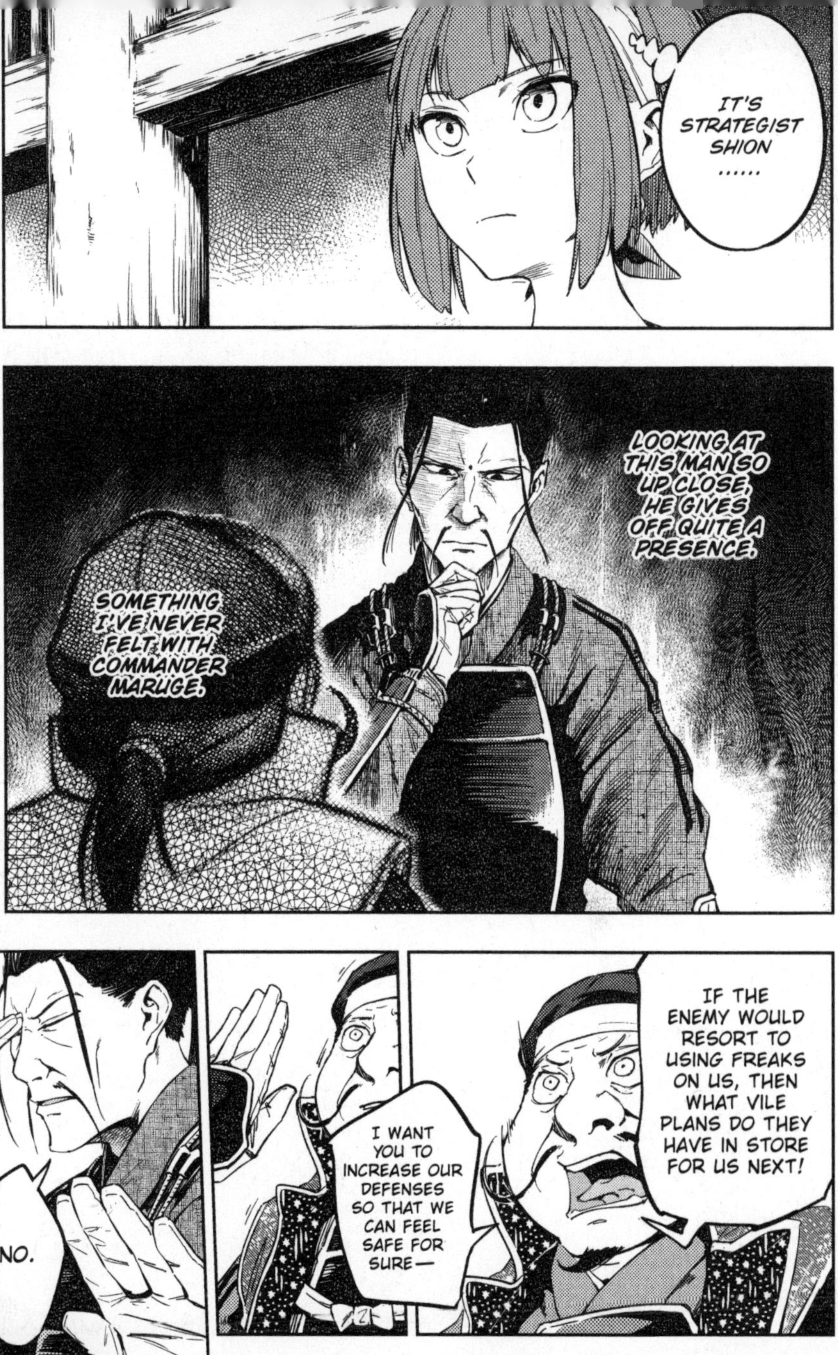
IT'S STRATEGIST SHION ......
LOOKING AT THIS MAN SO UP CLOSE, HE GIVES OFF QUITE A PRESENCE.
SOMETHING I'VE NEVER FELT WITH COMMANDER MARUGE.
IF THE ENEMY WOULD RESORT TO USING FREAKS ON US, THEN WHAT VILE PLANS DO THEY HAVE IN STORE FOR US NEXT!
I WANT YOU TO INCREASE OUR DEFENSES SO THAT WE CAN FEEL SAFE FOR SURE—
NO.

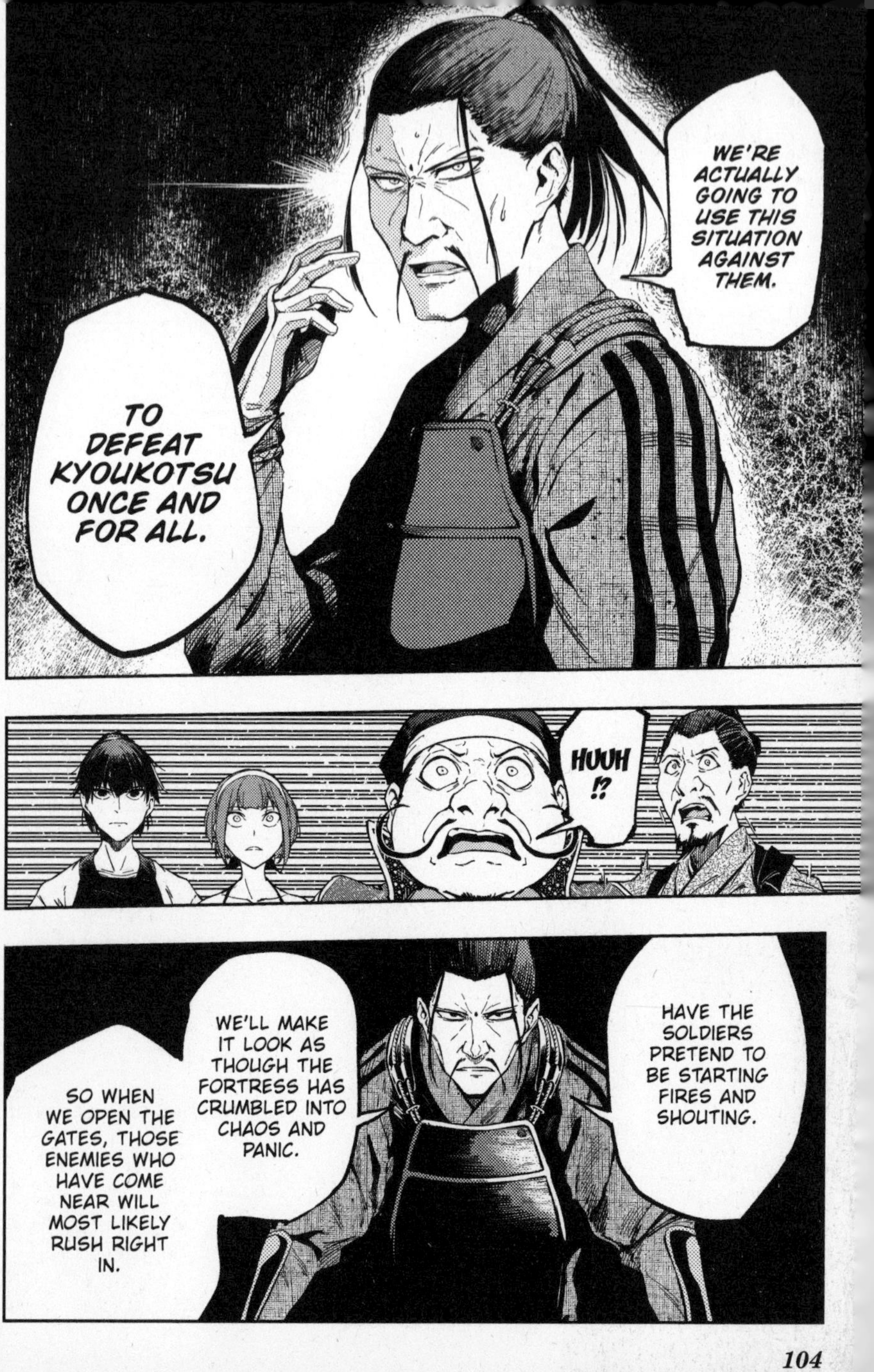
WE'RE ACTUALLY GOING TO USE THIS SITUATION AGAINST THEM.
TO DEFEAT KYOUKOTSU ONCE AND FOR ALL.
HUUH !?
HAVE THE SOLDIERS PRETEND TO BE STARTING FIRES AND SHOUTING.
WE'LL MAKE IT LOOK AS THOUGH THE FORTRESS HAS CRUMBLED INTO CHAOS AND PANIC.
SO WHEN WE OPEN THE GATES, THOSE ENEMIES WHO HAVE COME NEAR WILL MOST LIKELY RUSH RIGHT IN.

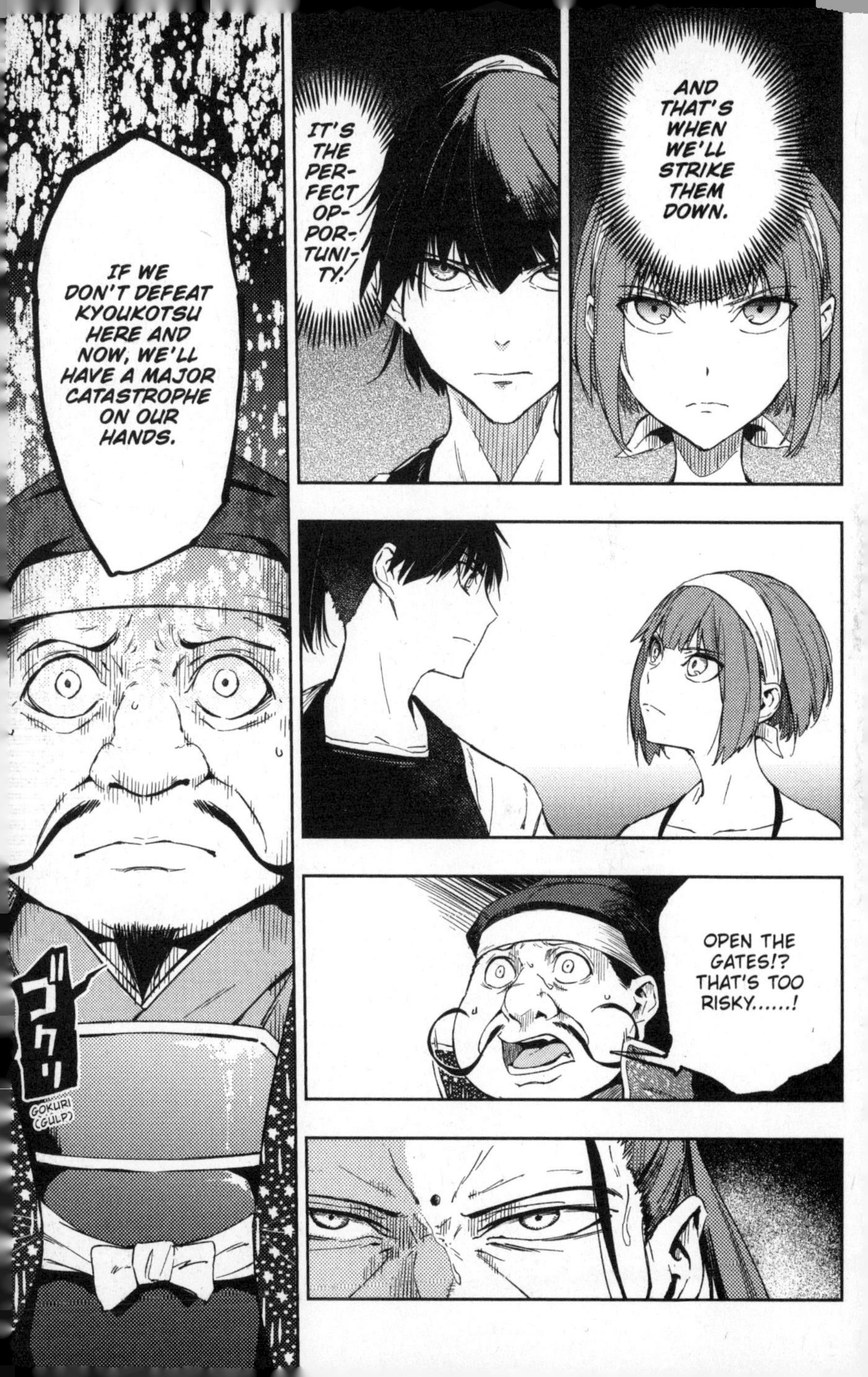
AND THAT'S WHEN WE'LL STRIKE THEM DOWN.
IT'S THE PERFECT OPPORTUNITY!
OPEN THE GATES!? THAT'S TOO RISKY......!
IF WE DON'T DEFEAT KYOUKOTSU HERE AND NOW, WE'LL HAVE A MAJOR CATASTROPHE ON OUR HANDS.
ゴクリ
GOKURI (GULP)

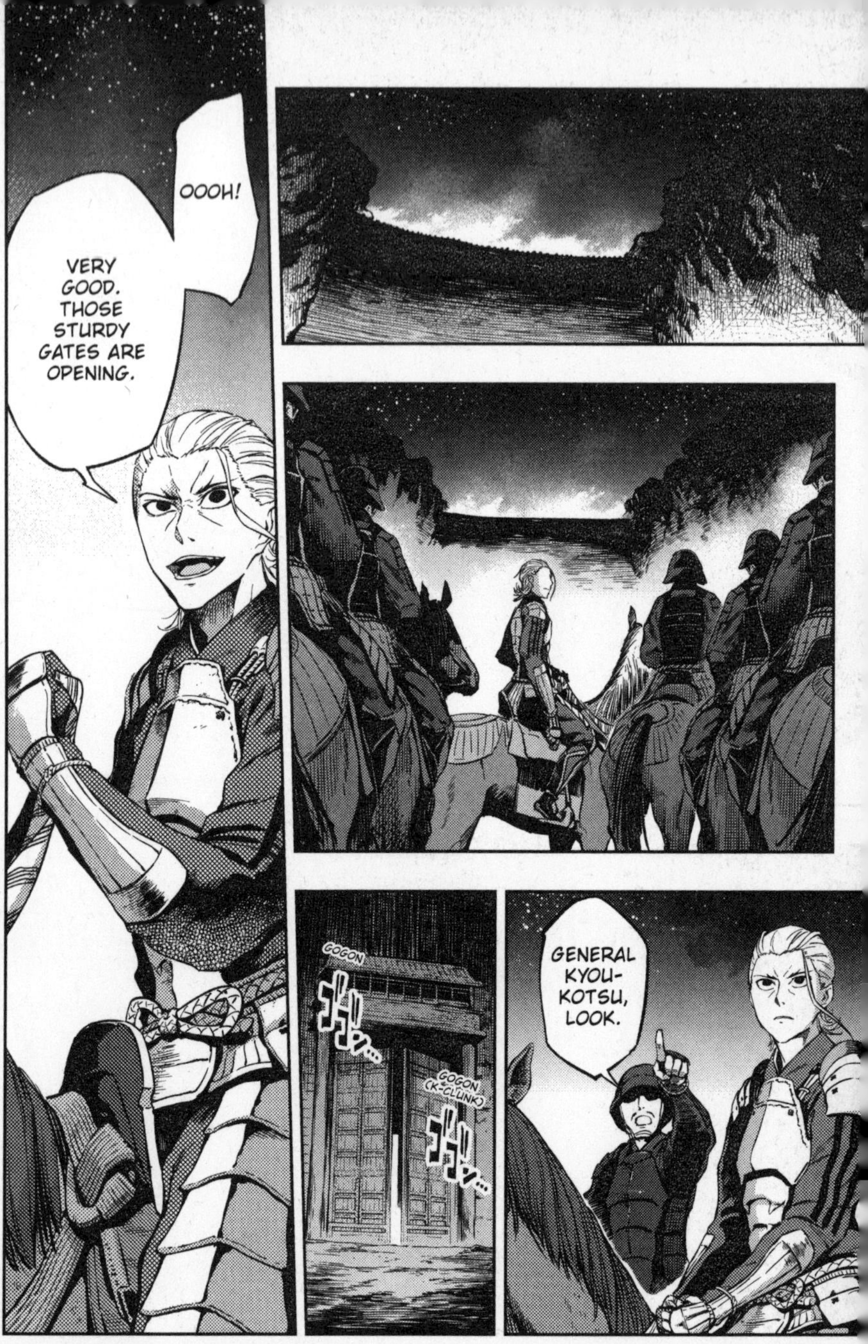
GENERAL KYOU-KOTSU, LOOK.
GOGON
GOGON (K-CLUNK)
OOOH!
VERY GOOD. THOSE STURDY GATES ARE OPENING.

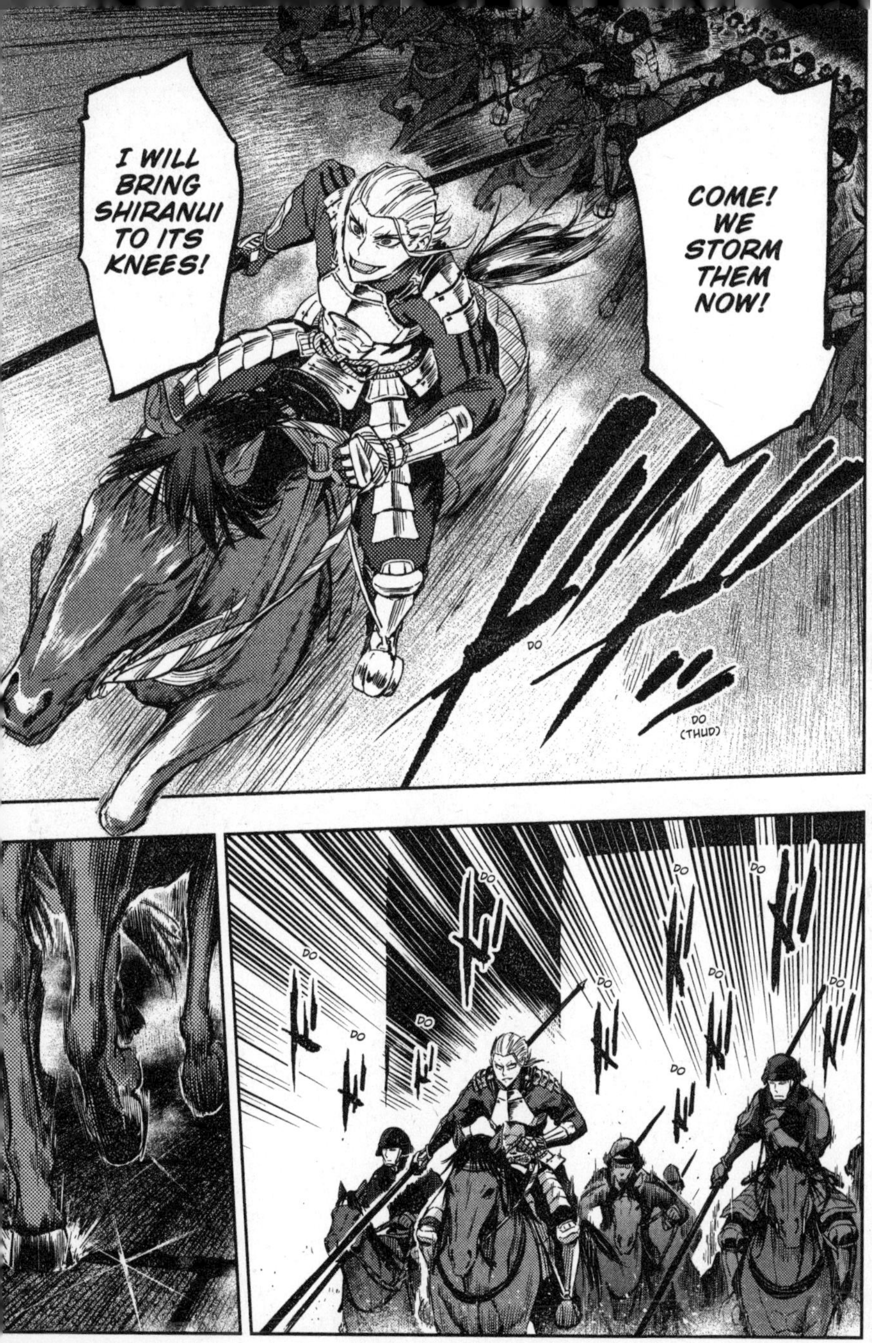
COME! WE STORM THEM NOW!
I WILL BRING SHIRANUI TO ITS KNEES!
DO
DO (THUD)
DO
DO
DO
DO
DO
DO
DO
DO
DO
DO
DO

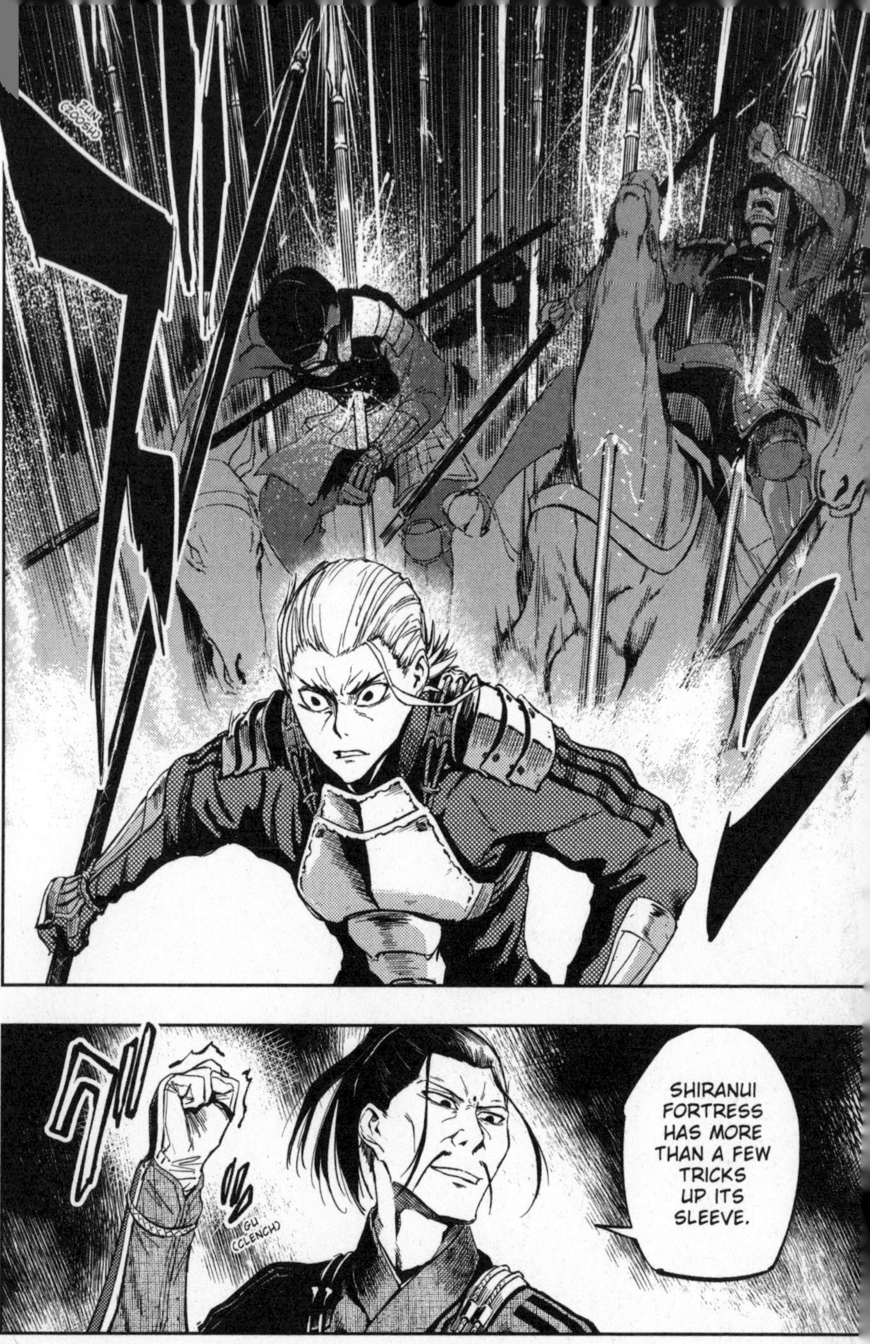
ZUN (ZOOSH)
SHIRANUI FORTRESS HAS MORE THAN A FEW TRICKS UP ITS SLEEVE.
GU (CLENCH)

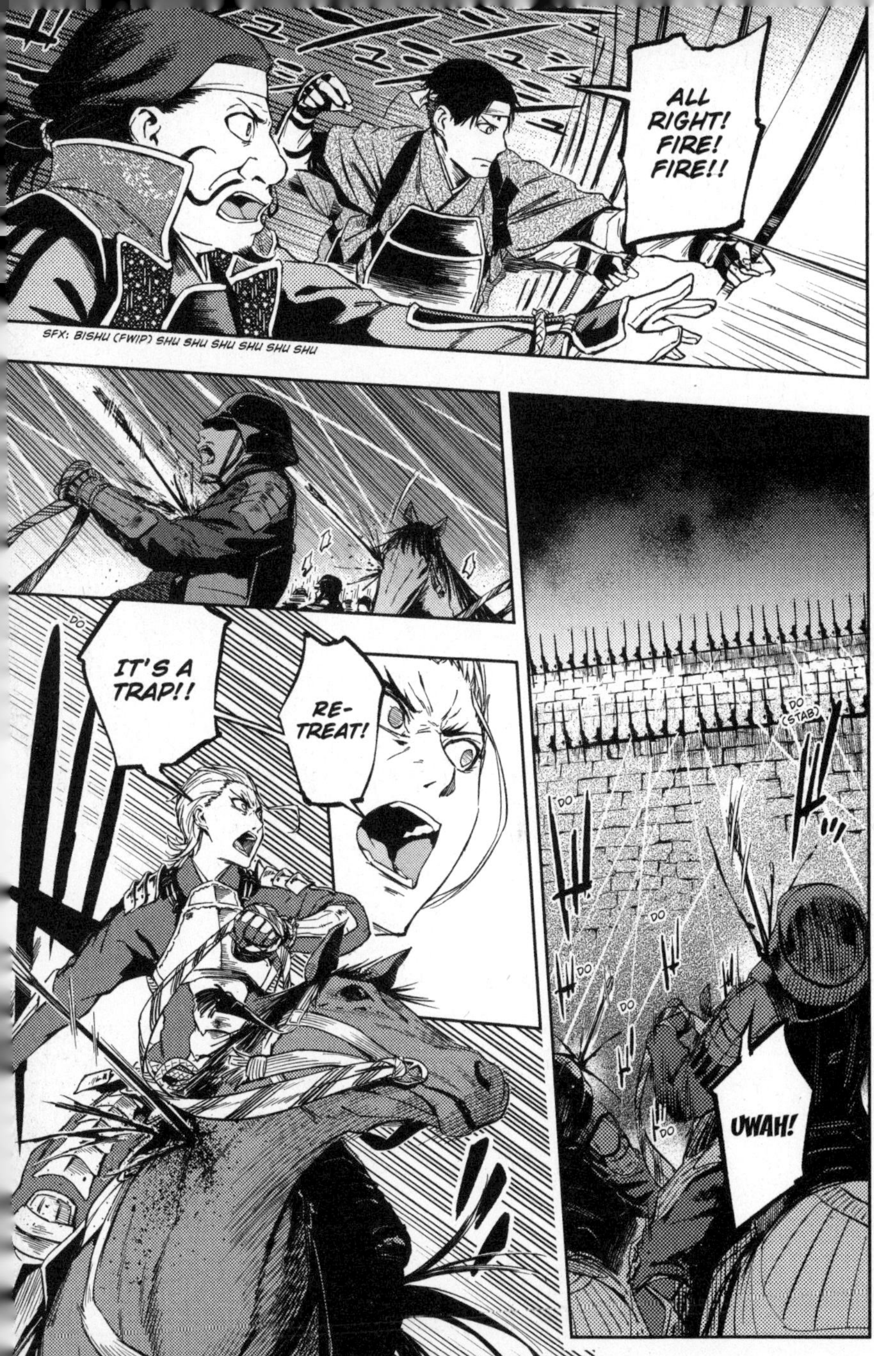
ALL RIGHT! FIRE! FIRE!!
SFX: BISHU (FWIP) SHU SHU SHU SHU SHU SHU
DO (STAB)
DO
DO
DO
DO
DO
UWAH!
DO
IT'S A TRAP!!
RE-TREAT!

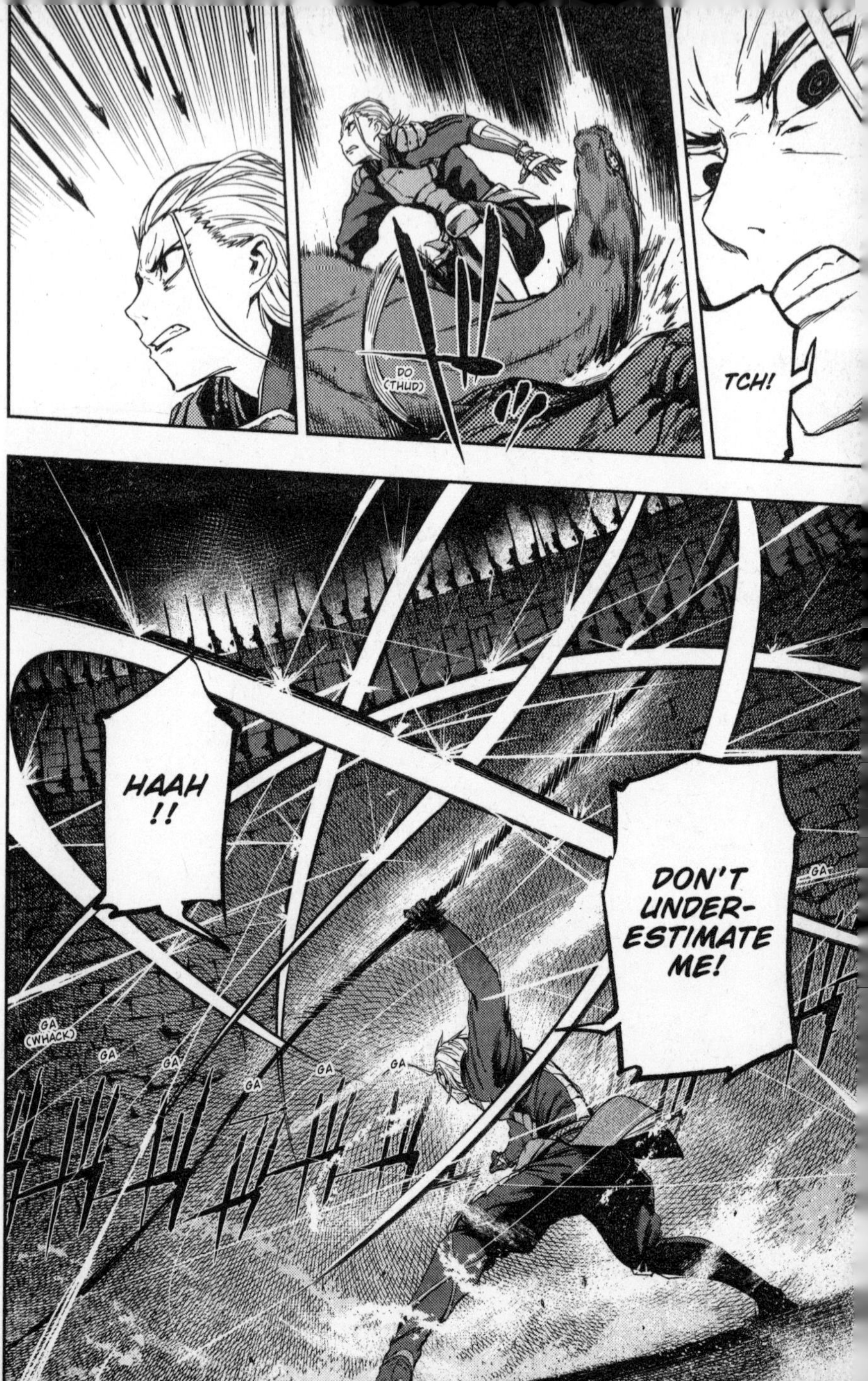
TCH!
DO (THUD)
GA
DON'T UNDER-ESTIMATE ME!
HAAH!!
GA
GA
GA
GA
GA
GA (WHACK)

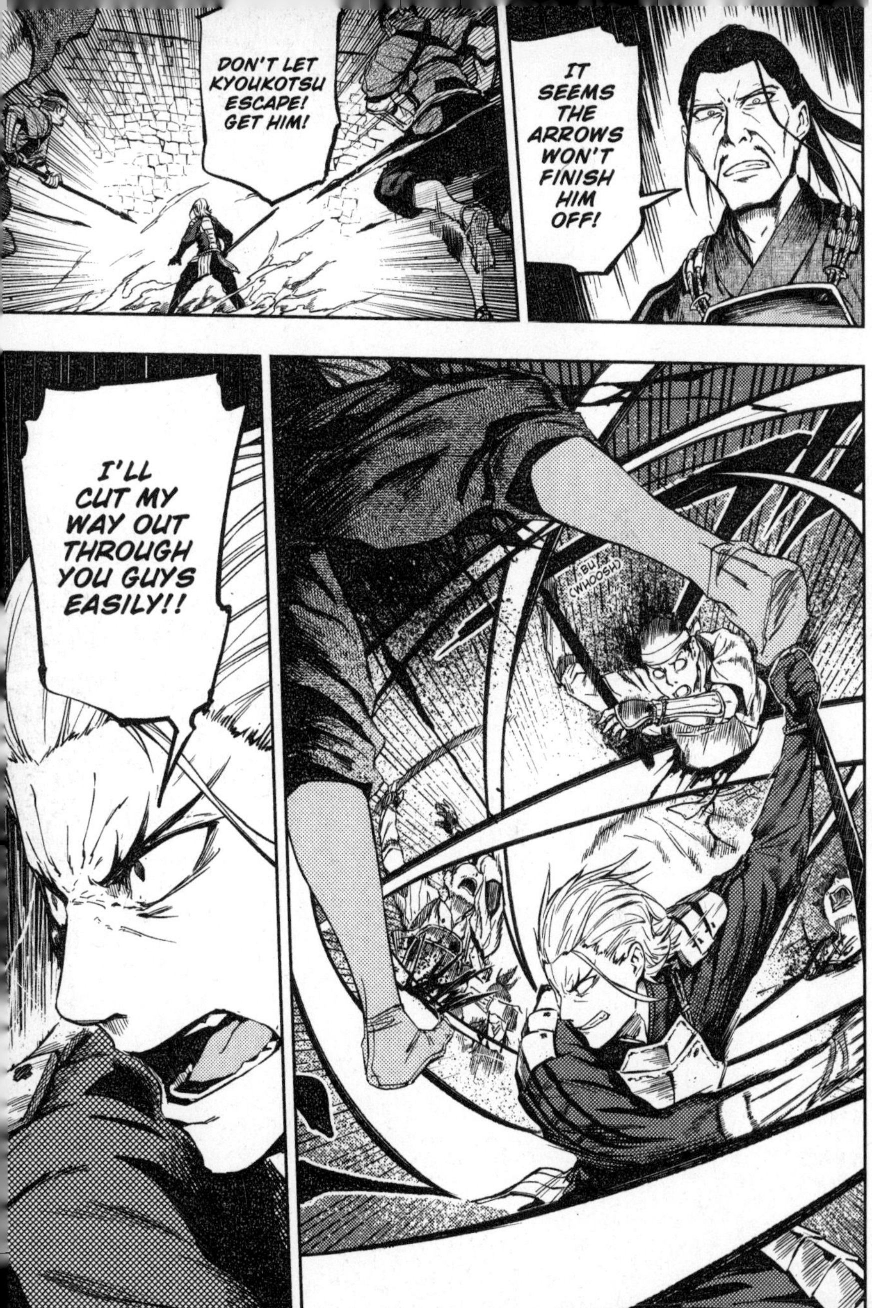
IT SEEMS THE ARROWS WON'T FINISH HIM OFF!
DON'T LET KYOUKOTSU ESCAPE! GET HIM!
BU (WHOOSH)
I'LL CUT MY WAY OUT THROUGH YOU GUYS EASILY!!

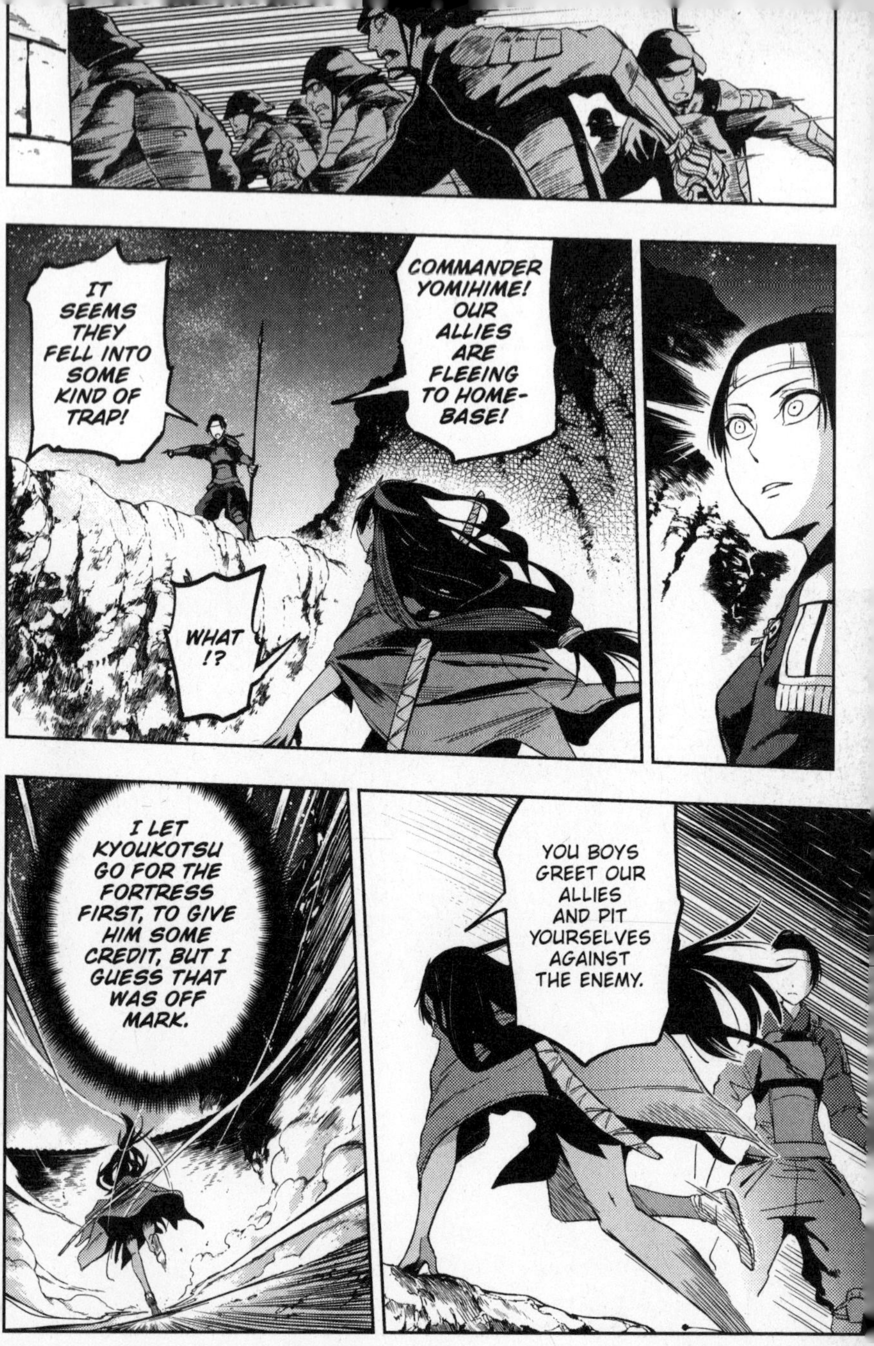
COMMANDER YOMIHIME! OUR ALLIES ARE FLEEING TO HOME-BASE!
IT SEEMS THEY FELL INTO SOME KIND OF TRAP!
WHAT!?
YOU BOYS GREET OUR ALLIES AND PIT YOURSELVES AGAINST THE ENEMY.
I LET KYOUKOTSU GO FOR THE FORTRESS FIRST, TO GIVE HIM SOME CREDIT, BUT I GUESS THAT WAS OFF MARK.

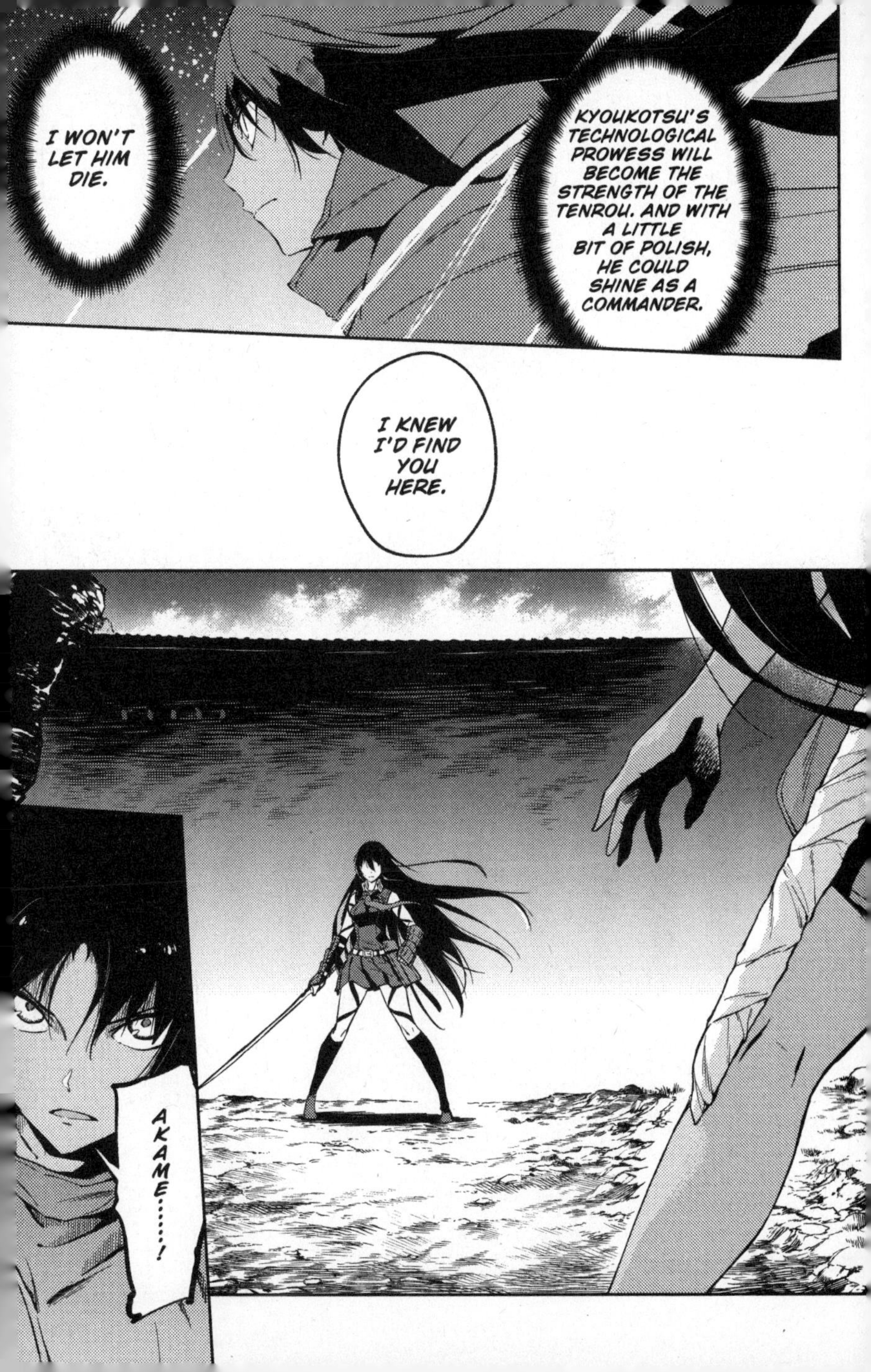
KYOUKOTSU'S TECHNOLOGICAL PROWESS WILL BECOME THE STRENGTH OF THE TENROU. AND WITH A LITTLE BIT OF POLISH, HE COULD SHINE AS A COMMANDER.
I WON'T LET HIM DIE.
I KNEW I'D FIND YOU HERE.
AKAME......!

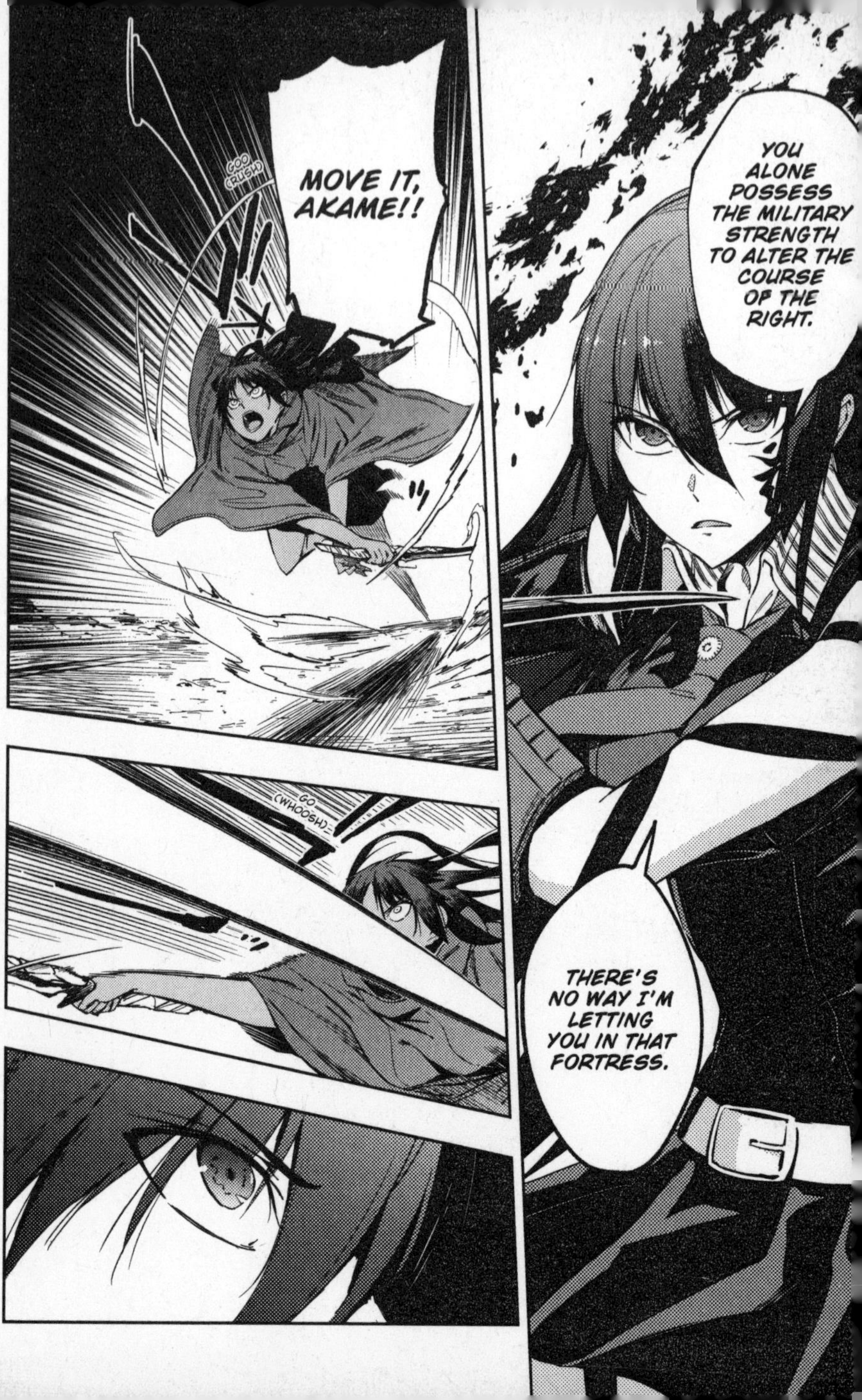
YOU ALONE POSSESS THE MILITARY STRENGTH TO ALTER THE COURSE OF THE RIGHT.
THERE'S NO WAY I'M LETTING YOU IN THAT FORTRESS.
MOVE IT, AKAME!!
GOO (RUSH)
GO (WHOOSH)

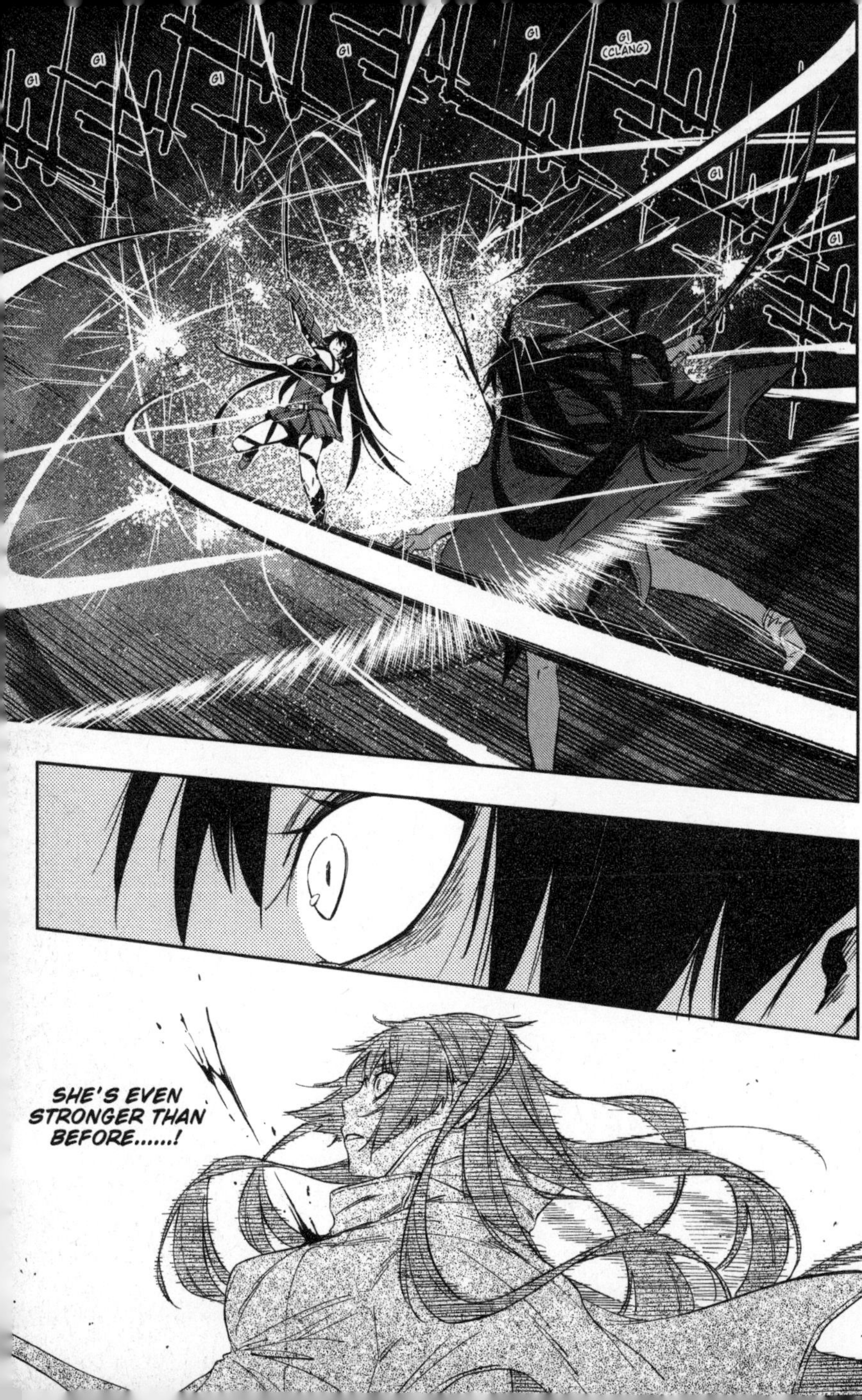
GI
GI
(CLANG)
GI
GI
GI
GI
GI
GI
SHE'S EVEN STRONGER THAN BEFORE......!

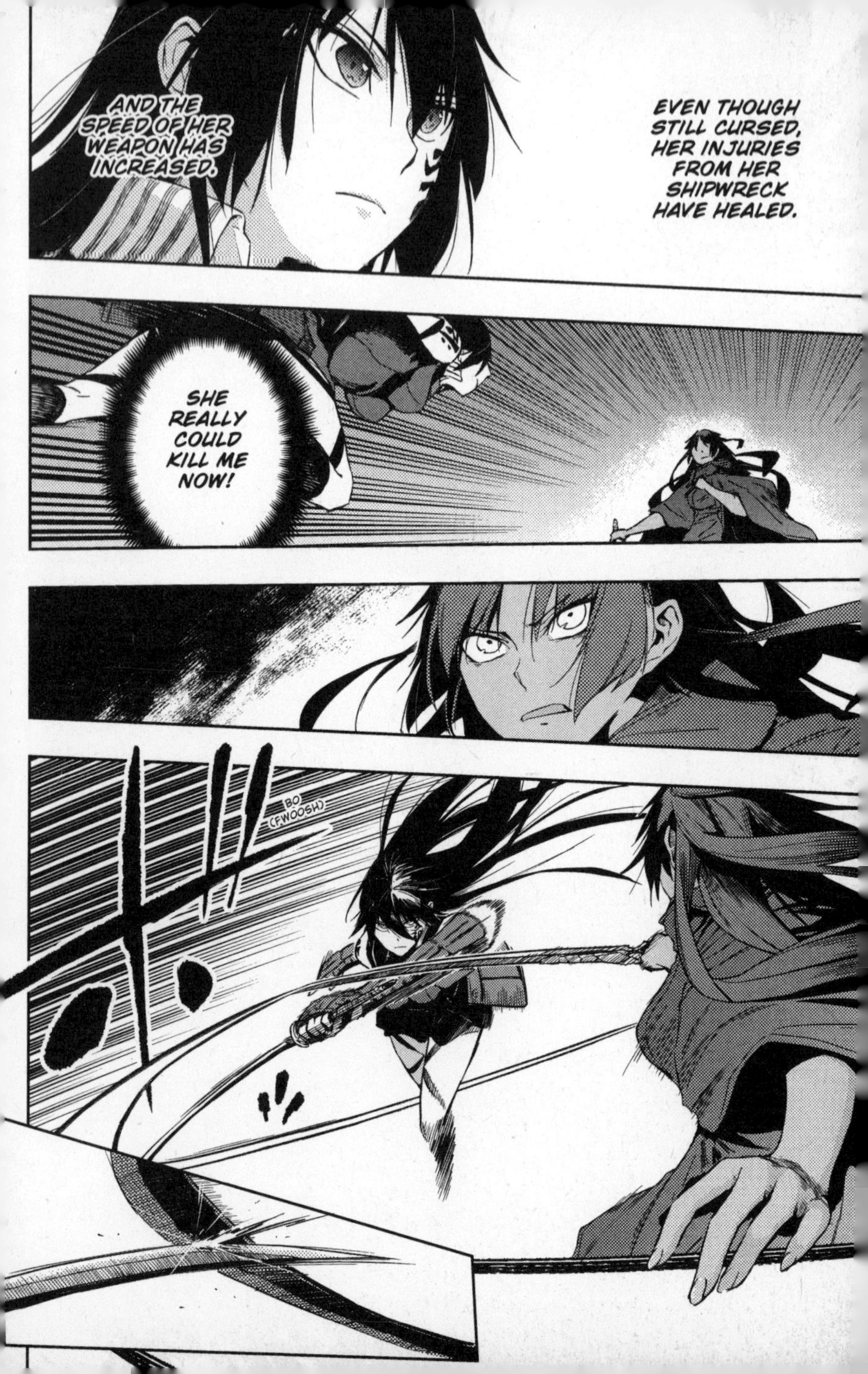
EVEN THOUGH STILL CURSED, HER INJURIES FROM HER SHIPWRECK HAVE HEALED.
AND THE SPEED OF HER WEAPON HAS INCREASED.
SHE REALLY COULD KILL ME NOW!
BO (FWOOSH)

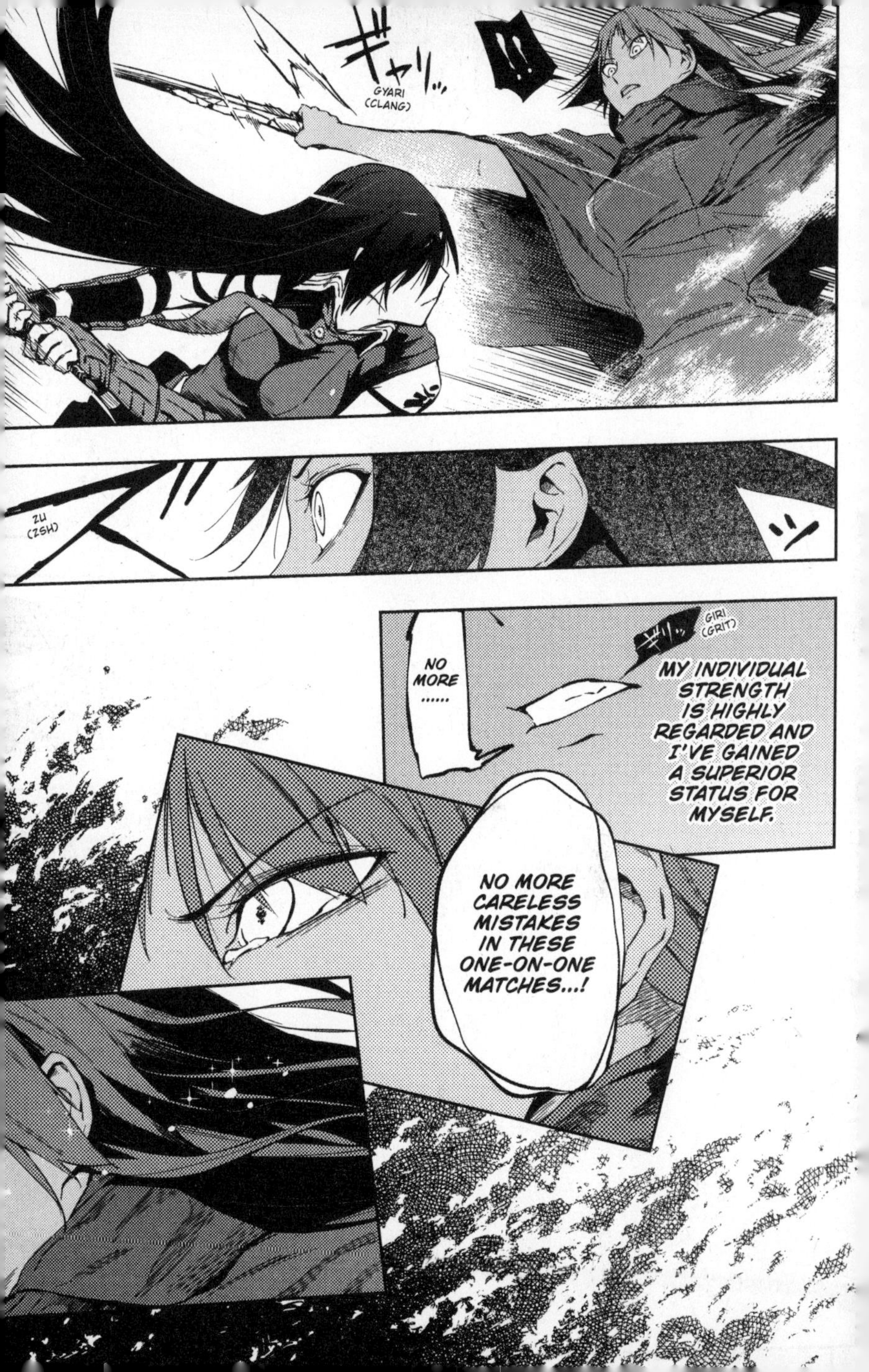
GYARI
(CLANG)
ZU
(ZSH)
GIRI
(GRIT)
MY INDIVIDUAL STRENGTH IS HIGHLY REGARDED AND I'VE GAINED A SUPERIOR STATUS FOR MYSELF.
NO MORE ......
NO MORE CARELESS MISTAKES IN THESE ONE-ON-ONE MATCHES...!

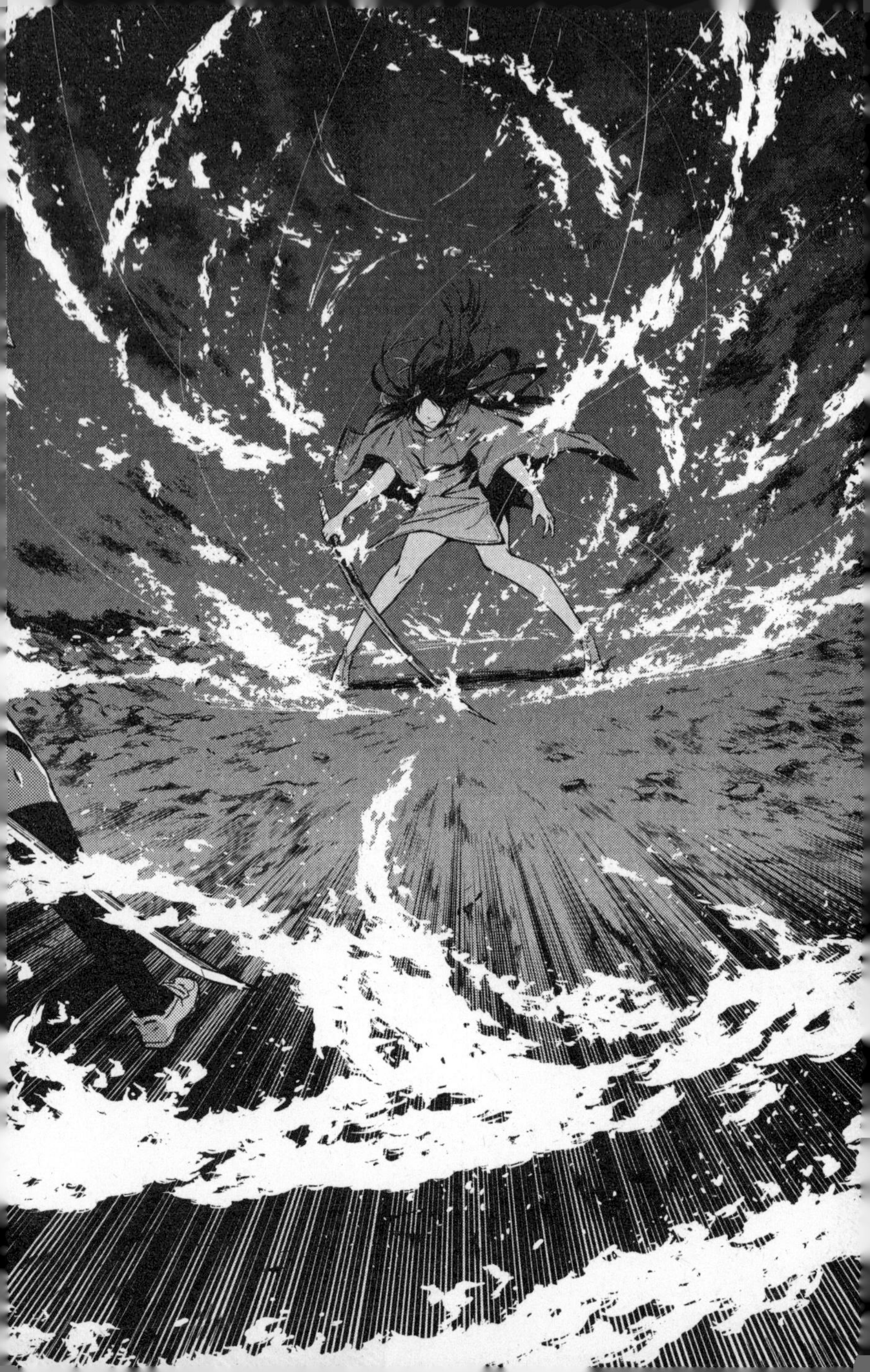

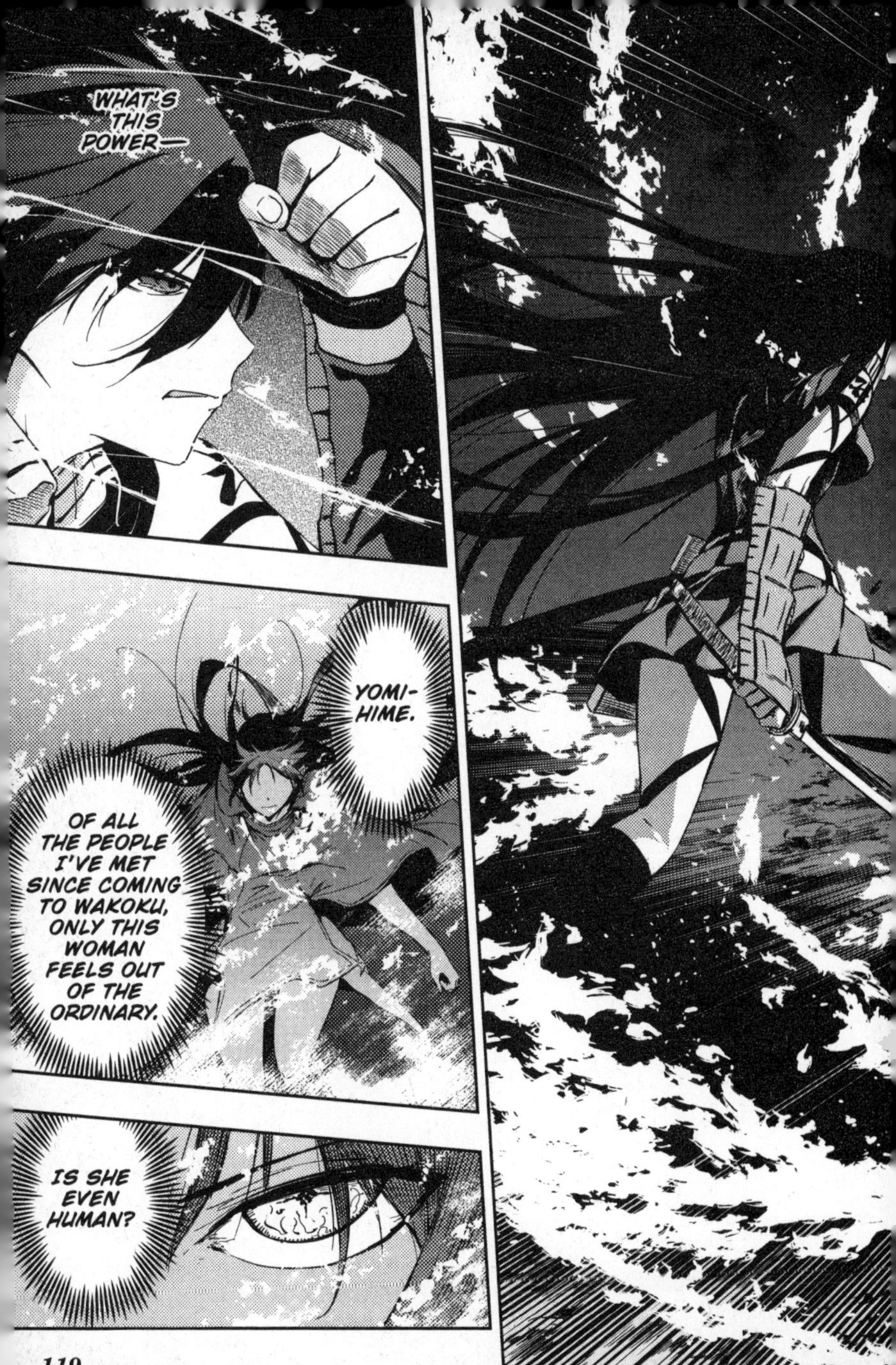
WHAT'S THIS POWER—
YOMI-HIME.
OF ALL THE PEOPLE I'VE MET SINCE COMING TO WAKOKU, ONLY THIS WOMAN FEELS OUT OF THE ORDINARY.
IS SHE EVEN HUMAN?

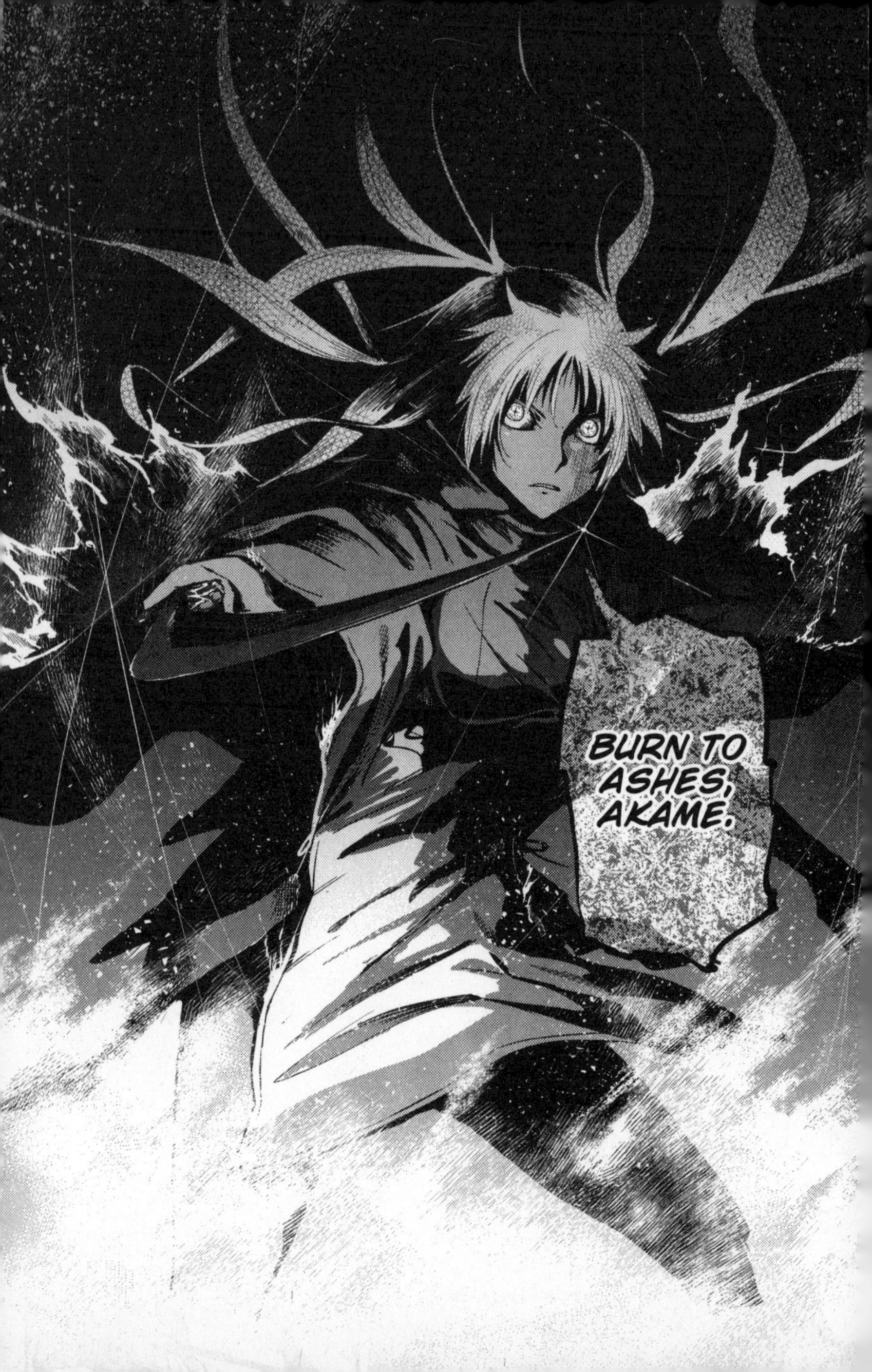
BURN TO ASHES, AKAME.

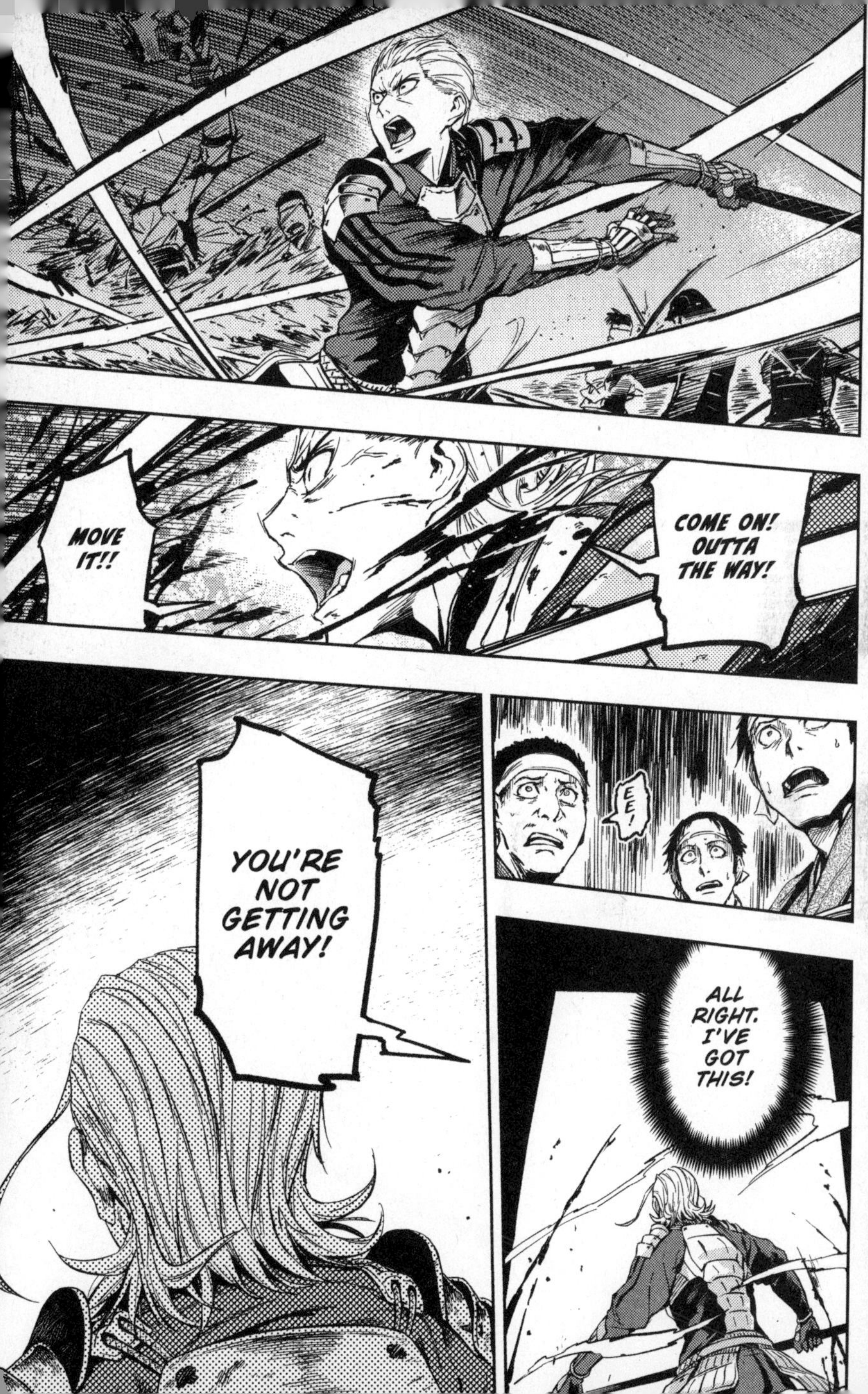
COME ON! OUTTA THE WAY!
MOVE IT!!
EE!
ALL RIGHT. I'VE GOT THIS!
YOU'RE NOT GETTING AWAY!

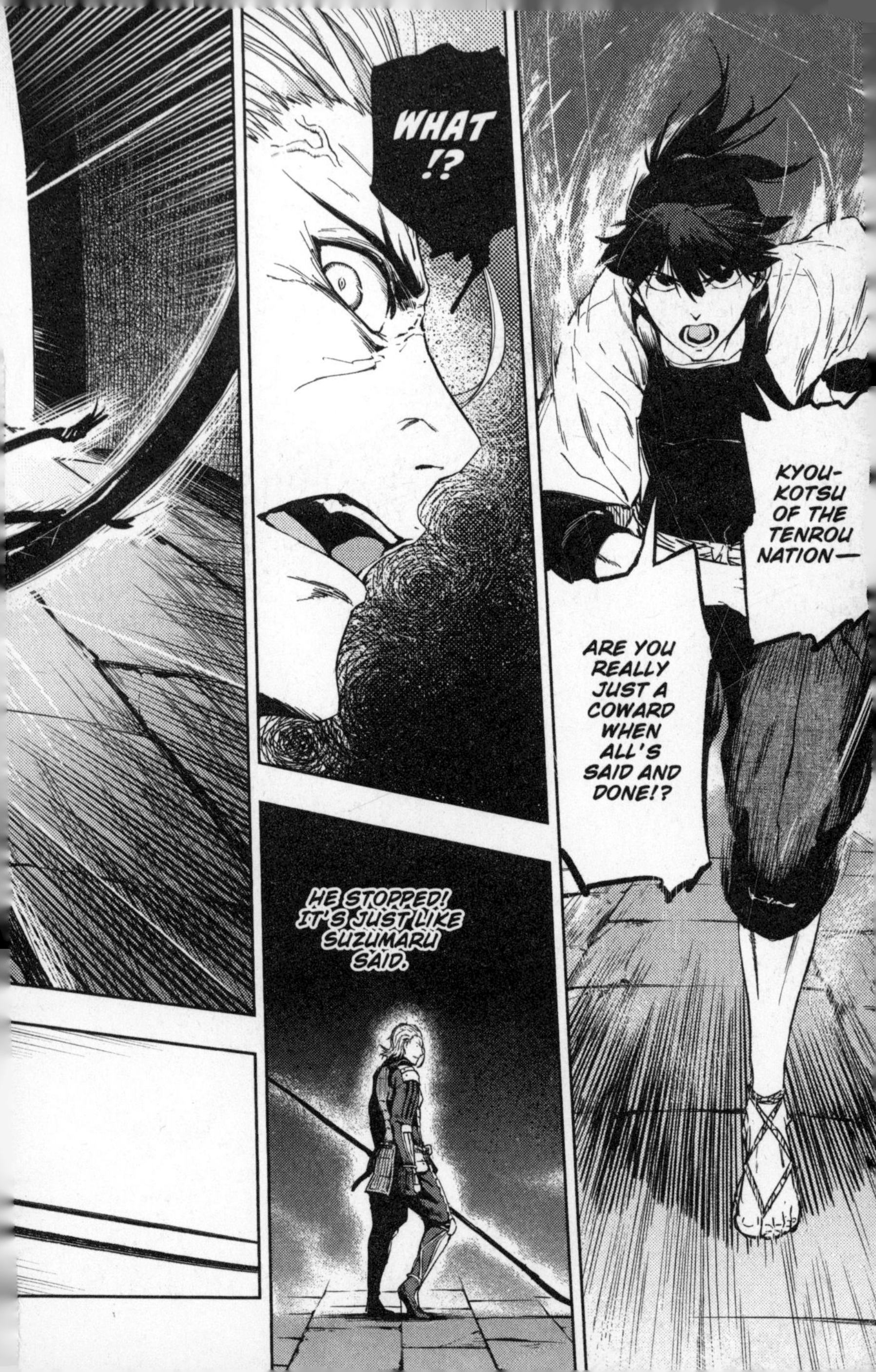
KYOU-KOTSU OF THE TENROU NATION—
ARE YOU REALLY JUST A COWARD WHEN ALL'S SAID AND DONE!?
WHAT !?
HE STOPPED! IT'S JUST LIKE SUZUMARU SAID.

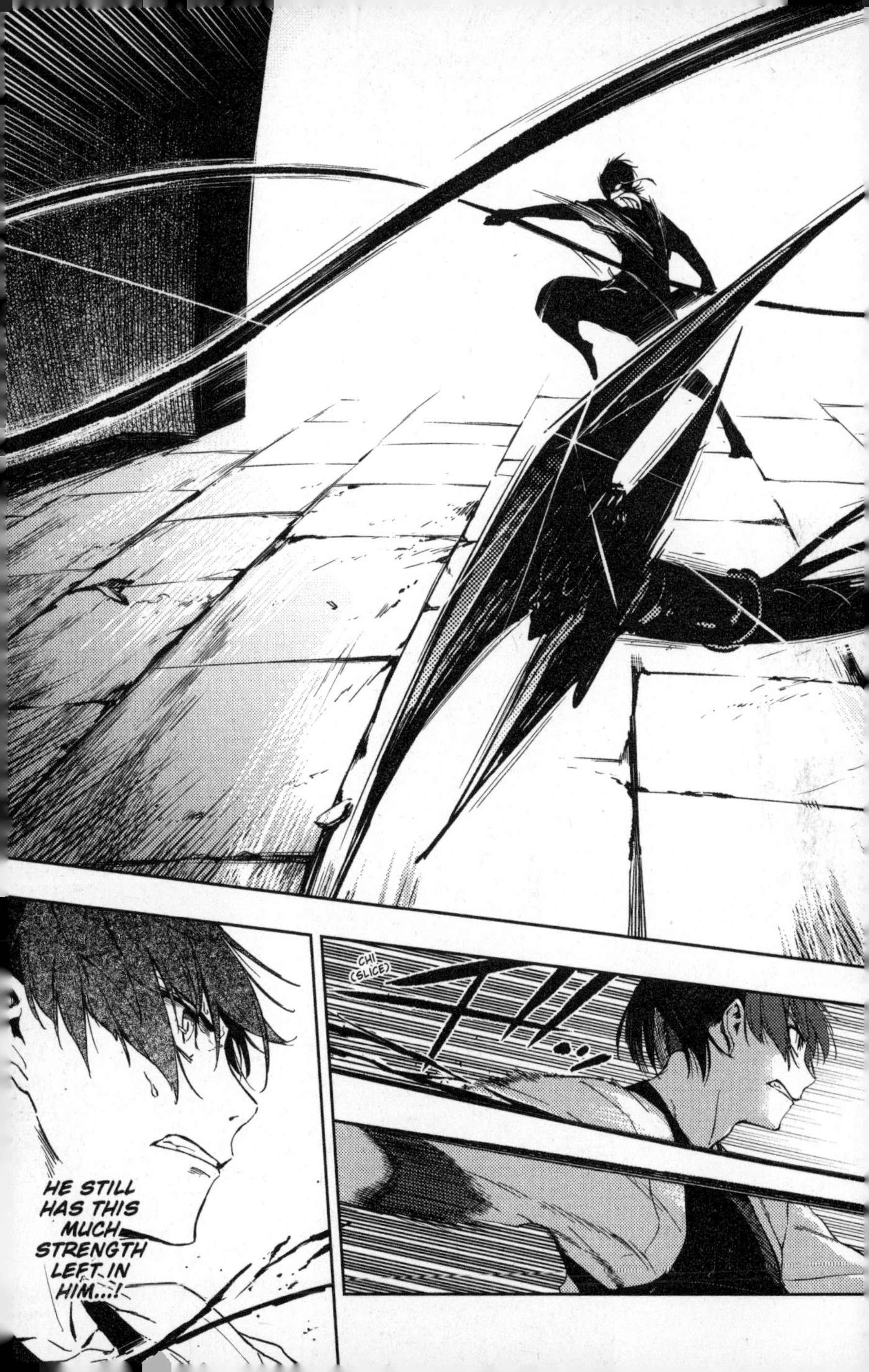
CHI
(SLICE)
HE STILL HAS THIS MUCH STRENGTH LEFT IN HIM...!

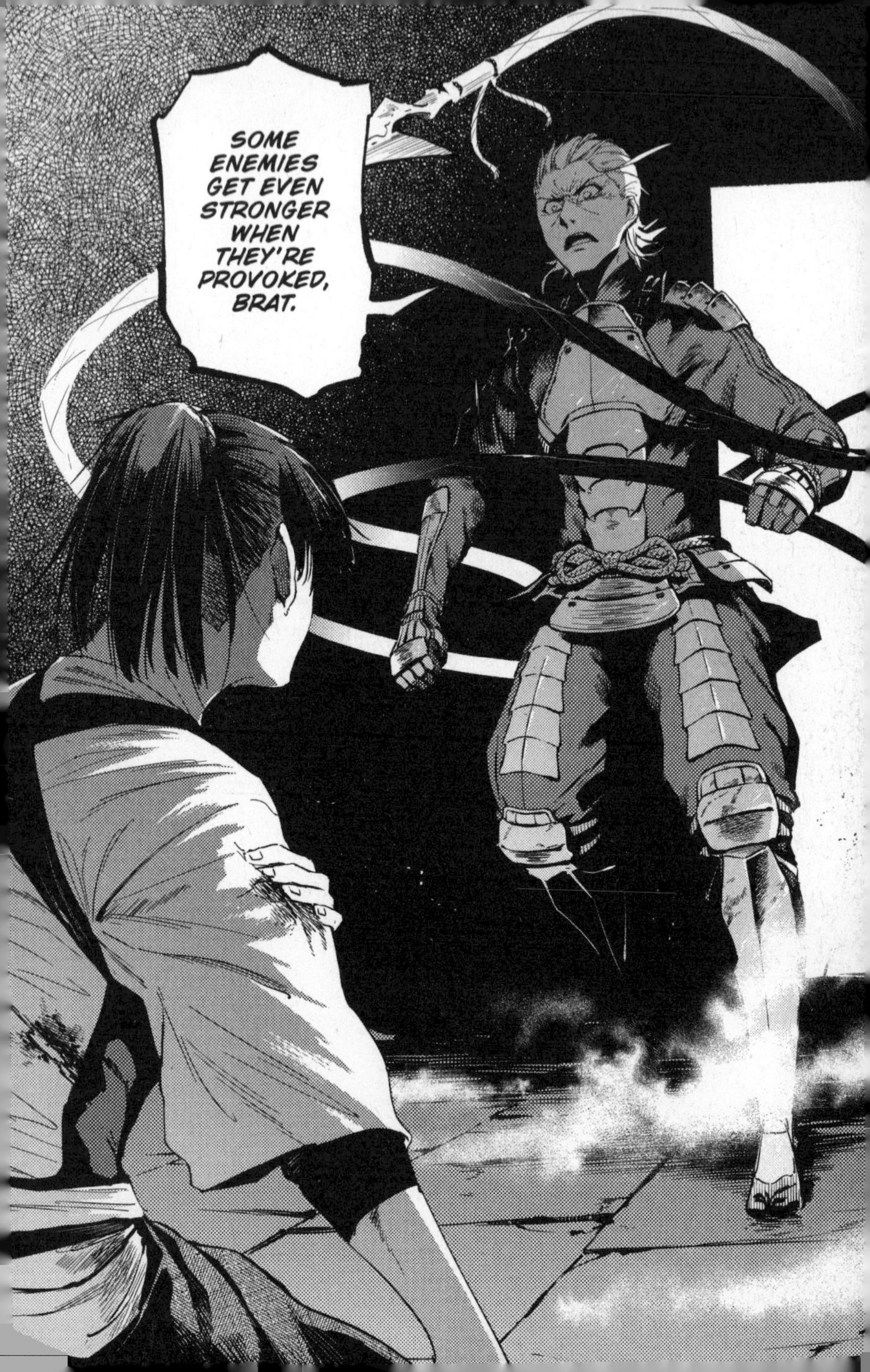
SOME ENEMIES GET EVEN STRONGER WHEN THEY'RE PROVOKED, BRAT.

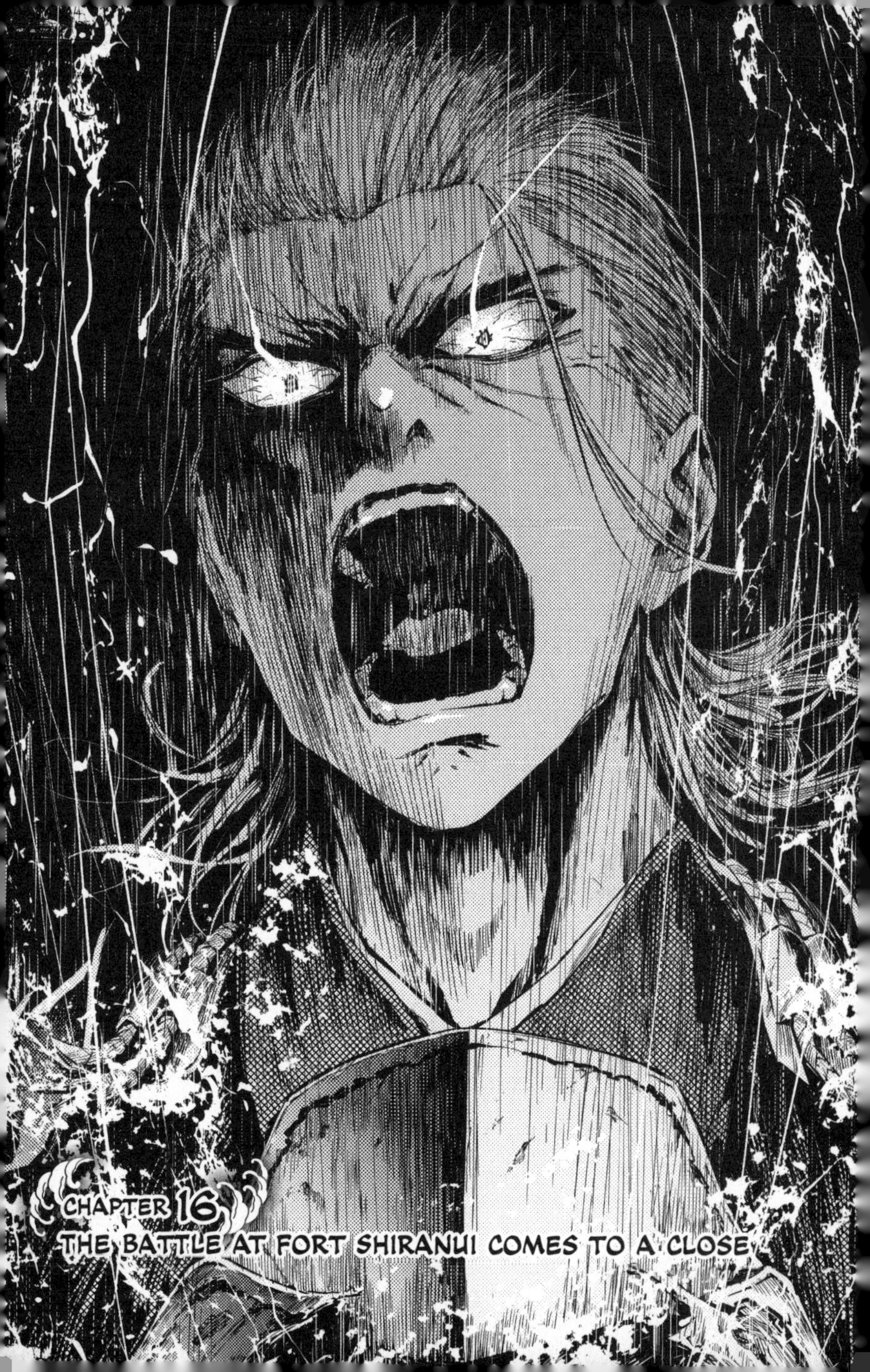
CHAPTER 16
THE BATTLE AT FORT SHIRANUI COMES TO A CLOSE

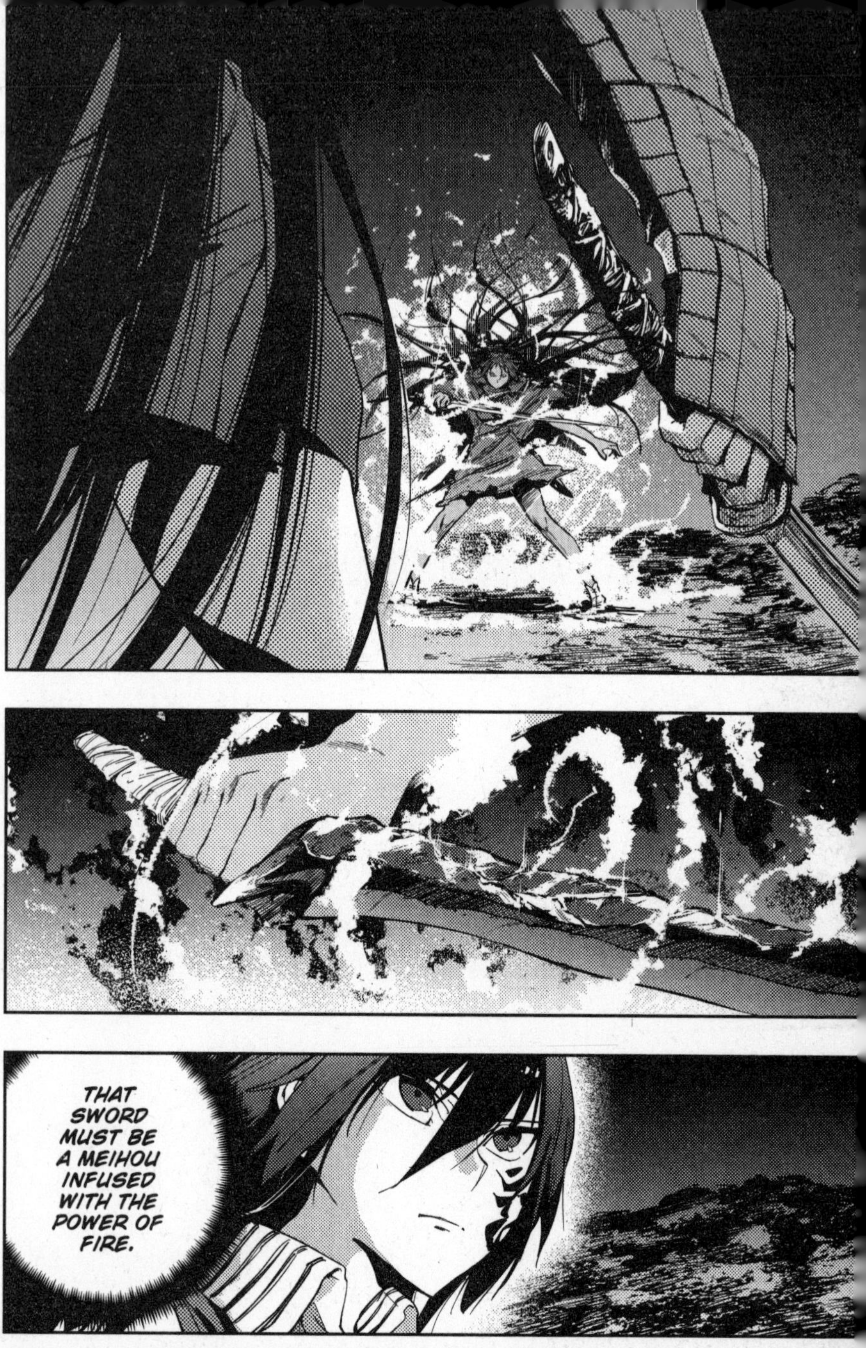
THAT SWORD MUST BE A MEIHOU INFUSED WITH THE POWER OF FIRE.

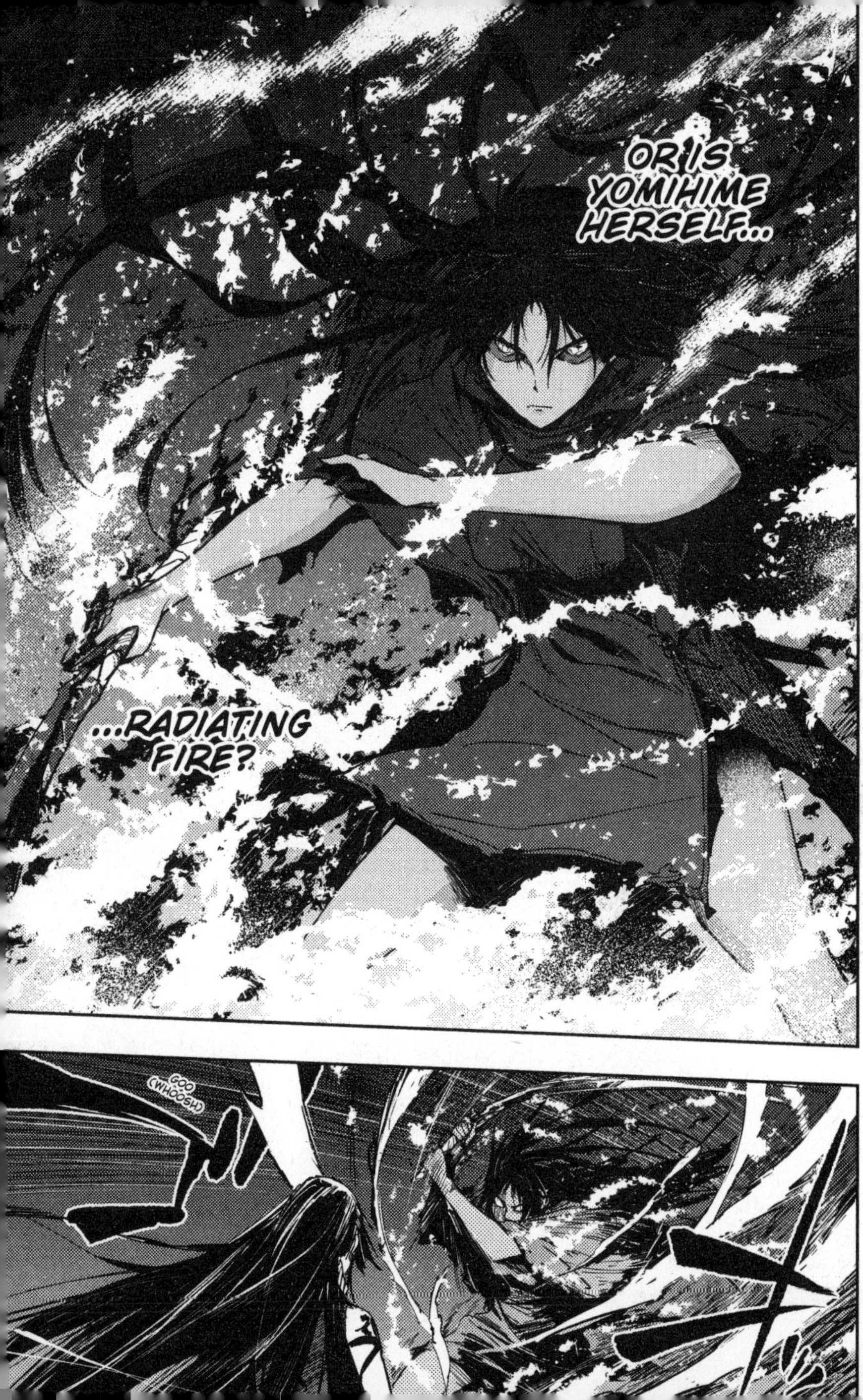
OR IS YOMIHIME HERSELF...
...RADIATING FIRE?
GOO (WHOOSH)

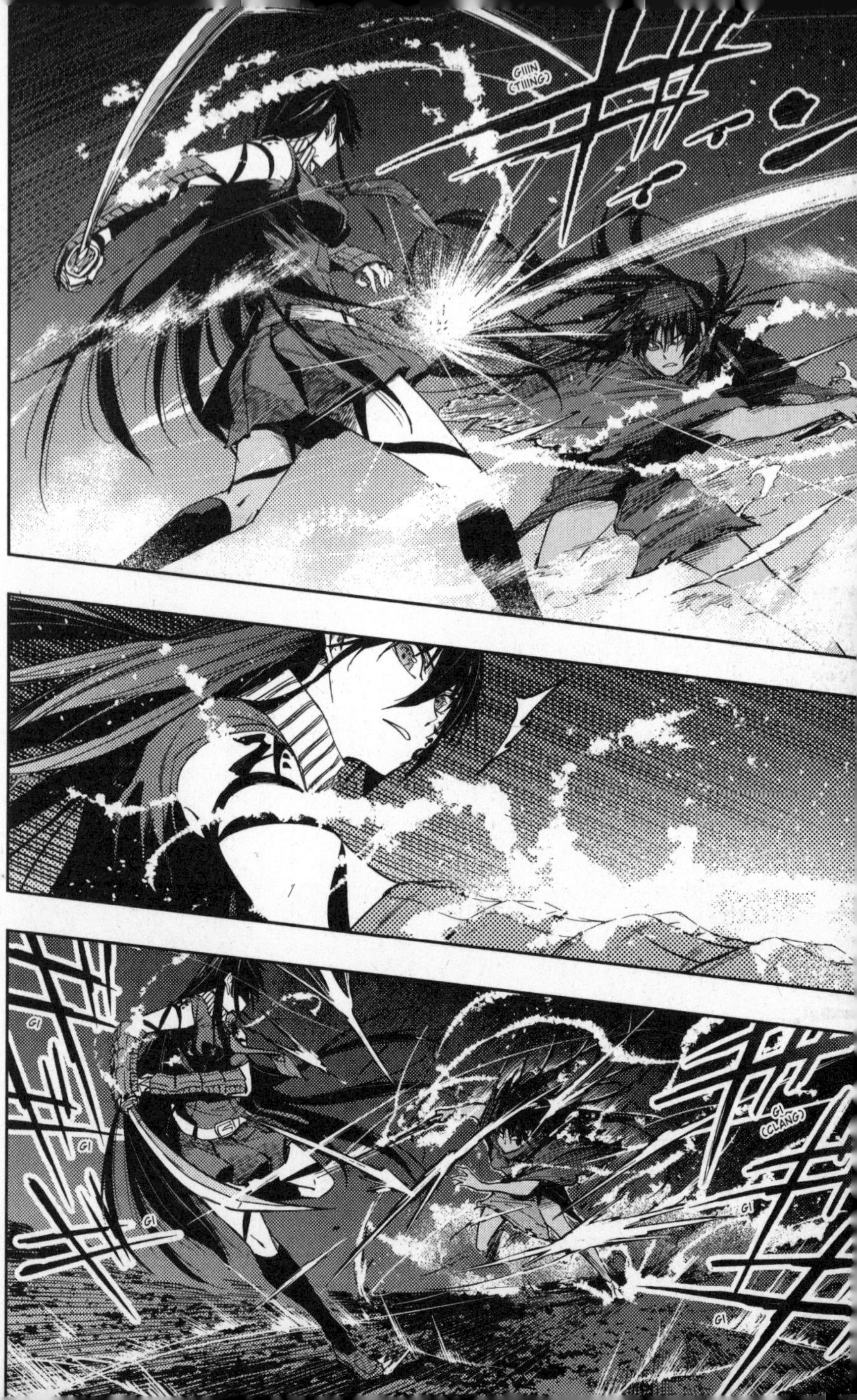
GIIIN
(TIIING)
GI
(CLANG)
GI
GI
GI
GI
GI

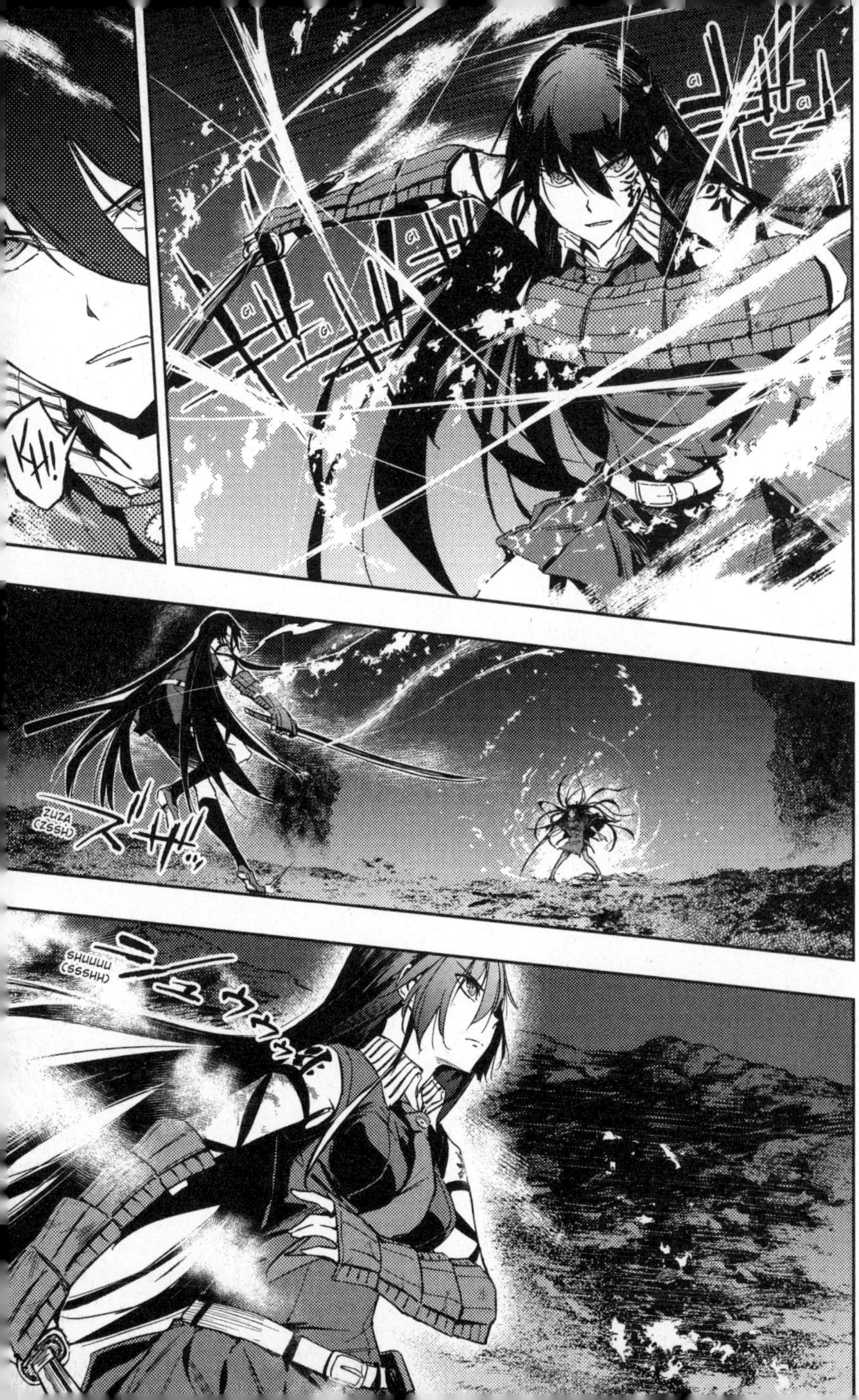
GI
GI
GI
GI
GI
KH!
ZUZA (ZSSH)
SHUUUU (SSSHH)

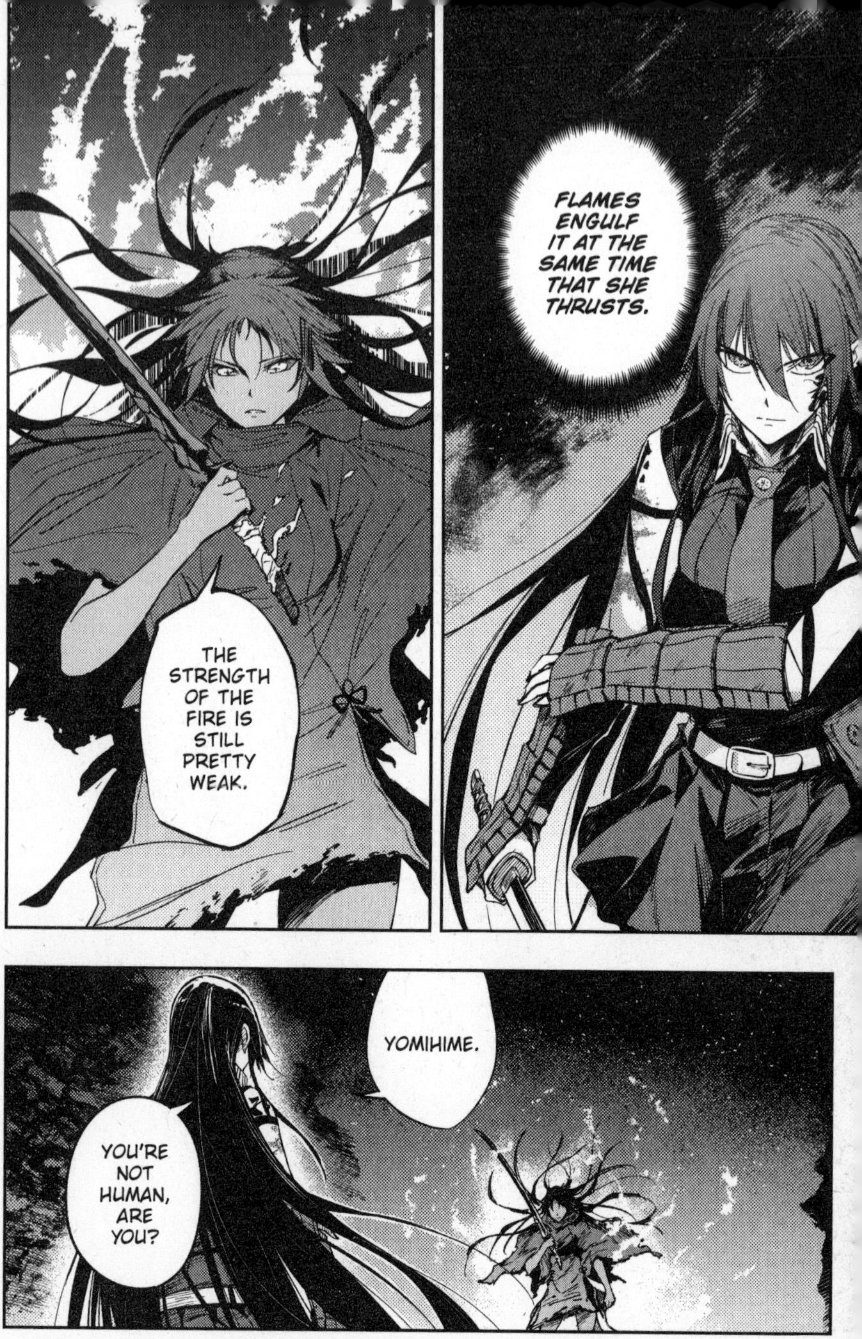
FLAMES ENGULF IT AT THE SAME TIME THAT SHE THRUSTS.
THE STRENGTH OF THE FIRE IS STILL PRETTY WEAK.
YOMIHIME.
YOU'RE NOT HUMAN, ARE YOU?

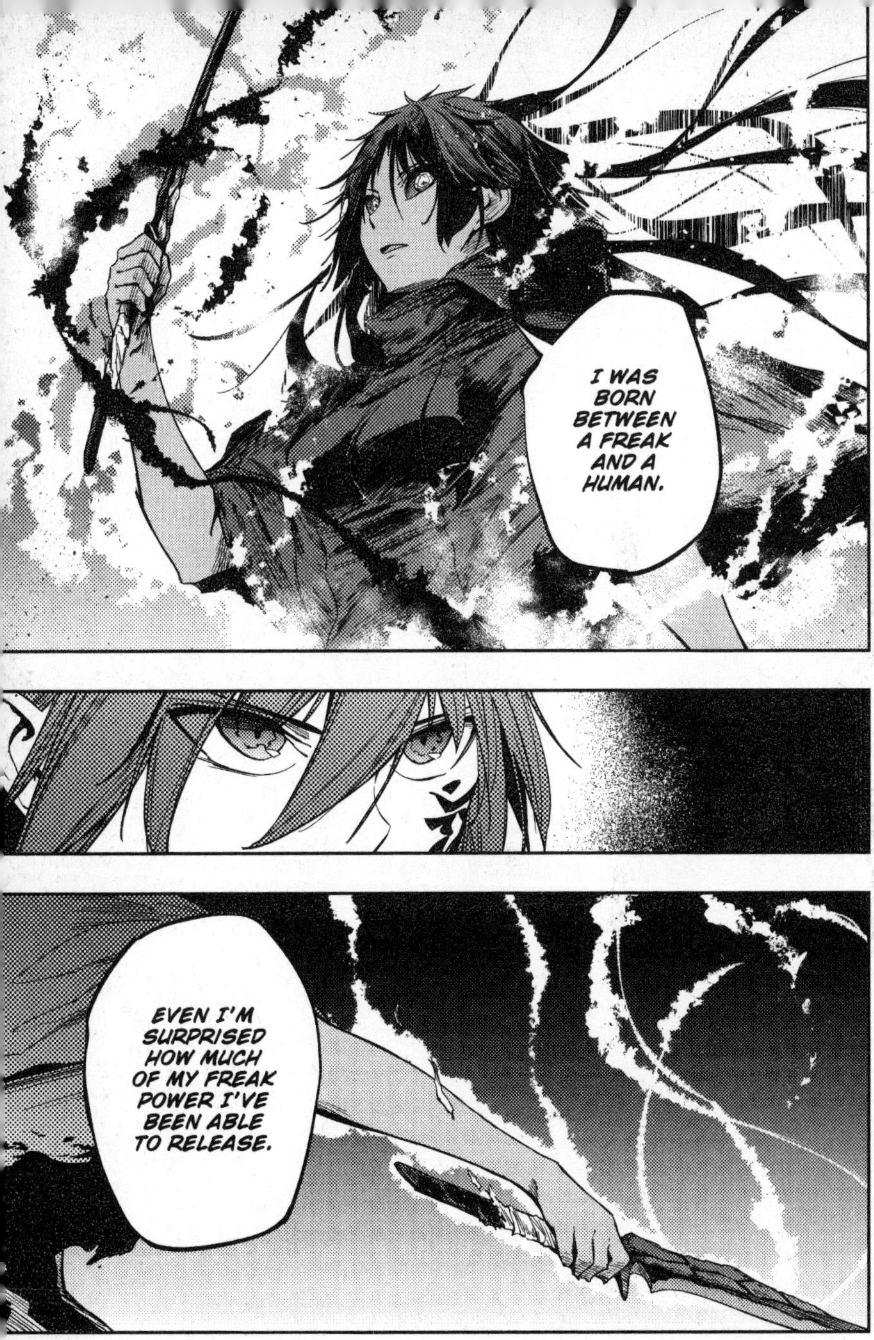
I WAS BORN BETWEEN A FREAK AND A HUMAN.
EVEN I'M SURPRISED HOW MUCH OF MY FREAK POWER I'VE BEEN ABLE TO RELEASE.

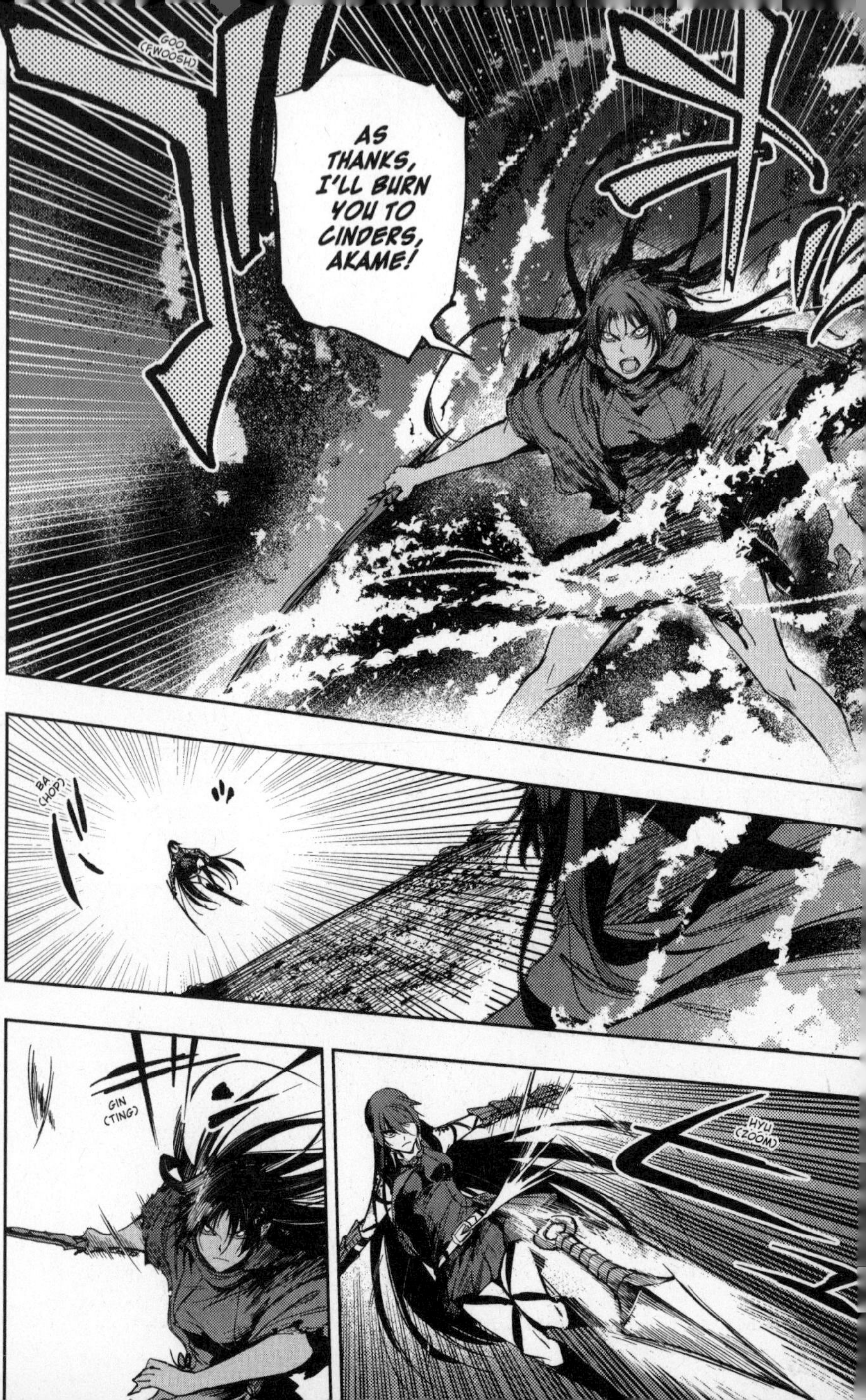
GOO (FWOOSH)
AS THANKS, I'LL BURN YOU TO CINDERS, AKAME!
BA (HOP)
HYU (ZOOM)
GIN (TING)

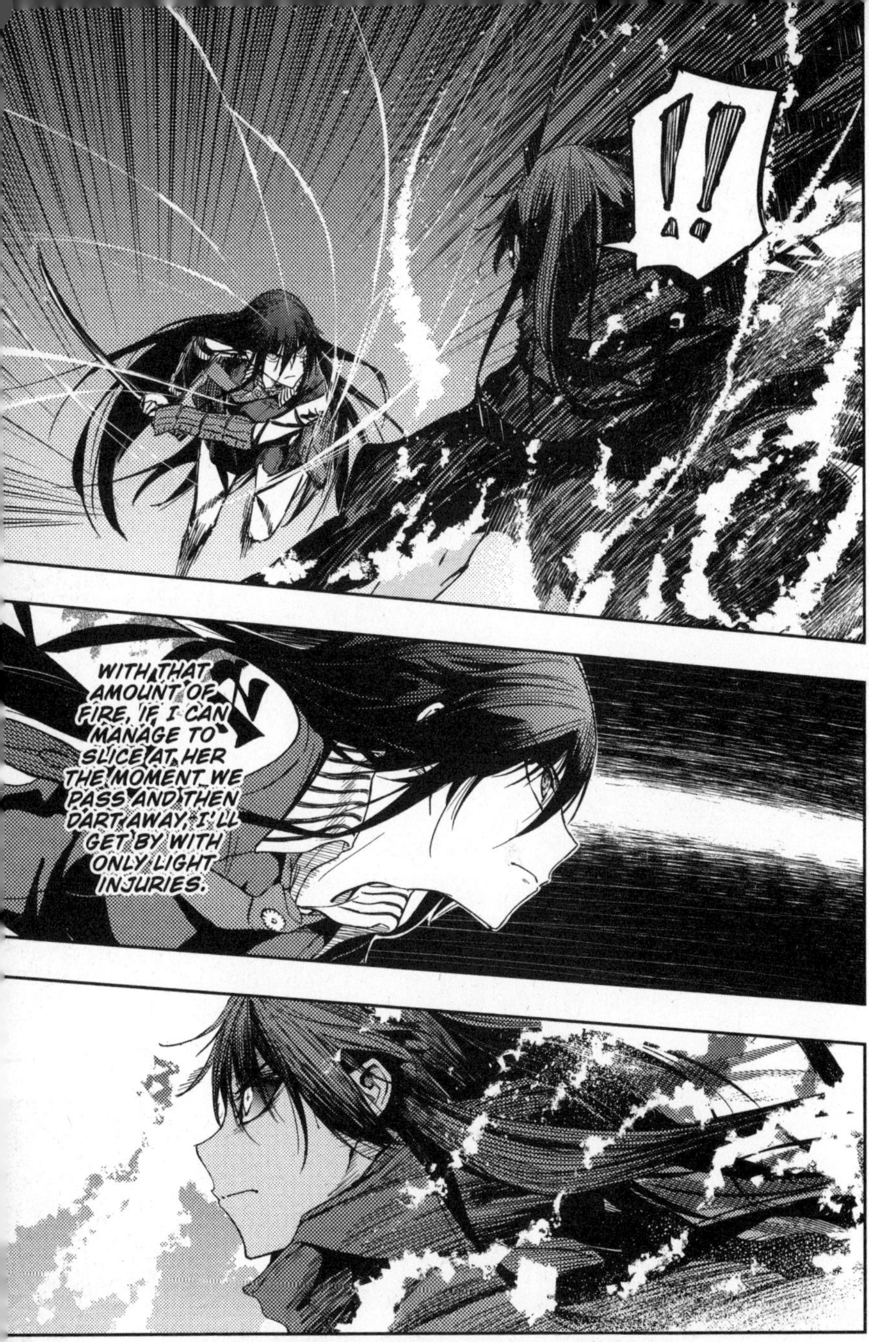
!!
WITH THAT AMOUNT OF FIRE, IF I CAN MANAGE TO SLICE AT HER THE MOMENT WE PASS AND THEN DART AWAY, I'LL GET BY WITH ONLY LIGHT INJURIES.

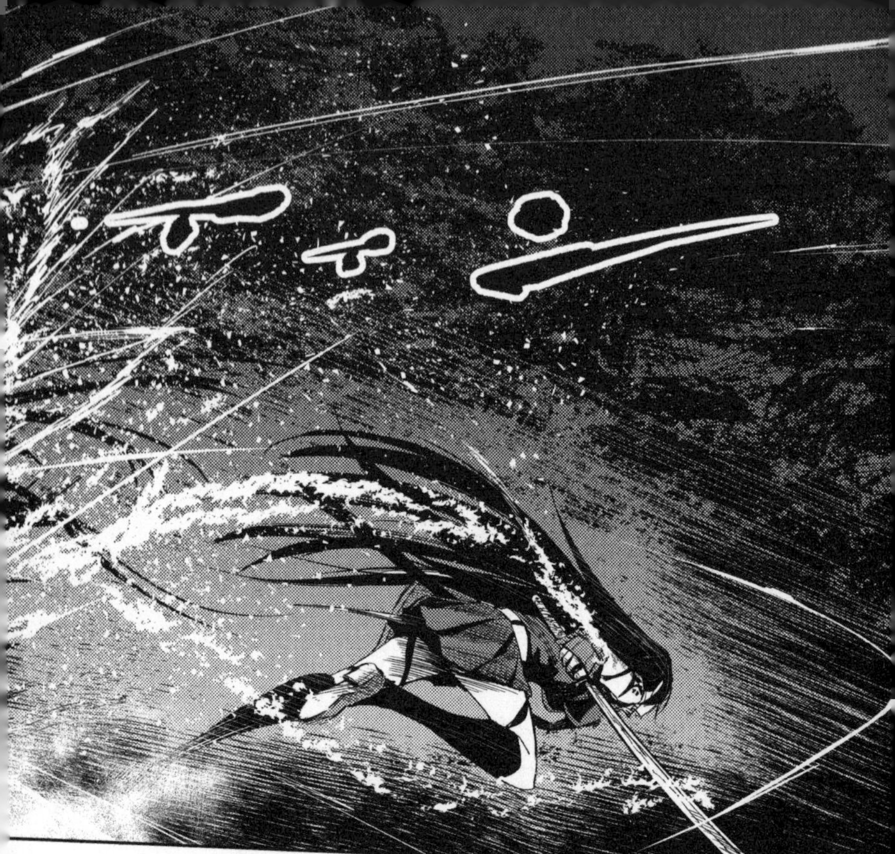

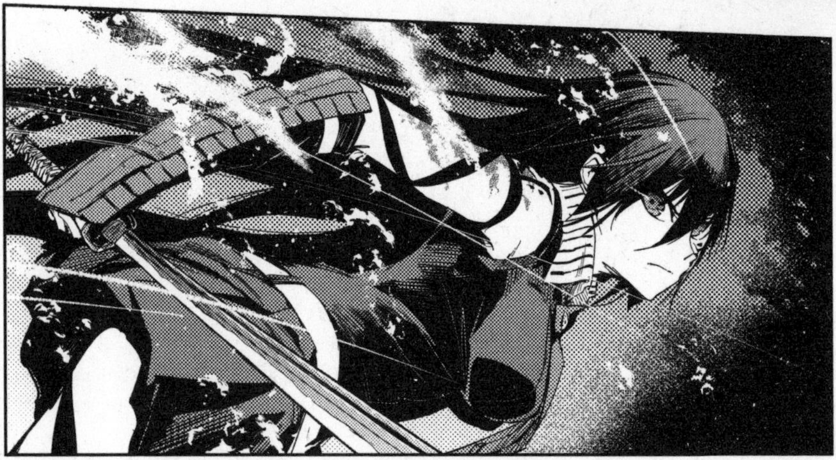

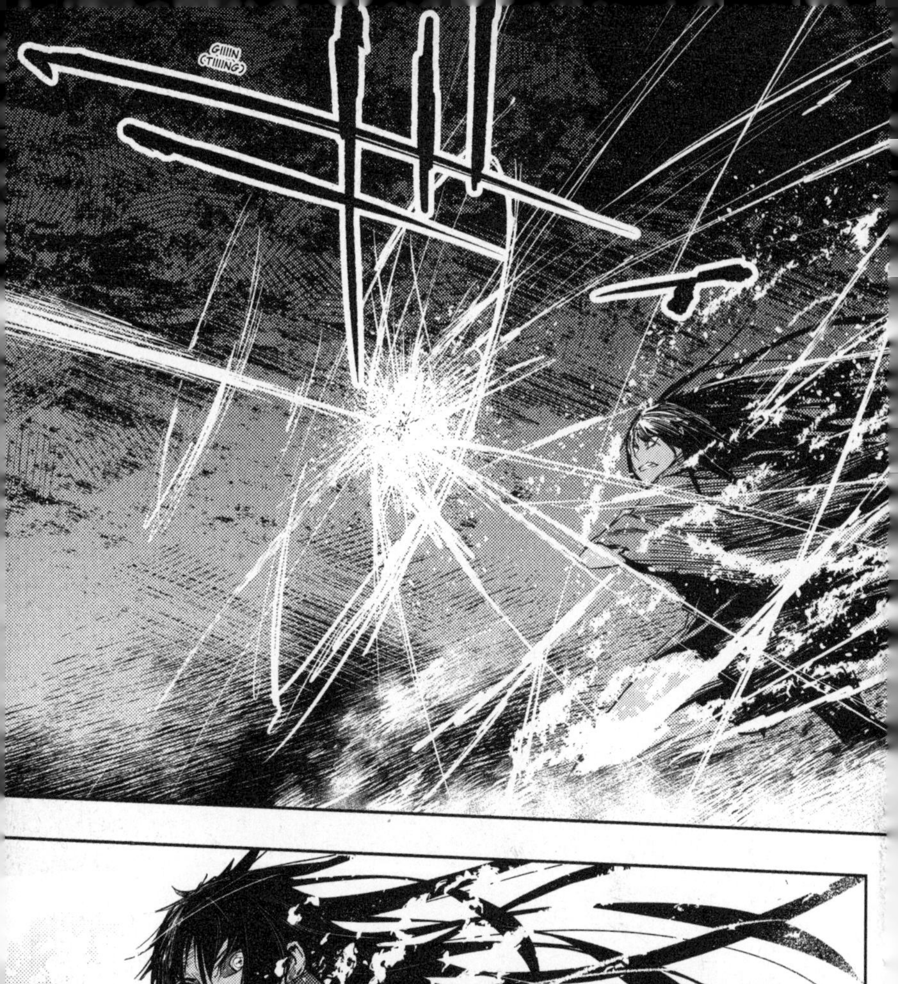
GIIIIN
(TIIIING)
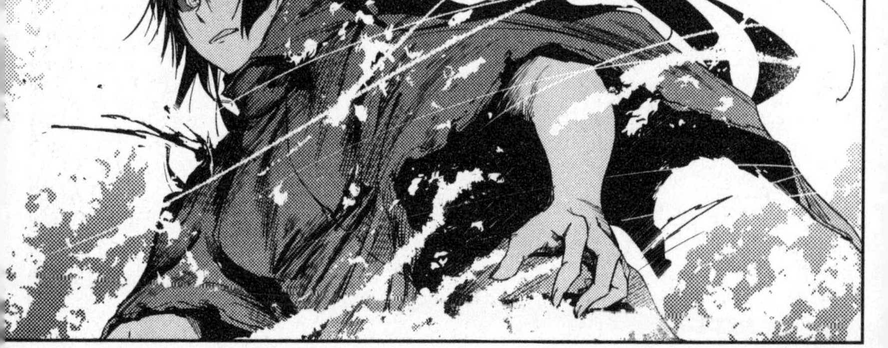

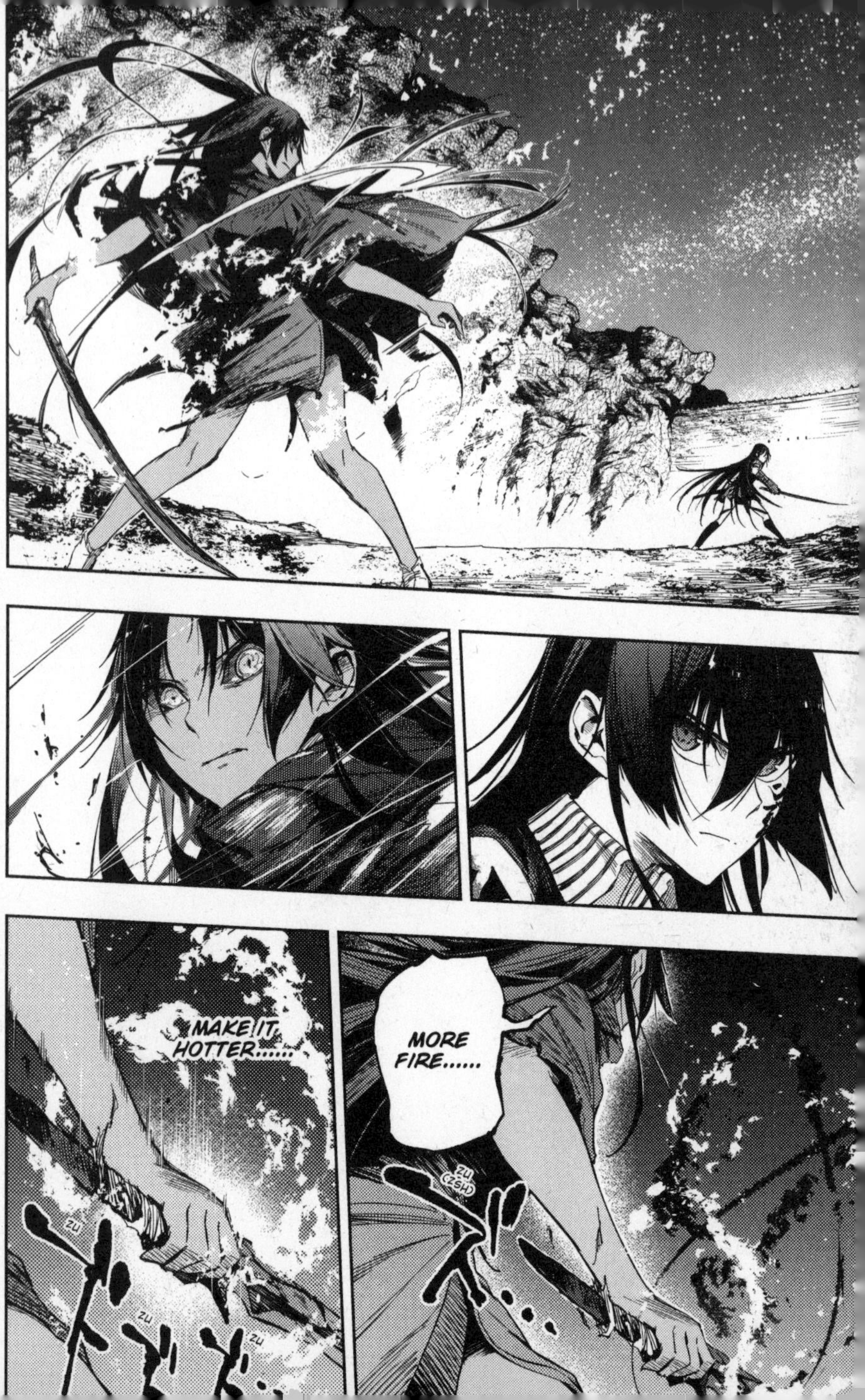
MORE FIRE......
ZU (ZSH)
MAKE IT HOTTER......
ZU
ZU
ZU

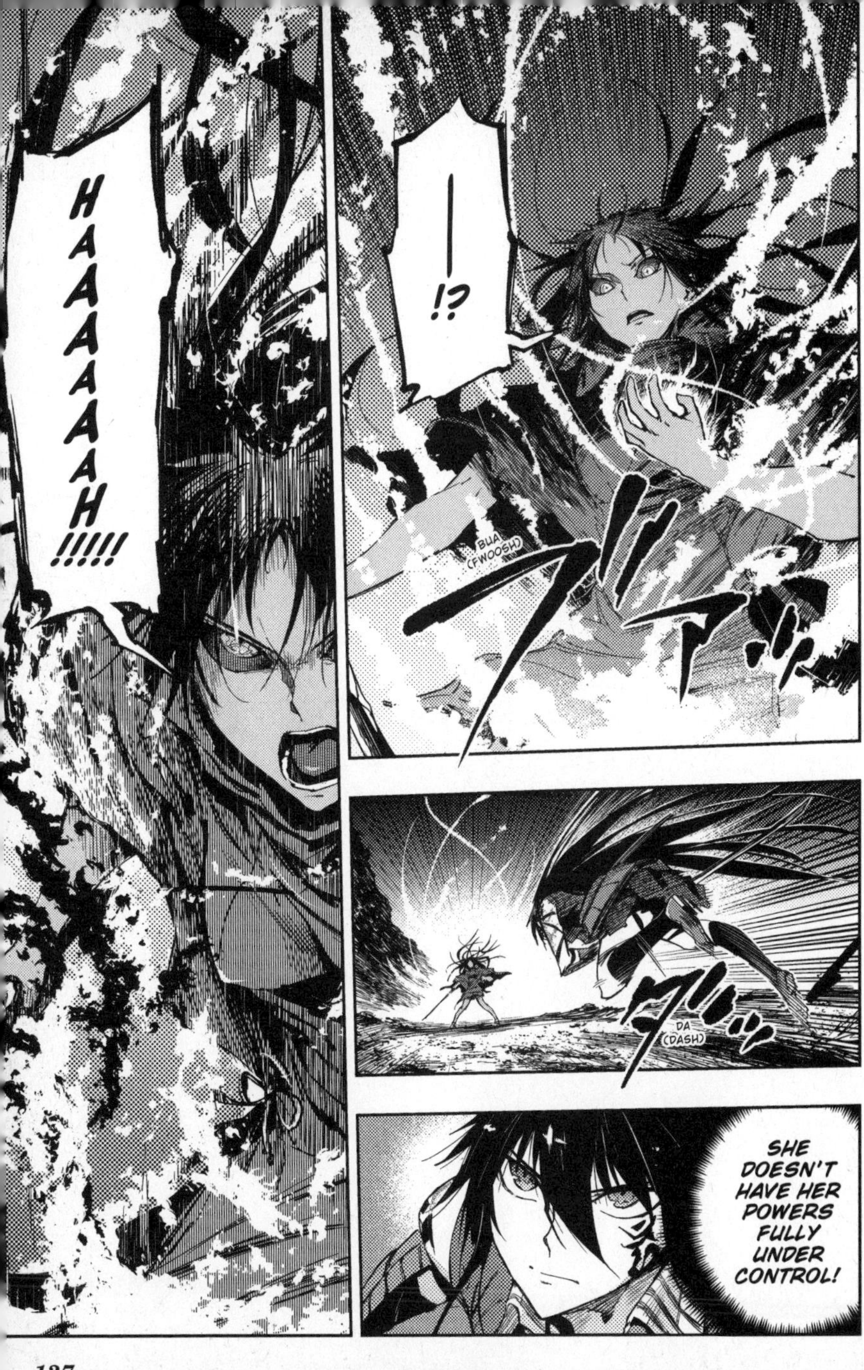
—!?
BUA (FWOOSH)
DA (DASH)
SHE DOESN'T HAVE HER POWERS FULLY UNDER CONTROL!
HAAAAAAAH!!!!!

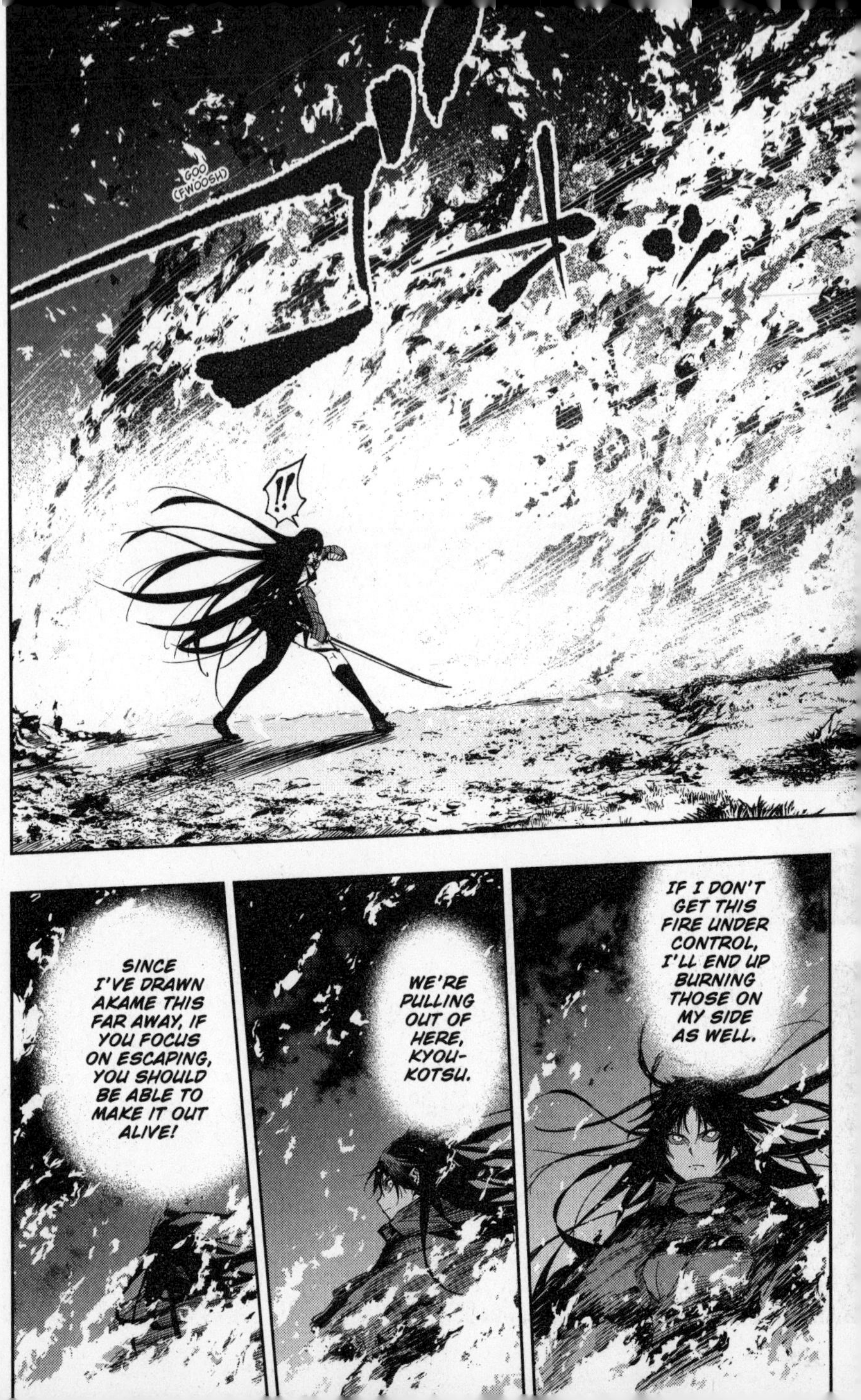
GOO (FWOOSH)
!!
IF I DON'T GET THIS FIRE UNDER CONTROL, I'LL END UP BURNING THOSE ON MY SIDE AS WELL.
WE'RE PULLING OUT OF HERE, KYOU-KOTSU.
SINCE I'VE DRAWN AKAME THIS FAR AWAY, IF YOU FOCUS ON ESCAPING, YOU SHOULD BE ABLE TO MAKE IT OUT ALIVE!

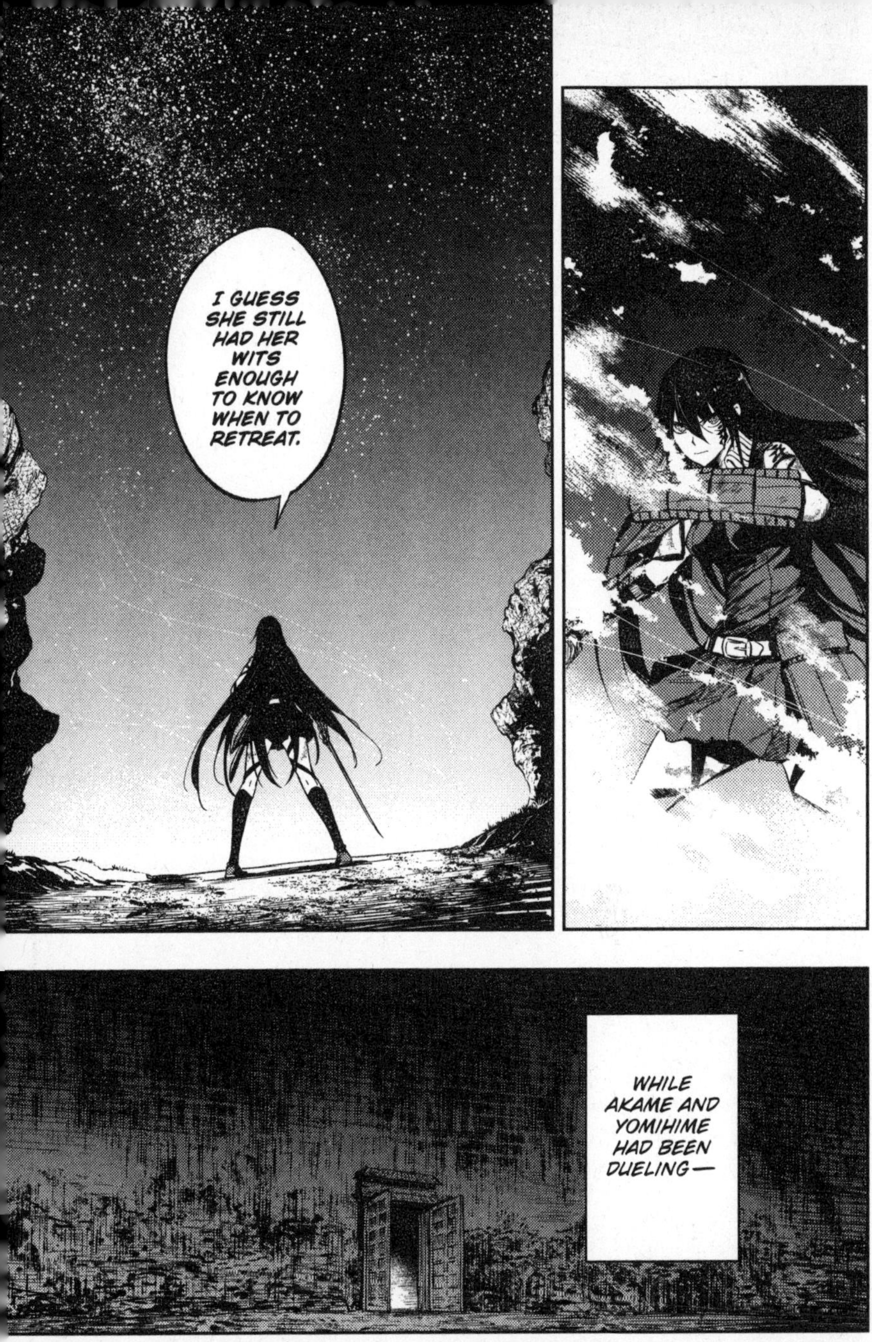
I GUESS SHE STILL HAD HER WITS ENOUGH TO KNOW WHEN TO RETREAT.
WHILE AKAME AND YOMIHIME HAD BEEN DUELING—

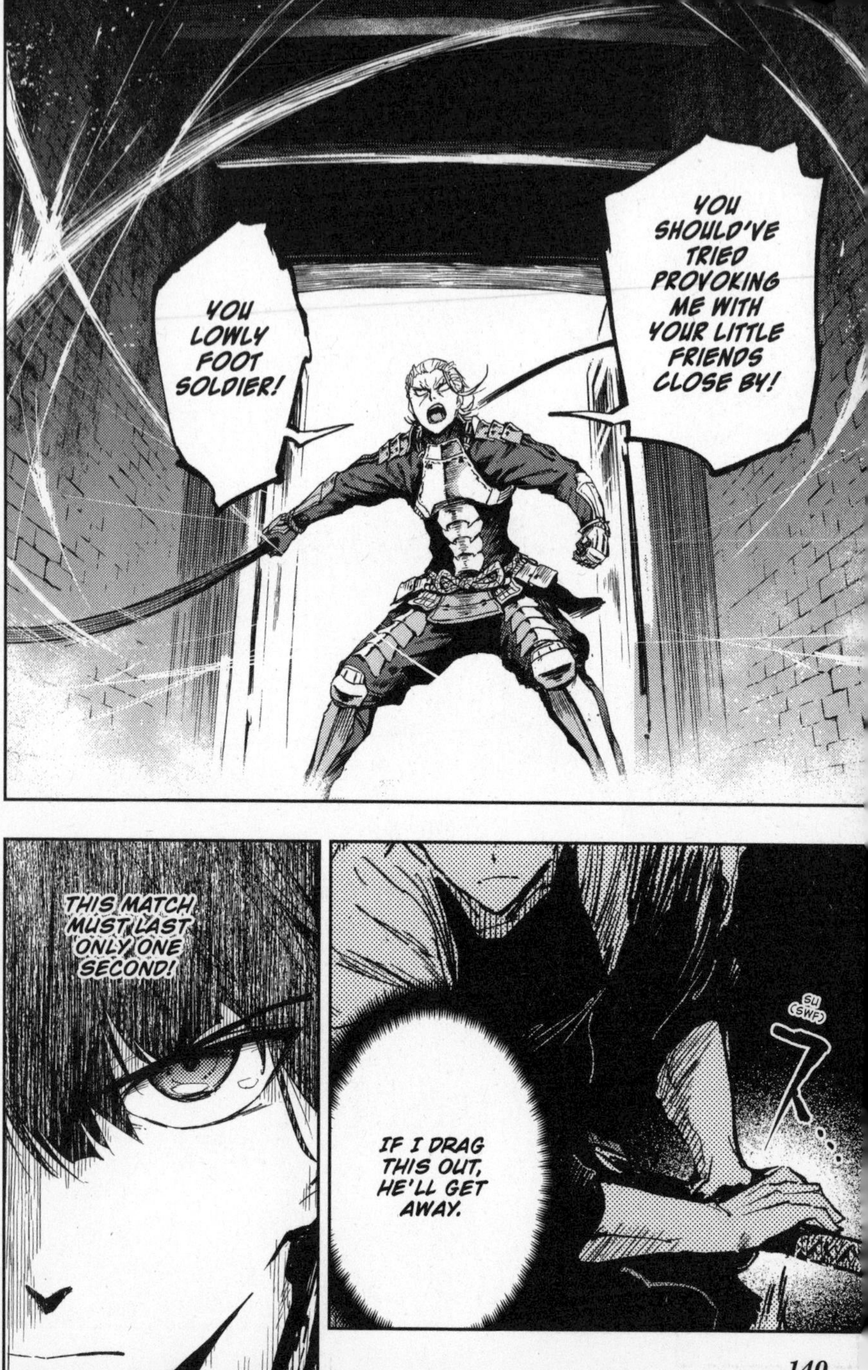
YOU SHOULD'VE TRIED PROVOKING ME WITH YOUR LITTLE FRIENDS CLOSE BY!
YOU LOWLY FOOT SOLDIER!
SU (SWF)
IF I DRAG THIS OUT, HE'LL GET AWAY.
THIS MATCH MUST LAST ONLY ONE SECOND!

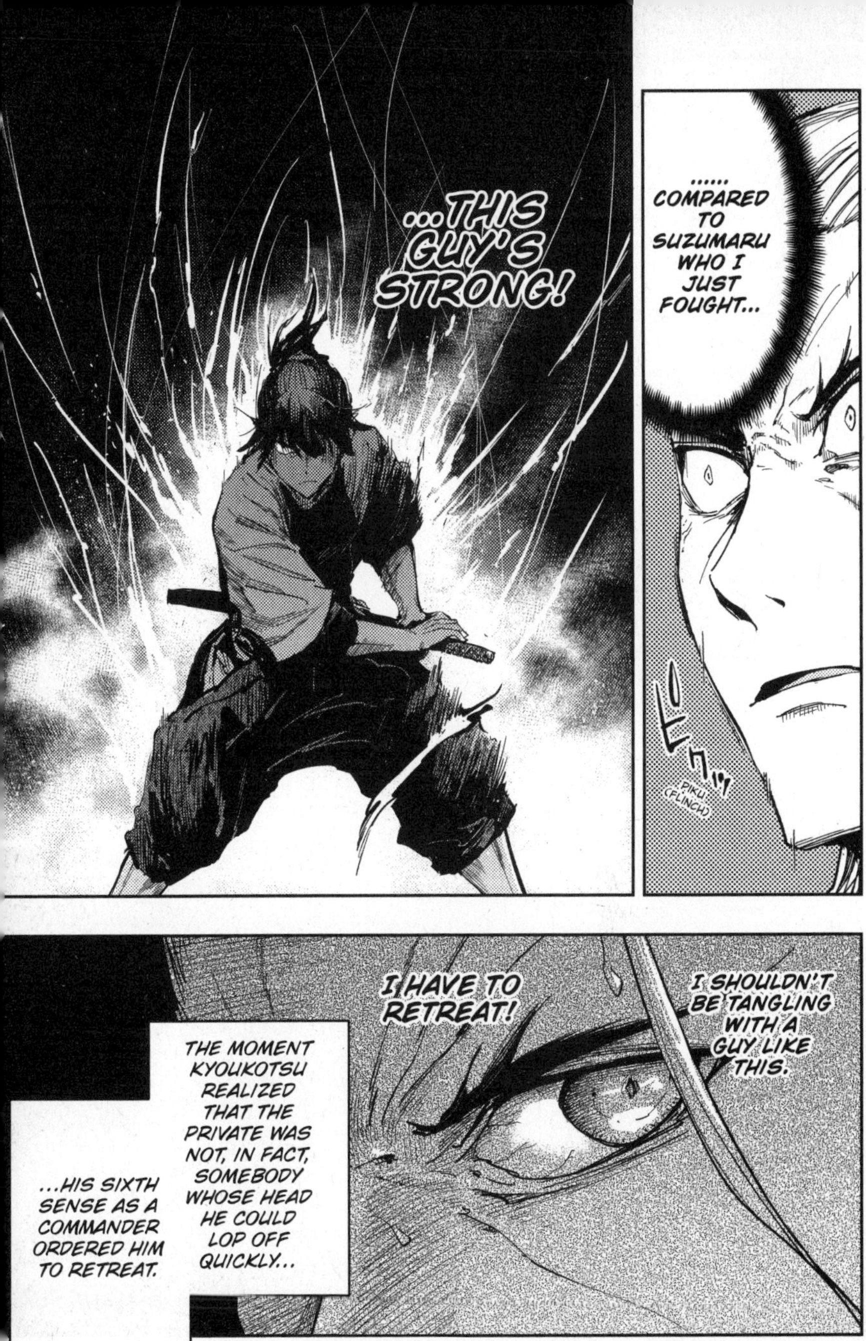
......COMPARED TO SUZUMARU WHO I JUST FOUGHT...
PIKU (FLINCH)
...THIS GUY'S STRONG!
I SHOULDN'T BE TANGLING WITH A GUY LIKE THIS.
I HAVE TO RETREAT!
THE MOMENT KYOUKOTSU REALIZED THAT THE PRIVATE WAS NOT, IN FACT, SOMEBODY WHOSE HEAD HE COULD LOP OFF QUICKLY...
...HIS SIXTH SENSE AS A COMMANDER ORDERED HIM TO RETREAT.

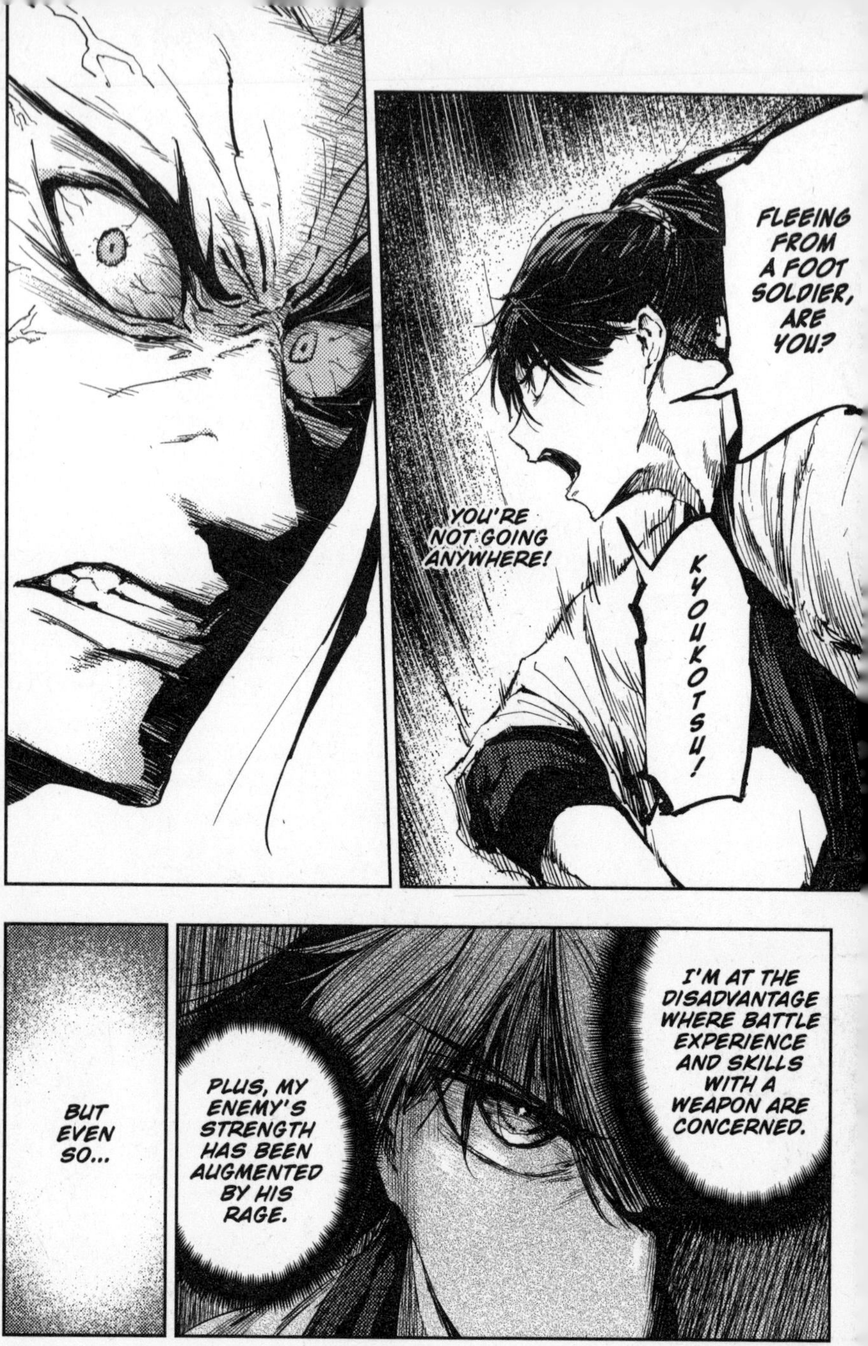
FLEEING FROM A FOOT SOLDIER, ARE YOU?
KYOUKOTSU!
YOU'RE NOT GOING ANYWHERE!
I'M AT THE DISADVANTAGE WHERE BATTLE EXPERIENCE AND SKILLS WITH A WEAPON ARE CONCERNED.
PLUS, MY ENEMY'S STRENGTH HAS BEEN AUGMENTED BY HIS RAGE.
BUT EVEN SO...

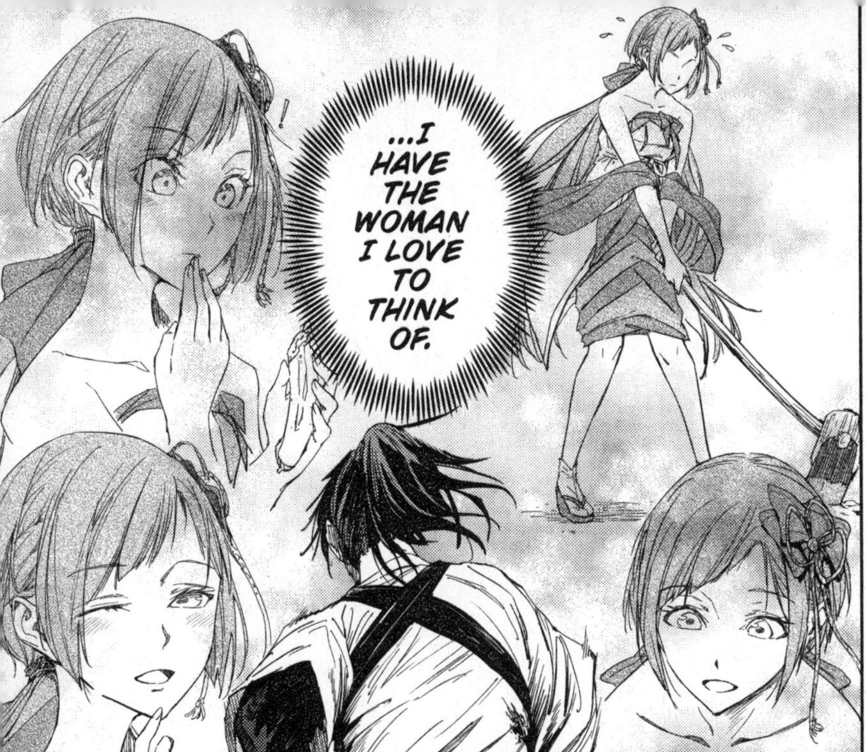
...I HAVE THE WOMAN I LOVE TO THINK OF.

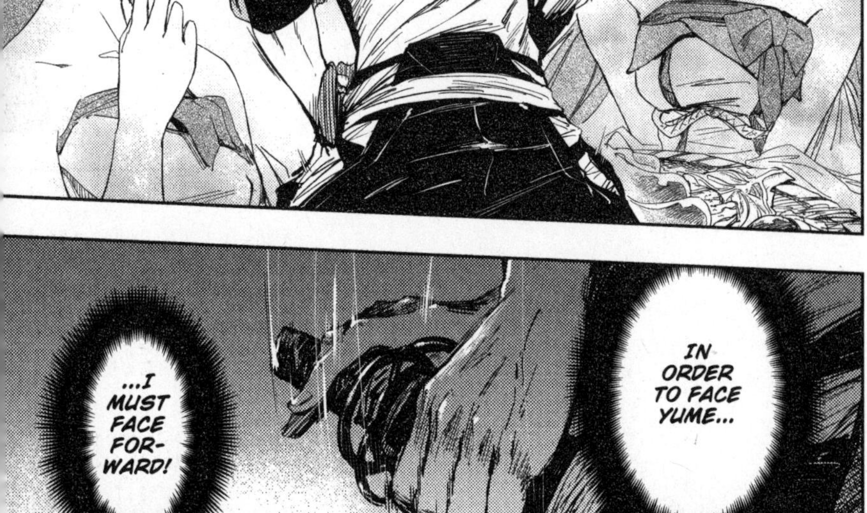
IN ORDER TO FACE YUME...
...I MUST FACE FOR-WARD!

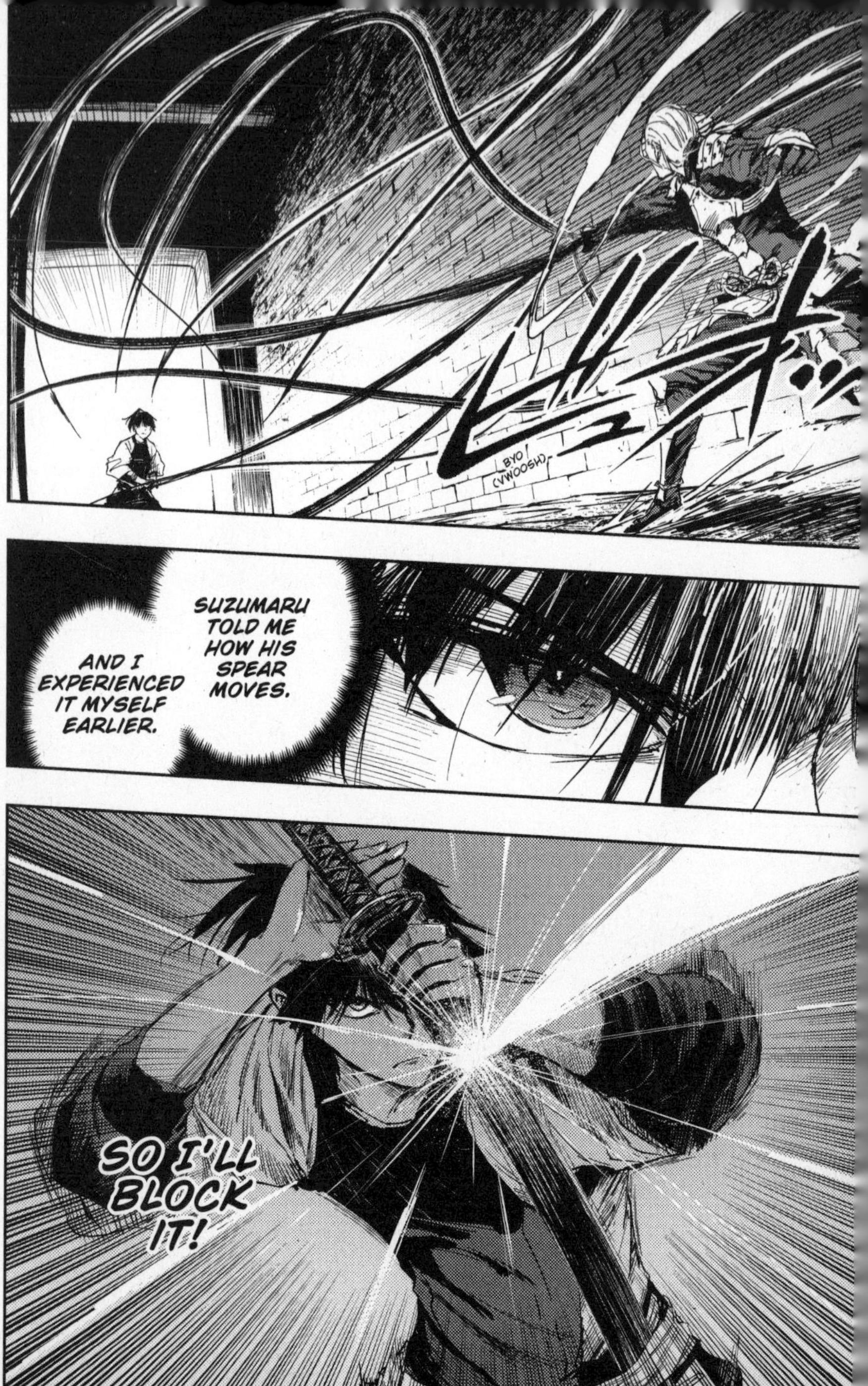
BYO
(VWOOSH)
SUZUMARU TOLD ME HOW HIS SPEAR MOVES.
AND I EXPERIENCED IT MYSELF EARLIER.
SO I'LL BLOCK IT!

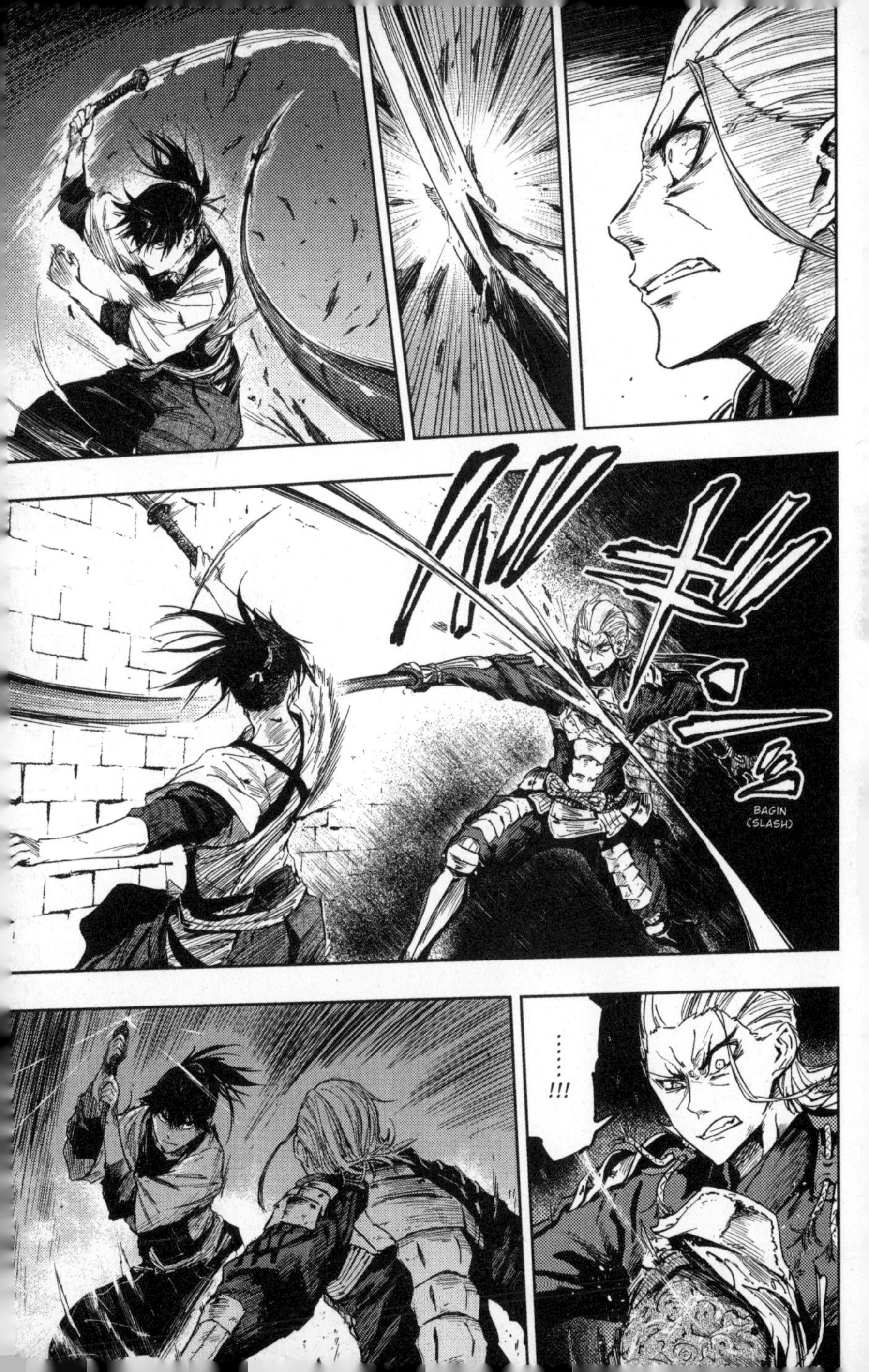
BAGIN
(SLASH)
......!!!

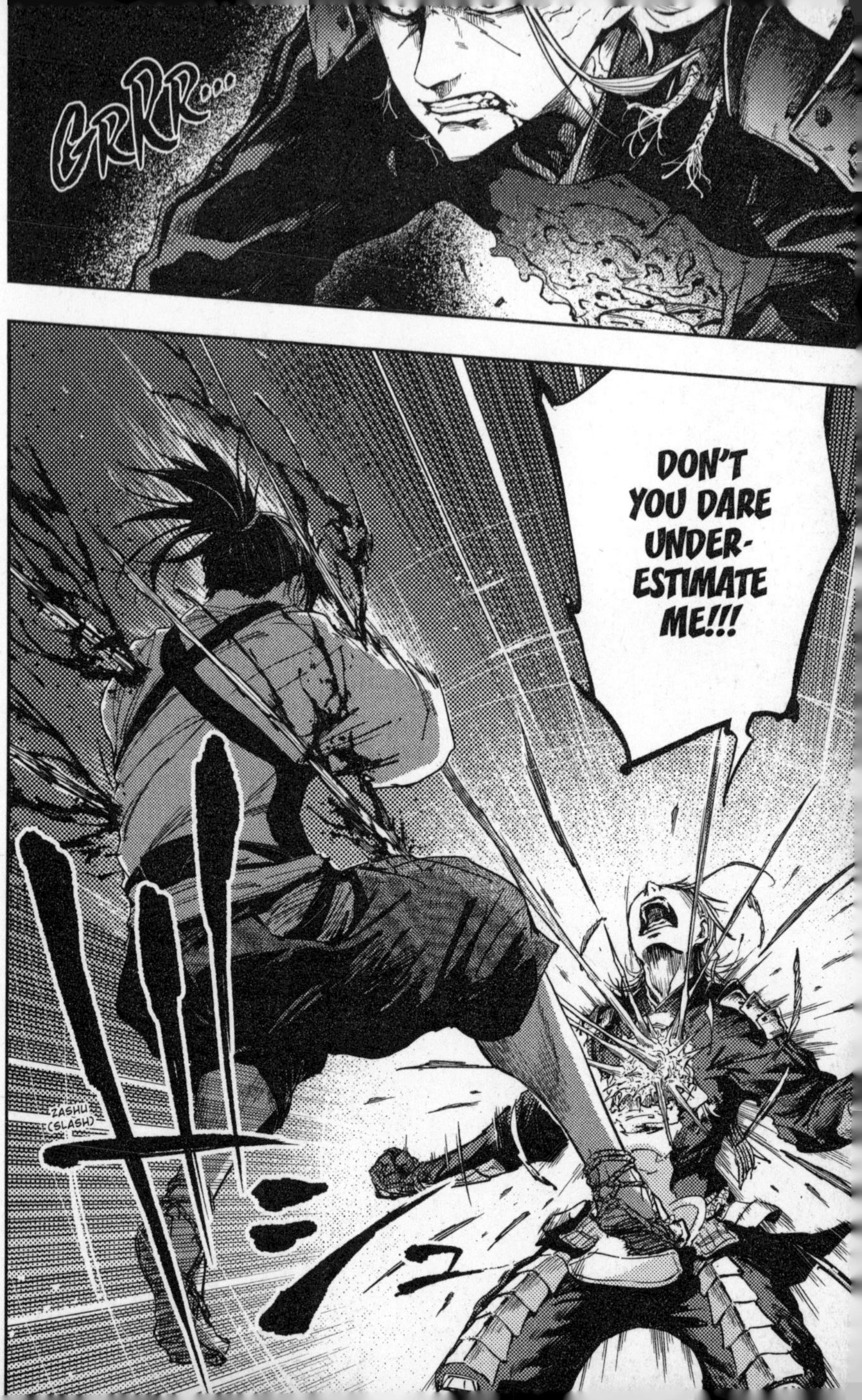
GRRR...
DON'T YOU DARE UNDER-ESTIMATE ME!!!
ZASHU (SLASH)

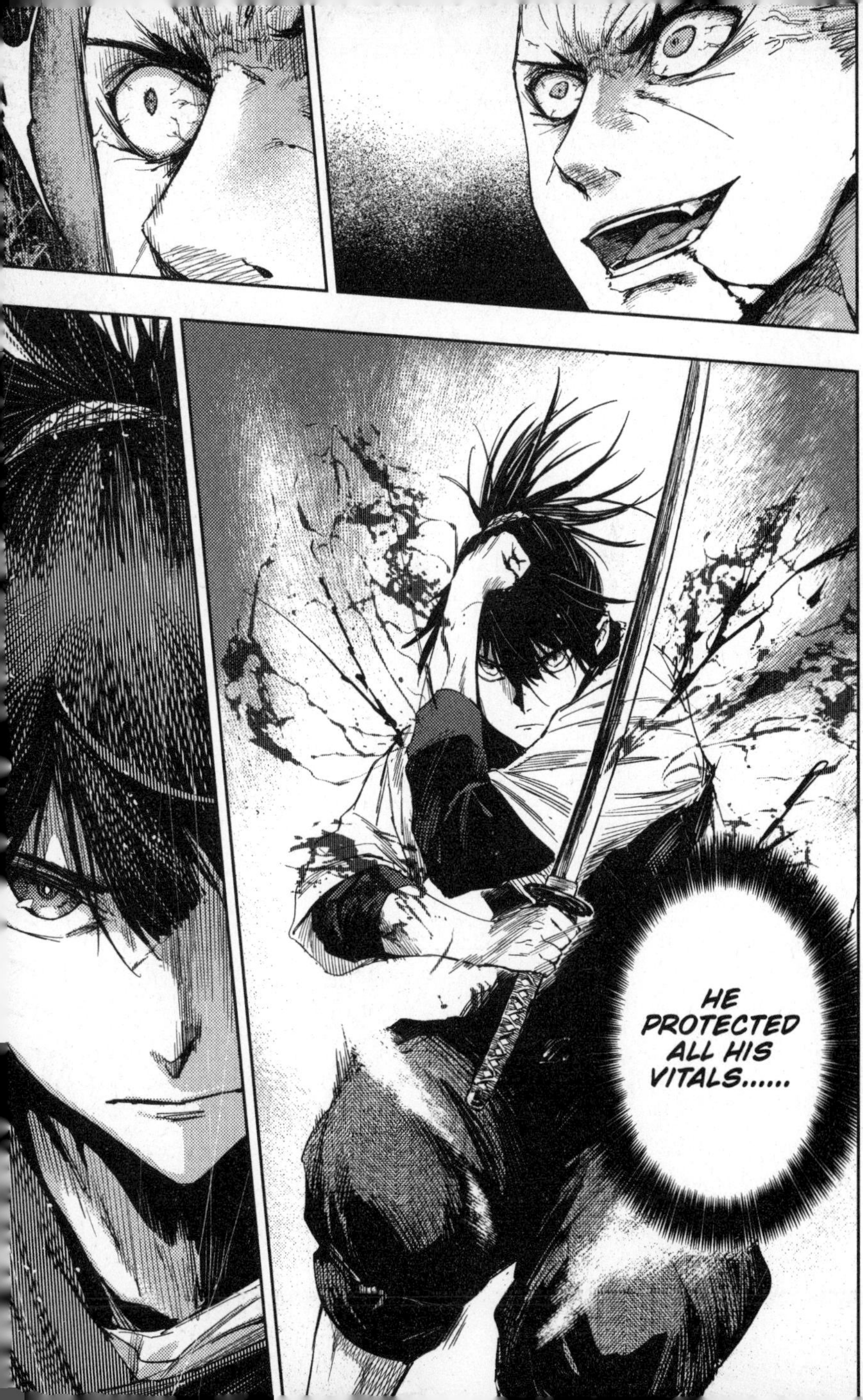
HE PROTECTED ALL HIS VITALS......

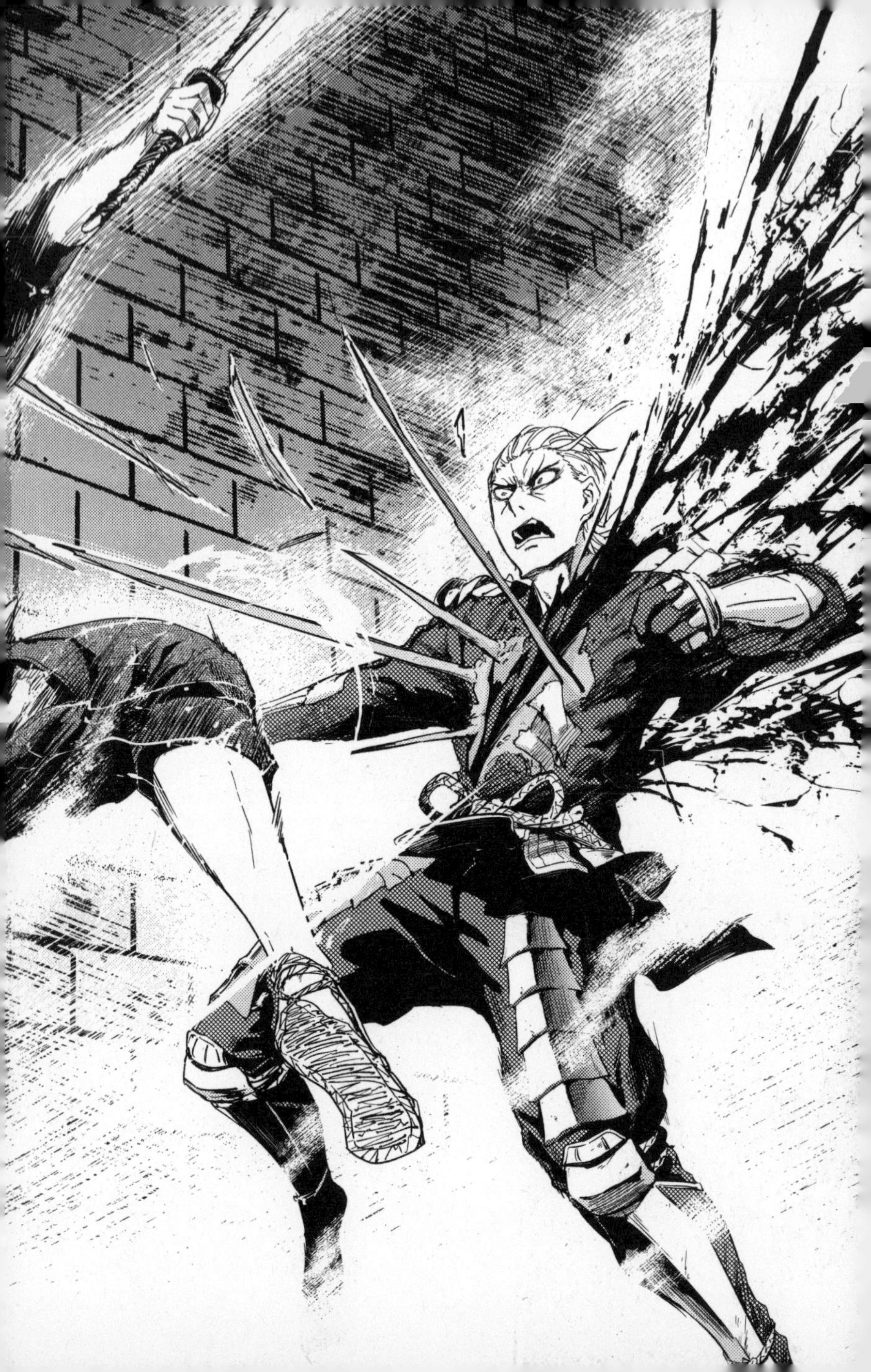
!

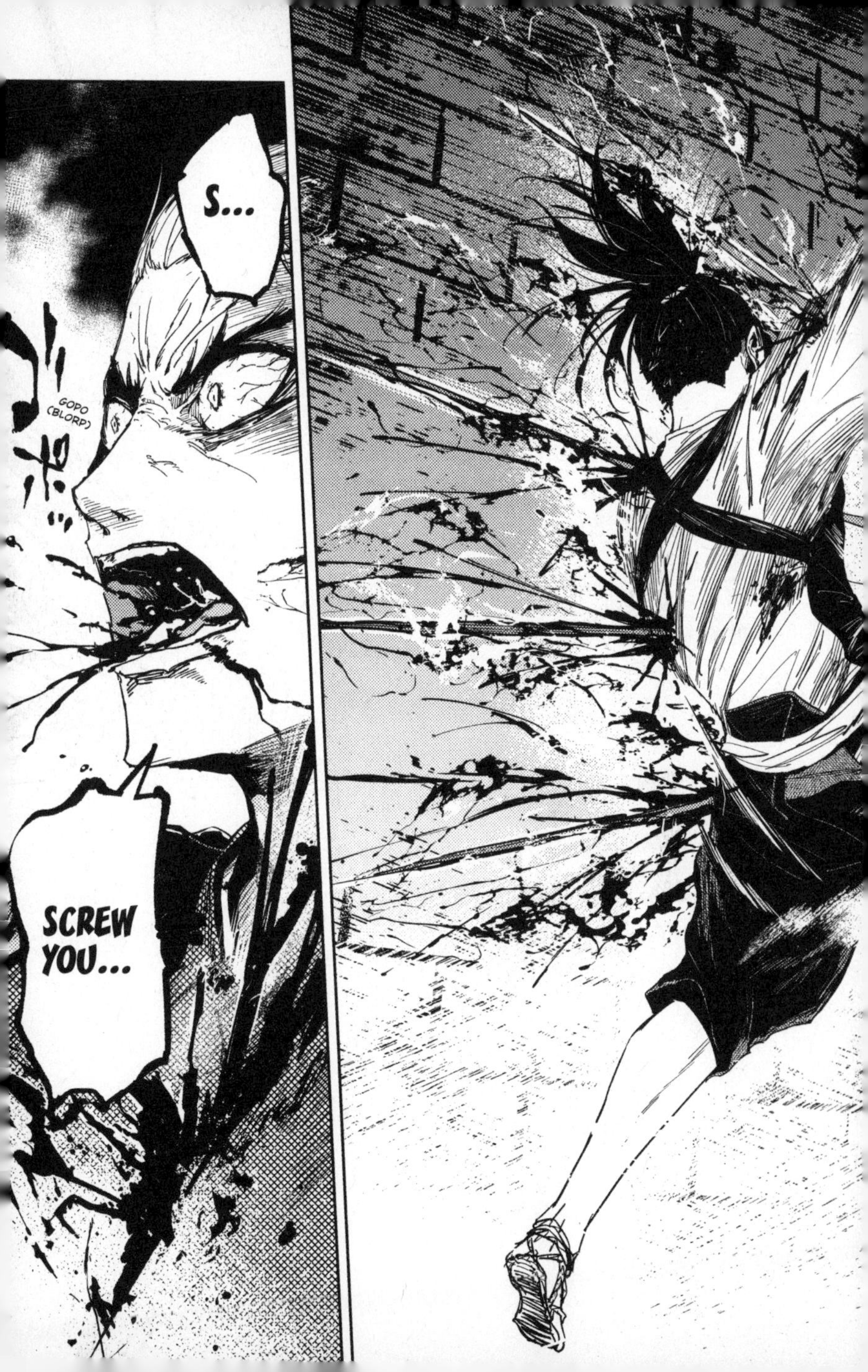
S...
GOPO (BLORP)
SCREW YOU...

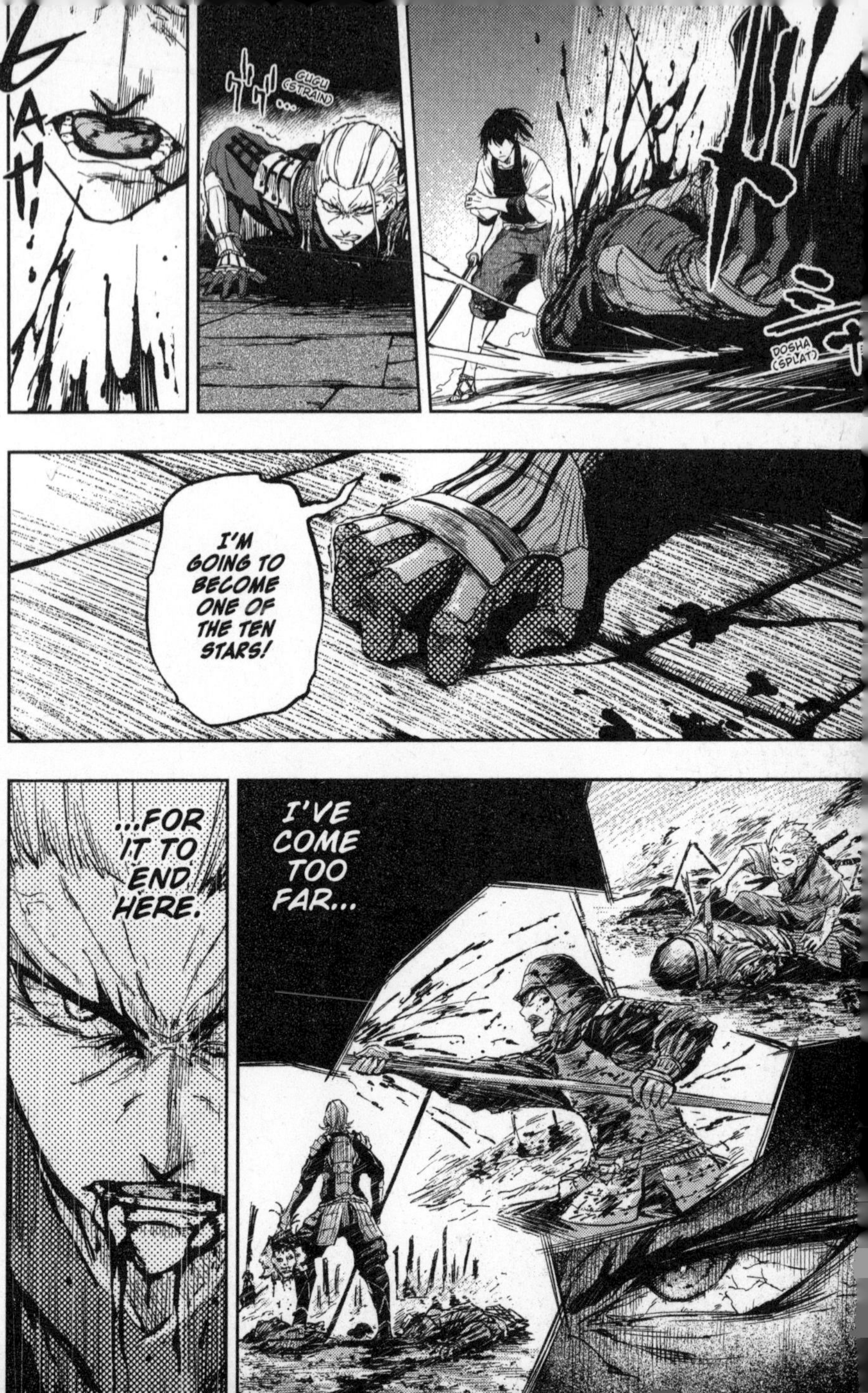
DOSHA (SPLAT)
GUGU (STRAIN)
...
GAH!!
I'M GOING TO BECOME ONE OF THE TEN STARS!
I'VE COME TOO FAR...
...FOR IT TO END HERE.

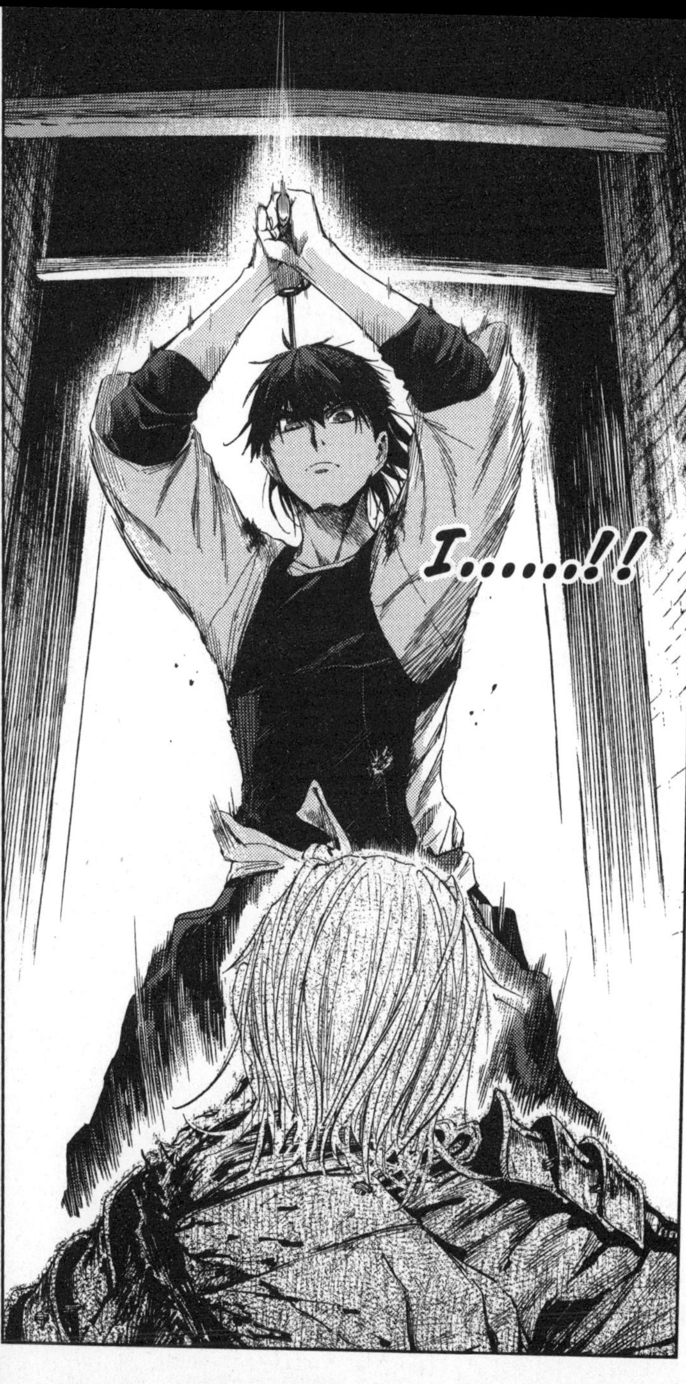
I......!!

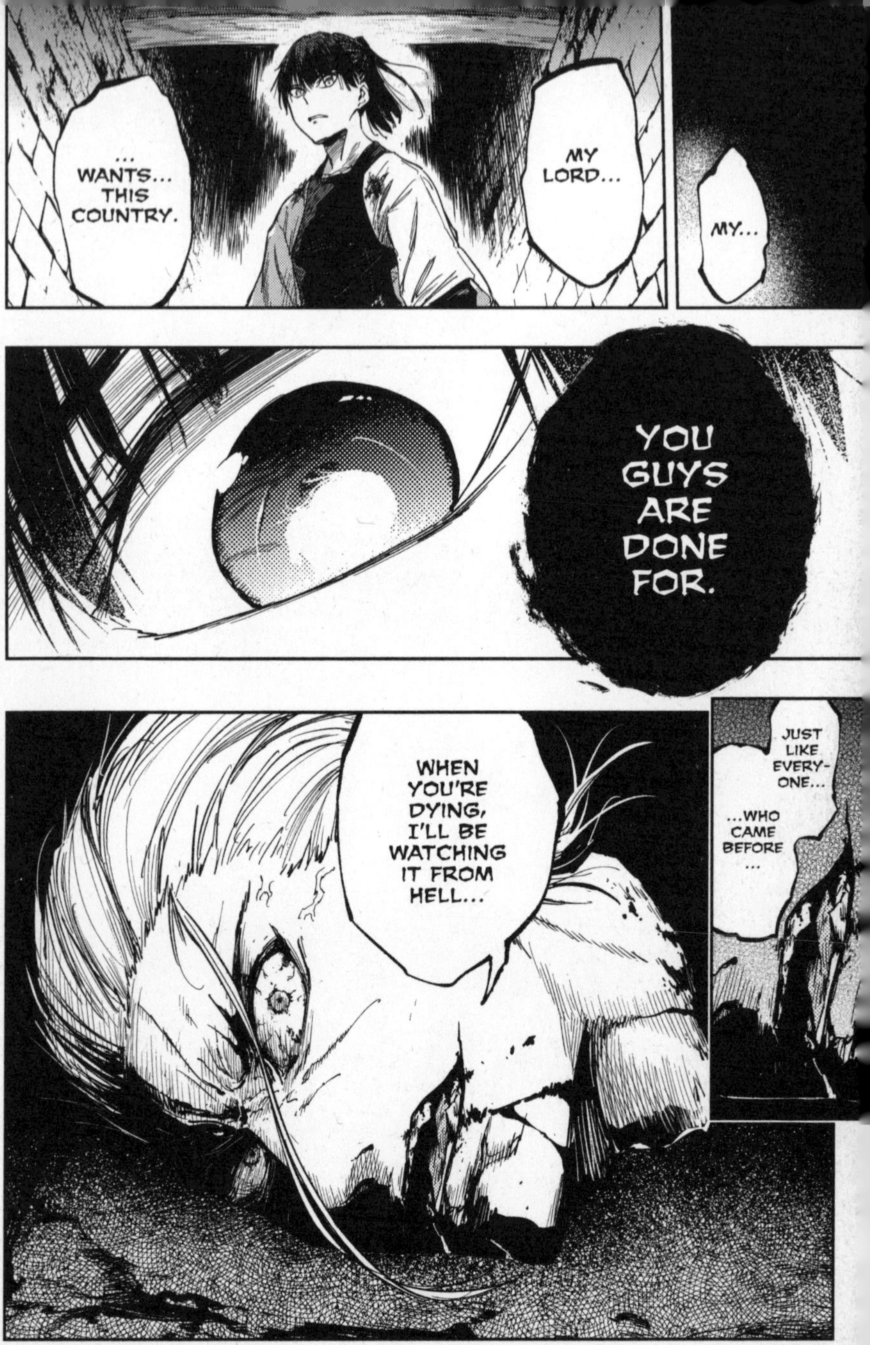
MY...
MY LORD...
... WANTS... THIS COUNTRY.
YOU GUYS ARE DONE FOR.
JUST LIKE EVERY-ONE...
...WHO CAME BEFORE ...
WHEN YOU'RE DYING, I'LL BE WATCHING IT FROM HELL...

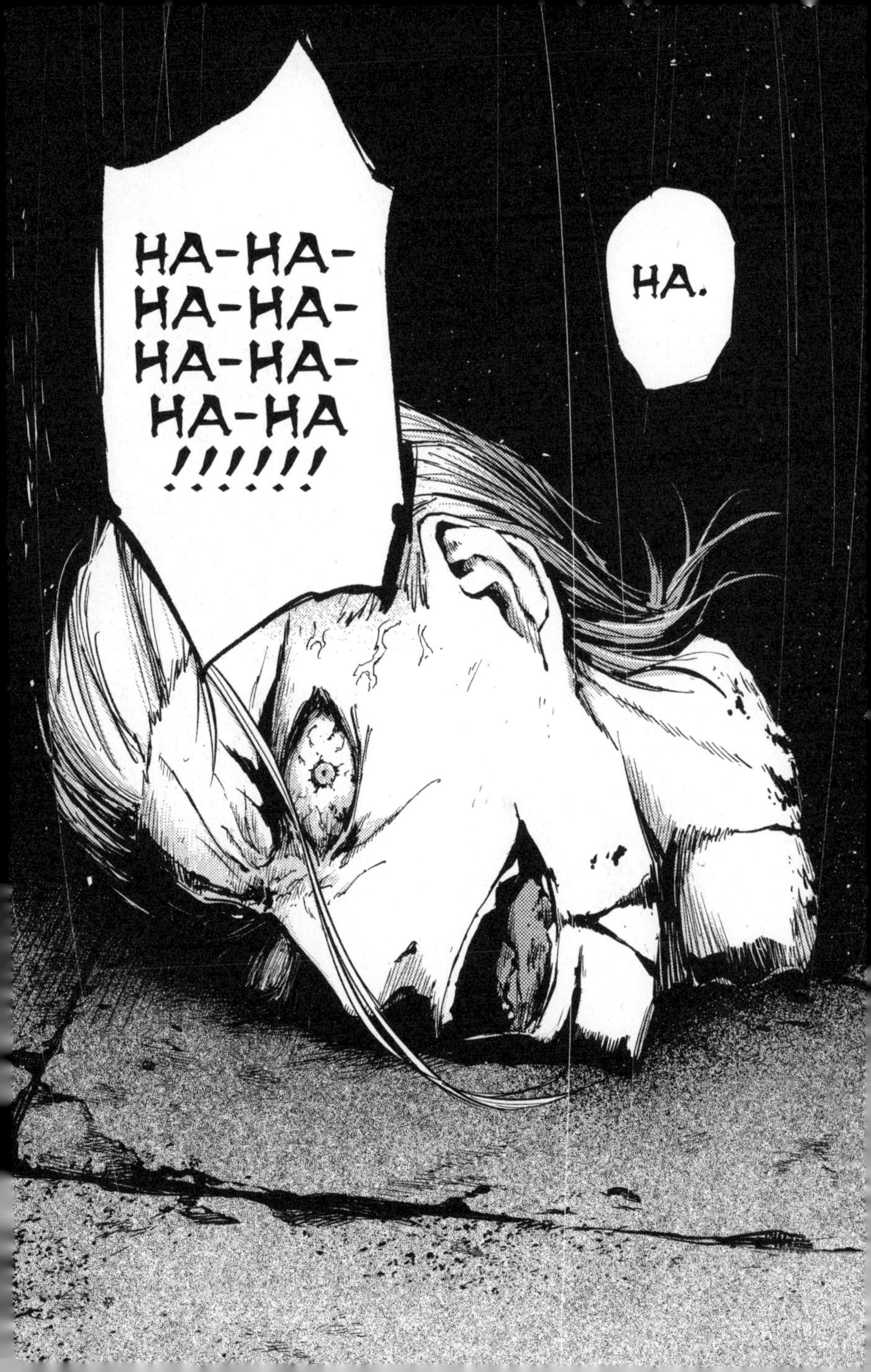
HA.
HA-HA-HA-HA-HA-HA-HA-HA!!!!!!!

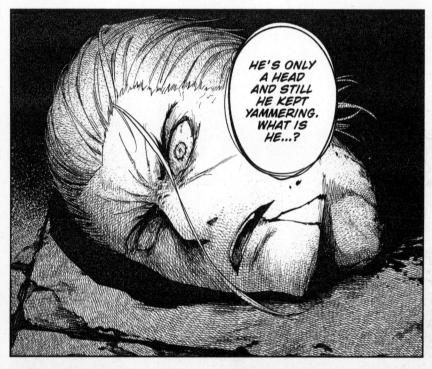

HE'S ONLY
A HEAD
AND STILL
HE KEPT
YAMMERING.
WHAT IS
HE...?

PON
(PAT)

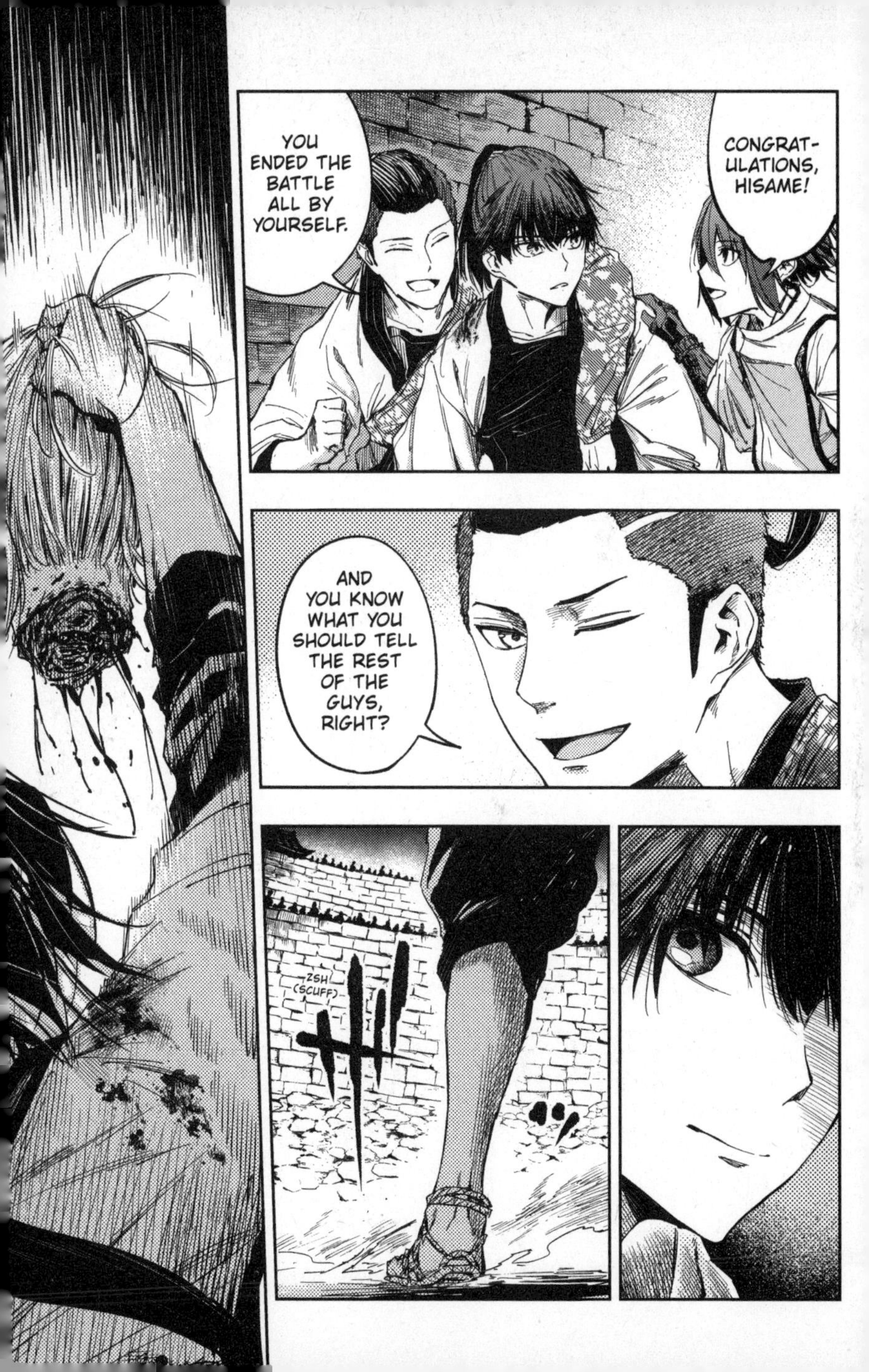
CONGRAT-ULATIONS, HISAME!
YOU ENDED THE BATTLE ALL BY YOURSELF.
AND YOU KNOW WHAT YOU SHOULD TELL THE REST OF THE GUYS, RIGHT?
ZSH (SCUFF)

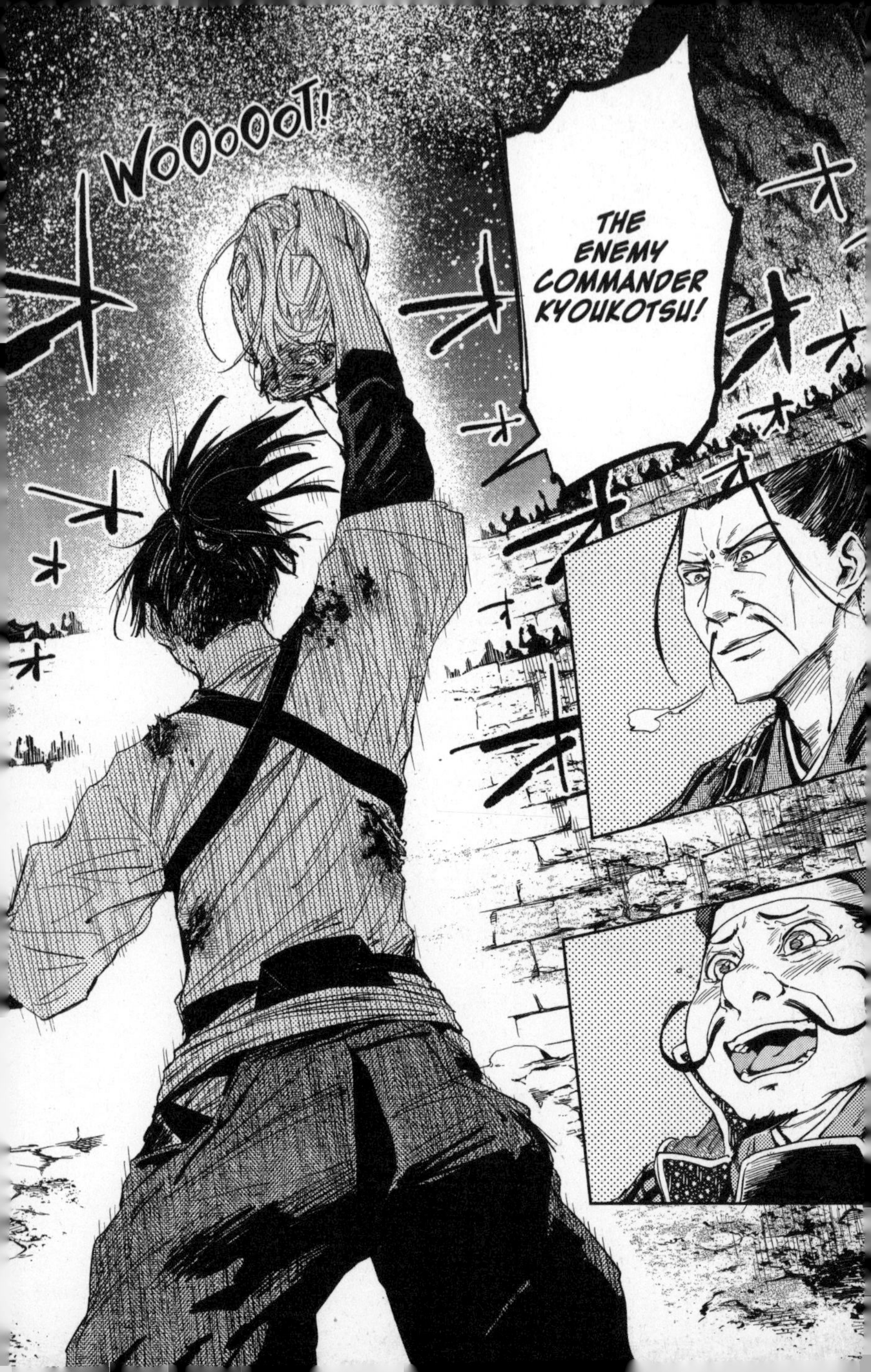
THE ENEMY COMMANDER KYOUKOTSU!
WOOOOOT!

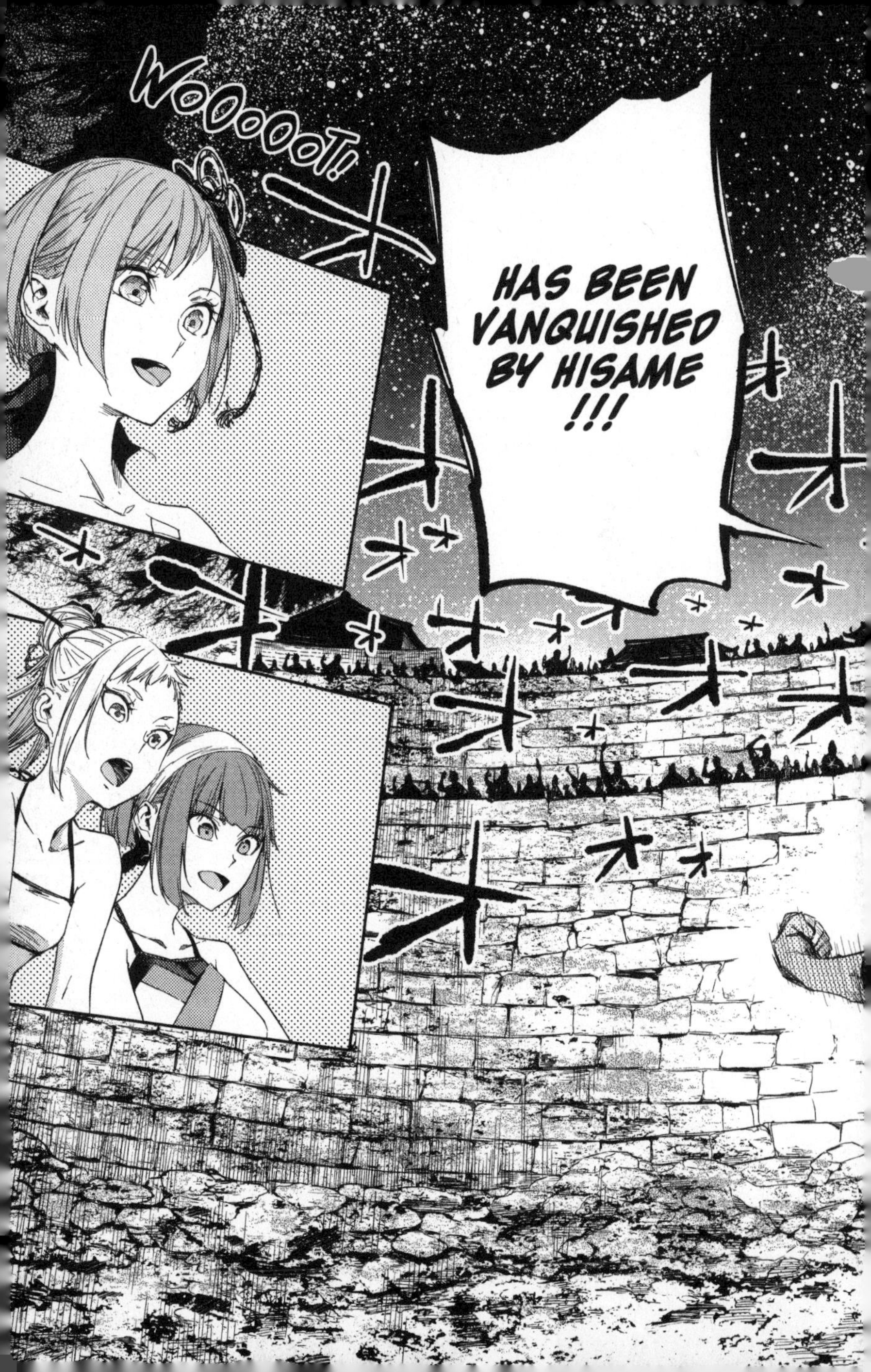
HAS BEEN VANQUISHED BY HISAME !!!
WOOOOOOT!

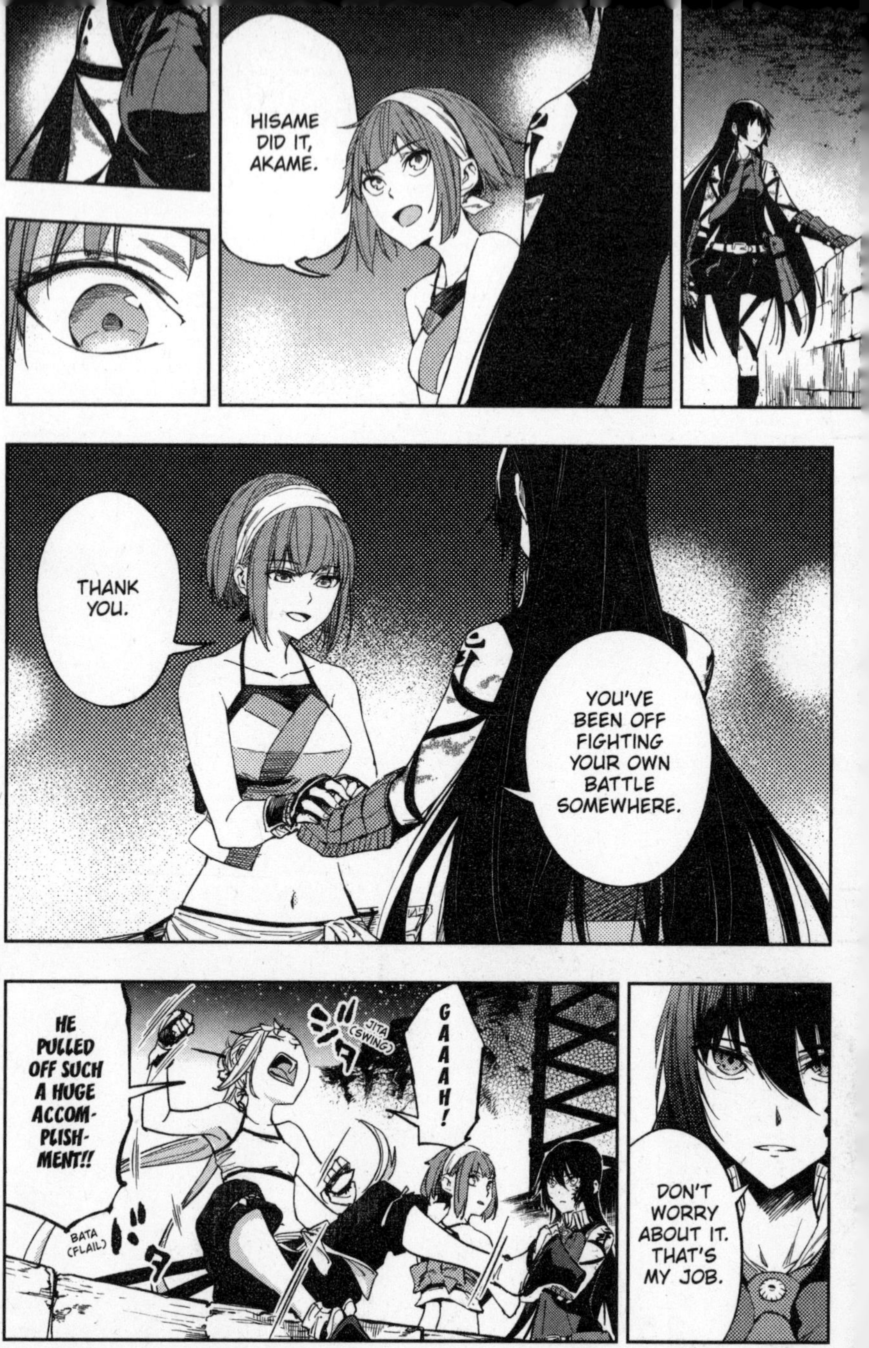
HISAME DID IT, AKAME.
THANK YOU.
YOU'VE BEEN OFF FIGHTING YOUR OWN BATTLE SOMEWHERE.
DON'T WORRY ABOUT IT. THAT'S MY JOB.
GAAAH!
JITA (SWING)
HE PULLED OFF SUCH A HUGE ACCOM-PLISH-MENT!!
BATA (FLAIL)

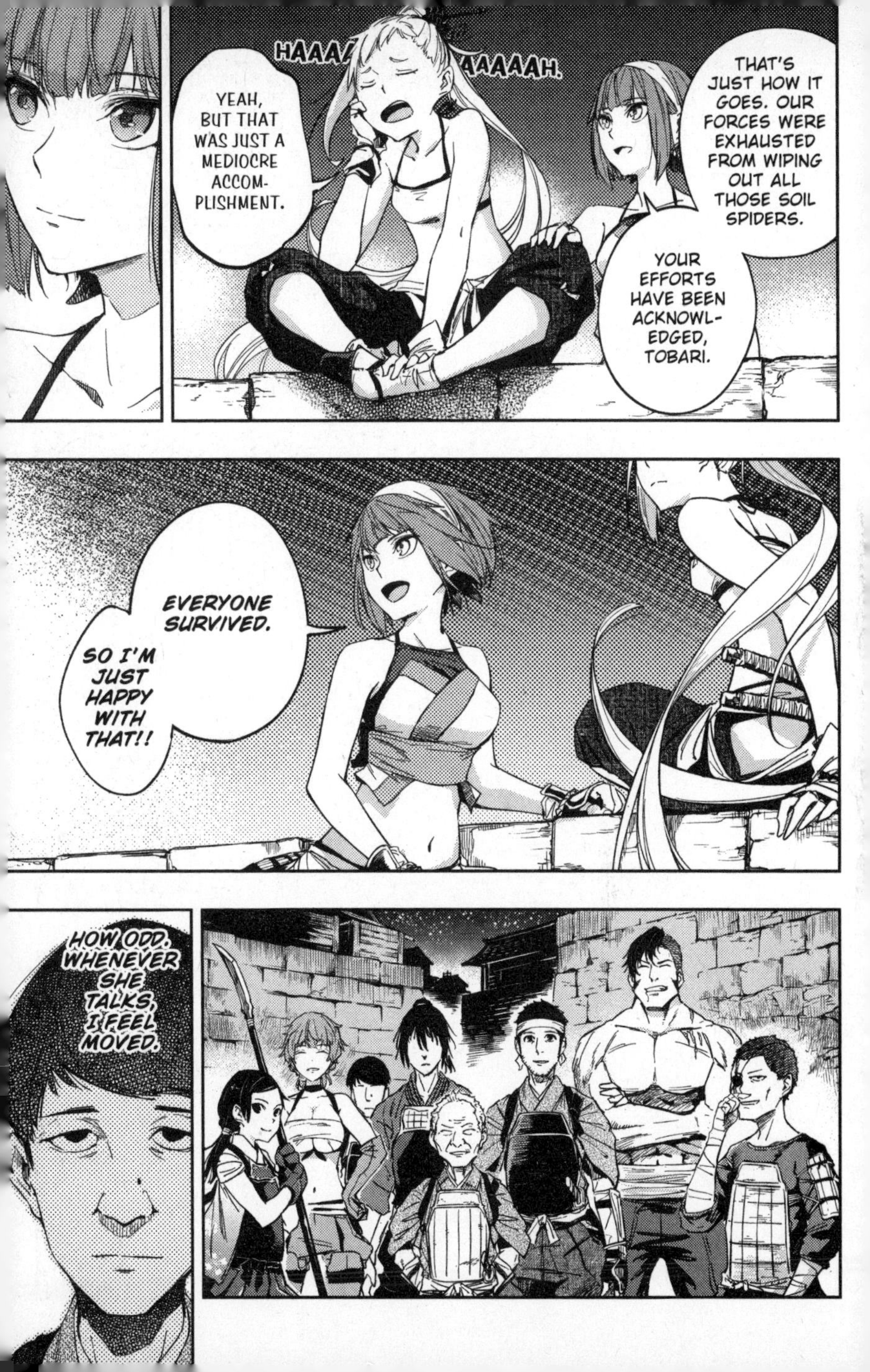
THAT'S JUST HOW IT GOES. OUR FORCES WERE EXHAUSTED FROM WIPING OUT ALL THOSE SOIL SPIDERS.
HAAAA AAAAAH.
YEAH, BUT THAT WAS JUST A MEDIOCRE ACCOM-PLISHMENT.
YOUR EFFORTS HAVE BEEN ACKNOWL-EDGED, TOBARI.
EVERYONE SURVIVED.
SO I'M JUST HAPPY WITH THAT!!
HOW ODD. WHENEVER SHE TALKS, I FEEL MOVED.

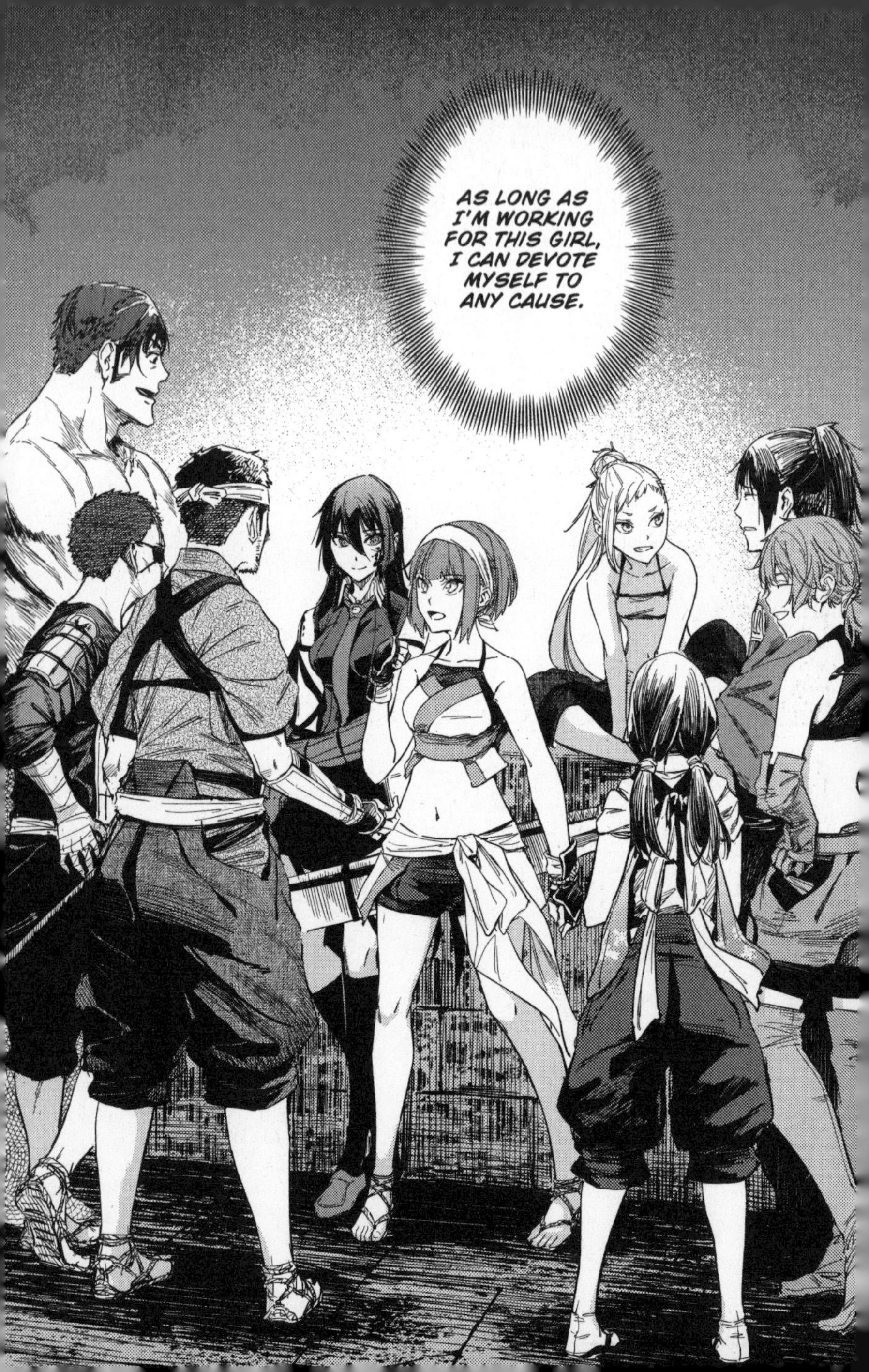
AS LONG AS I'M WORKING FOR THIS GIRL, I CAN DEVOTE MYSELF TO ANY CAUSE.

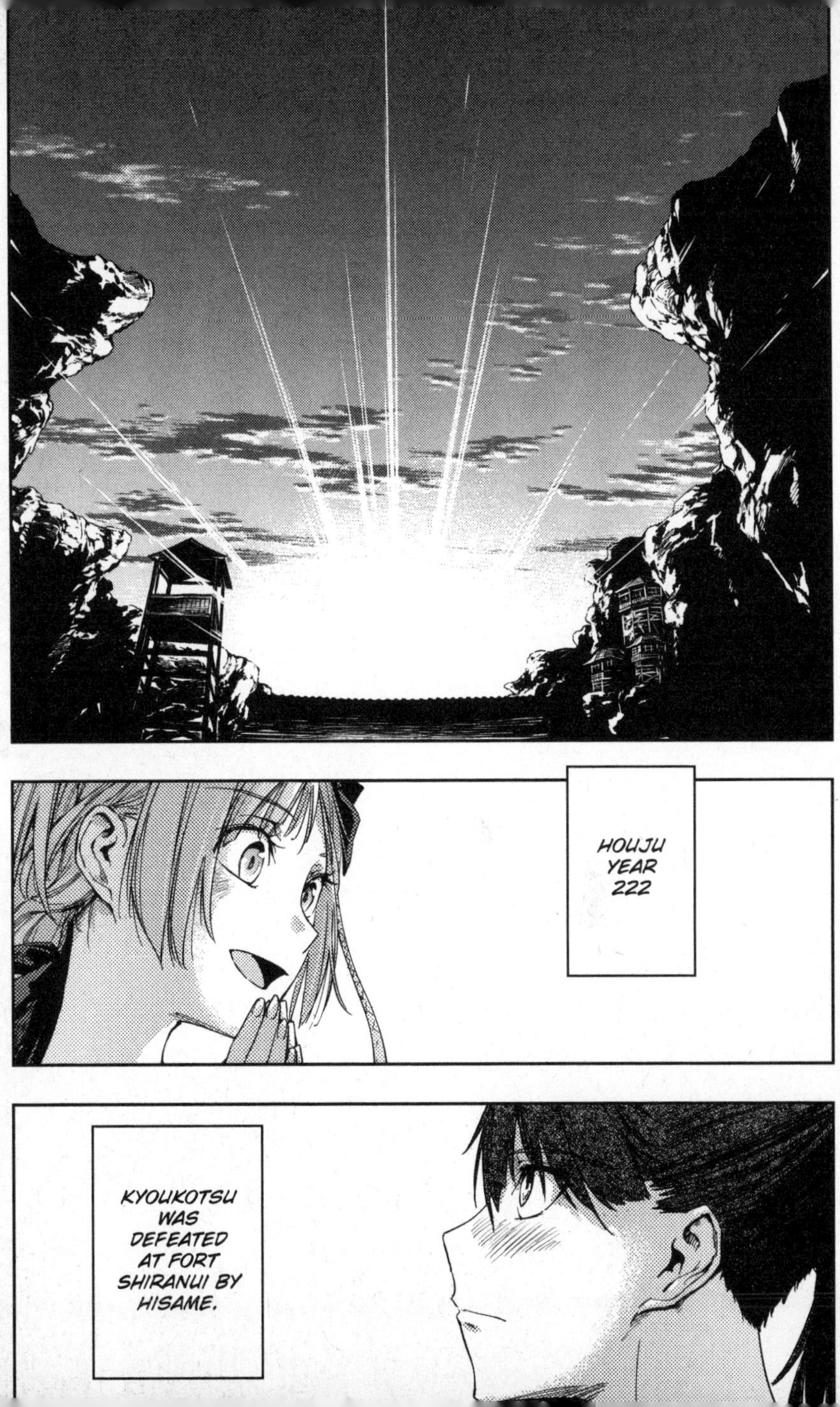
HOUJU YEAR 222
KYOUKOTSU WAS DEFEATED AT FORT SHIRANUI BY HISAME.

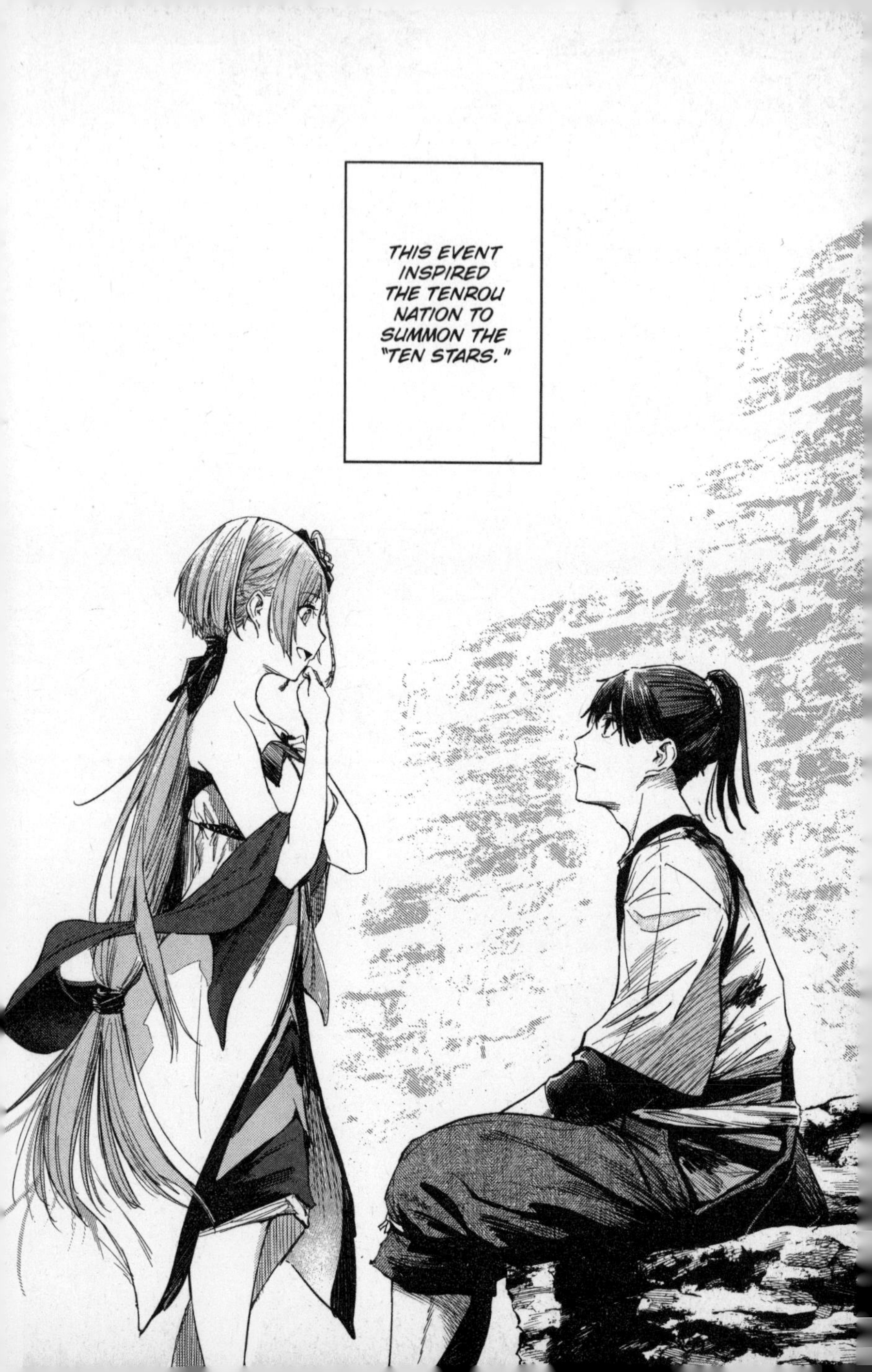
THIS EVENT INSPIRED THE TENROU NATION TO SUMMON THE "TEN STARS."

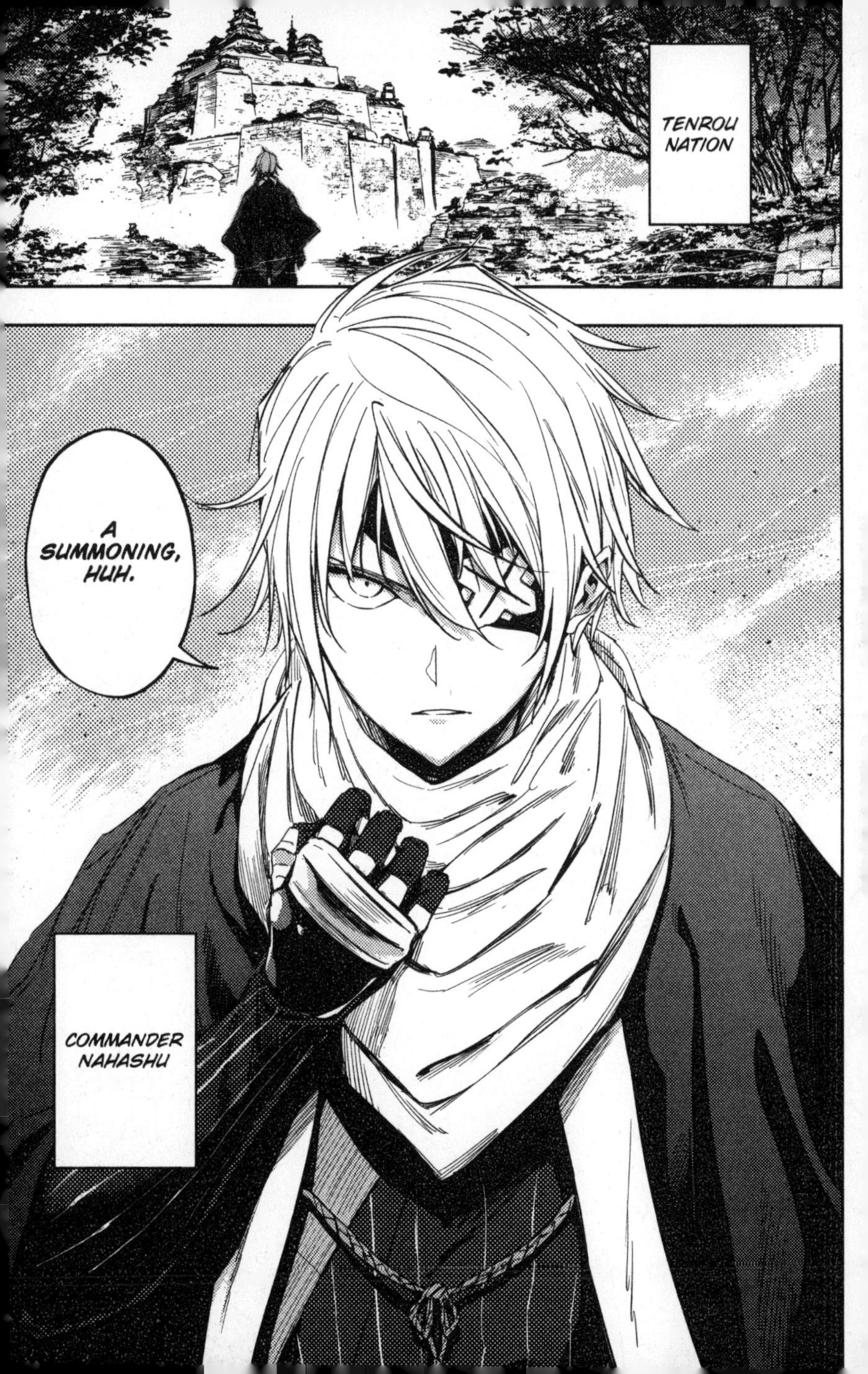
TENROU NATION
A SUMMONING, HUH.
COMMANDER NAHASHU

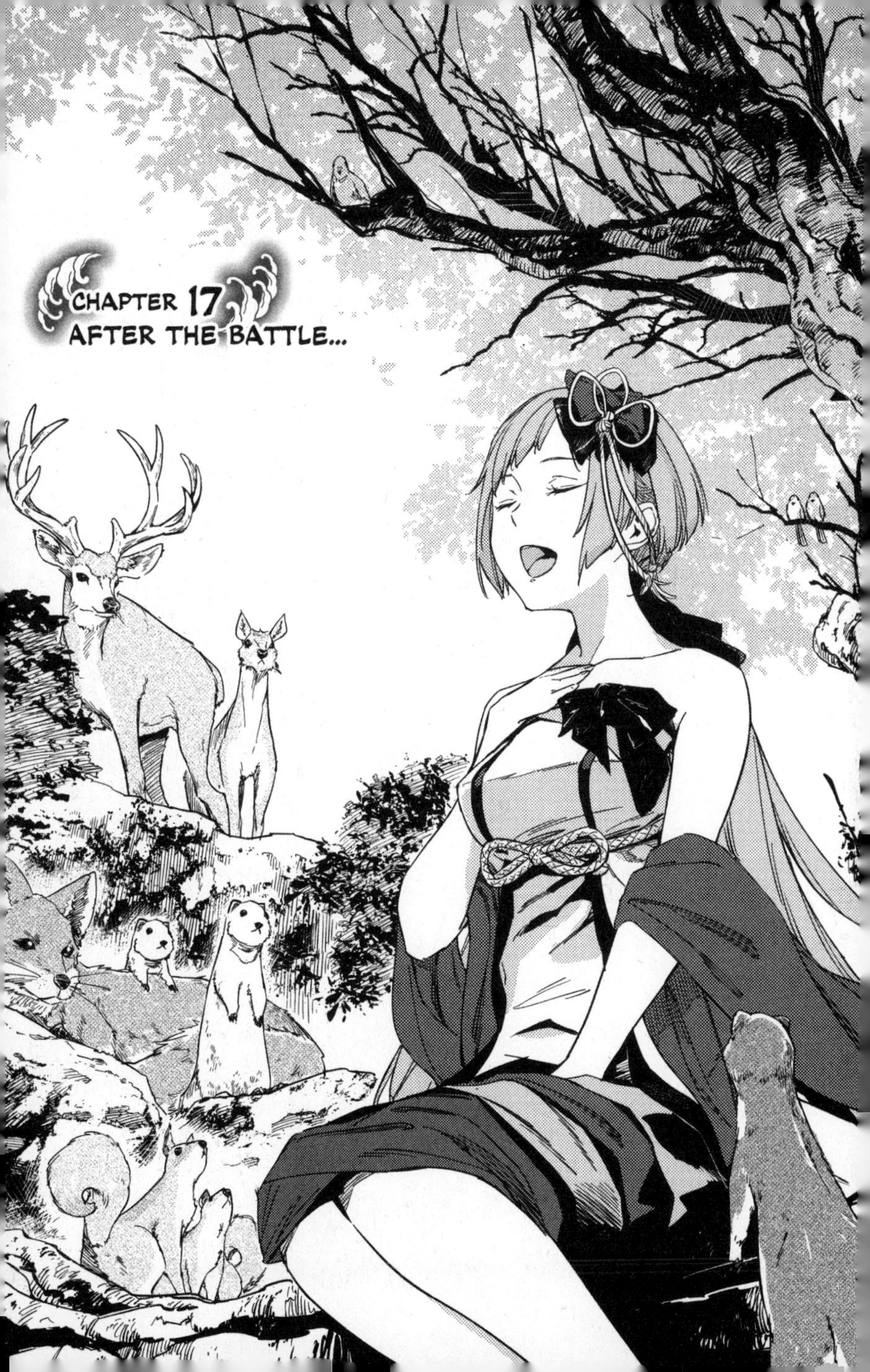
CHAPTER 17
AFTER THE BATTLE...

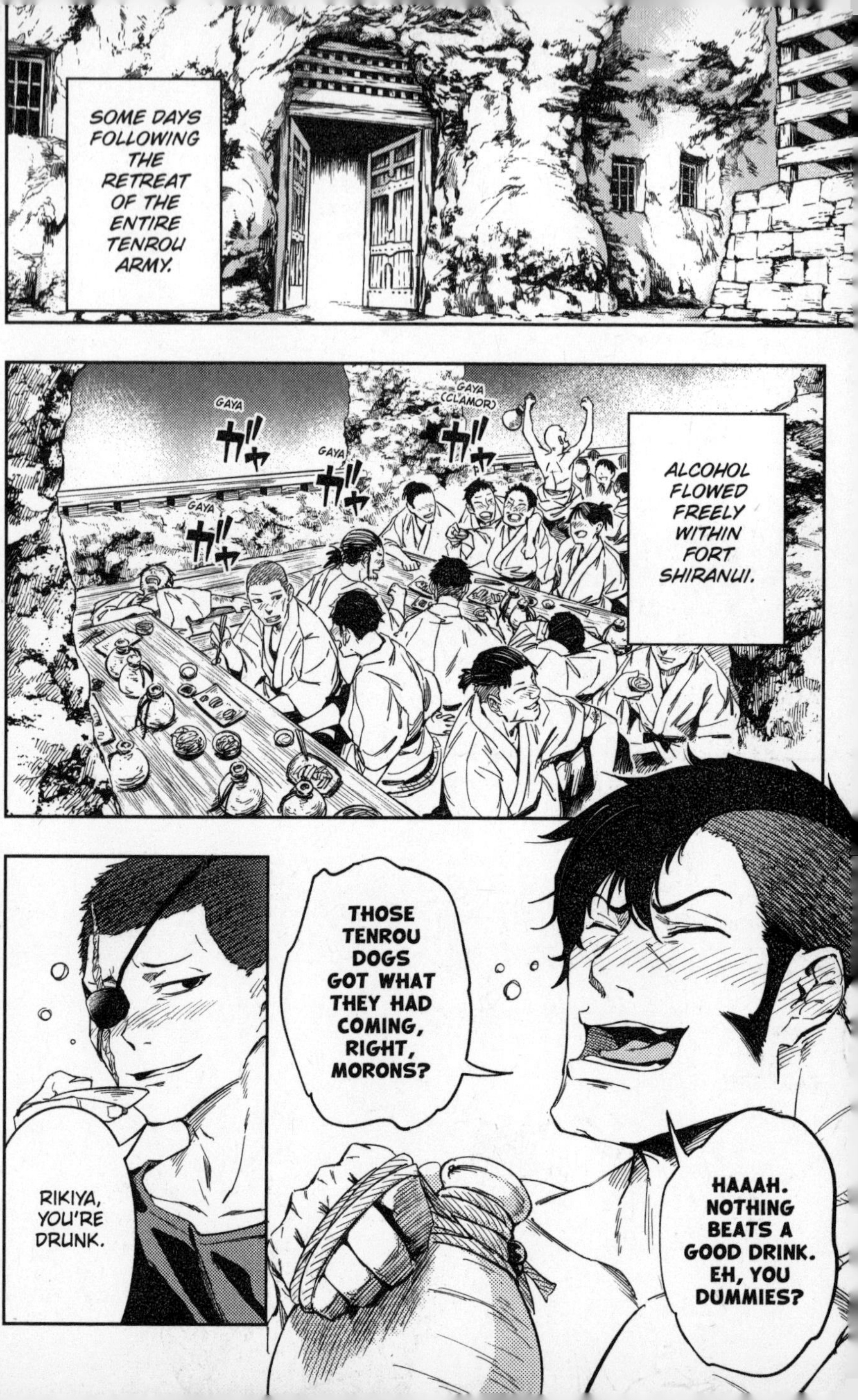
SOME DAYS FOLLOWING THE RETREAT OF THE ENTIRE TENROU ARMY.
ALCOHOL FLOWED FREELY WITHIN FORT SHIRANUI.
GAYA (CLAMOR)
ガヤ
GAYA
ガヤ
GAYA
ガヤ
GAYA
ガヤ
THOSE TENROU DOGS GOT WHAT THEY HAD COMING, RIGHT, MORONS?
HAAAH. NOTHING BEATS A GOOD DRINK. EH, YOU DUMMIES?
RIKIYA, YOU'RE DRUNK.

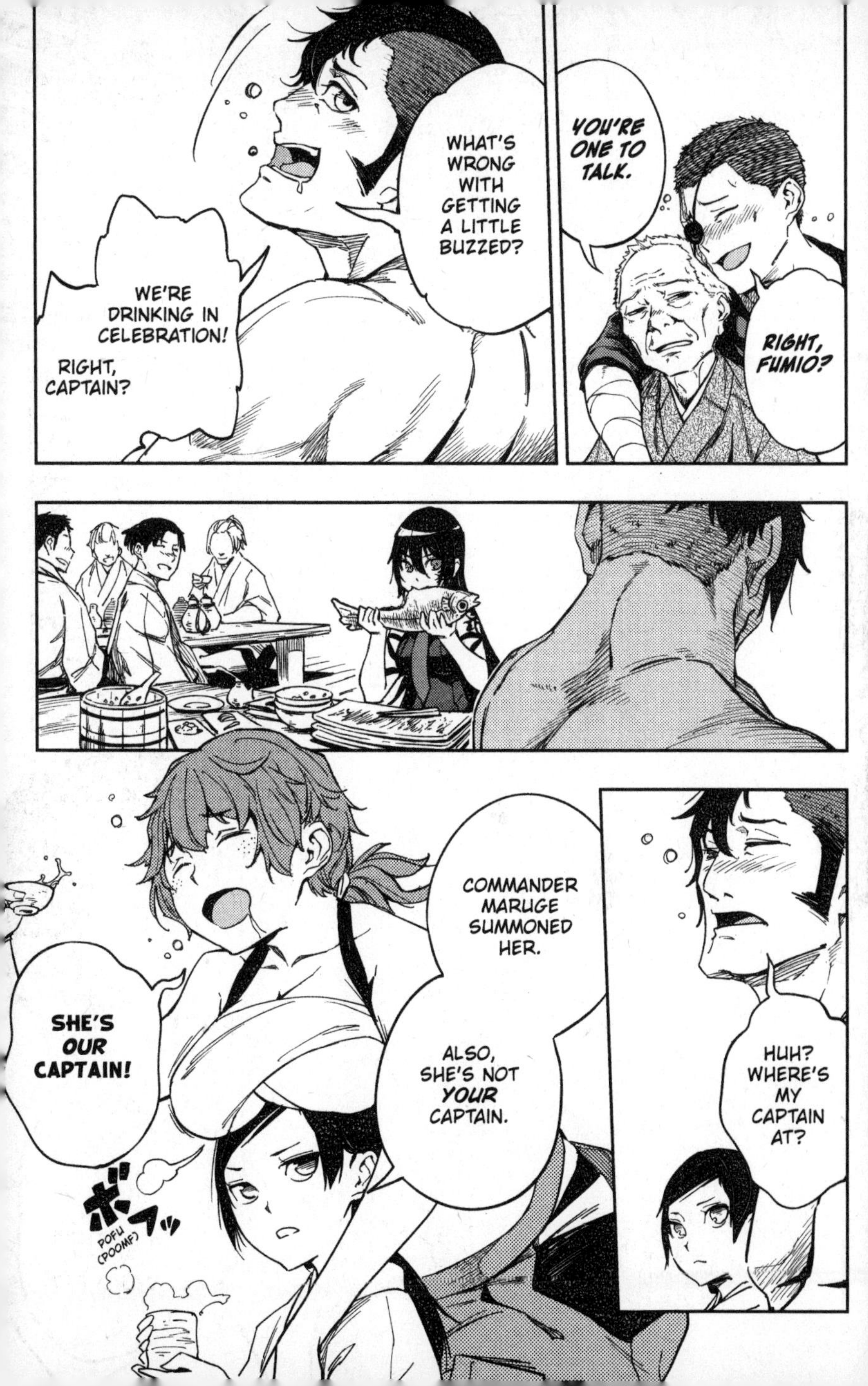
YOU'RE ONE TO TALK.
RIGHT, FUMIO?
WHAT'S WRONG WITH GETTING A LITTLE BUZZED?
WE'RE DRINKING IN CELEBRATION!
RIGHT, CAPTAIN?
HUH? WHERE'S MY CAPTAIN AT?
COMMANDER MARUGE SUMMONED HER.
ALSO, SHE'S NOT *YOUR* CAPTAIN.
SHE'S *OUR* CAPTAIN!
ボフッ
POFU (POOMF)

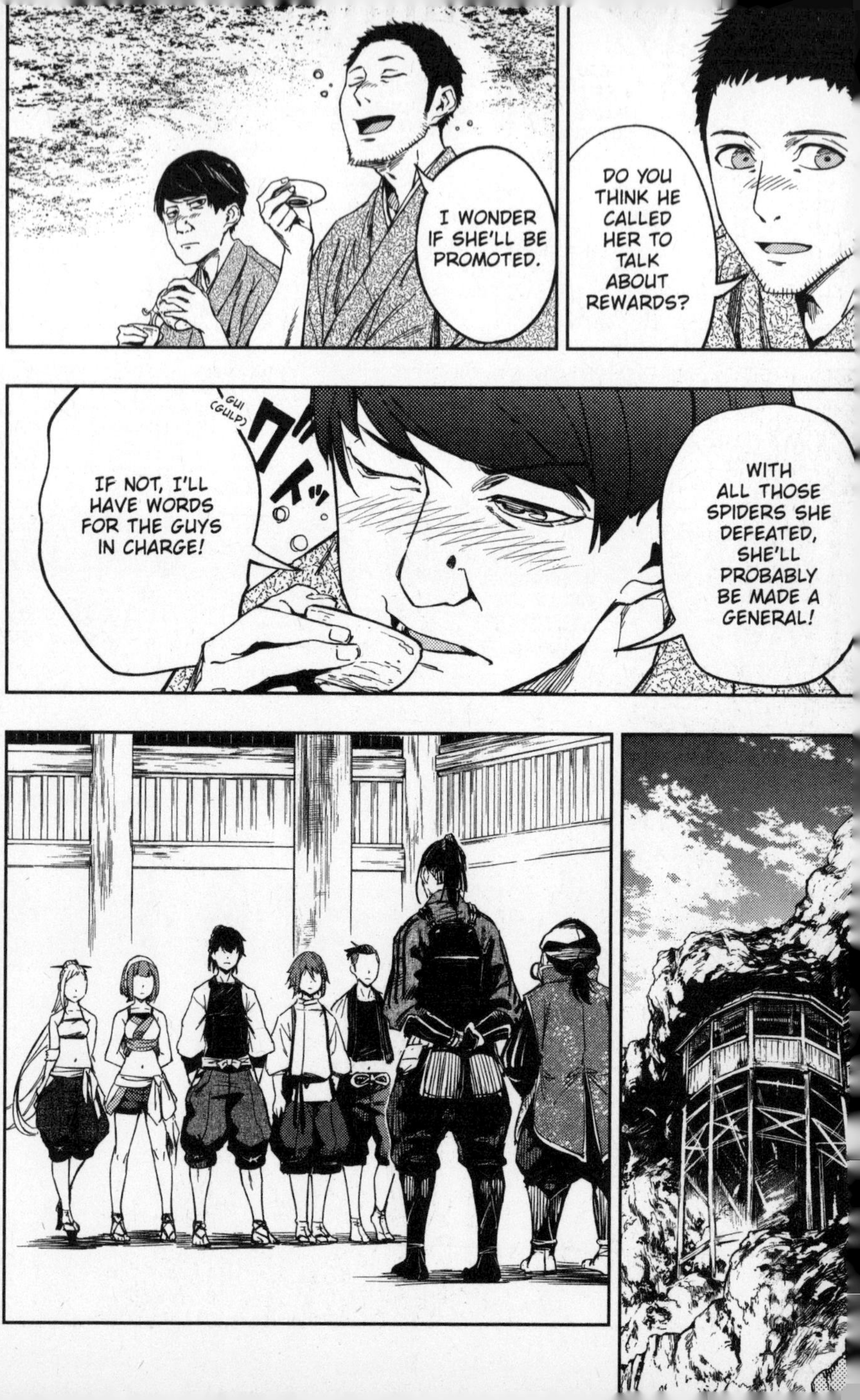
DO YOU THINK HE CALLED HER TO TALK ABOUT REWARDS?
I WONDER IF SHE'LL BE PROMOTED.
WITH ALL THOSE SPIDERS SHE DEFEATED, SHE'LL PROBABLY BE MADE A GENERAL!
GUI (GULP)
IF NOT, I'LL HAVE WORDS FOR THE GUYS IN CHARGE!

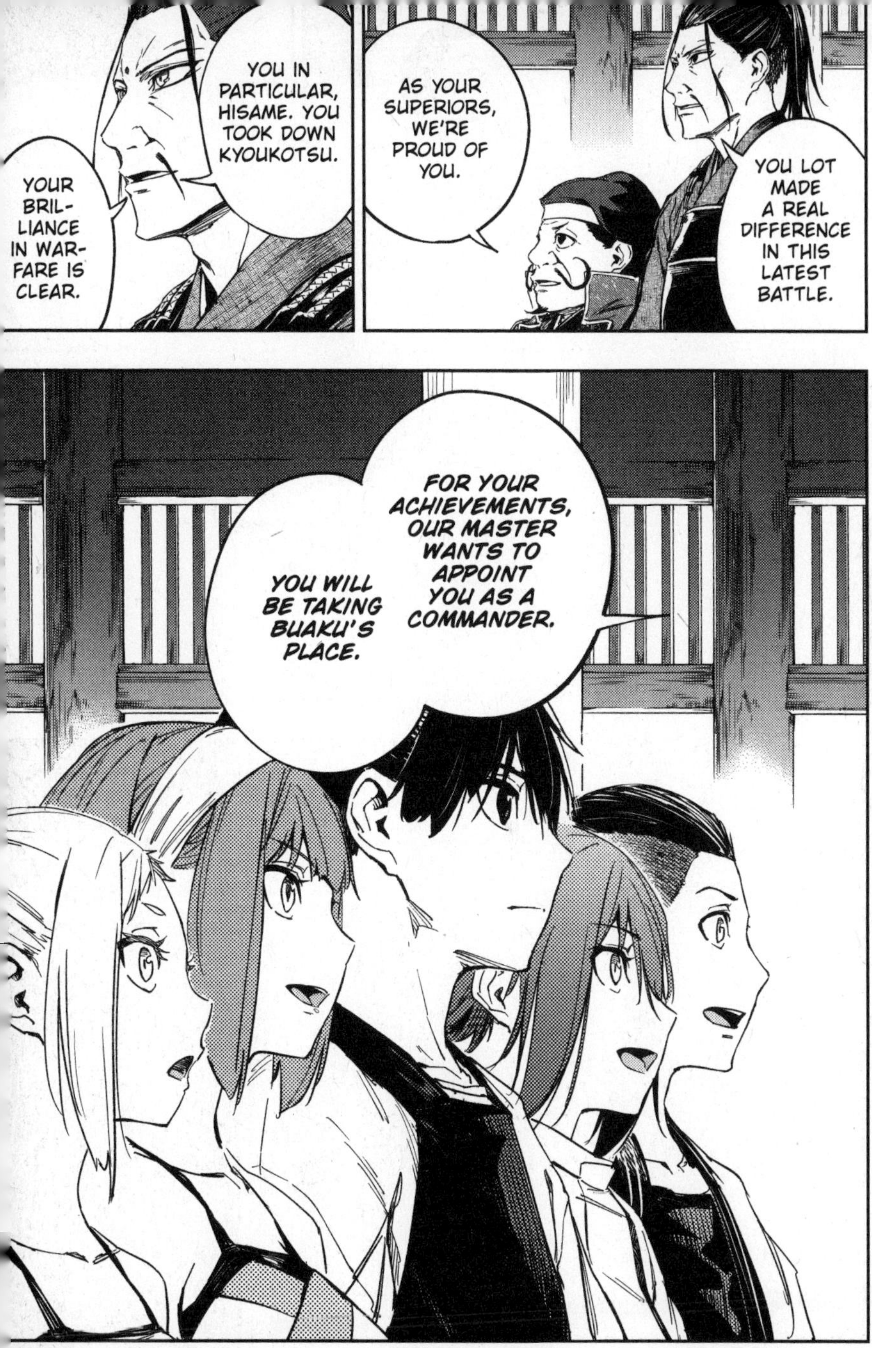
YOU LOT MADE A REAL DIFFERENCE IN THIS LATEST BATTLE.
AS YOUR SUPERIORS, WE'RE PROUD OF YOU.
YOU IN PARTICULAR, HISAME. YOU TOOK DOWN KYOUKOTSU.
YOUR BRILLIANCE IN WARFARE IS CLEAR.
FOR YOUR ACHIEVEMENTS, OUR MASTER WANTS TO APPOINT YOU AS A COMMANDER.
YOU WILL BE TAKING BUAKU'S PLACE.

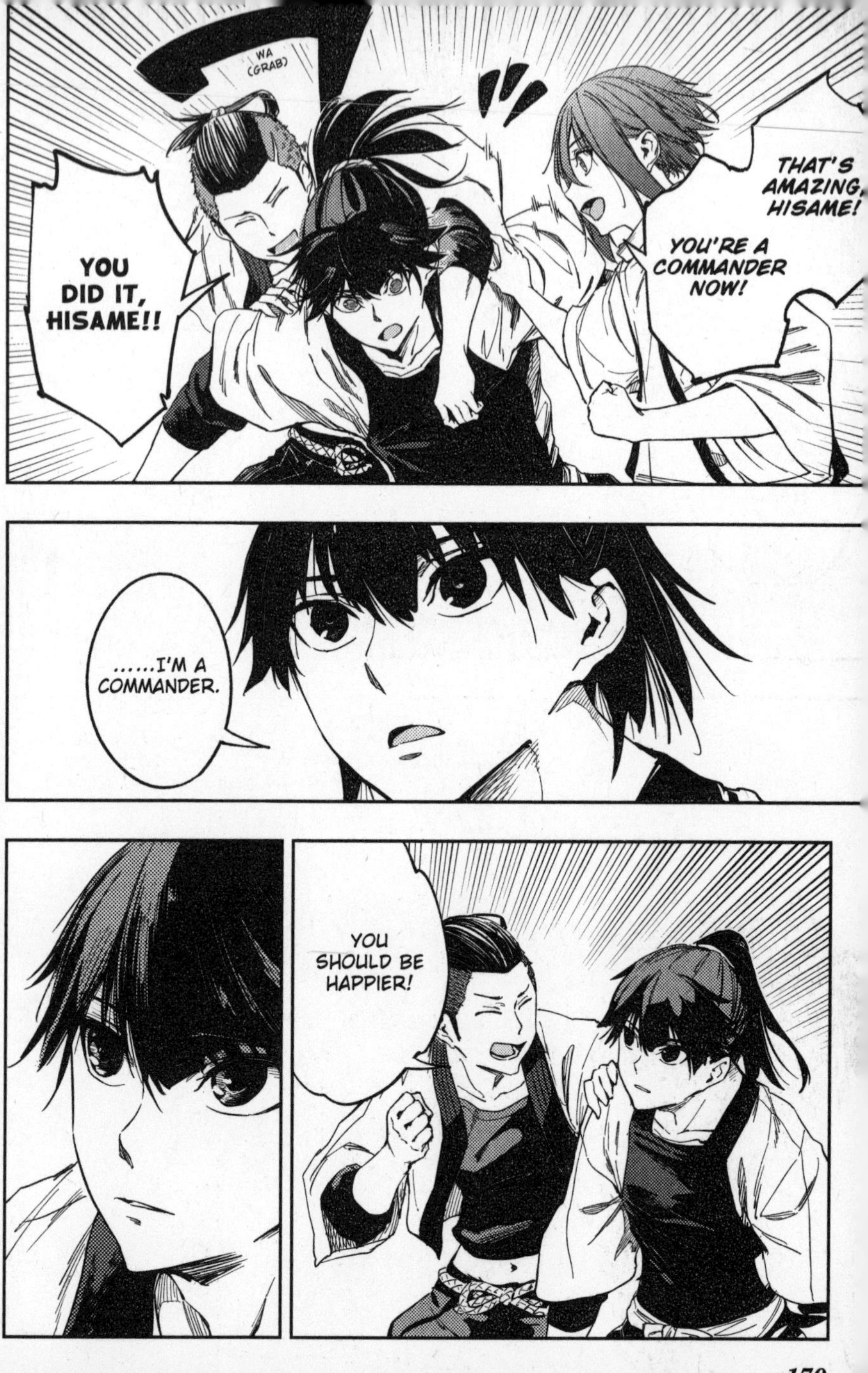
THAT'S AMAZING, HISAME!
YOU'RE A COMMANDER NOW!
WA (GRAB)
YOU DID IT, HISAME!!
......I'M A COMMANDER.
YOU SHOULD BE HAPPIER!

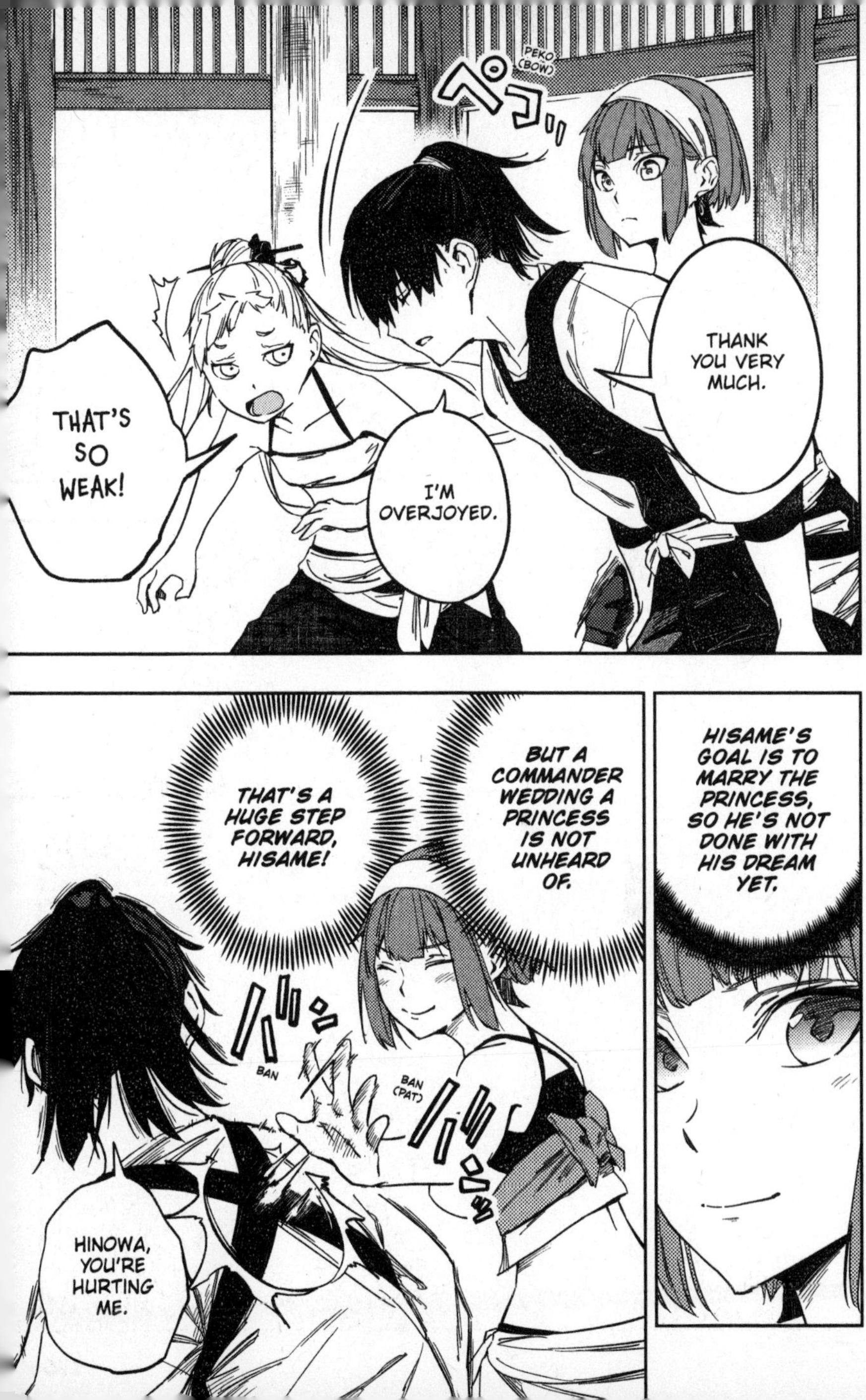
PEKO (BOW)
THANK YOU VERY MUCH.
I'M OVERJOYED.
THAT'S SO WEAK!
HISAME'S GOAL IS TO MARRY THE PRINCESS, SO HE'S NOT DONE WITH HIS DREAM YET.
BUT A COMMANDER WEDDING A PRINCESS IS NOT UNHEARD OF.
THAT'S A HUGE STEP FORWARD, HISAME!
BAN (PAT)
BAN
HINOWA, YOU'RE HURTING ME.

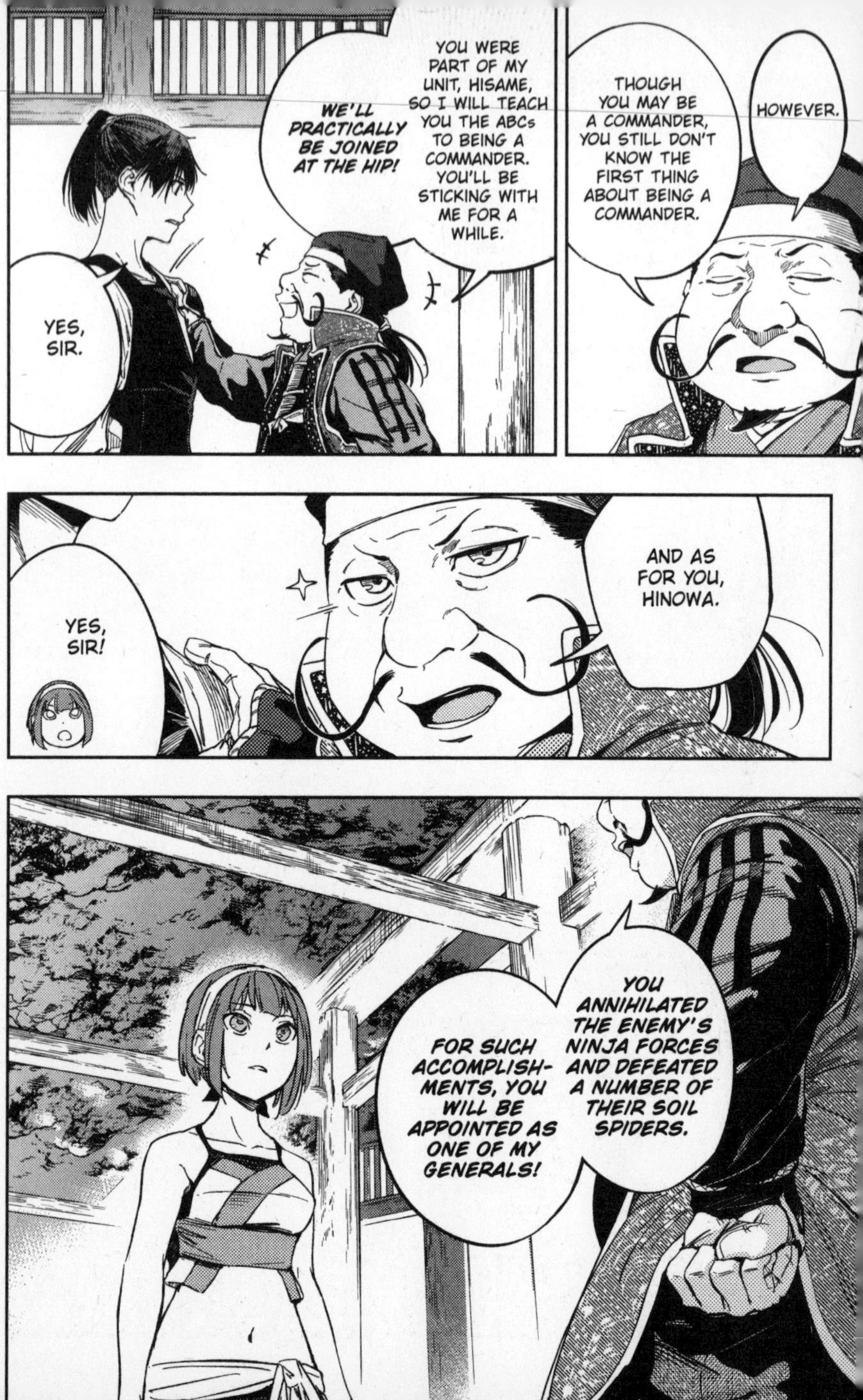
HOWEVER.
THOUGH YOU MAY BE A COMMANDER, YOU STILL DON'T KNOW THE FIRST THING ABOUT BEING A COMMANDER.
YOU WERE PART OF MY UNIT, HISAME, SO I WILL TEACH YOU THE ABCs TO BEING A COMMANDER. YOU'LL BE STICKING WITH ME FOR A WHILE.
WE'LL PRACTICALLY BE JOINED AT THE HIP!
YES, SIR.
AND AS FOR YOU, HINOWA.
YES, SIR!
YOU ANNIHILATED THE ENEMY'S NINJA FORCES AND DEFEATED A NUMBER OF THEIR SOIL SPIDERS.
FOR SUCH ACCOMPLISHMENTS, YOU WILL BE APPOINTED AS ONE OF MY GENERALS!

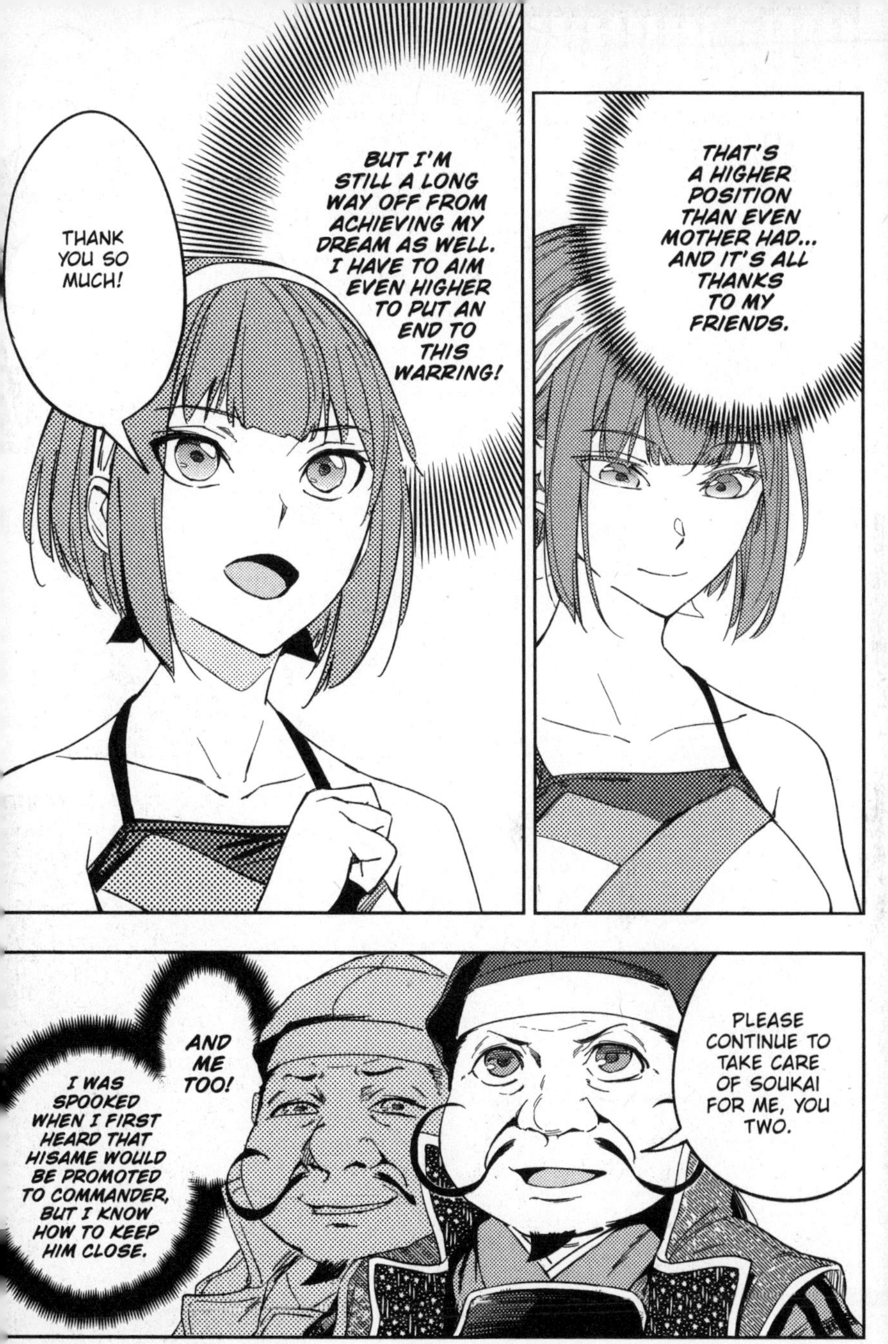
THAT'S A HIGHER POSITION THAN EVEN MOTHER HAD... AND IT'S ALL THANKS TO MY FRIENDS.
BUT I'M STILL A LONG WAY OFF FROM ACHIEVING MY DREAM AS WELL. I HAVE TO AIM EVEN HIGHER TO PUT AN END TO THIS WARRING!
THANK YOU SO MUCH!
PLEASE CONTINUE TO TAKE CARE OF SOUKAI FOR ME, YOU TWO.
AND ME TOO!
I WAS SPOOKED WHEN I FIRST HEARD THAT HISAME WOULD BE PROMOTED TO COMMANDER, BUT I KNOW HOW TO KEEP HIM CLOSE.

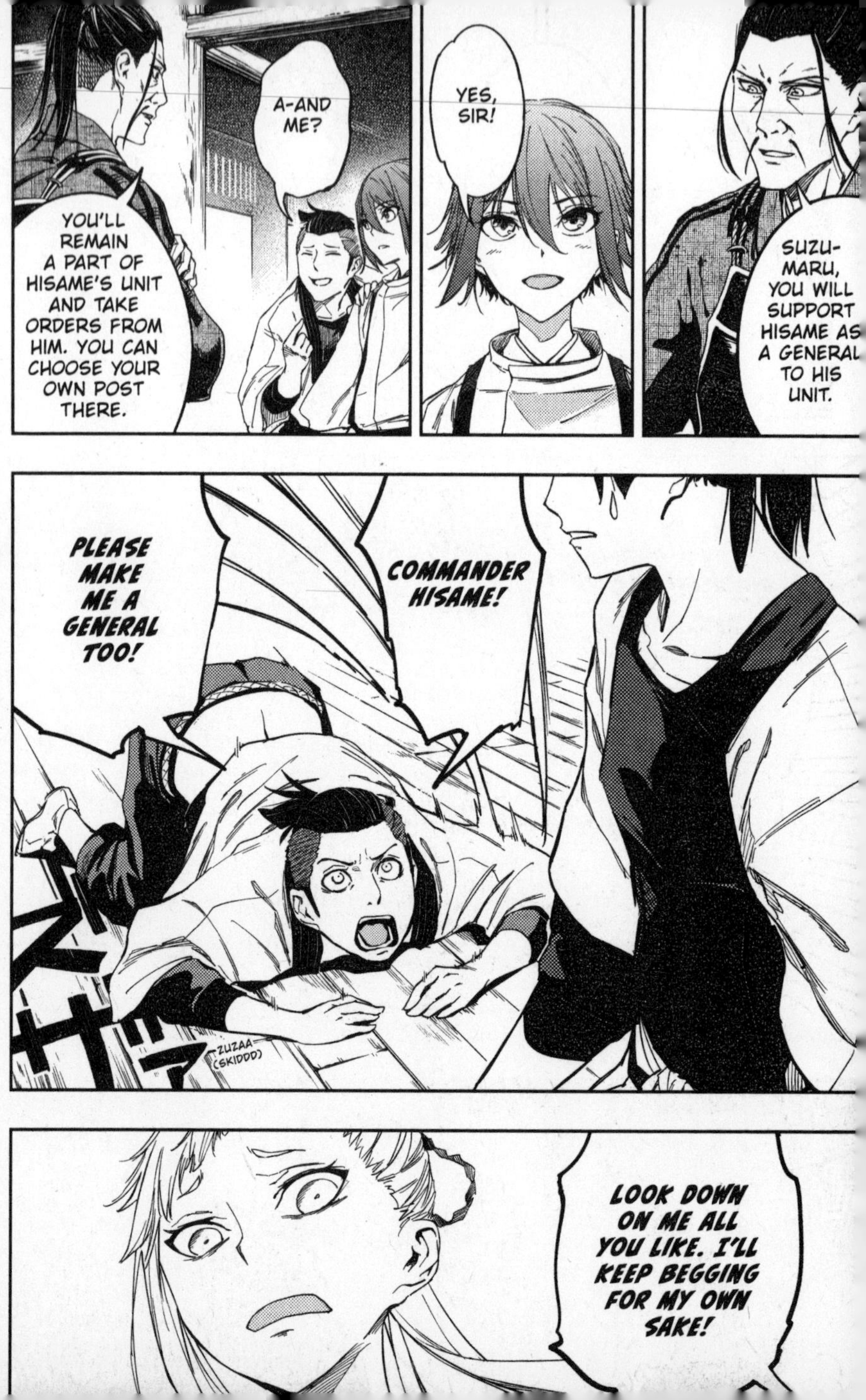
SUZU-MARU, YOU WILL SUPPORT HISAME AS A GENERAL TO HIS UNIT.
YES, SIR!
A-AND ME?
YOU'LL REMAIN A PART OF HISAME'S UNIT AND TAKE ORDERS FROM HIM. YOU CAN CHOOSE YOUR OWN POST THERE.
COMMANDER HISAME!
PLEASE MAKE ME A GENERAL TOO!
ZUZAA (SKIDDD)
LOOK DOWN ON ME ALL YOU LIKE. I'LL KEEP BEGGING FOR MY OWN SAKE!

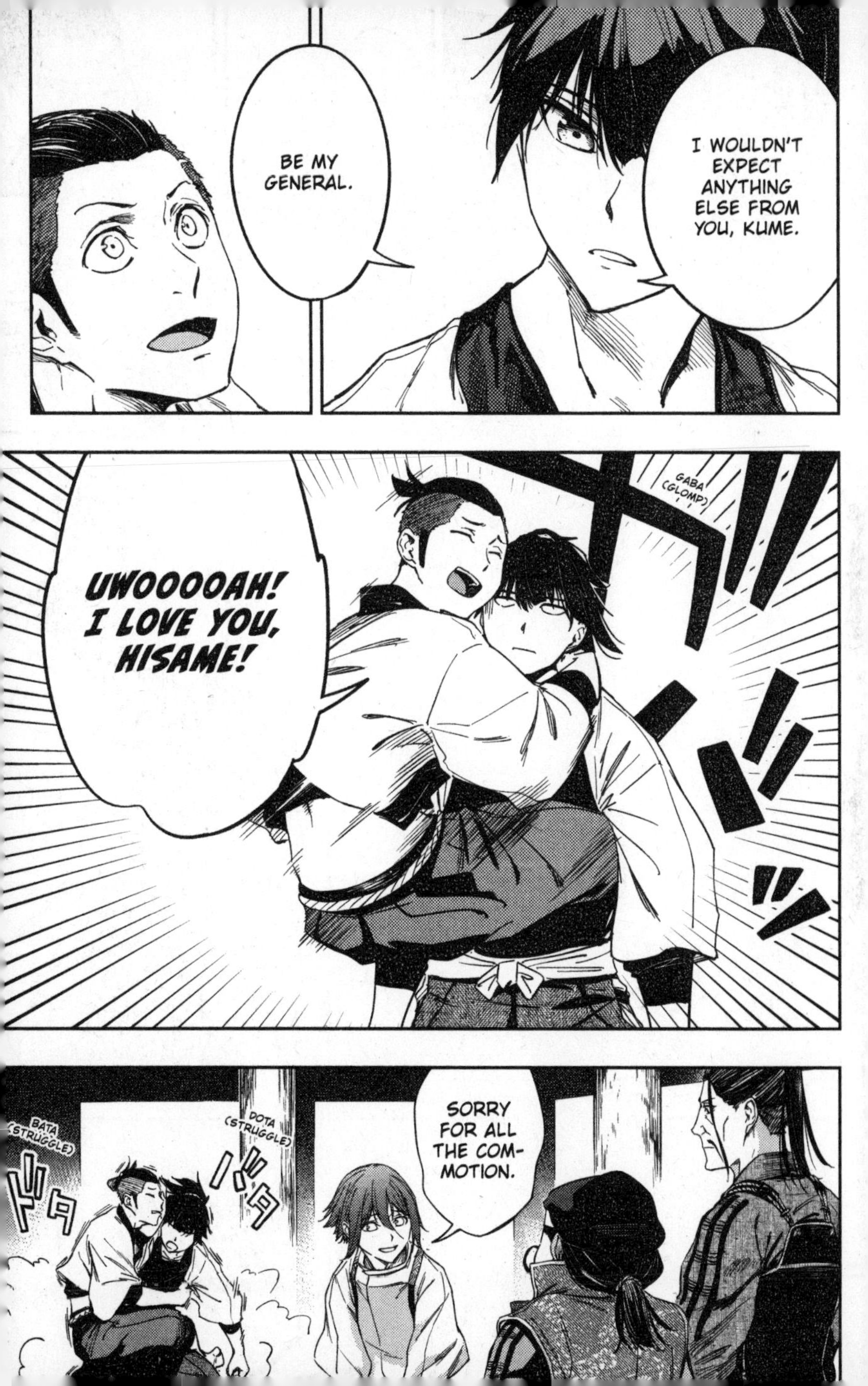
I WOULDN'T EXPECT ANYTHING ELSE FROM YOU, KUME.
BE MY GENERAL.
GABA (GLOMP)
UWOOOOAH! I LOVE YOU, HISAME!
SORRY FOR ALL THE COM-MOTION.
DOTA (STRUGGLE)
BATA (STRUGGLE)

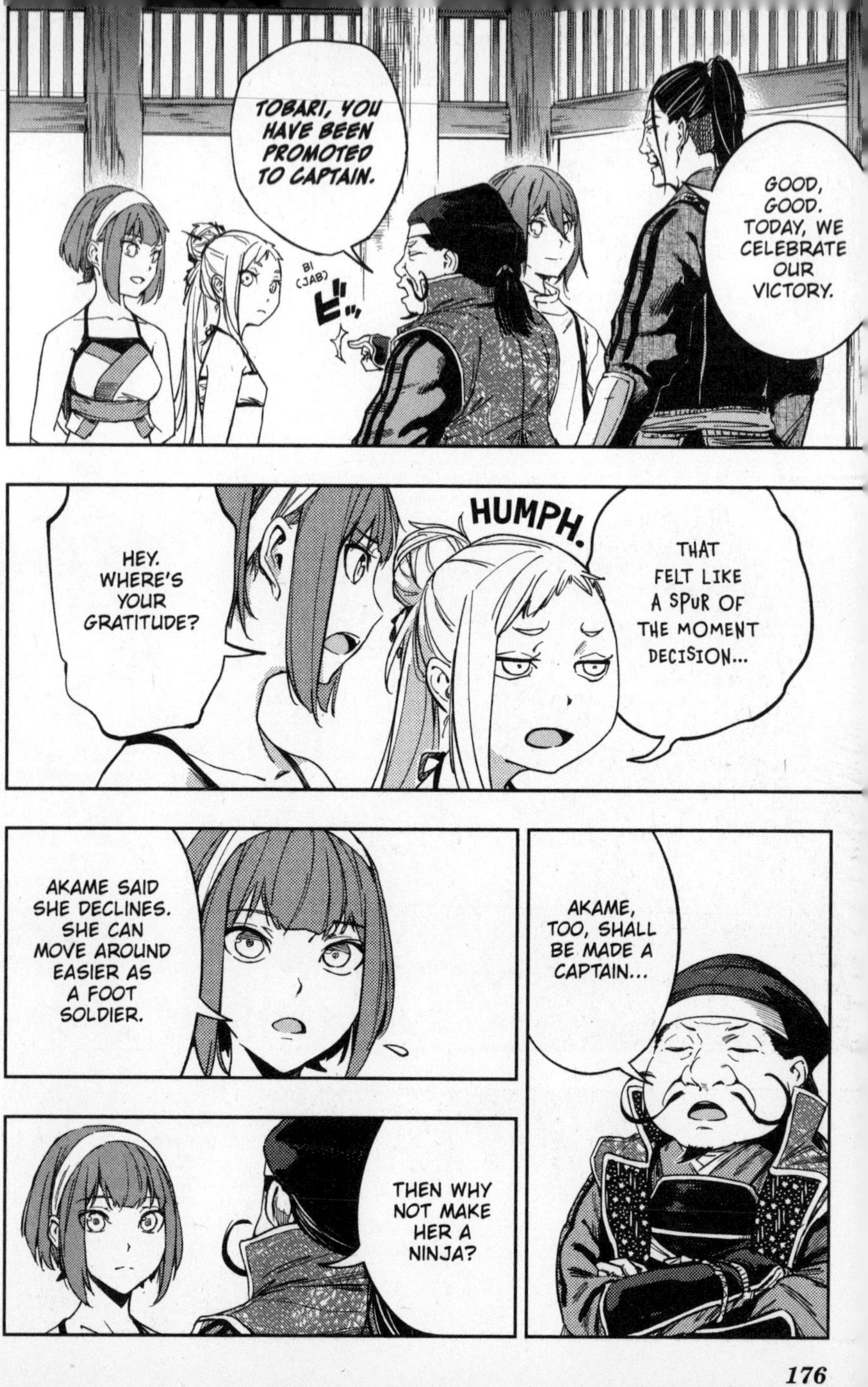
GOOD, GOOD. TODAY, WE CELEBRATE OUR VICTORY.
TOBARI, YOU HAVE BEEN PROMOTED TO CAPTAIN.
BI (JAB)
ビッ
HUMPH.
THAT FELT LIKE A SPUR OF THE MOMENT DECISION...
HEY. WHERE'S YOUR GRATITUDE?
AKAME, TOO, SHALL BE MADE A CAPTAIN...
AKAME SAID SHE DECLINES. SHE CAN MOVE AROUND EASIER AS A FOOT SOLDIER.
THEN WHY NOT MAKE HER A NINJA?

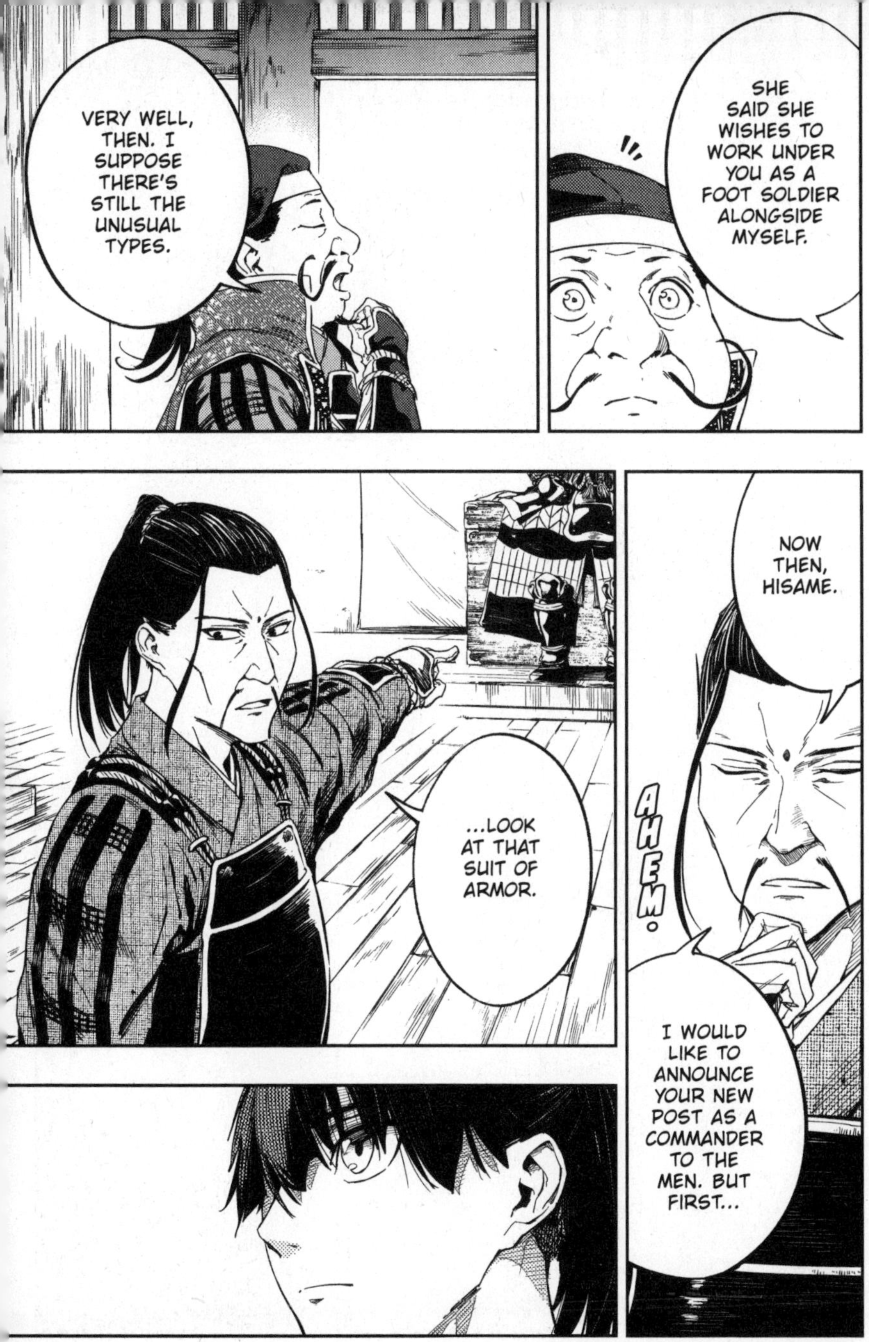
SHE SAID SHE WISHES TO WORK UNDER YOU AS A FOOT SOLDIER ALONGSIDE MYSELF.
VERY WELL, THEN. I SUPPOSE THERE'S STILL THE UNUSUAL TYPES.
NOW THEN, HISAME.
AHEM.
I WOULD LIKE TO ANNOUNCE YOUR NEW POST AS A COMMANDER TO THE MEN. BUT FIRST...
...LOOK AT THAT SUIT OF ARMOR.

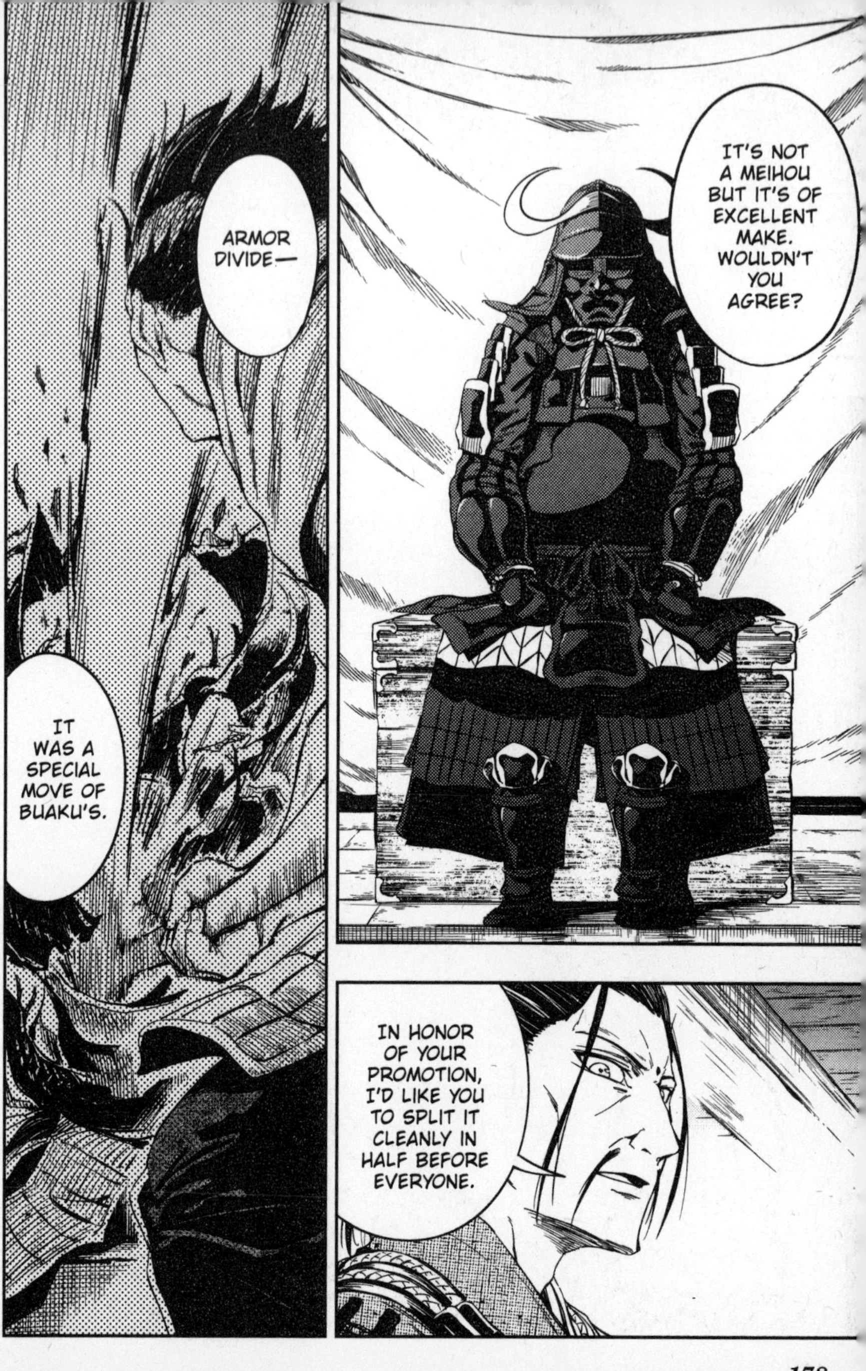
IT'S NOT A MEIHOU BUT IT'S OF EXCELLENT MAKE. WOULDN'T YOU AGREE?
IN HONOR OF YOUR PROMOTION, I'D LIKE YOU TO SPLIT IT CLEANLY IN HALF BEFORE EVERYONE.
ARMOR DIVIDE—
IT WAS A SPECIAL MOVE OF BUAKU'S.

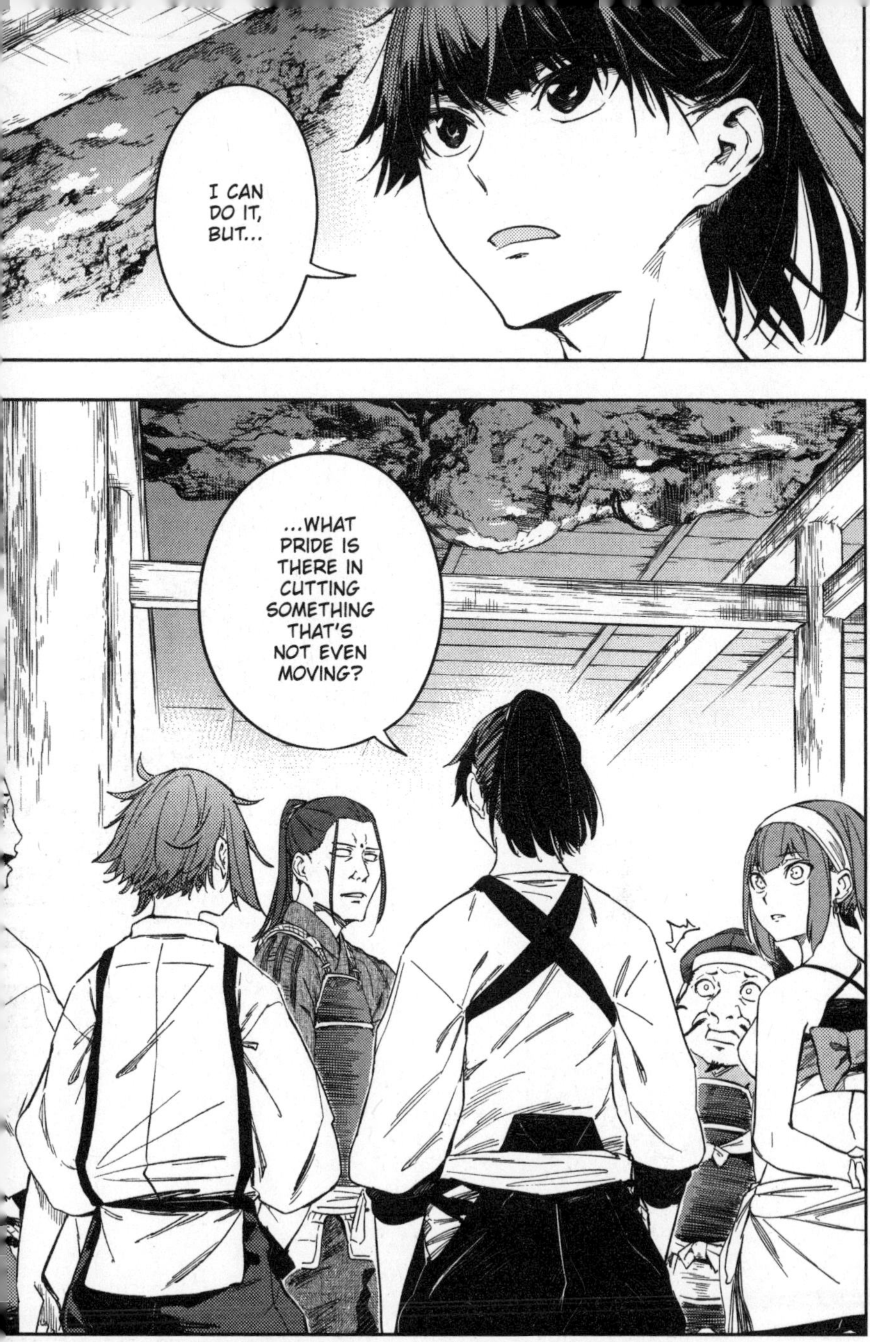
I CAN DO IT, BUT...
...WHAT PRIDE IS THERE IN CUTTING SOMETHING THAT'S NOT EVEN MOVING?

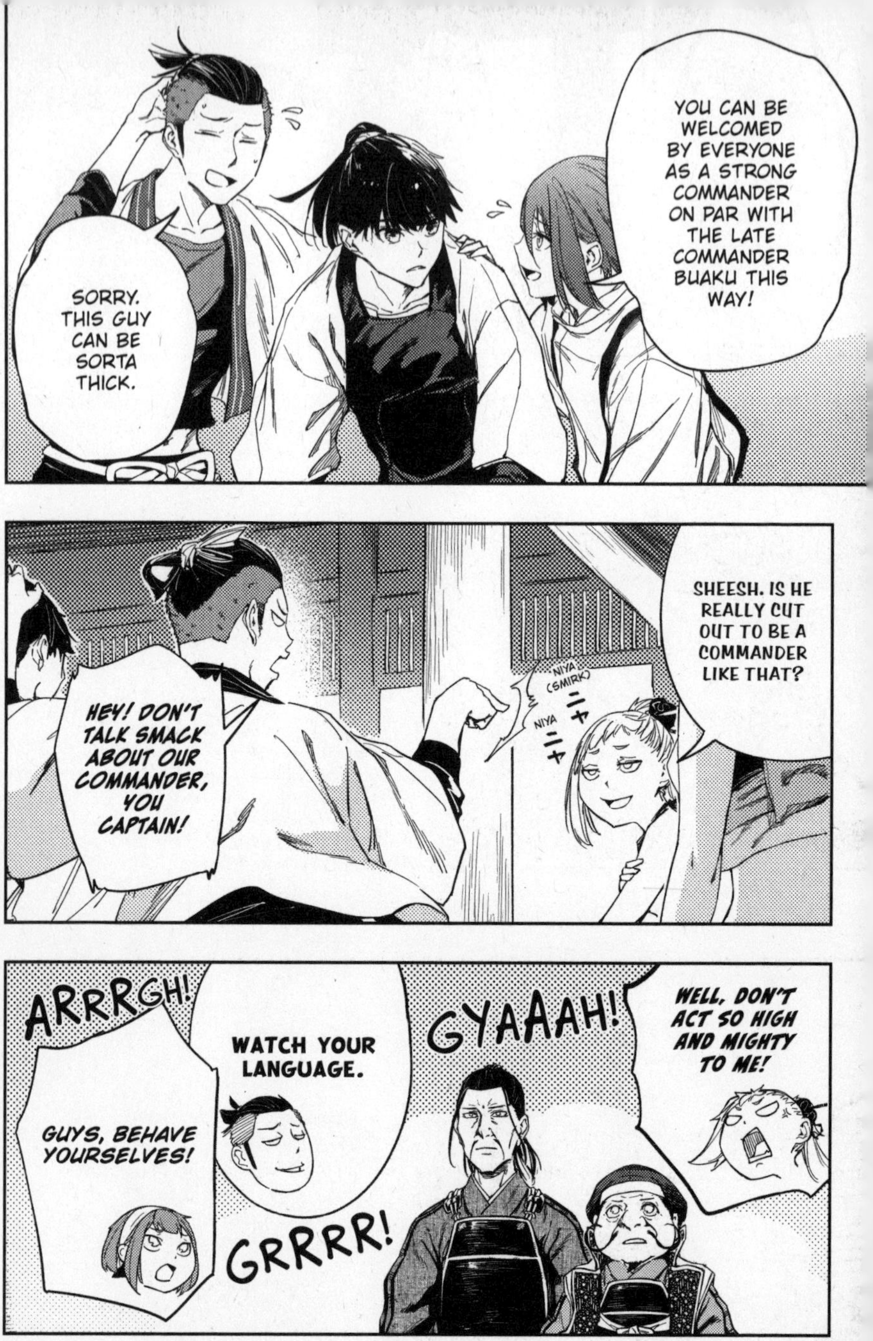
YOU CAN BE WELCOMED BY EVERYONE AS A STRONG COMMANDER ON PAR WITH THE LATE COMMANDER BUAKU THIS WAY!
SORRY. THIS GUY CAN BE SORTA THICK.
SHEESH. IS HE REALLY CUT OUT TO BE A COMMANDER LIKE THAT?
ニヤ ニヤ
NIYA NIYA (SMIRK)
HEY! DON'T TALK SMACK ABOUT OUR COMMANDER, YOU CAPTAIN!
WELL, DON'T ACT SO HIGH AND MIGHTY TO ME!
GYAAAH!
WATCH YOUR LANGUAGE.
ARRRGH!
GUYS, BEHAVE YOURSELVES!
GRRRR!

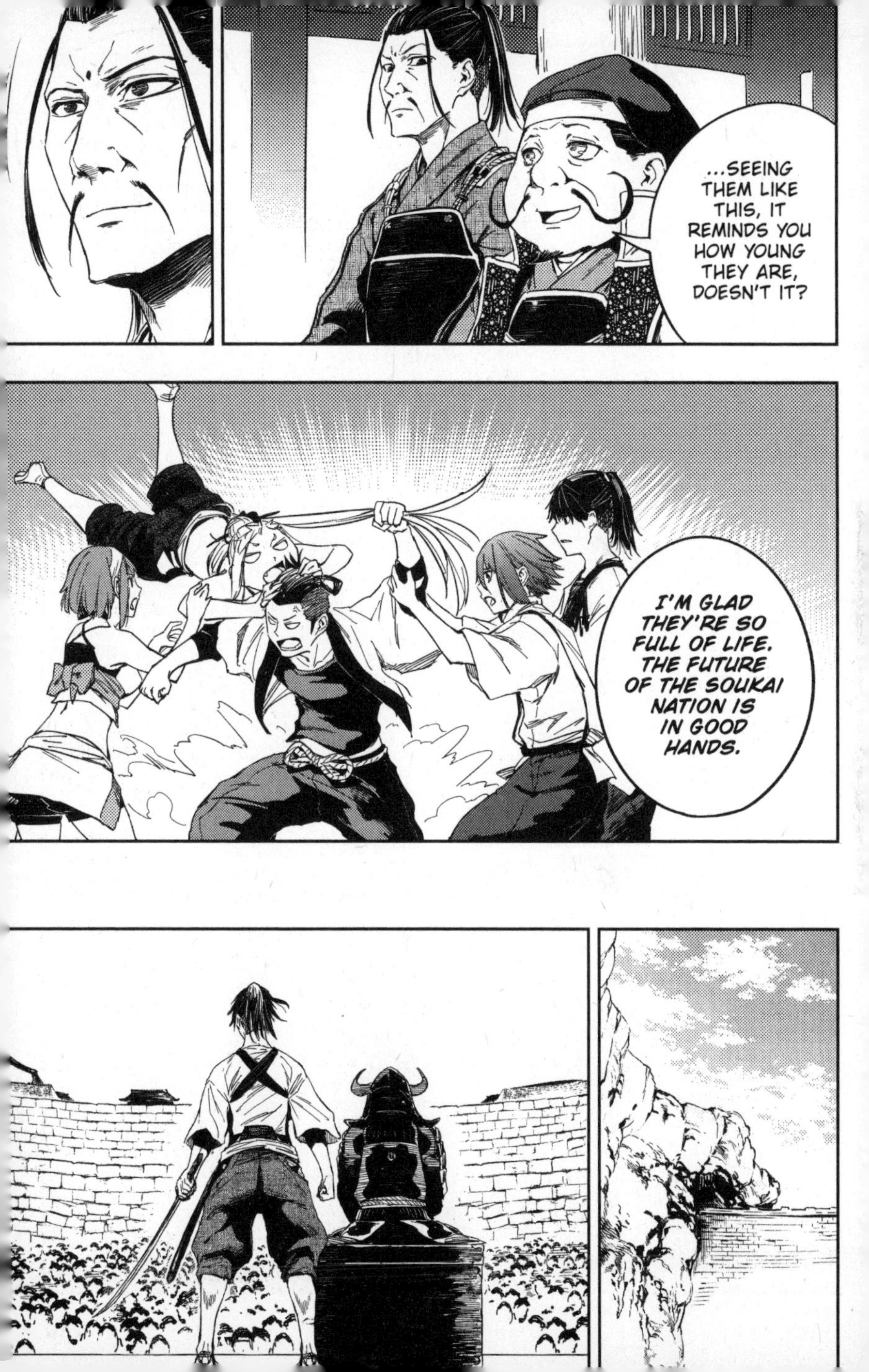
...SEEING THEM LIKE THIS, IT REMINDS YOU HOW YOUNG THEY ARE, DOESN'T IT?
I'M GLAD THEY'RE SO FULL OF LIFE. THE FUTURE OF THE SOUKAI NATION IS IN GOOD HANDS.

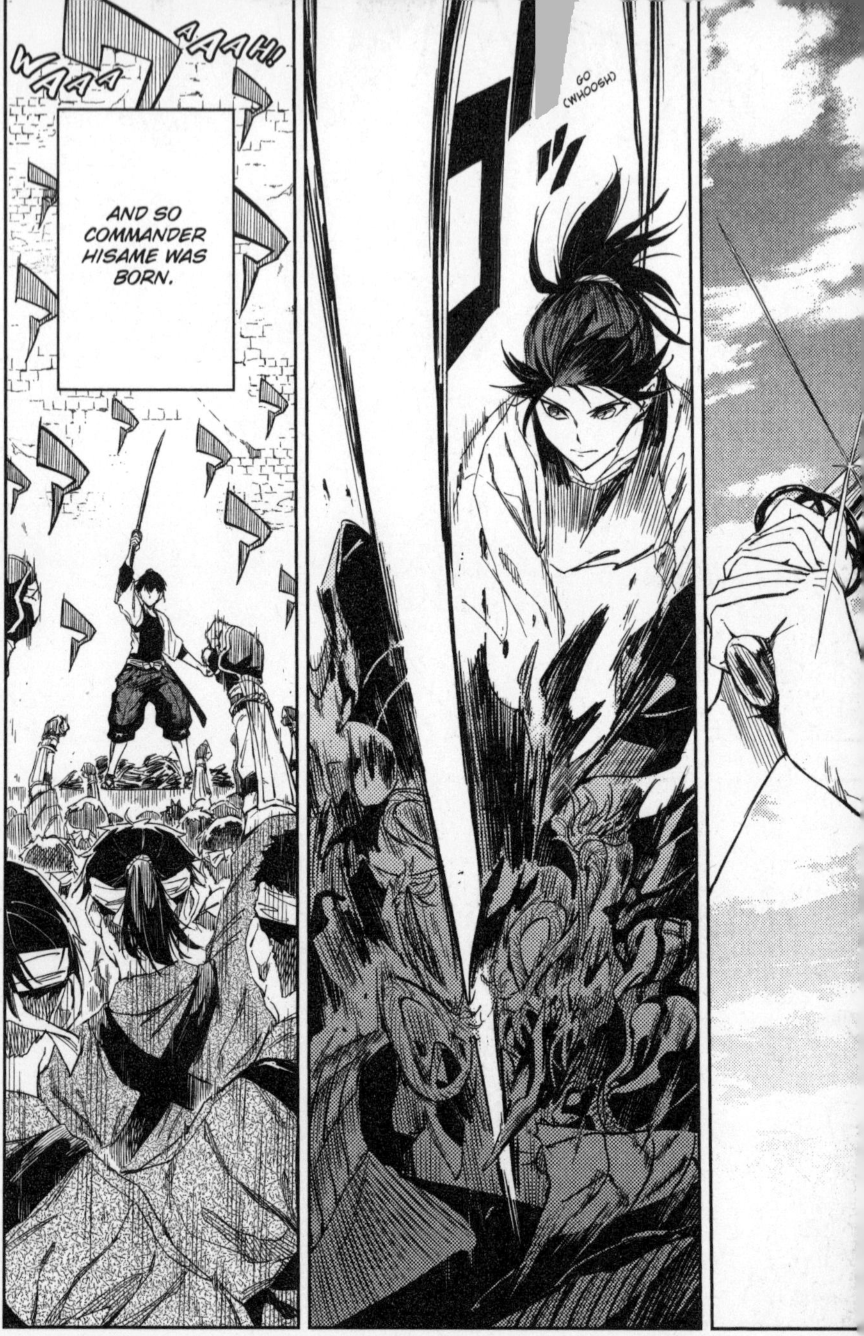
GO
(WHOOSH)
WAAA AAAH!!
AND SO COMMANDER HISAME WAS BORN.

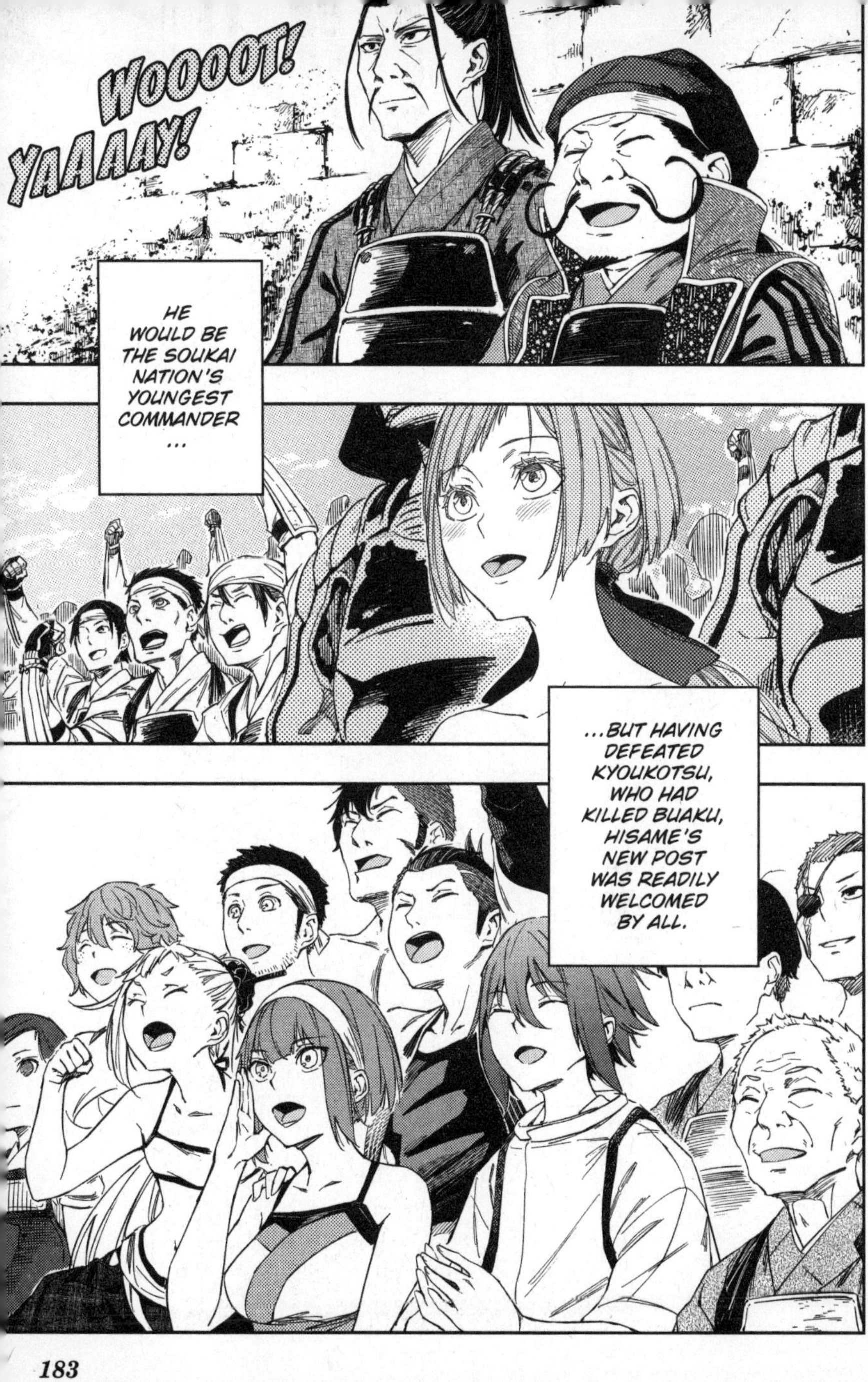
WOOOOOT!
YAAAAAY!
HE WOULD BE THE SOUKAI NATION'S YOUNGEST COMMANDER ...
...BUT HAVING DEFEATED KYOUKOTSU, WHO HAD KILLED BUAKU, HISAME'S NEW POST WAS READILY WELCOMED BY ALL.

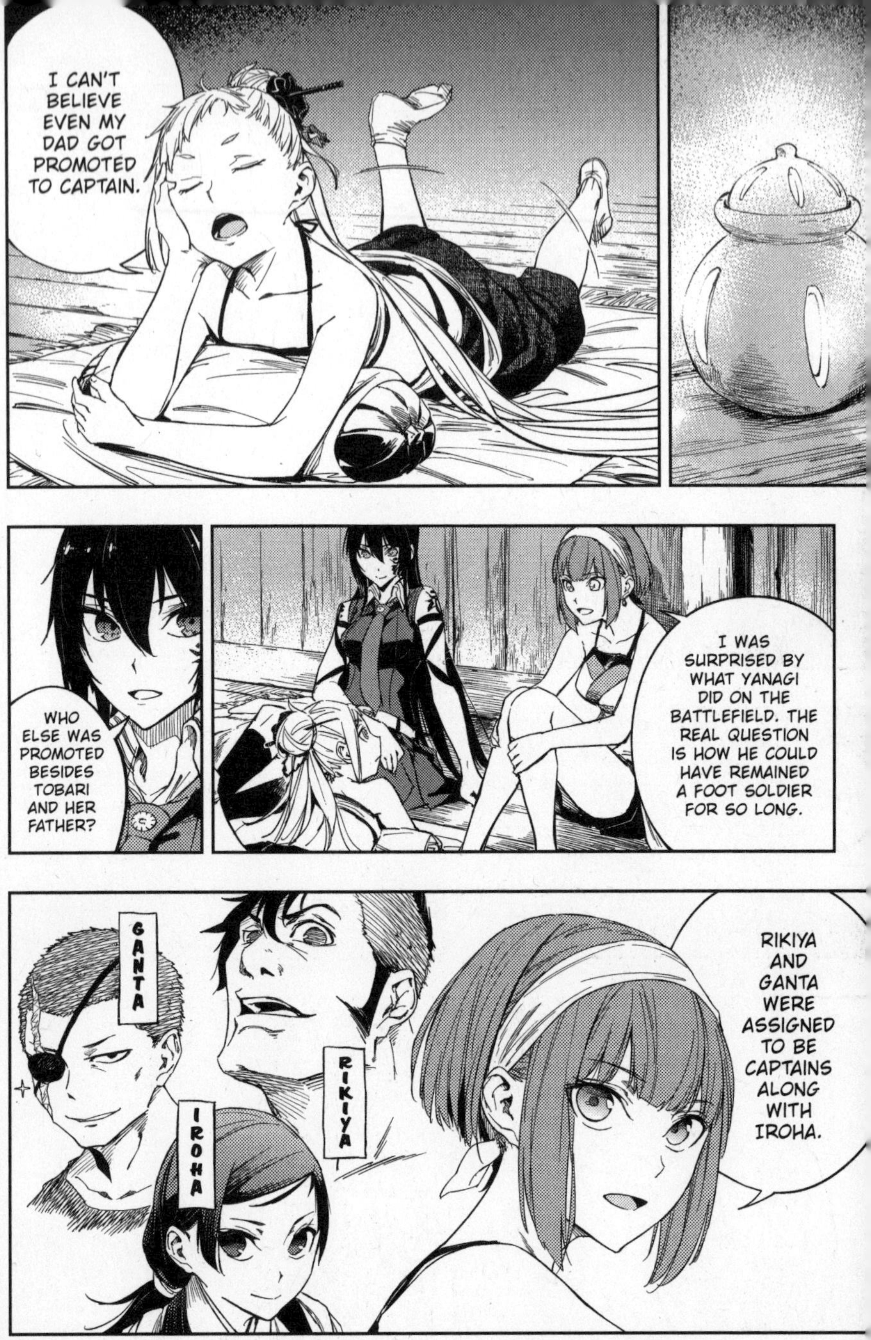
I CAN'T BELIEVE EVEN MY DAD GOT PROMOTED TO CAPTAIN.
I WAS SURPRISED BY WHAT YANAGI DID ON THE BATTLEFIELD. THE REAL QUESTION IS HOW HE COULD HAVE REMAINED A FOOT SOLDIER FOR SO LONG.
WHO ELSE WAS PROMOTED BESIDES TOBARI AND HER FATHER?
RIKIYA AND GANTA WERE ASSIGNED TO BE CAPTAINS ALONG WITH IROHA.
GANTA
RIKIYA
IROHA

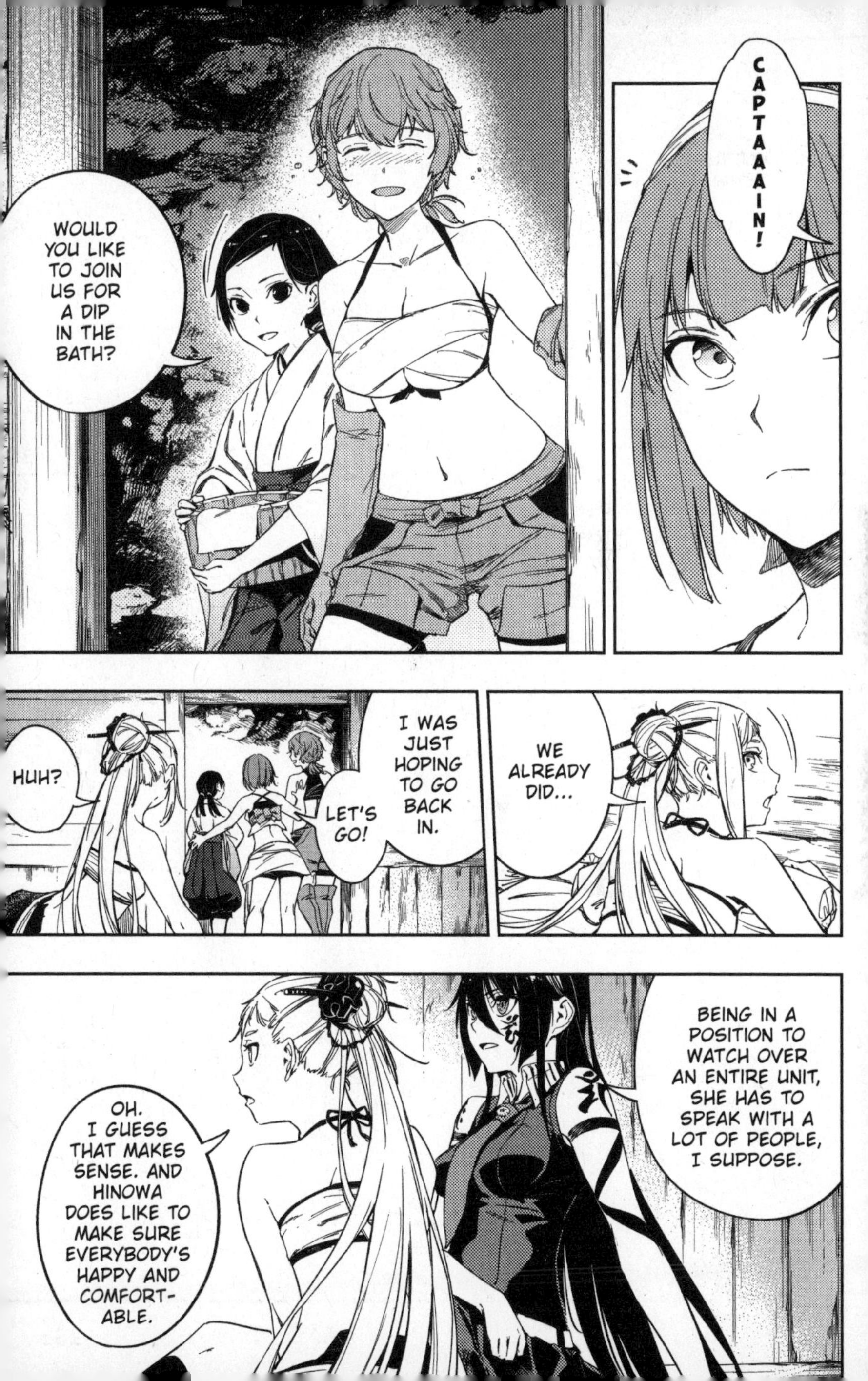
CAPTAAAAIN!
WOULD YOU LIKE TO JOIN US FOR A DIP IN THE BATH?
WE ALREADY DID...
I WAS JUST HOPING TO GO BACK IN.
LET'S GO!
HUH?
BEING IN A POSITION TO WATCH OVER AN ENTIRE UNIT, SHE HAS TO SPEAK WITH A LOT OF PEOPLE, I SUPPOSE.
OH. I GUESS THAT MAKES SENSE. AND HINOWA DOES LIKE TO MAKE SURE EVERYBODY'S HAPPY AND COMFORT-ABLE.

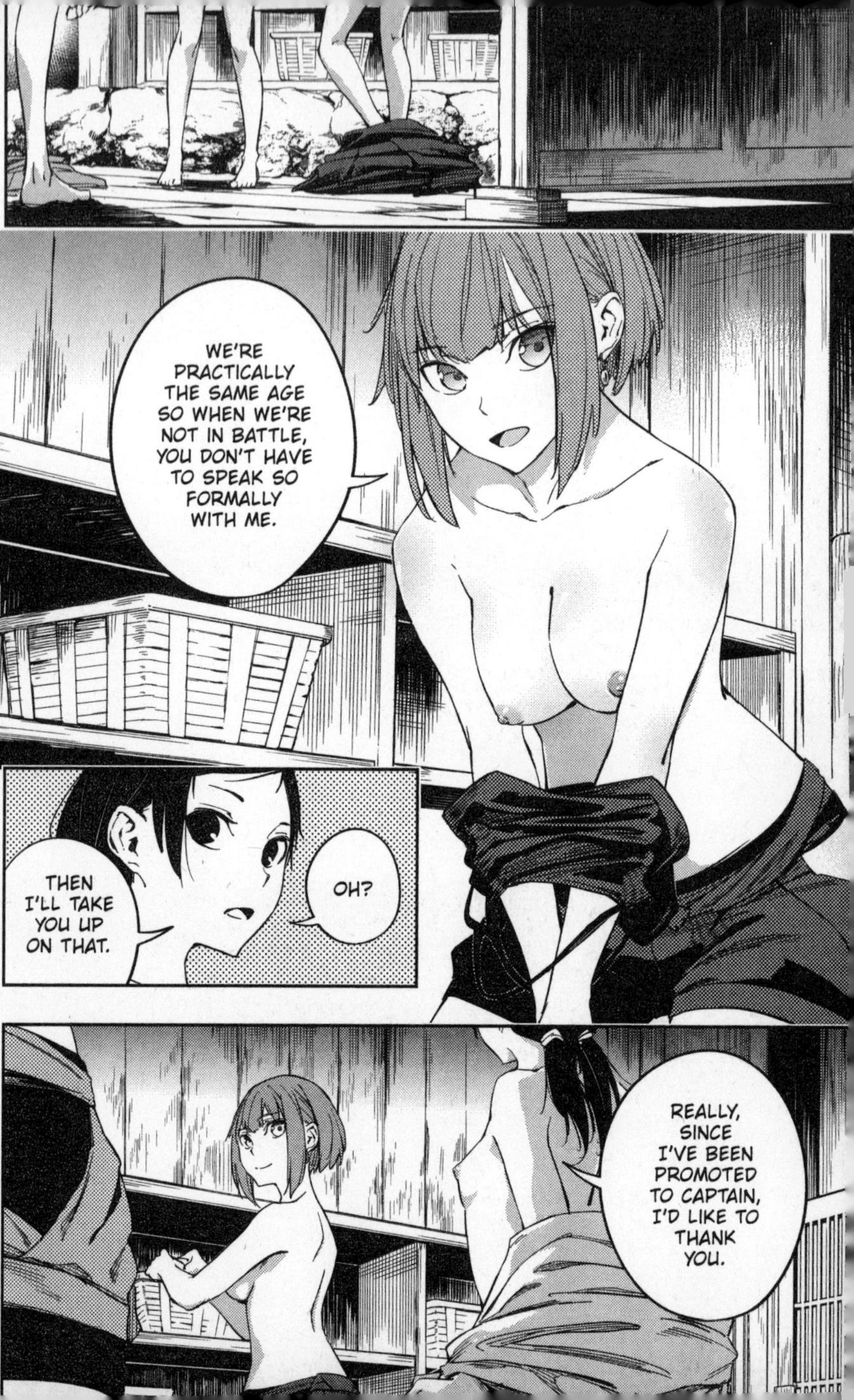
WE'RE PRACTICALLY THE SAME AGE SO WHEN WE'RE NOT IN BATTLE, YOU DON'T HAVE TO SPEAK SO FORMALLY WITH ME.
OH?
THEN I'LL TAKE YOU UP ON THAT.
REALLY, SINCE I'VE BEEN PROMOTED TO CAPTAIN, I'D LIKE TO THANK YOU.

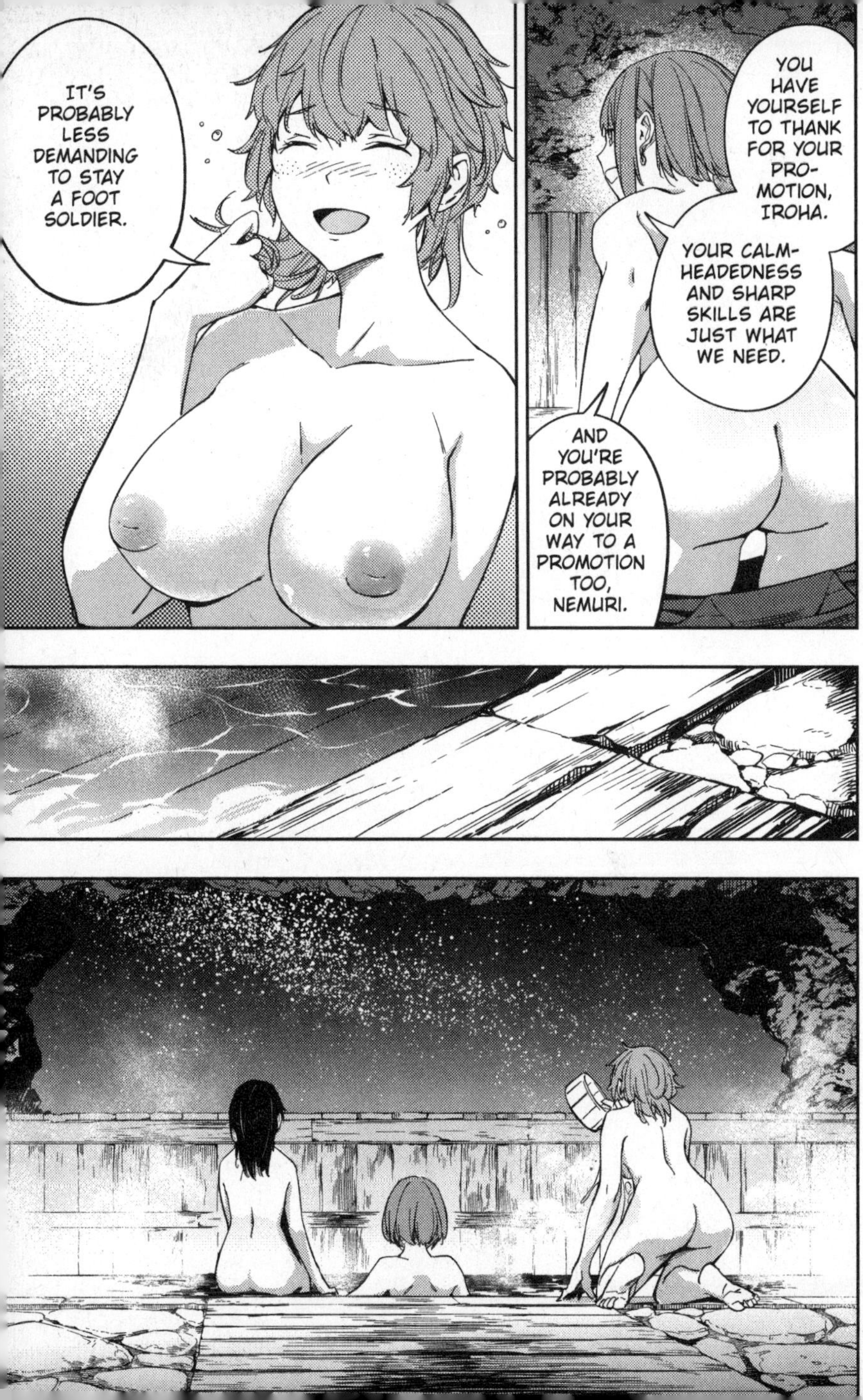
YOU HAVE YOURSELF TO THANK FOR YOUR PRO-MOTION, IROHA.
YOUR CALM-HEADEDNESS AND SHARP SKILLS ARE JUST WHAT WE NEED.
AND YOU'RE PROBABLY ALREADY ON YOUR WAY TO A PROMOTION TOO, NEMURI.
IT'S PROBABLY LESS DEMANDING TO STAY A FOOT SOLDIER.

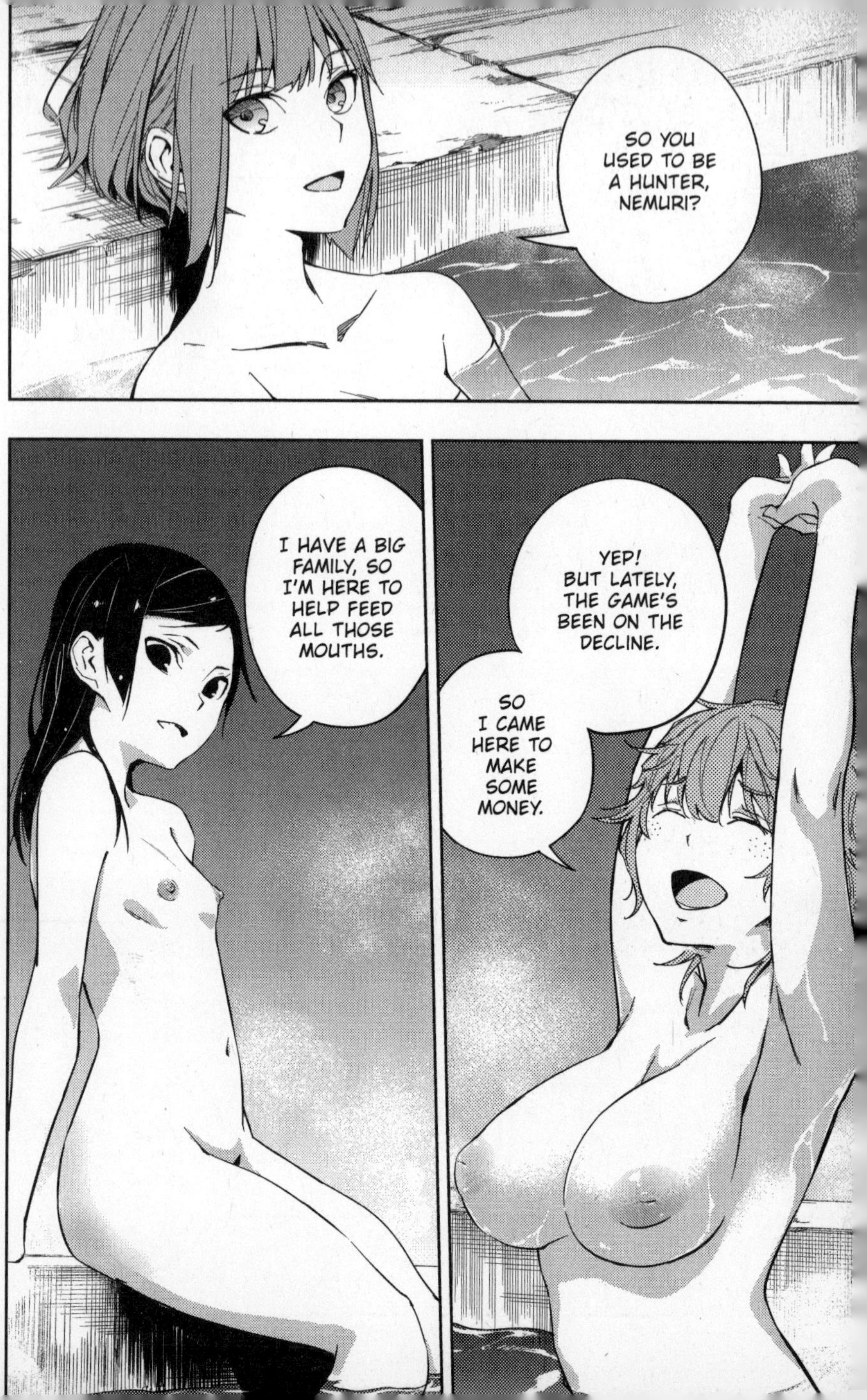
SO YOU USED TO BE A HUNTER, NEMURI?
YEP! BUT LATELY, THE GAME'S BEEN ON THE DECLINE.
SO I CAME HERE TO MAKE SOME MONEY.
I HAVE A BIG FAMILY, SO I'M HERE TO HELP FEED ALL THOSE MOUTHS.

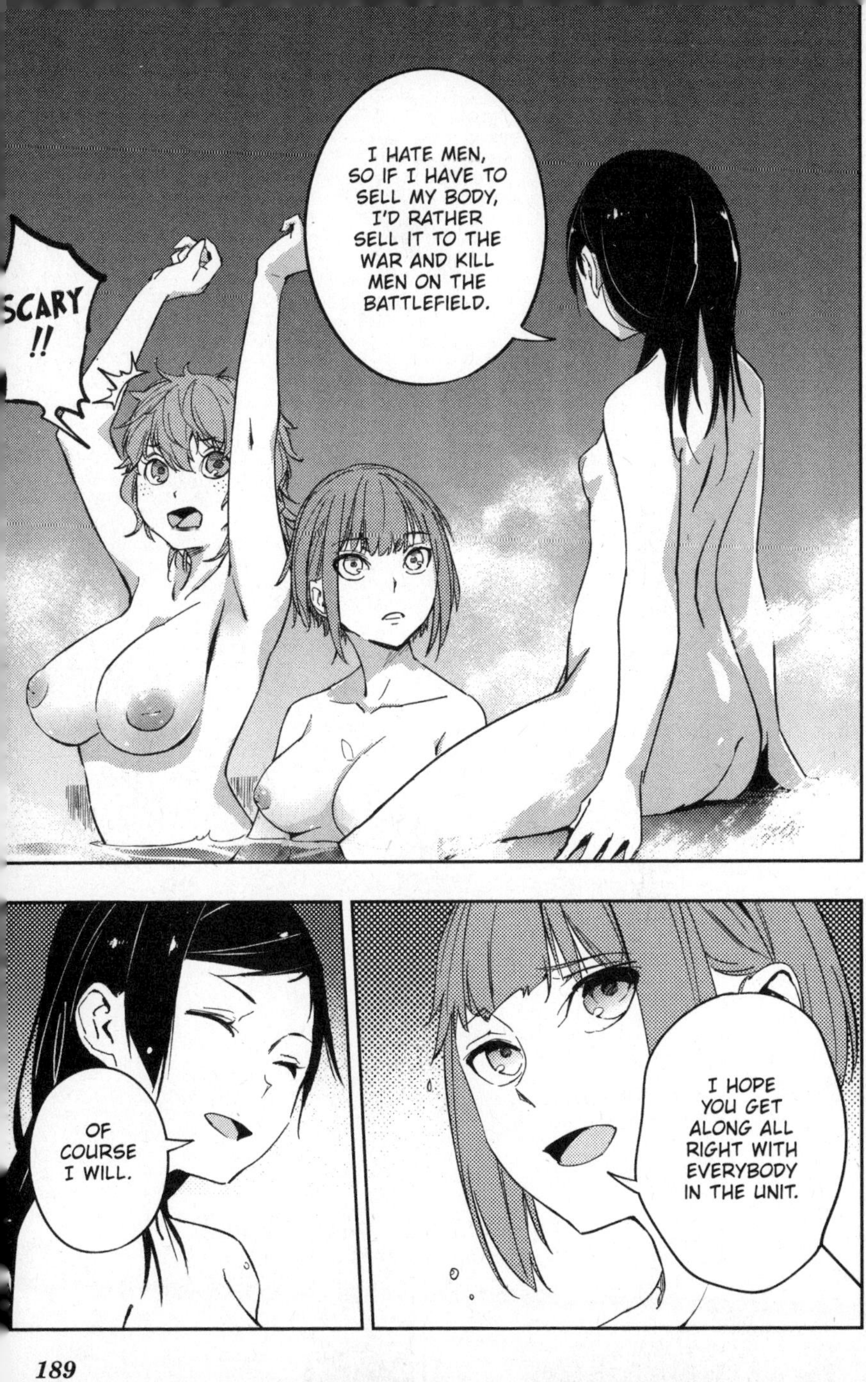
I HATE MEN, SO IF I HAVE TO SELL MY BODY, I'D RATHER SELL IT TO THE WAR AND KILL MEN ON THE BATTLEFIELD.
SCARY!!
I HOPE YOU GET ALONG ALL RIGHT WITH EVERYBODY IN THE UNIT.
OF COURSE I WILL.

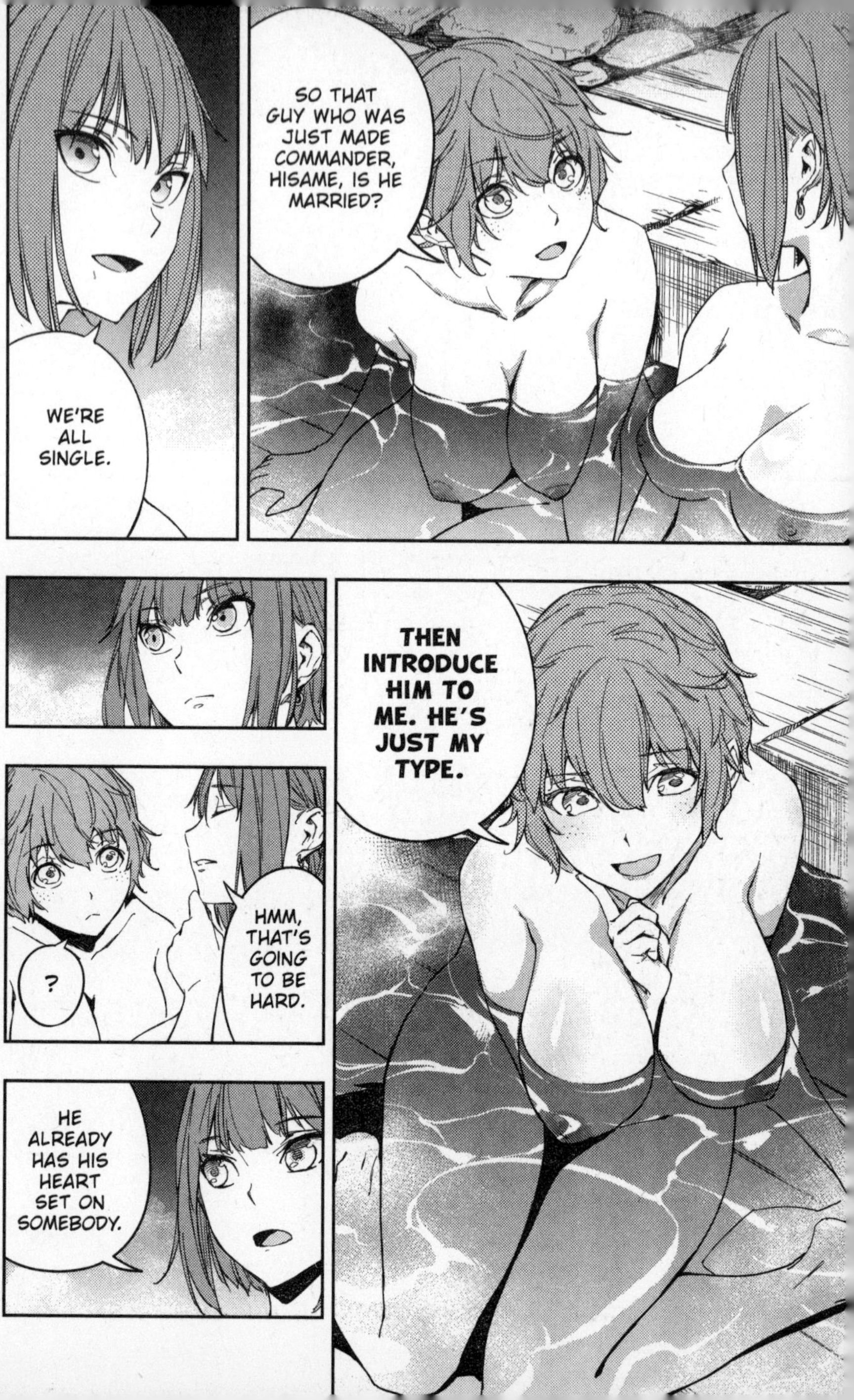
SO THAT GUY WHO WAS JUST MADE COMMANDER, HISAME, IS HE MARRIED?
WE'RE ALL SINGLE.
THEN INTRODUCE HIM TO ME. HE'S JUST MY TYPE.
HMM, THAT'S GOING TO BE HARD.
?
HE ALREADY HAS HIS HEART SET ON SOMEBODY.

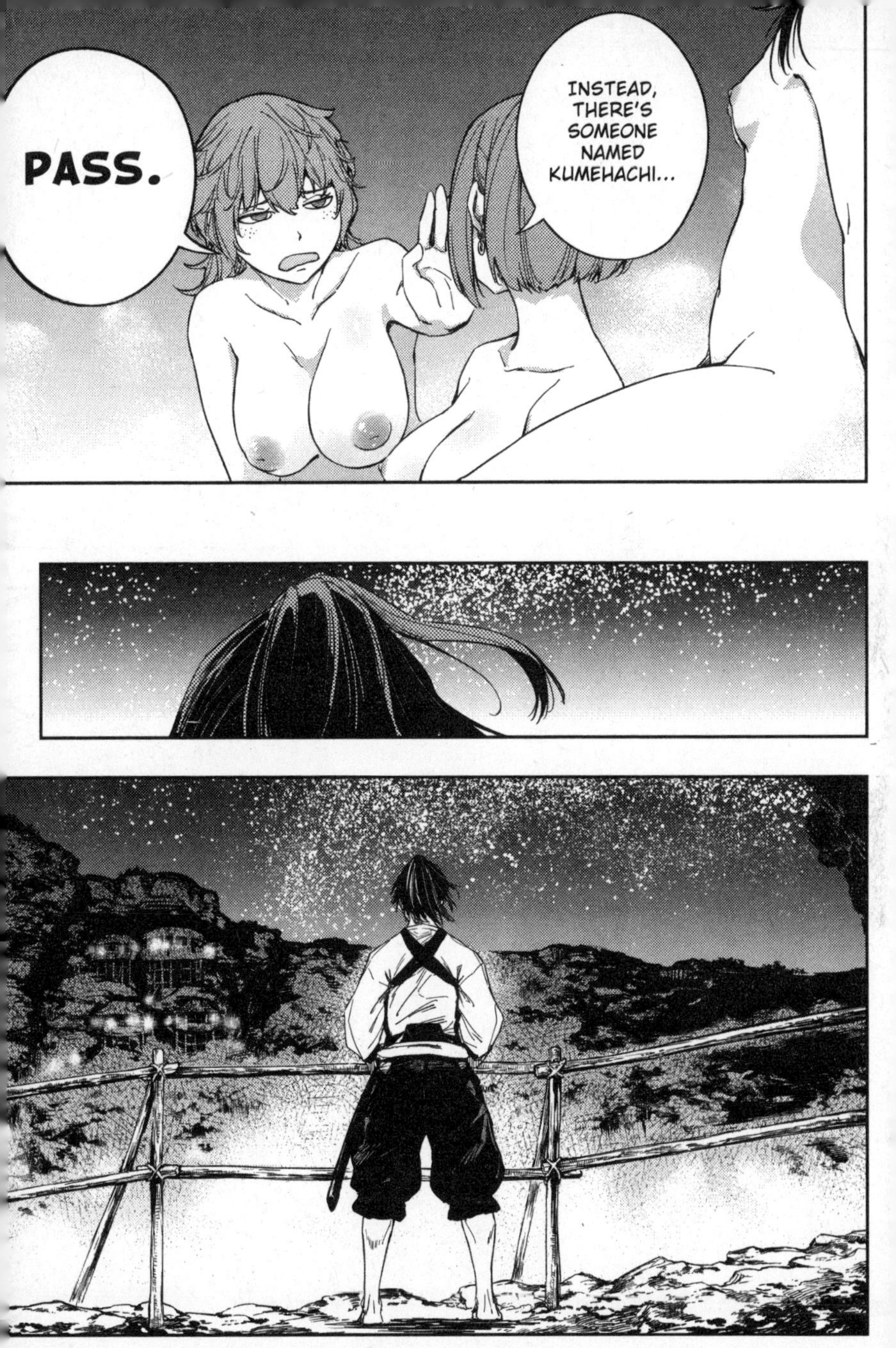
INSTEAD, THERE'S SOMEONE NAMED KUMEHACHI...
PASS.

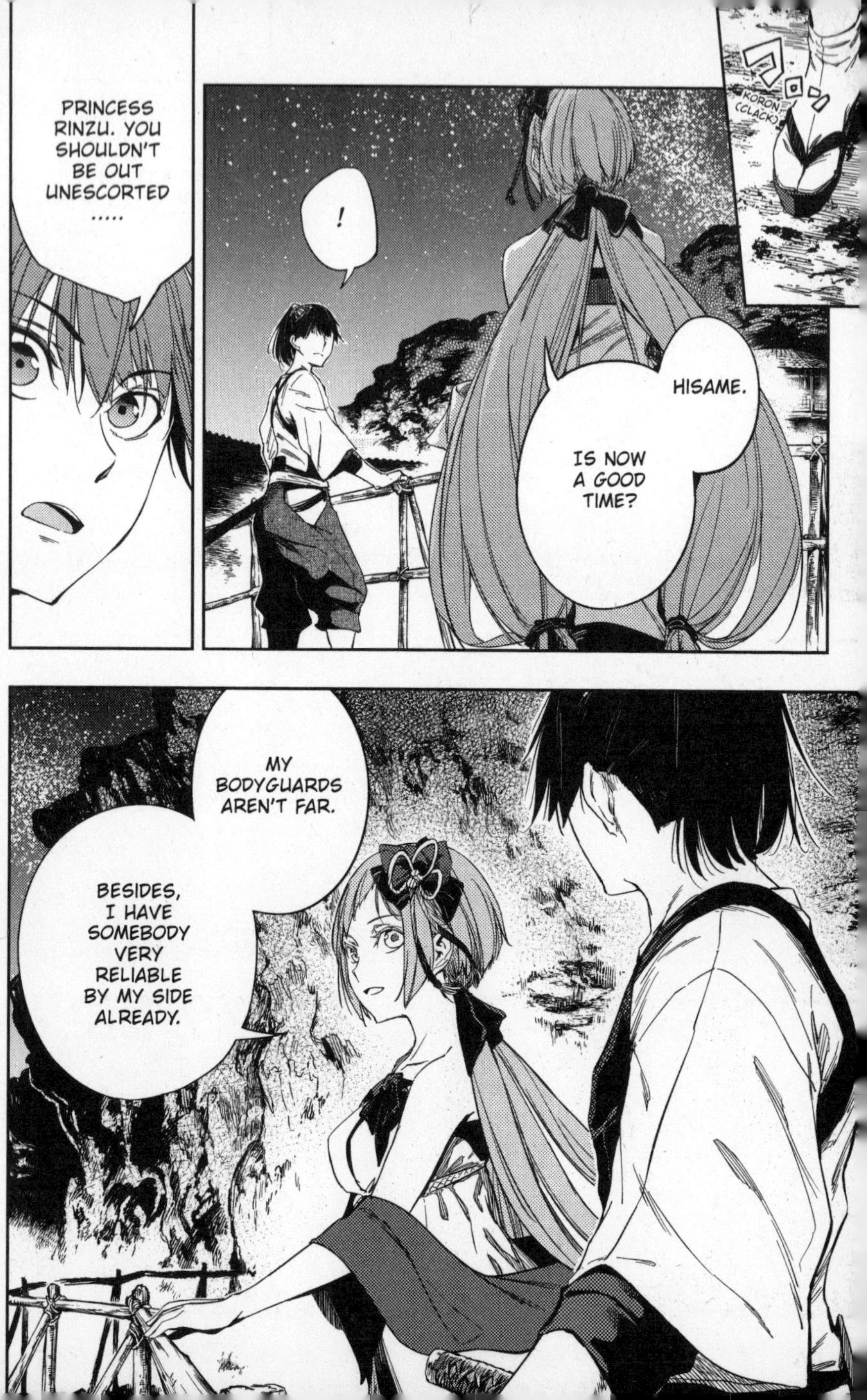
KORON (CLACK)
HISAME. IS NOW A GOOD TIME?
!
PRINCESS RINZU. YOU SHOULDN'T BE OUT UNESCORTED .....
MY BODYGUARDS AREN'T FAR.
BESIDES, I HAVE SOMEBODY VERY RELIABLE BY MY SIDE ALREADY.

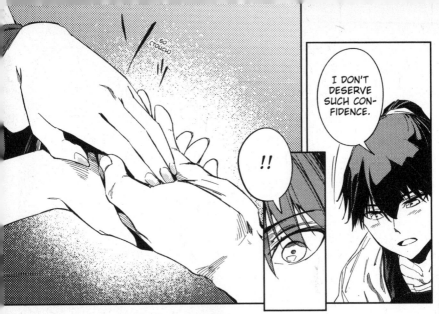

SO
(TOUCH)

!!

I DON'T DESERVE SUCH CON- FIDENCE.

I WANT TO THANK YOU AGAIN FOR SAVING ME. THAT WAS VERY CLOSE.

I'M A MAN OF THE SOUKAI NATION. WHAT ELSE COULD I HAVE DONE?

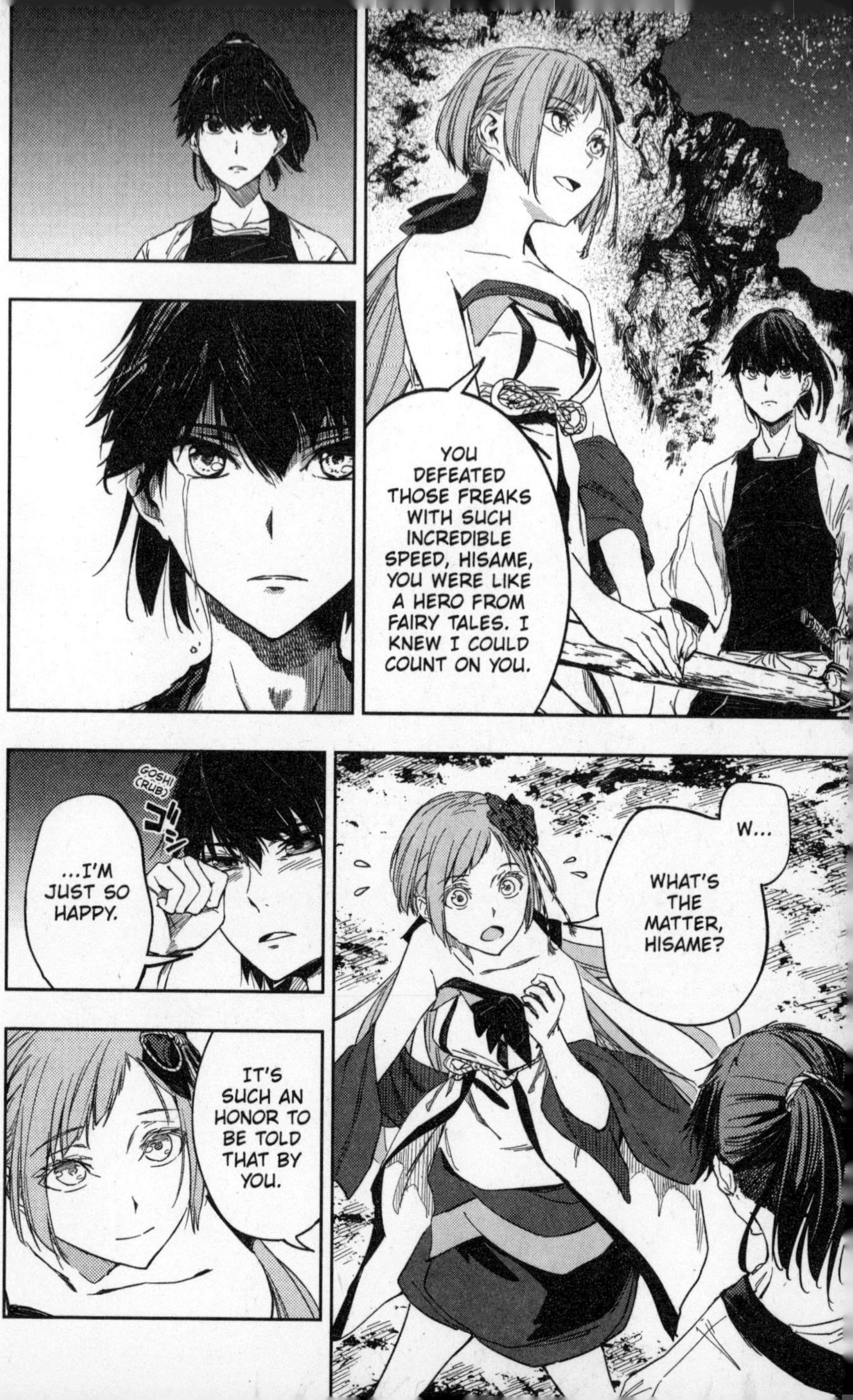
YOU DEFEATED THOSE FREAKS WITH SUCH INCREDIBLE SPEED, HISAME, YOU WERE LIKE A HERO FROM FAIRY TALES. I KNEW I COULD COUNT ON YOU.
W...
WHAT'S THE MATTER, HISAME?
GOSHI (RUB)
...I'M JUST SO HAPPY.
IT'S SUCH AN HONOR TO BE TOLD THAT BY YOU.

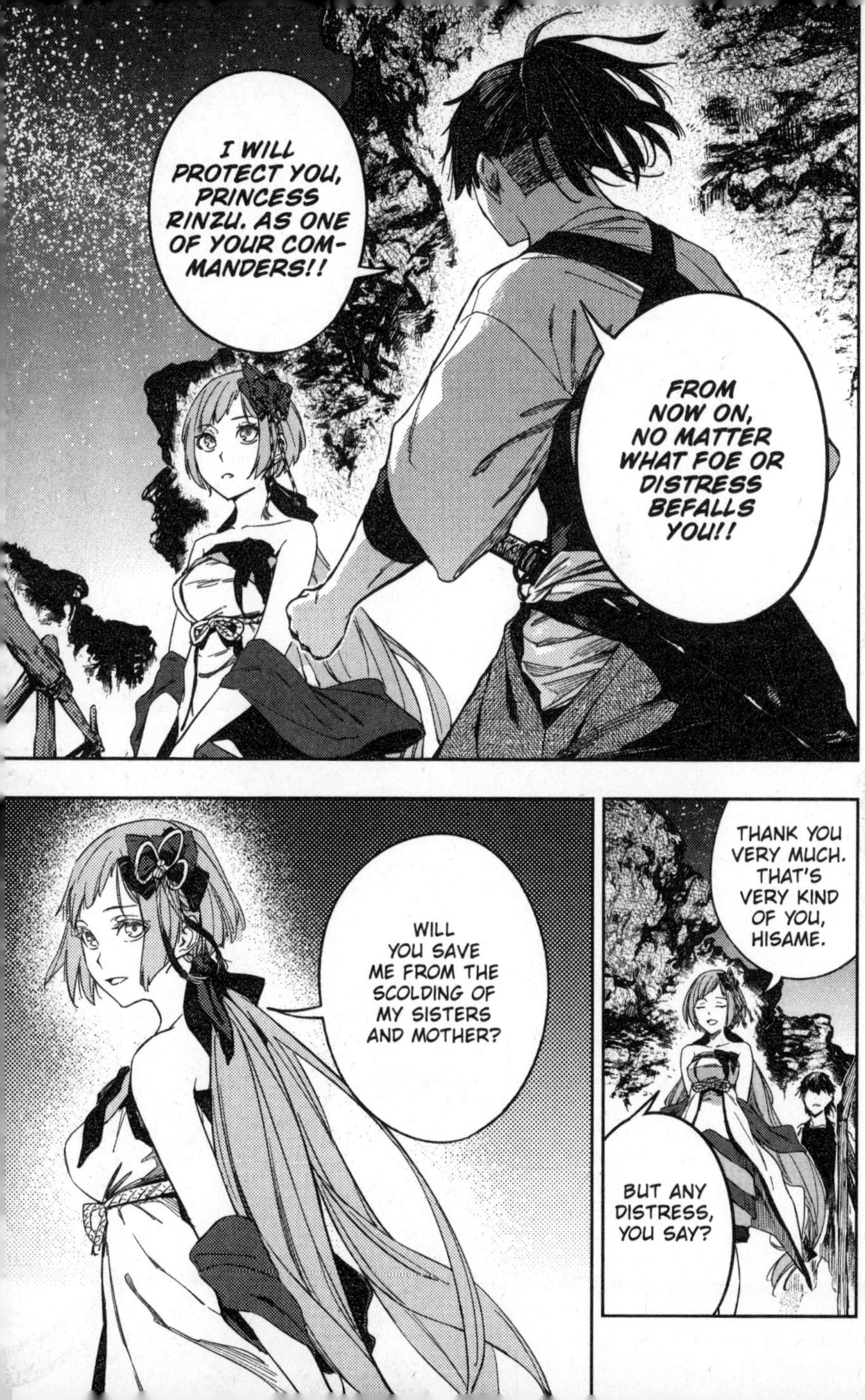
I WILL PROTECT YOU, PRINCESS RINZU. AS ONE OF YOUR COM-MANDERS!!
FROM NOW ON, NO MATTER WHAT FOE OR DISTRESS BEFALLS YOU!!
THANK YOU VERY MUCH. THAT'S VERY KIND OF YOU, HISAME.
BUT ANY DISTRESS, YOU SAY?
WILL YOU SAVE ME FROM THE SCOLDING OF MY SISTERS AND MOTHER?

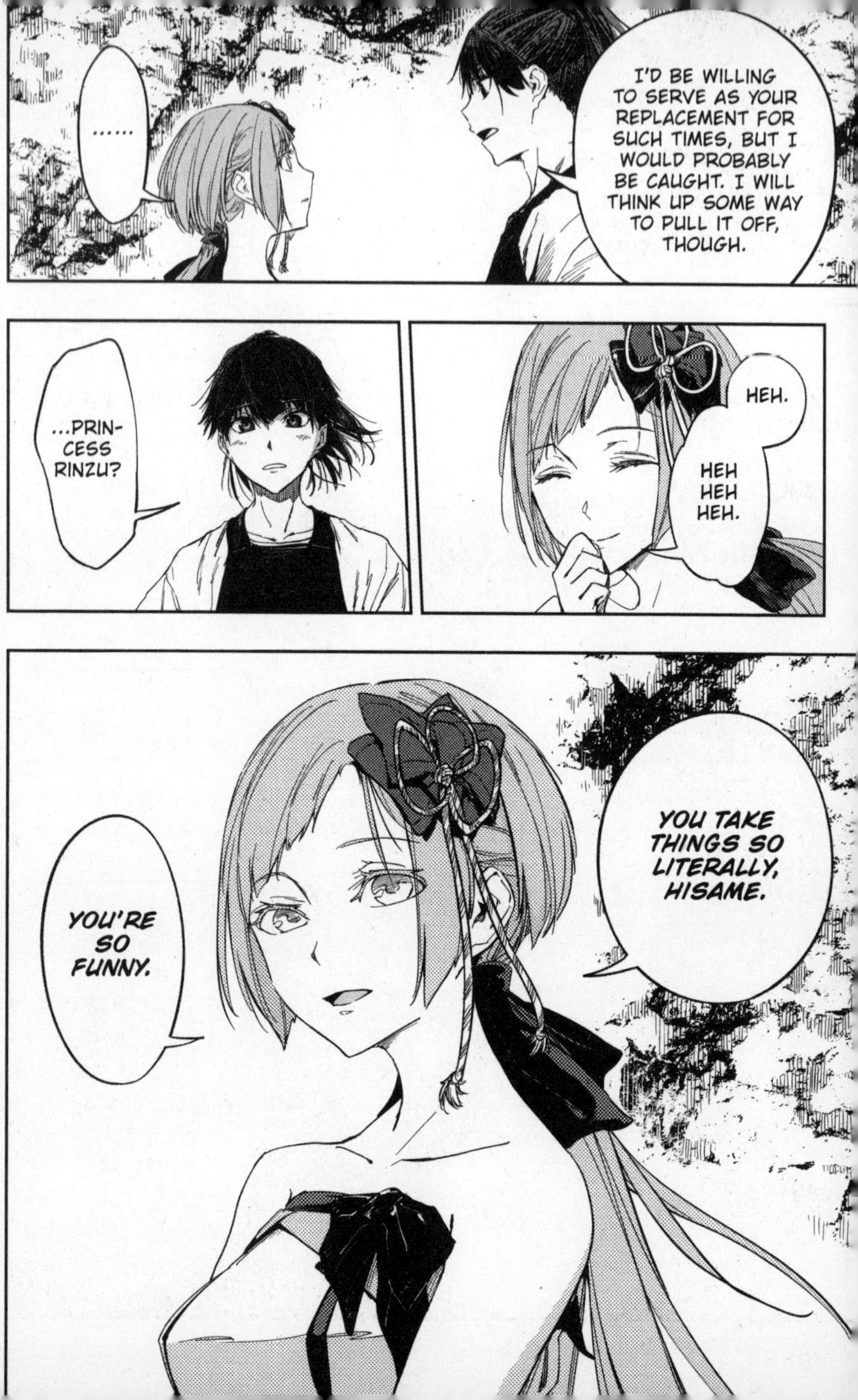
I'D BE WILLING TO SERVE AS YOUR REPLACEMENT FOR SUCH TIMES, BUT I WOULD PROBABLY BE CAUGHT. I WILL THINK UP SOME WAY TO PULL IT OFF, THOUGH.
......
HEH.
HEH HEH HEH.
...PRIN-CESS RINZU?
YOU TAKE THINGS SO LITERALLY, HISAME.
YOU'RE SO FUNNY.

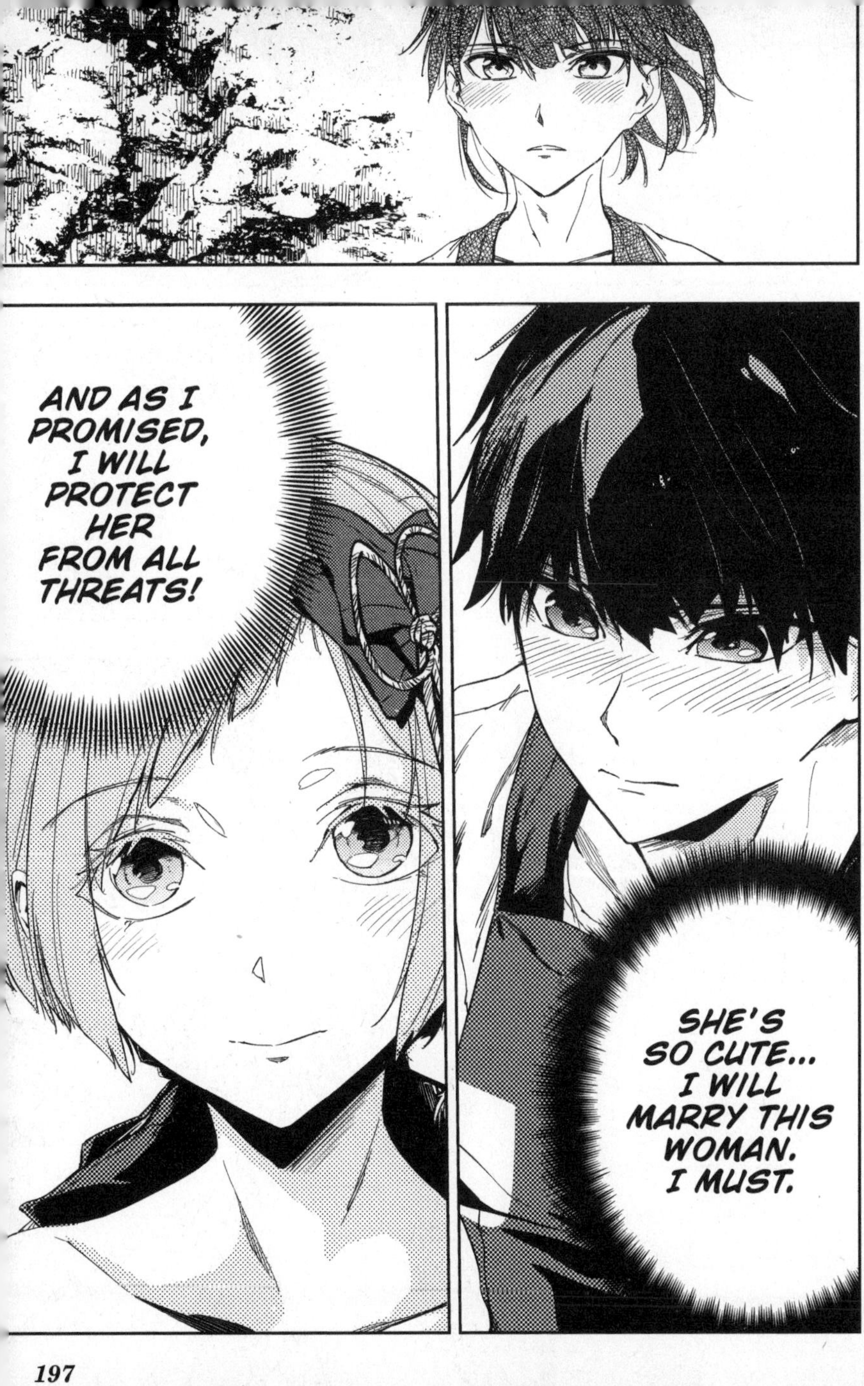
SHE'S SO CUTE... I WILL MARRY THIS WOMAN. I MUST.
AND AS I PROMISED, I WILL PROTECT HER FROM ALL THREATS!

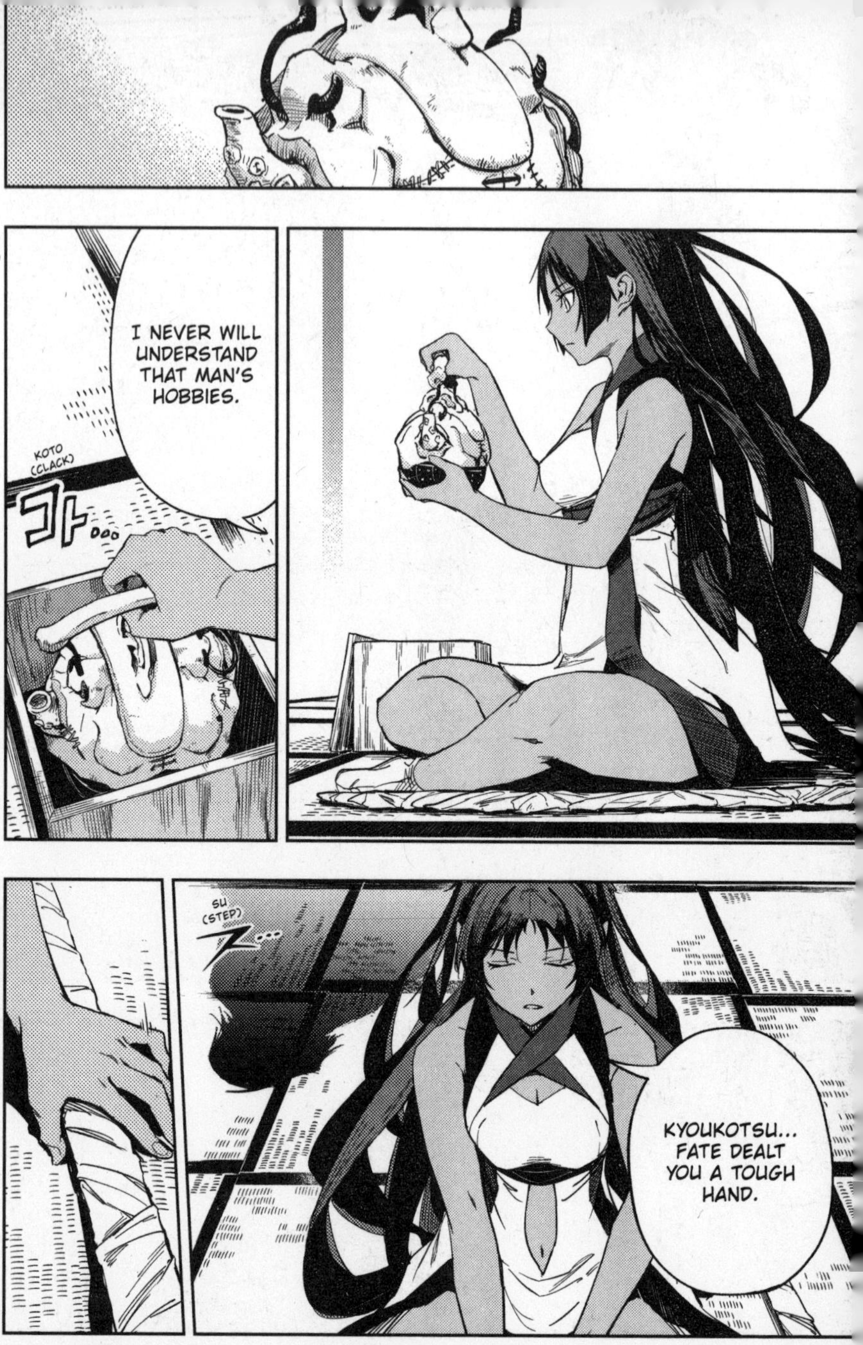
KOTO (CLACK)
I NEVER WILL UNDERSTAND THAT MAN'S HOBBIES.
SU (STEP)
KYOUKOTSU... FATE DEALT YOU A TOUGH HAND.

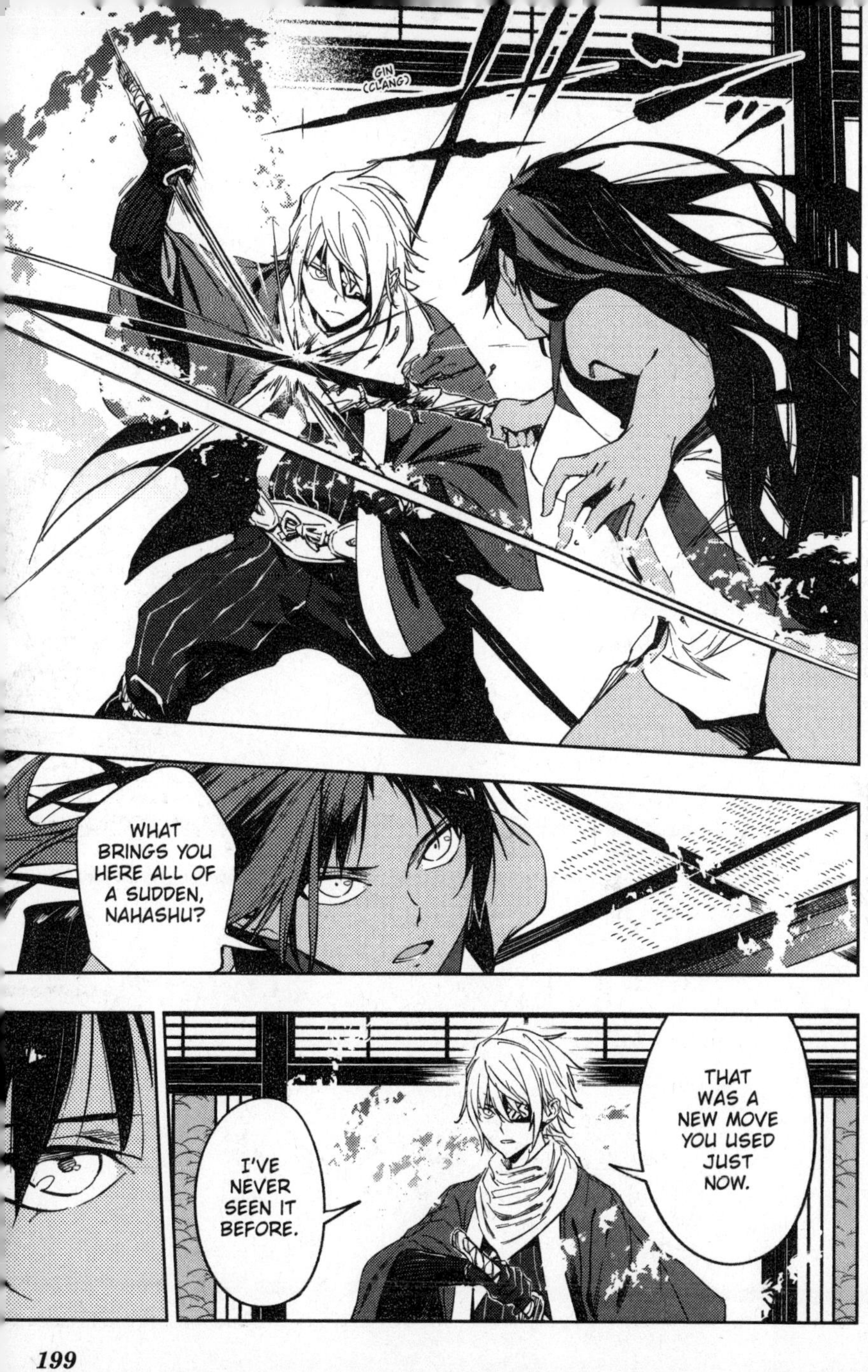
GIN (CLANG)
WHAT BRINGS YOU HERE ALL OF A SUDDEN, NAHASHU?
THAT WAS A NEW MOVE YOU USED JUST NOW.
I'VE NEVER SEEN IT BEFORE.

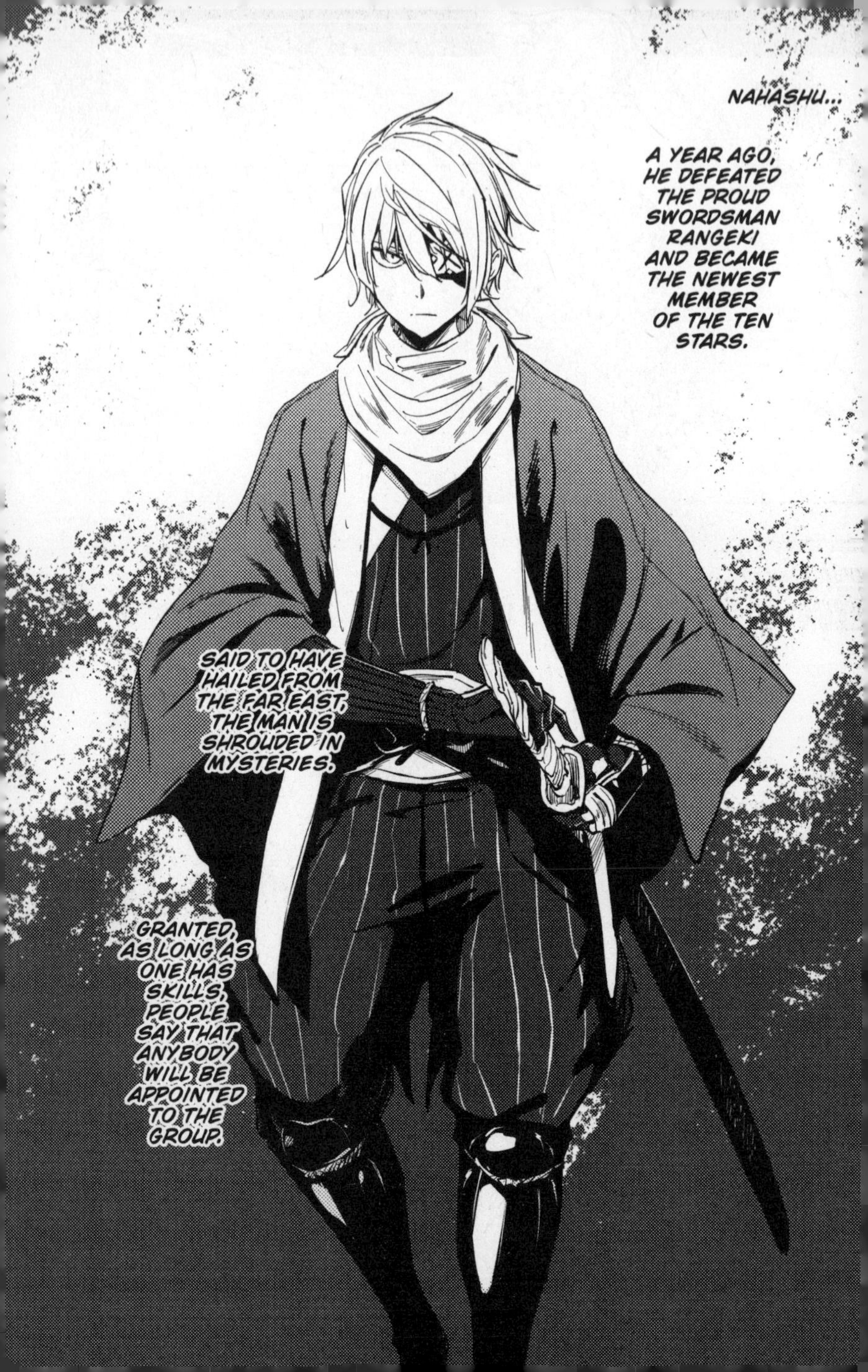
NAHASHU...
A YEAR AGO, HE DEFEATED THE PROUD SWORDSMAN RANGEKI AND BECAME THE NEWEST MEMBER OF THE TEN STARS.
SAID TO HAVE HAILED FROM THE FAR EAST, THE MAN IS SHROUDED IN MYSTERIES.
GRANTED, AS LONG AS ONE HAS SKILLS, PEOPLE SAY THAT ANYBODY WILL BE APPOINTED TO THE GROUP.

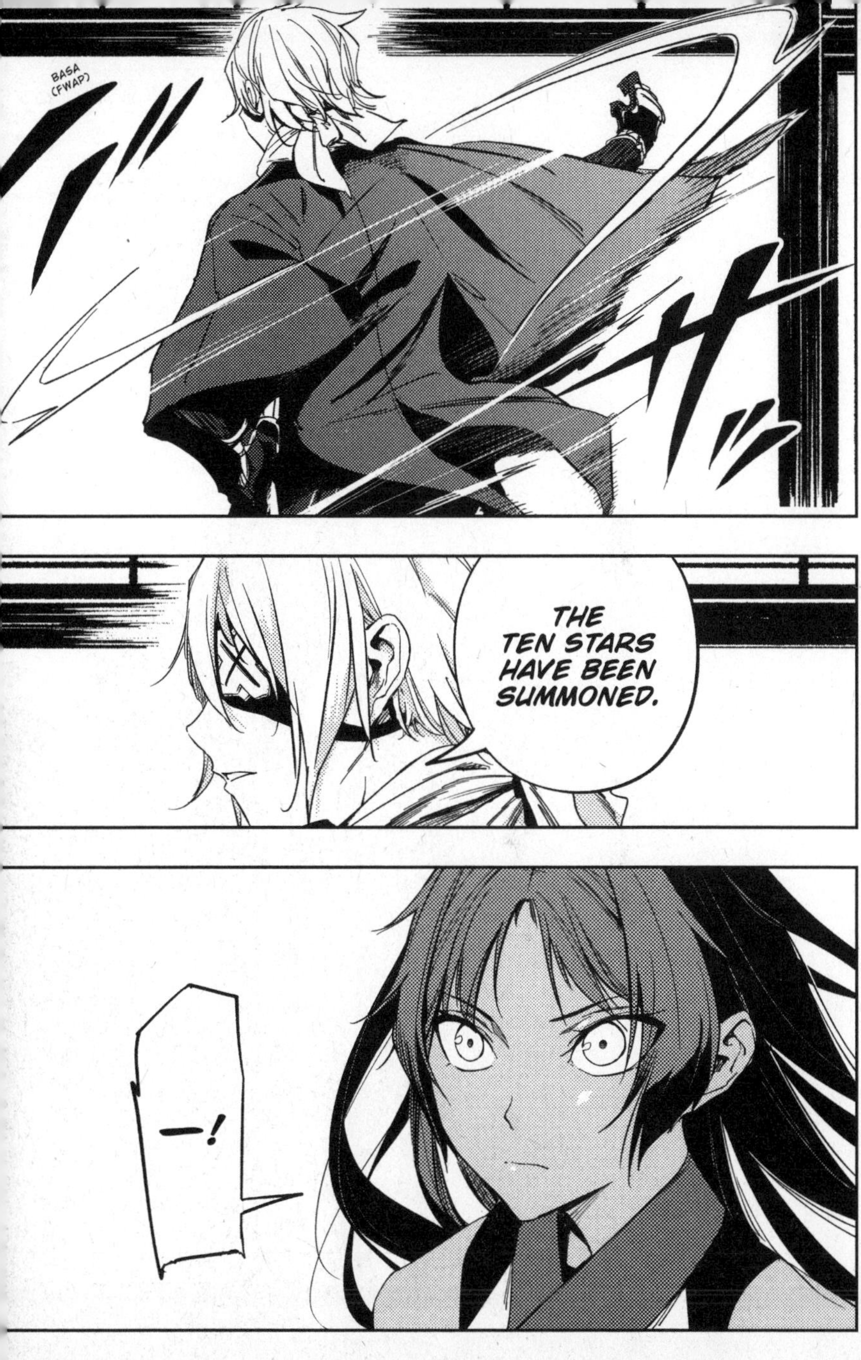
BASA (FWAP)
THE TEN STARS HAVE BEEN SUMMONED.
—!

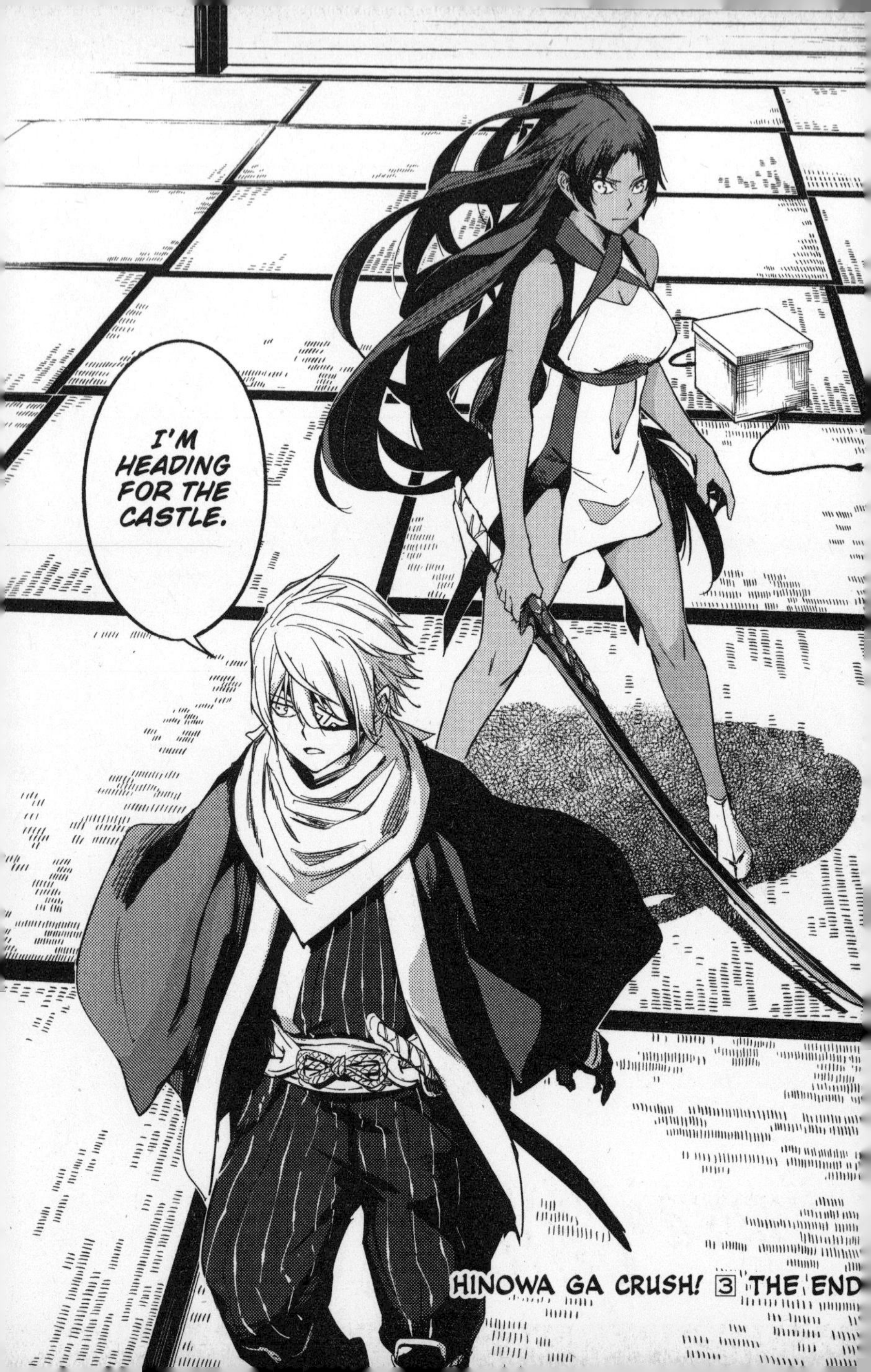
I'M HEADING FOR THE CASTLE.
HINOWA GA CRUSH! 3 THE END

Translation Notes

PAGE 21
A *gashadokuro* is a traditional Japanese
demon that looks like a giant skeleton.

Hinowa ga CRUSH!

Takahiro's PostScript

HELLO, EVERYONE. THIS IS THE WRITER OF THIS MANGA, TAKAHIRO. I'D LIKE TO TAKE THIS OPPORTUNITY TO TOUCH UPON EVERYONE IN HINOWA'S UNIT.

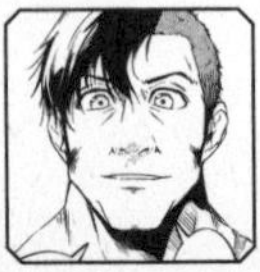

★*RIKIYA*

HE'S 45 YEARS OLD AND USUALLY MADE HIS LIVING WORKING SECURITY FOR HIS VILLAGE. HE'S CONFIDENT IN HIS STRENGTH AND PRETTY STRONG, BUT HIS PERSONALITY IS SURPRISINGLY DELICATE AND SENSITIVE.

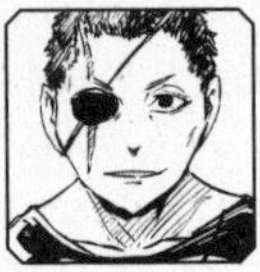

★*GANTA*

HE'S 42 YEARS OLD AND IS A BORN MERCENARY WITH LOTS OF EXPERIENCE ON THE BATTLEFIELD. HE CAN USE A VARIETY OF WEAPONS, HAS NERVES OF STEEL, AND KEEPS A COOL HEAD.

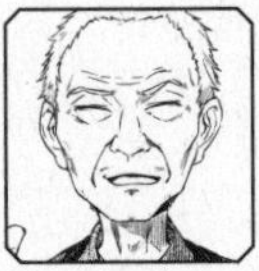

★*GRAMPS WHO KNOWS HIS STUFF*

A SEASONED WARRIOR WHO HAS LIVED THROUGH COUNTLESS BATTLES. HE'S GOOD AT EXPLAINING THINGS AND WILL OFTEN FILL PEOPLE IN ON A GIVEN SITUATION. HIS HOBBIES INCLUDE WRITING WAR STORIES.

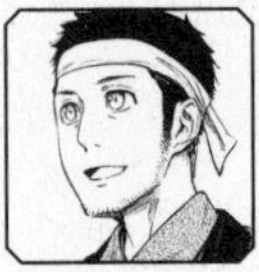

★*FUMIO*

HE WORKED FOR HINOWA'S MOTHER AND IS THE STRONGEST HINOWA-BELIEVER IN HER UNIT. HE'S NOT THAT SKILLED, BUT HE TRIES HIS BEST.

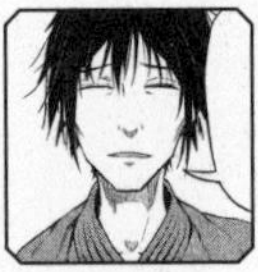

★*YANAGI*

39 YEARS OLD, HE'S TOBARI'S FATHER. HE'S A BIT OF A COWARD, BUT WILL ACT WHEN THE SITUATION CALLS FOR IT. SINCE HIS SUPERIORS HAVE ALWAYS TAKEN THE CREDIT FOR HIS ACCOMPLISHMENTS, HE'S BEEN STUCK AS A FOOT SOLDIER HIS ENTIRE CAREER.

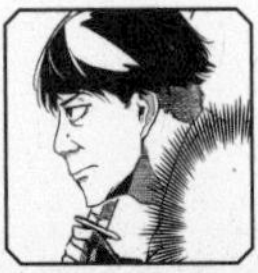

★*KOBU*

35 YEARS OLD, HE WORKED IN COMMERCE IN THE SOKAI NATION, BUT AFTER A DISPUTE WITH HIS EMPLOYER, HE WAS KICKED OUT OF THE BUSINESS AND BARRED FROM EVER WORKING IN THAT INDUSTRY AGAIN. HE HAS A SARCASTIC STREAK.

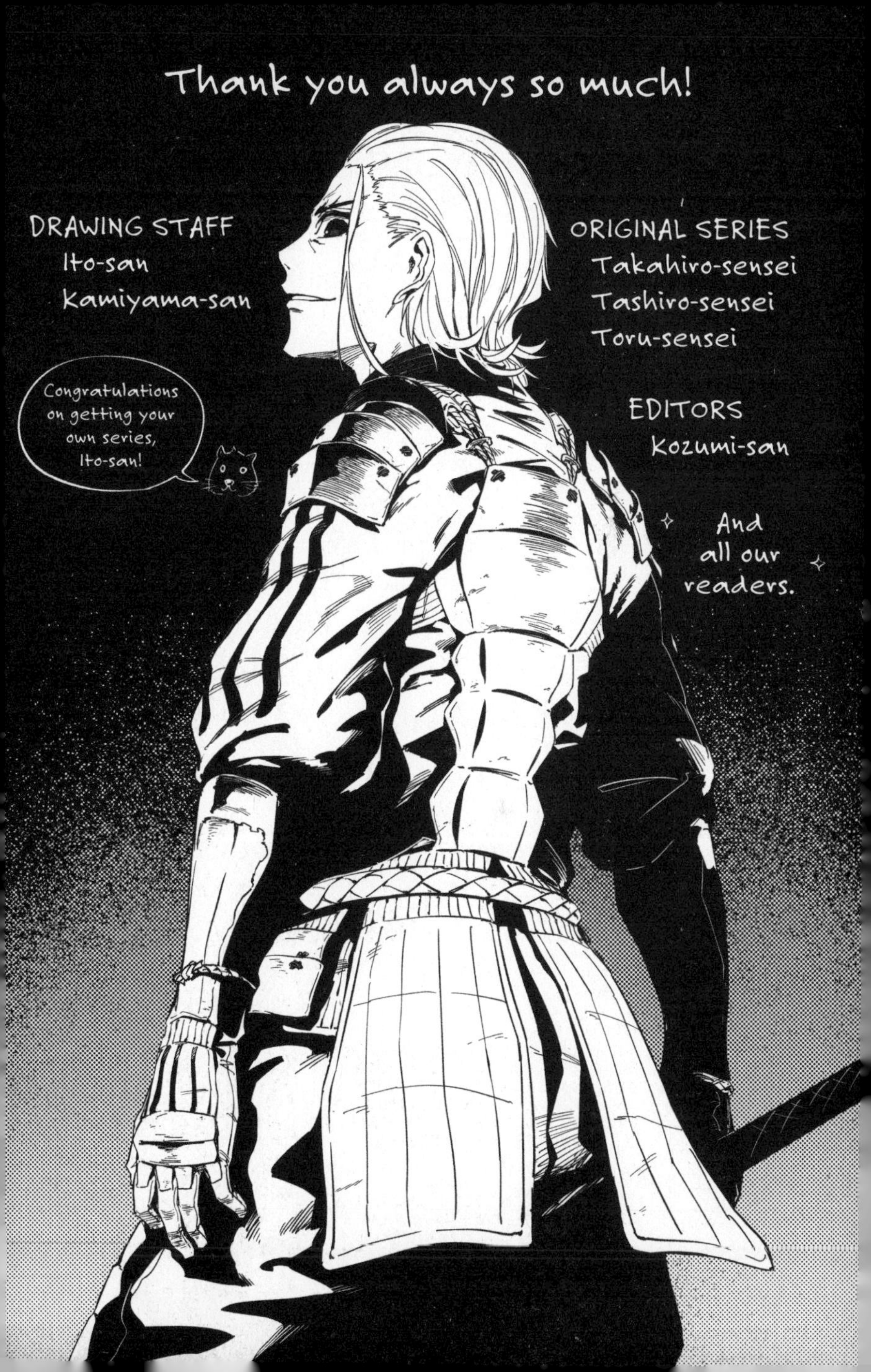
Thank you always so much!
DRAWING STAFF
Ito-san
Kamiyama-san
ORIGINAL SERIES
Takahiro-sensei
Tashiro-sensei
Toru-sensei
Congratulations on getting your own series, Ito-san!
EDITORS
Kozumi-san
And all our readers.

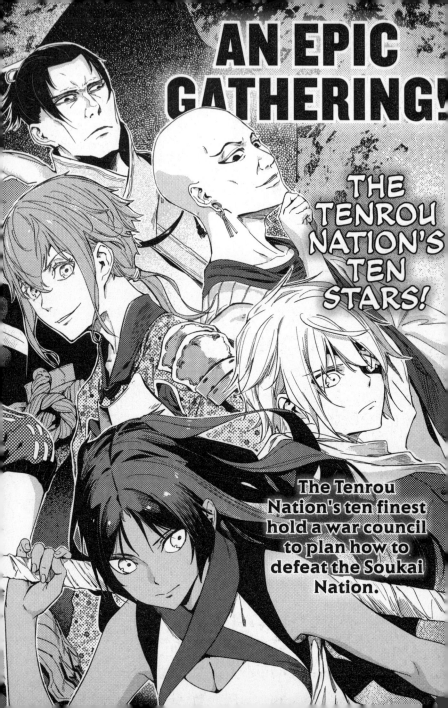

AN EPIC GATHERING!

THE TENROU NATION'S TEN STARS!

The Tenrou Nation's ten finest hold a war council to plan how to defeat the Soukai Nation.

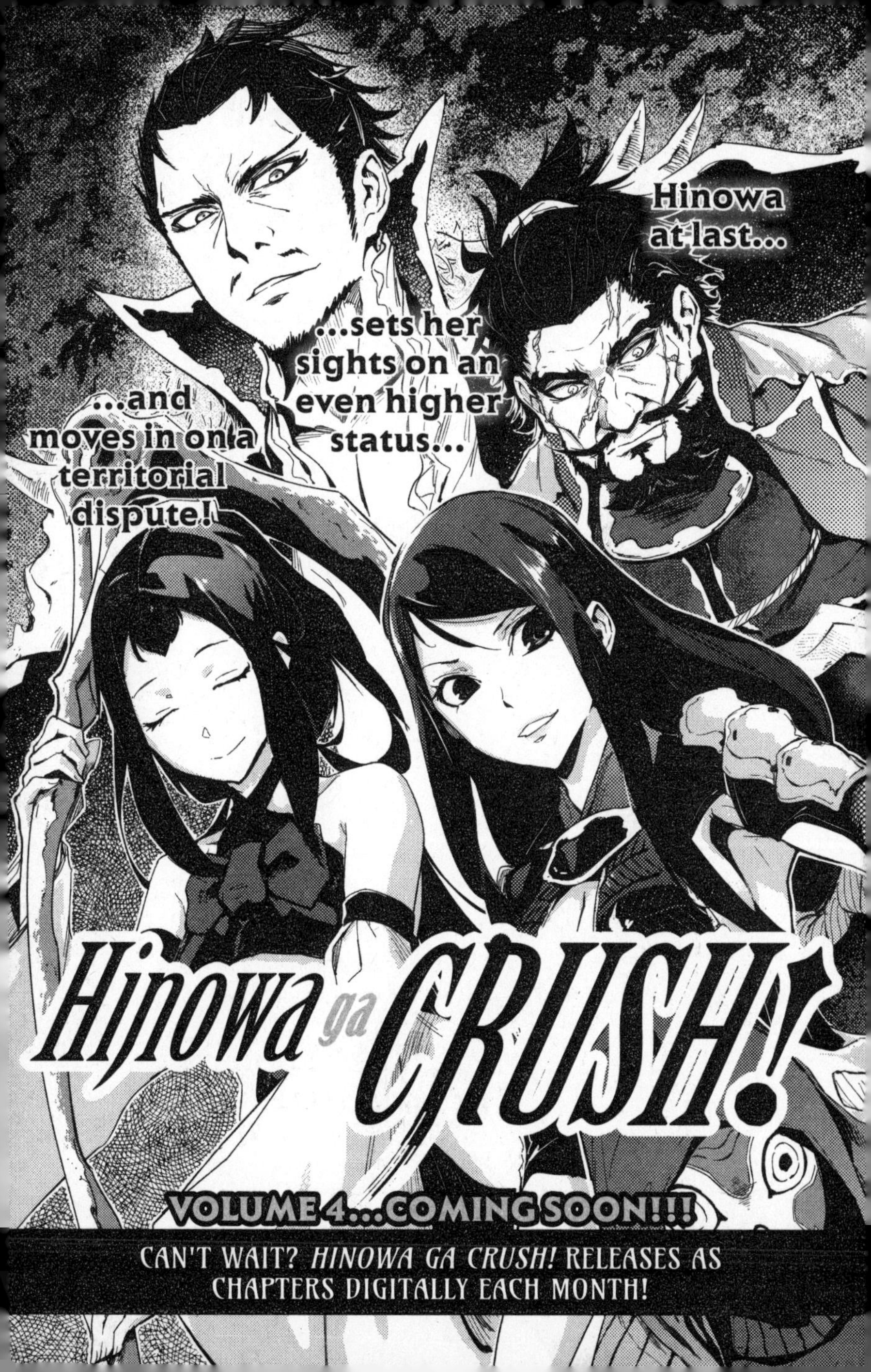
Hinowa at last...
...sets her sights on an even higher status...
...and moves in on a territorial dispute!
Hinowa ga CRUSH!
VOLUME 4...COMING SOON!!!
CAN'T WAIT? *HINOWA GA CRUSH!* RELEASES AS CHAPTERS DIGITALLY EACH MONTH!

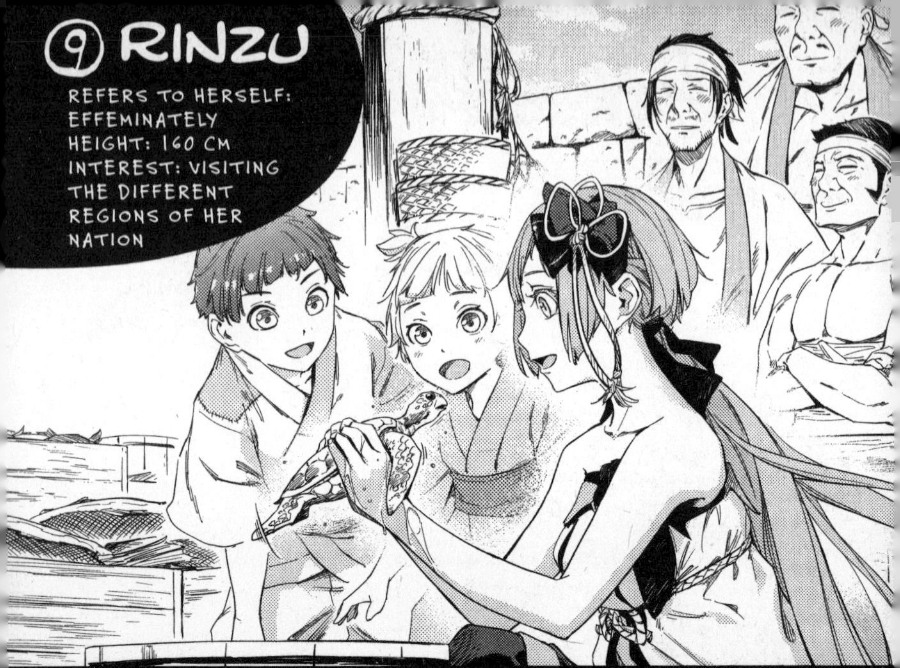
9 RINZU
REFERS TO HERSELF: EFFEMINATELY
HEIGHT: 160 CM
INTEREST: VISITING THE DIFFERENT REGIONS OF HER NATION

HINOWA GA CRUSH!

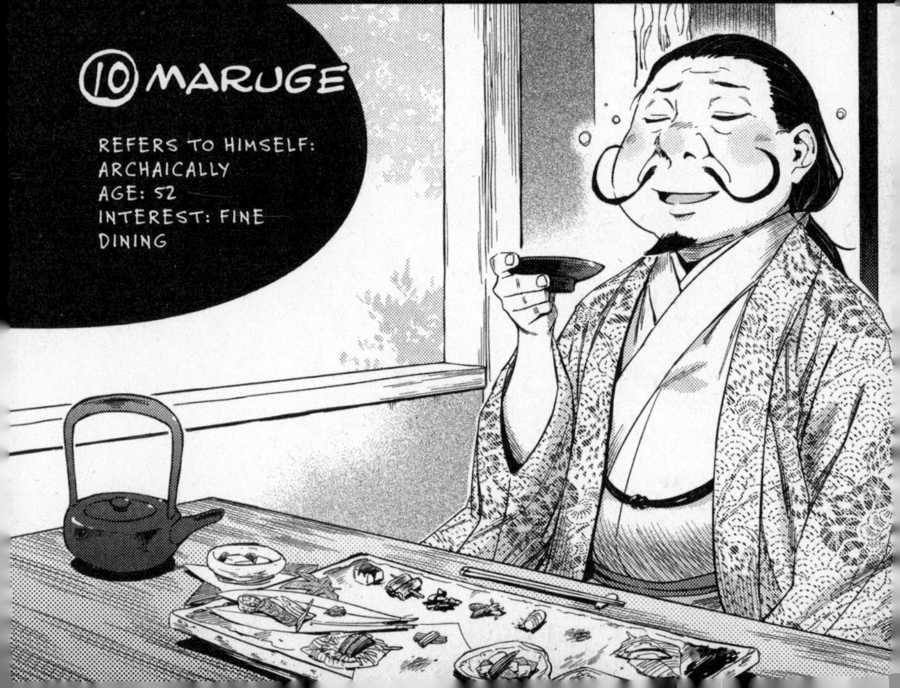
10 MARUGE
REFERS TO HIMSELF: ARCHAICALLY
AGE: 52
INTEREST: FINE DINING

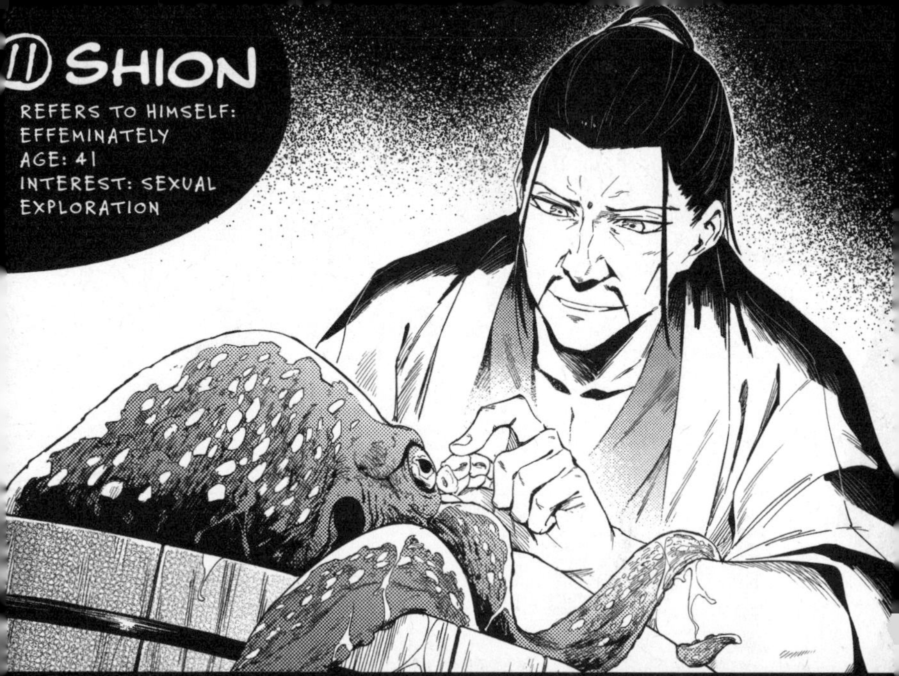
11 SHION
REFERS TO HIMSELF: EFFEMINATELY
AGE: 41
INTEREST: SEXUAL EXPLORATION

CHARACTER DIRECTORY

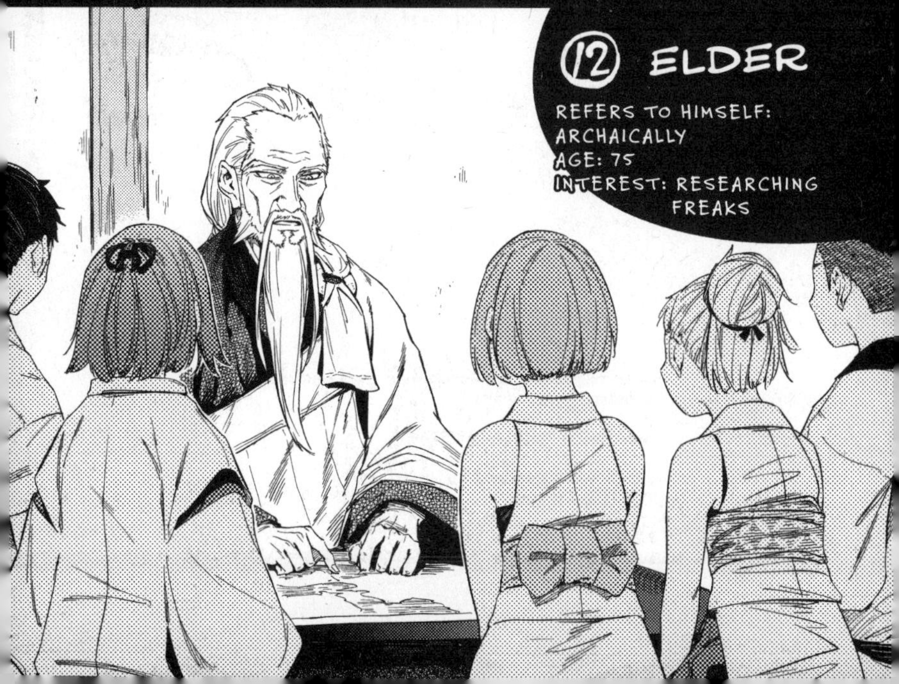
12 ELDER
REFERS TO HIMSELF: ARCHAICALLY
AGE: 75
INTEREST: RESEARCHING FREAKS

Hinowa ga Chusii!

STORY: **TAKAHIRO**   ART: **strelka**

Translation: Christine Dashiell

Lettering: Rochelle Gancio

HINOWA GA YUKU! Volume 3 © 2019 Takahiro, strelka / SQUARE ENIX CO., LTD. First published in Japan in 2019 by SQUARE ENIX CO., LTD. English translation rights arranged with SQUARE ENIX CO., LTD. and Yen Press, LLC through Tuttle-Mori Agency, Inc., Tokyo.

English translation © 2019 by SQUARE ENIX CO., LTD.

Yen Press
150 West 30th Street, 19th Floor
New York, NY 10001

Visit us at yenpress.com
facebook.com/yenpress
twitter.com/yenpress
yenpress.tumblr.com
instagram.com/yenpress

First Yen Press Edition: December 2019
The chapters in this volume were originally published as ebooks by Yen Press.

Yen Press is an imprint of Yen Press, LLC.
The Yen Press name and logo are trademarks of Yen Press, LLC.

The publisher is not
owned by the p

Library of Cong

ISBNs: 978-1-9
      978-1-9

10 9 8 7 6 5 4

WOR

Printed in the United States of America